A LIFE FORCE

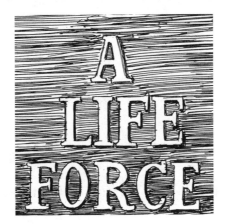

The Will Eisner Library

from W. W. Norton & Company

Hardcover Compilations

The Contract With God Trilogy: Life on Dropsie Avenue
Will Eisner's New York
Brush Strokes: My Life in Pictures

Paperbacks

A Contract With God
Dropsie Avenue: The Neighborhood
New York: The Big City
City People Notebook
Will Eisner Reader
The Dreamer
Invisible People
To the Heart of the Storm
Life on Another Planet
Family Matter
Minor Miracles
Name of the Game
The Building
The Plot: The Secret History of the Protocols of the Elders of Zion

Other Graphic Novels by Will Eisner

Fagin the Jew
Last Day in Vietnam

A Life Force

A Graphic Novel by

W. W. NORTON & COMPANY
New York • London

Copyright © 2006 by the Estate of Will Eisner
Copyright © 1983, 1984, 1985, 1988, 1995 by Will Eisner

All rights reserved
Printed in the United States of America
First published as a Norton paperback 2006

For information about permission to reproduce selections from this book, write to Permissions,
W. W. Norton & Company, Inc., 500 Fifth Avenue, New York, NY 10110

Manufacturing by RR Donnelley, Willard Division
Production: Julia Druskin and Sue Carlson

The Library of Congress has cataloged the one-volume edition as follows:
Eisner, Will.
The contract with God trilogy : life on Dropsie Avenue / Will Eisner.
p. cm.
Contents: A contract with God—A life force—Dropsie Avenue.
ISBN 0-393-06105-1
1. Graphic Novels. I. Title: Life on Dropsie Avenue. II. Eisner, Will. Contract with God.
III. Eisner, Will. Life force. IV. Eisner, Will. Dropsie Avenue. V. Title

PN6727.E4A6 2005
741.5'973—dc33
2005053944

ISBN-13: 978-0-393-32803-5 pbk.
ISBN-10: 0-393-32803-1 pbk.

W. W. Norton & Company, Inc., 500 Fifth Avenue, New York, N.Y. 10110
www.wwnorton.com

W. W. Norton & Company Ltd., Castle House, 75/76 Wells Street, London W1T 3QT

1 2 3 4 5 6 7 8 9 0

Contents

List of New Illustrations

A LIFE FORCE

Who Knows...who Knows,
why all the creatures of earth
struggle so to live.
Why they scurry about, run from
danger and continue to live
out a natural span,
seemingly in response to
a mysterious Life Force.

So, the question is
WHY? WHAT FOR?
Ask the insects...
Maybe they Know!

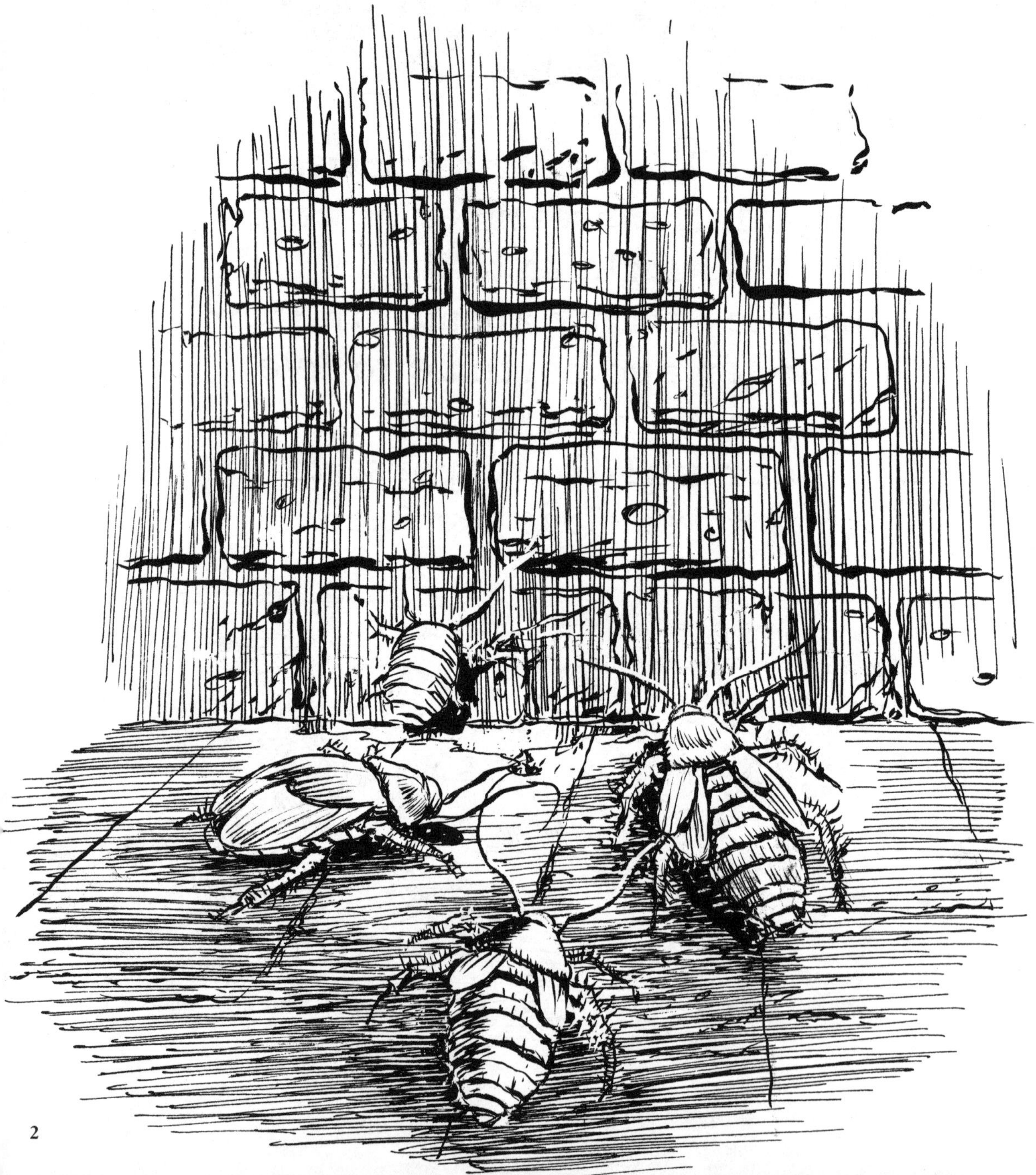

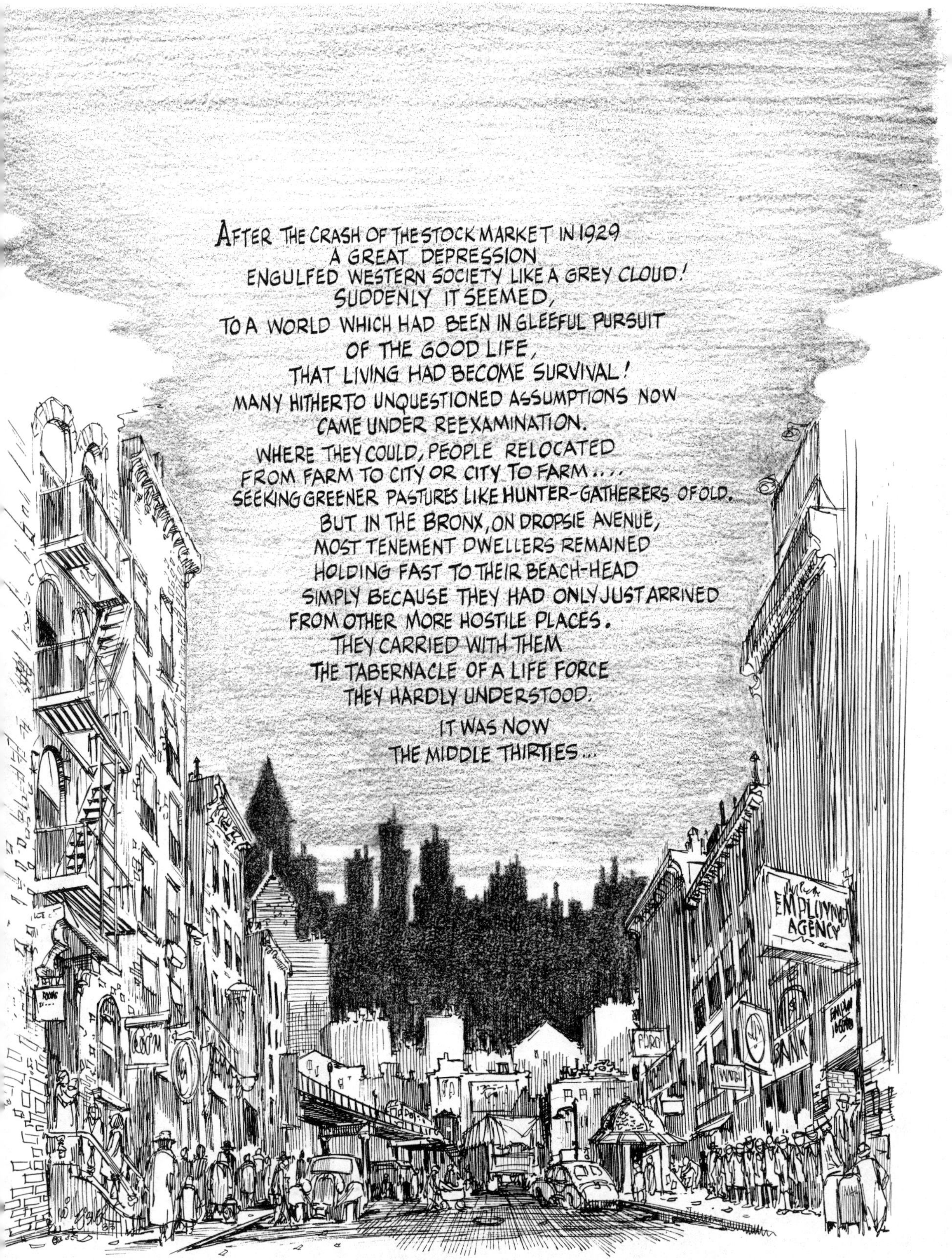
AFTER THE CRASH OF THE STOCK MARKET IN 1929
A GREAT DEPRESSION
ENGULFED WESTERN SOCIETY LIKE A GREY CLOUD!
SUDDENLY IT SEEMED,
TO A WORLD WHICH HAD BEEN IN GLEEFUL PURSUIT
OF THE GOOD LIFE,
THAT LIVING HAD BECOME SURVIVAL!
MANY HITHERTO UNQUESTIONED ASSUMPTIONS NOW
CAME UNDER REEXAMINATION.
WHERE THEY COULD, PEOPLE RELOCATED
FROM FARM TO CITY OR CITY TO FARM....
SEEKING GREENER PASTURES LIKE HUNTER-GATHERERS OF OLD.
BUT IN THE BRONX, ON DROPSIE AVENUE,
MOST TENEMENT DWELLERS REMAINED
HOLDING FAST TO THEIR BEACH-HEAD
SIMPLY BECAUSE THEY HAD ONLY JUST ARRIVED
FROM OTHER MORE HOSTILE PLACES.
THEY CARRIED WITH THEM
THE TABERNACLE OF A LIFE FORCE
THEY HARDLY UNDERSTOOD.
IT WAS NOW
THE MIDDLE THIRTIES...
AGENCY
BANK

1934

" . . . the withered leaves of industrial enterprise lie on every side . . . the savings of many thousands of families are gone . . . unemployed citizens face the grim problem of existence. . . ."

FRANKLIN D. ROOSEVELT
From his first Inaugural Address

ITEMS FROM THE NEW YORK PRESS

1500 HOMELESS LIVE IN ARMORY

69th REGIMENT HOUSES POOR

FEB. 7, 1934

Sheltered from the cold, over 1500 homeless people have found at least temporary refuge in the 69th Regiment Armory at Lexington Avenue and Twenty-Sixth Street in New York.

These victims of the depression, poorly clothed and dispirited, have been pouring into the huge building filling the drill floor and the mezzanine. Coming from the inclement pavements and wet doorways or dank subway kiosks, they encamp on the polished wooden floors.

SIMPLE GAMES OCCUPY THEIR TIME

In an effort to keep up morale, the men play checkers, jigsaw puzzles and hang around a piano played by a volunteer of surprising talent.

SLUMP CAN AFFECT PEOPLE'S HEALTH

INCREASE IN ILLNESS AND REDUCTION OF INCOME EFFECT.

In an article published on Jan. 14 by the *New York Times*, it was reported that the average annual income of a representative group of American wage-earners dropped from $1700 in 1929 to $900 this year.

The significance of the statistic is that historically an economic depression usually results in sickness and impaired vitality.

RATE OF DEATH SINCE 1929 HAS REDUCED

Strangely enough, the U.S. death rate has fallen despite the drop in living standards.

TWO MEN FAINT OF HUNGER IN CITY HALL WHILE WOMAN SCREAMS

MAYOR LA GUARDIA HALTS CONFERENCE

MARCH 2, 1934

According to the *New York Times*, two men in a group of twenty-two unemployed people besieged City Hall in the belief that the mayor would give them jobs in snow removal work, collapsed in the hall outside the Mayor's Office.

Both men, exhausted from lack of food, were immediately taken to the Beekman Street Hospital at Mayor Fiorello La Guardia's orders.

"WANT JOBS, NOT FOOD"

The men had worked the day before at snow clearing for the Sanitation Department until they were laid off for lack of work.

CHAPTER 1

IZZY THE COCKROACH AND THE MEANING OF LIFE

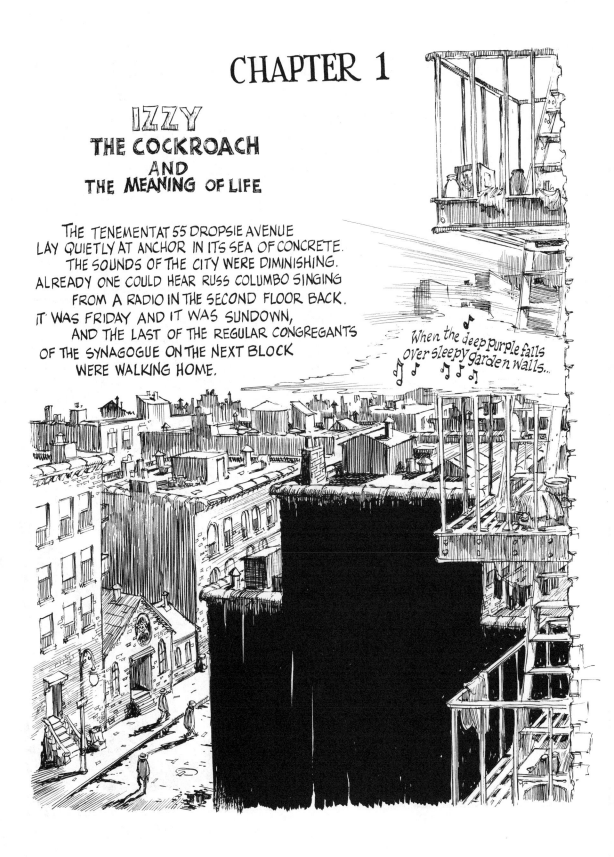

THE TENEMENT AT 55 DROPSIE AVENUE LAY QUIETLY AT ANCHOR IN ITS SEA OF CONCRETE. THE SOUNDS OF THE CITY WERE DIMINISHING. ALREADY ONE COULD HEAR RUSS COLUMBO SINGING FROM A RADIO IN THE SECOND FLOOR BACK. IT WAS FRIDAY AND IT WAS SUNDOWN, AND THE LAST OF THE REGULAR CONGREGANTS OF THE SYNAGOGUE ON THE NEXT BLOCK WERE WALKING HOME.

When the deep purple falls over sleepy garden walls...

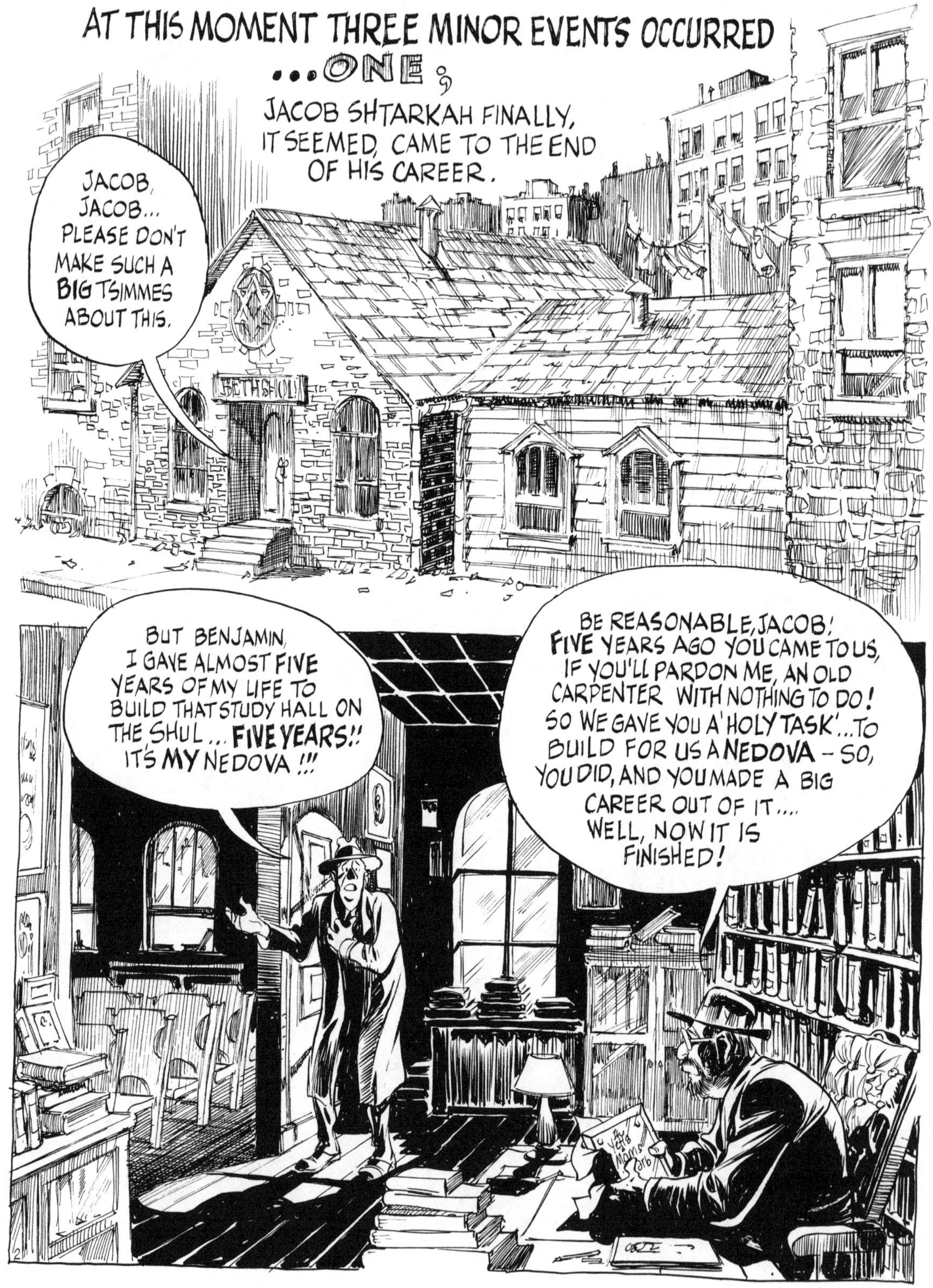
AT THIS MOMENT THREE MINOR EVENTS OCCURRED
...ONE
JACOB SHTARKAH FINALLY, IT SEEMED, CAME TO THE END OF HIS CAREER.
JACOB, JACOB... PLEASE DON'T MAKE SUCH A BIG TSIMMES ABOUT THIS.
BUT BENJAMIN, I GAVE ALMOST FIVE YEARS OF MY LIFE TO BUILD THAT STUDY HALL ON THE SHUL... FIVE YEARS!! IT'S MY NEDOVA !!!
BE REASONABLE, JACOB! FIVE YEARS AGO YOU CAME TO US, IF YOU'LL PARDON ME, AN OLD CARPENTER WITH NOTHING TO DO! SO WE GAVE YOU A 'HOLY TASK'... TO BUILD FOR US A NEDOVA – SO, YOU DID, AND YOU MADE A BIG CAREER OUT OF IT.... WELL, NOW IT IS FINISHED!

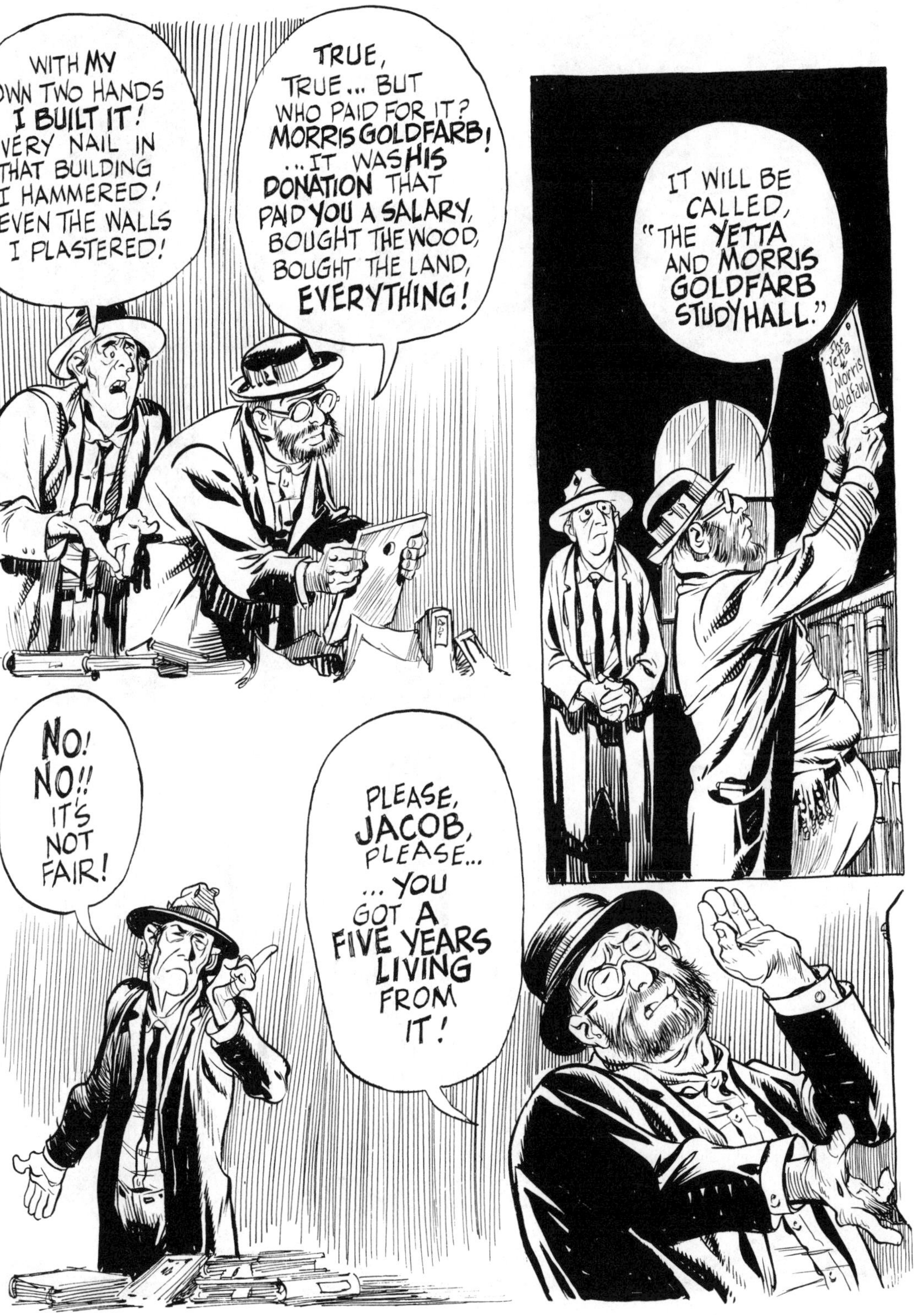

WITH MY OWN TWO HANDS I BUILT IT! EVERY NAIL IN THAT BUILDING I HAMMERED! EVEN THE WALLS I PLASTERED!
TRUE, TRUE... BUT WHO PAID FOR IT? MORRIS GOLDFARB! ...IT WAS HIS DONATION THAT PAID YOU A SALARY, BOUGHT THE WOOD, BOUGHT THE LAND, EVERYTHING!
IT WILL BE CALLED, "THE YETTA AND MORRIS GOLDFARB STUDY HALL."
NO! NO!! IT'S NOT FAIR!
PLEASE, JACOB, PLEASE... ...YOU GOT A FIVE YEARS LIVING FROM IT!

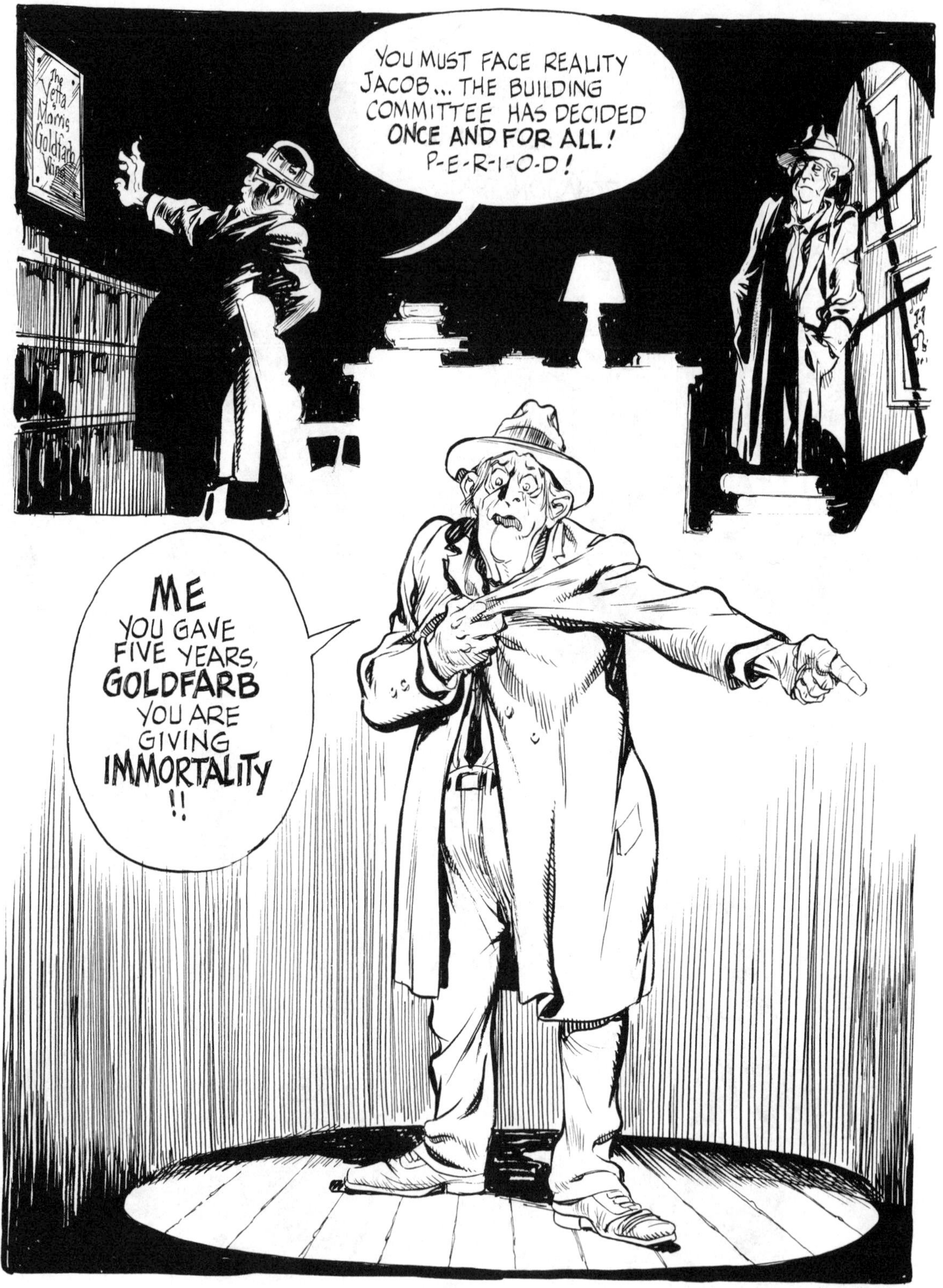
The Yetta & Morris Goldfarb Wing
YOU MUST FACE REALITY JACOB... THE BUILDING COMMITTEE HAS DECIDED ONCE AND FOR ALL! P-E-R-I-O-D!
ME YOU GAVE FIVE YEARS, GOLDFARB YOU ARE GIVING IMMORTALITY !!

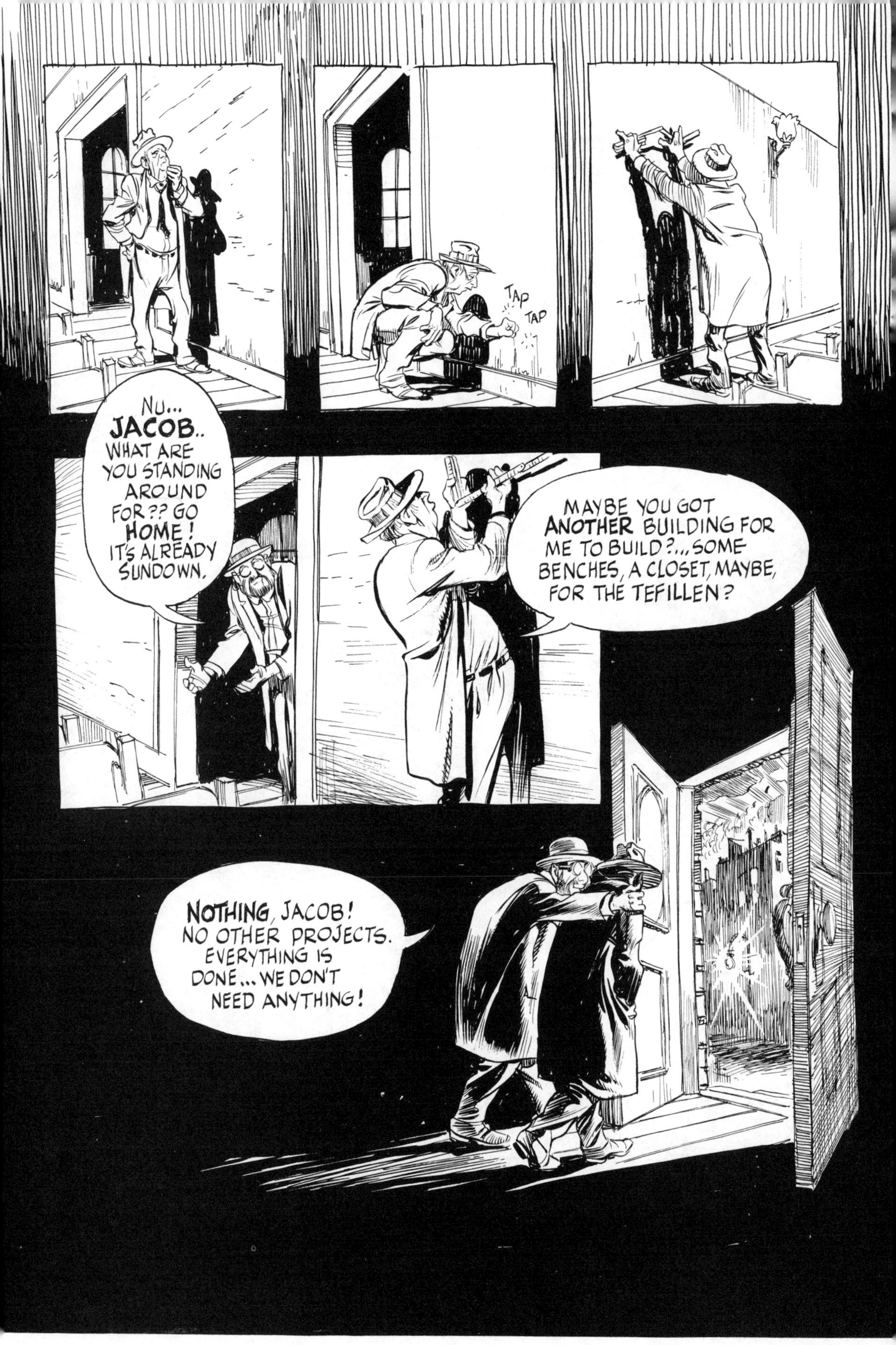
TAP
TAP
NU... JACOB.. WHAT ARE YOU STANDING AROUND FOR?? GO HOME! IT'S ALREADY SUNDOWN.
MAYBE YOU GOT ANOTHER BUILDING FOR ME TO BUILD?..., SOME BENCHES, A CLOSET, MAYBE, FOR THE TEFILLEN?
NOTHING, JACOB! NO OTHER PROJECTS. EVERYTHING IS DONE... WE DON'T NEED ANYTHING!

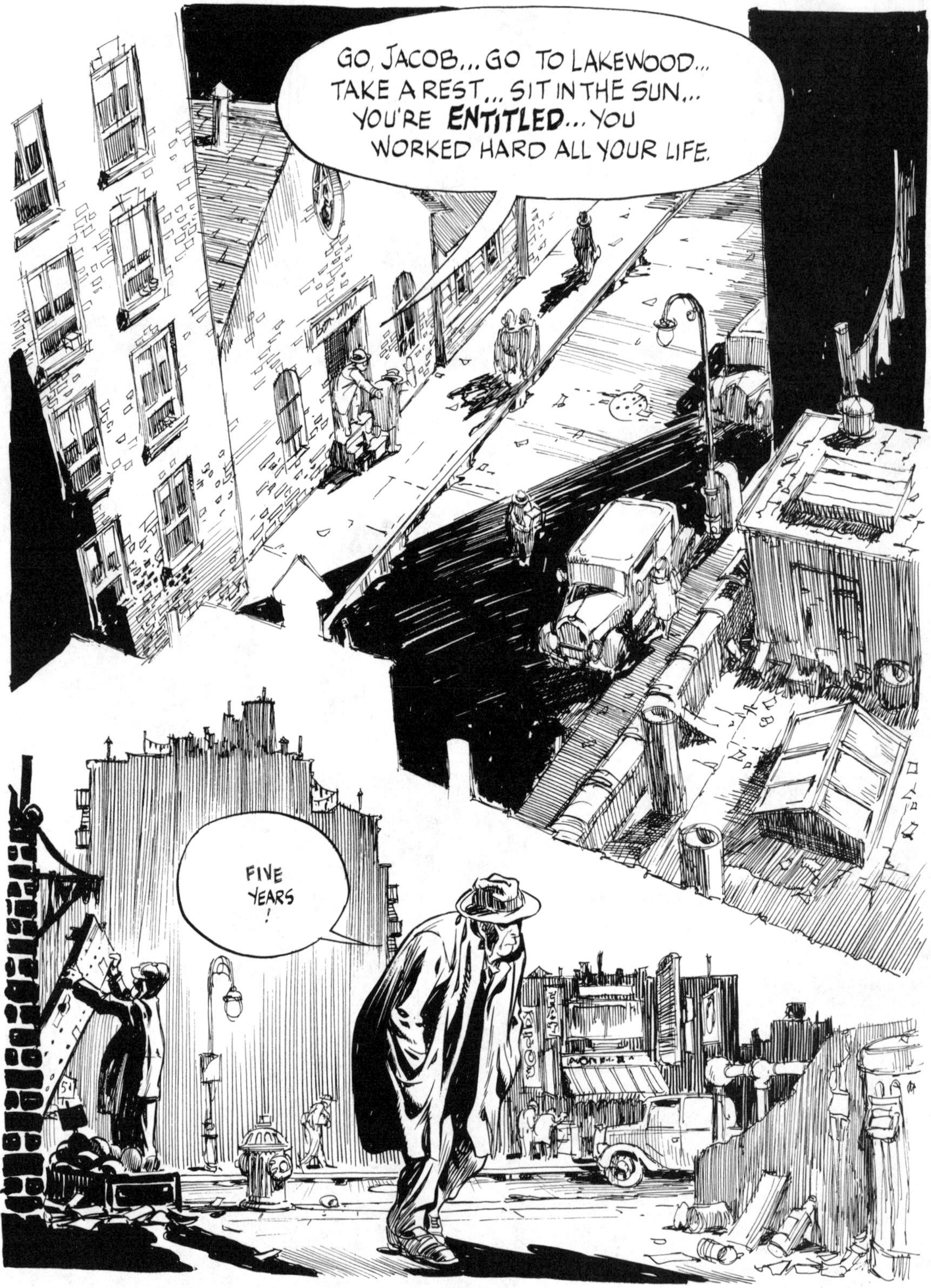
GO, JACOB... GO TO LAKEWOOD... TAKE A REST... SIT IN THE SUN... YOU'RE **ENTITLED**... YOU WORKED HARD ALL YOUR LIFE.
FIVE YEARS!

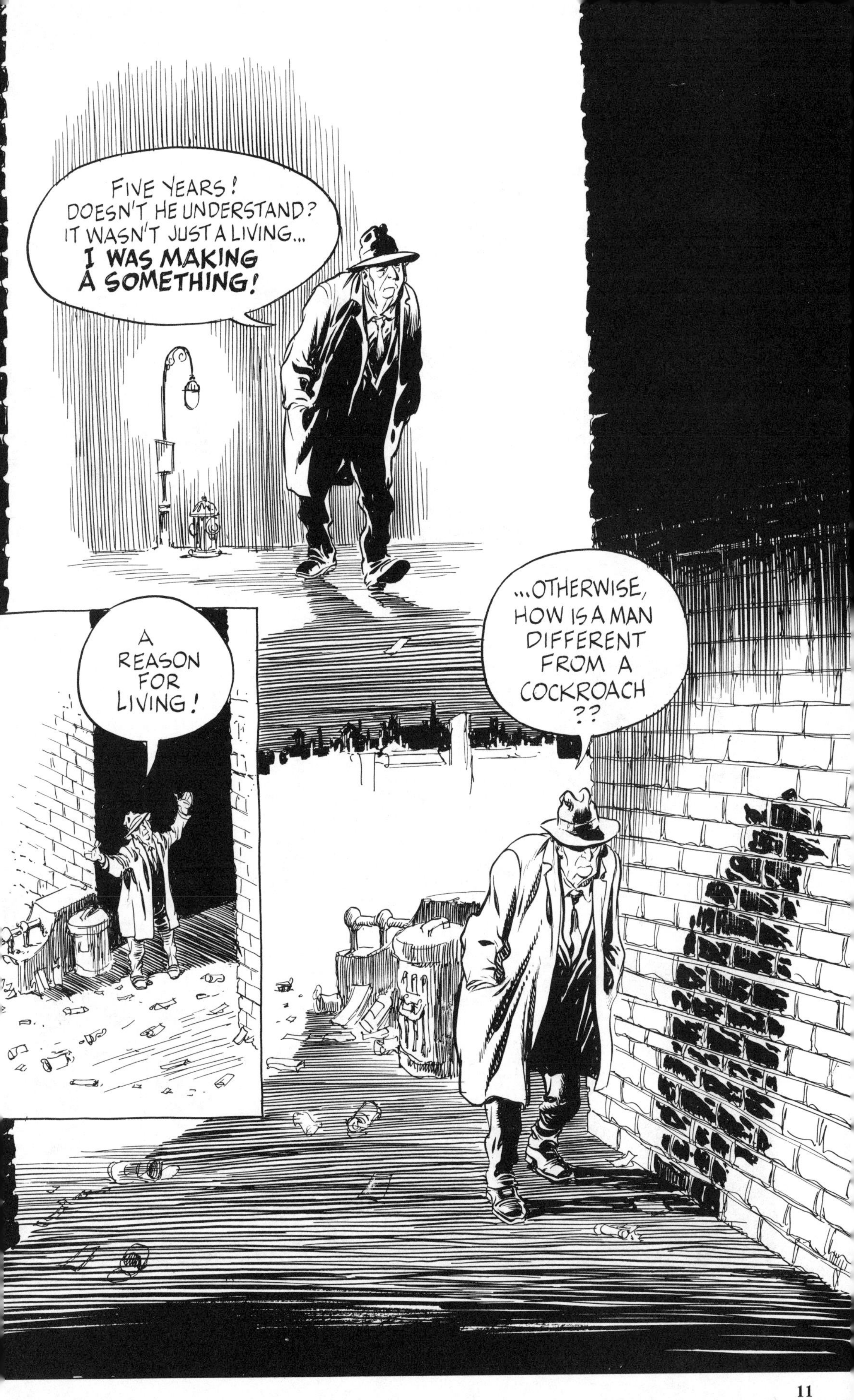
FIVE YEARS!
DOESN'T HE UNDERSTAND?
IT WASN'T JUST A LIVING...
I WAS MAKING
A SOMETHING!
A
REASON
FOR
LIVING!
...OTHERWISE,
HOW IS A MAN
DIFFERENT
FROM A
COCKROACH
??

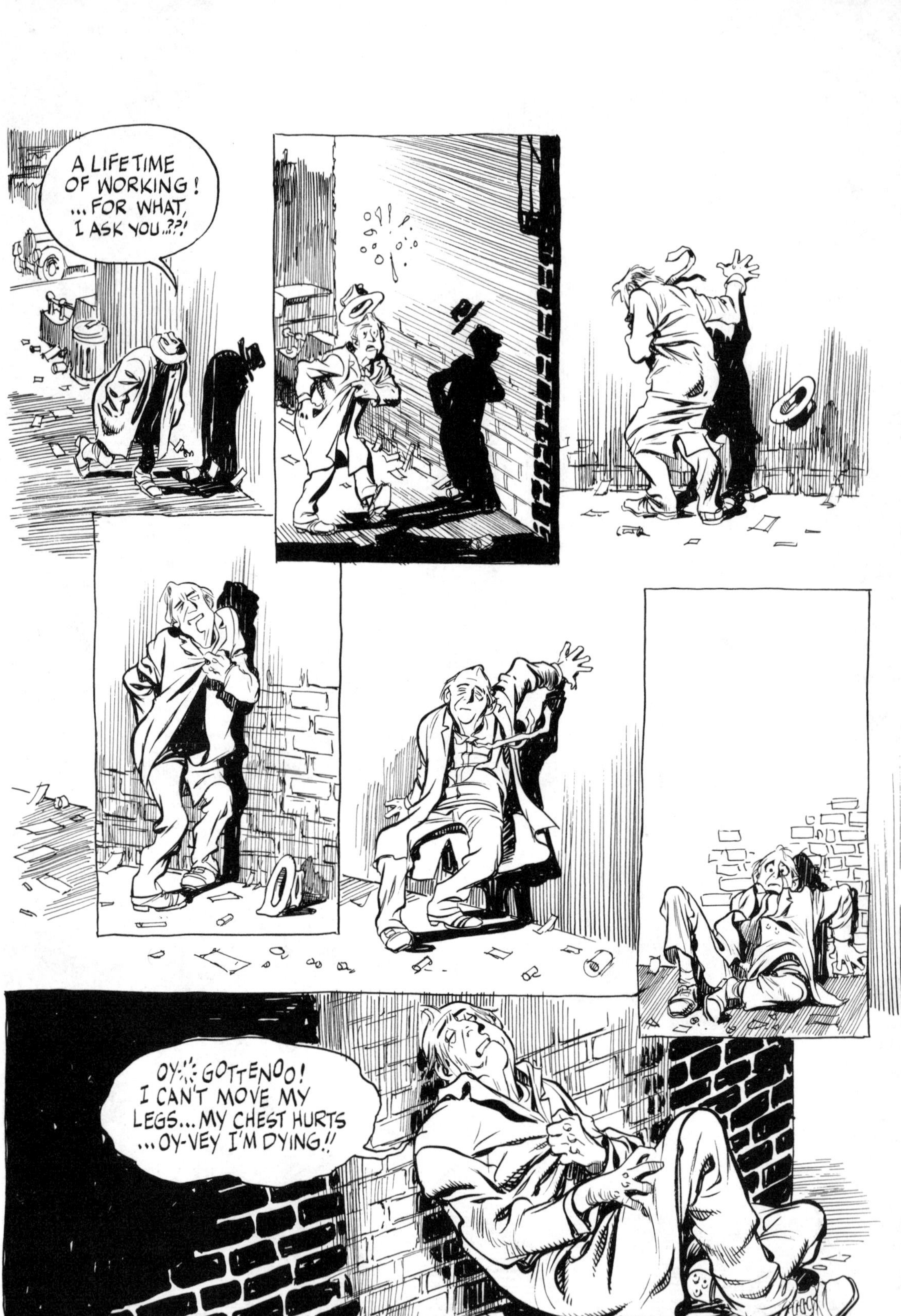
A LIFETIME OF WORKING! ...FOR WHAT, I ASK YOU..??!
OY! GOTTENOO! I CAN'T MOVE MY LEGS...MY CHEST HURTS ...OY-VEY I'M DYING!!

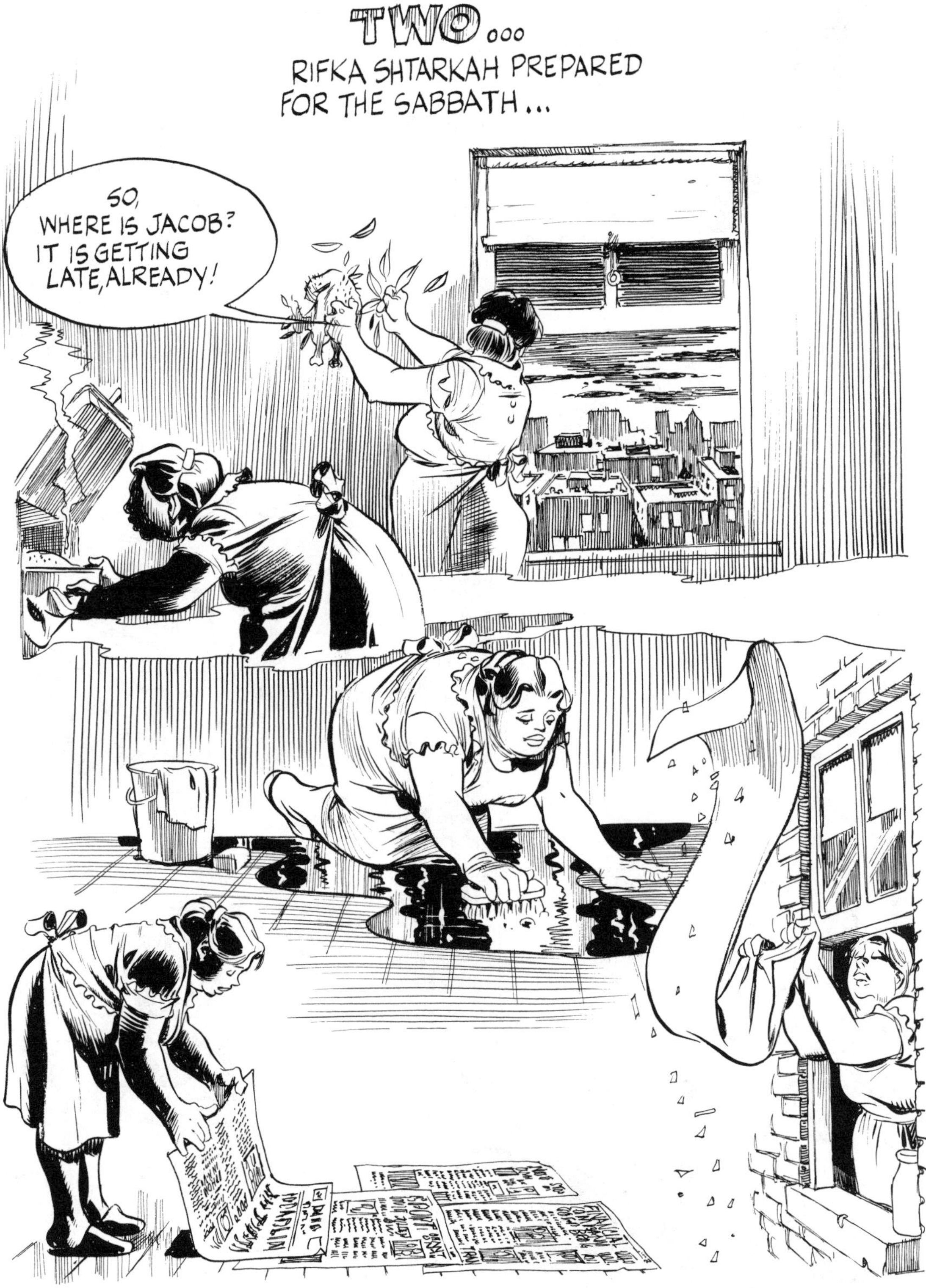
TWO...
RIFKA SHTARKAH PREPARED FOR THE SABBATH...
SO, WHERE IS JACOB? IT IS GETTING LATE, ALREADY!

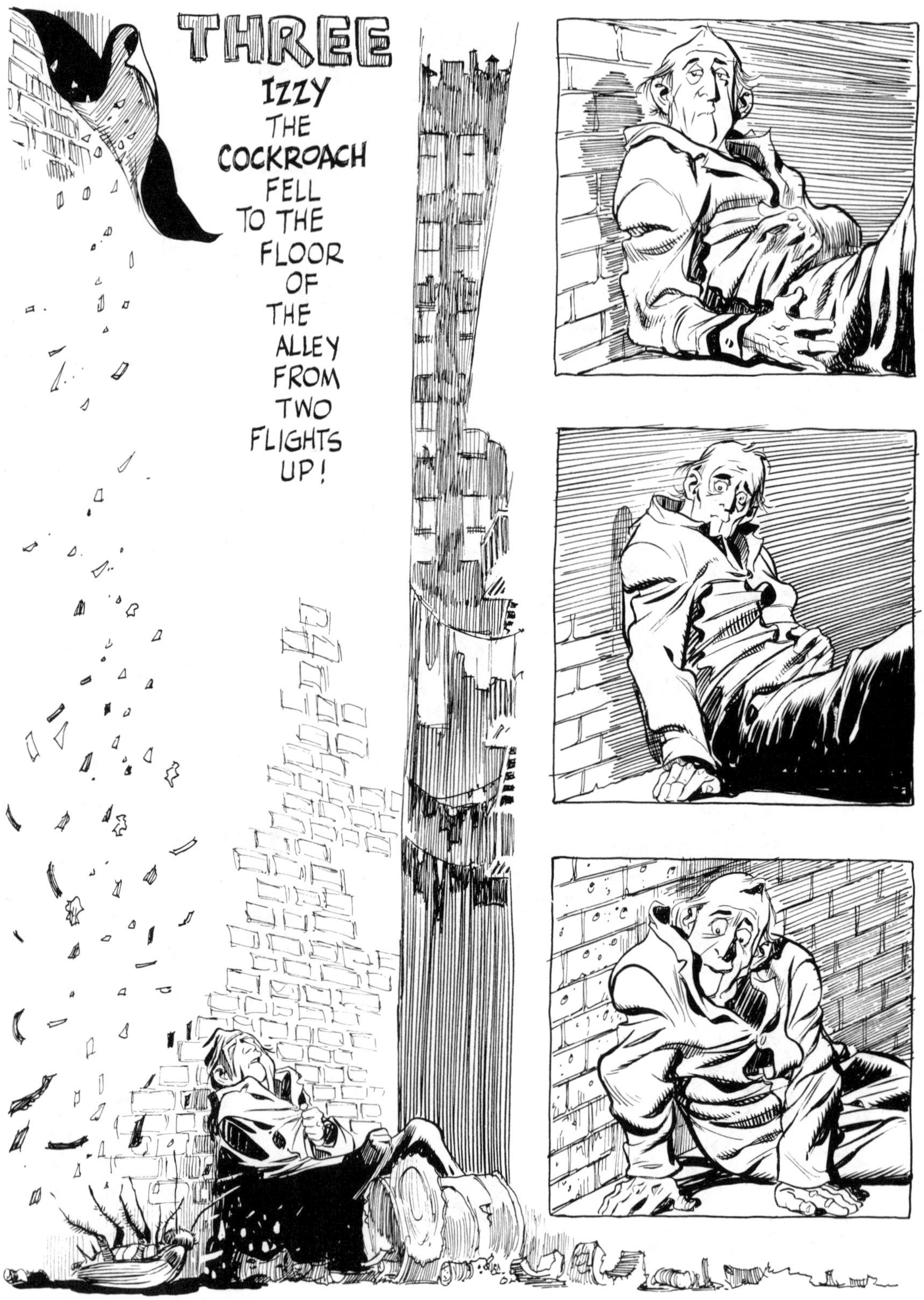
THREE
IZZY THE COCKROACH FELL TO THE FLOOR OF THE ALLEY FROM TWO FLIGHTS UP!

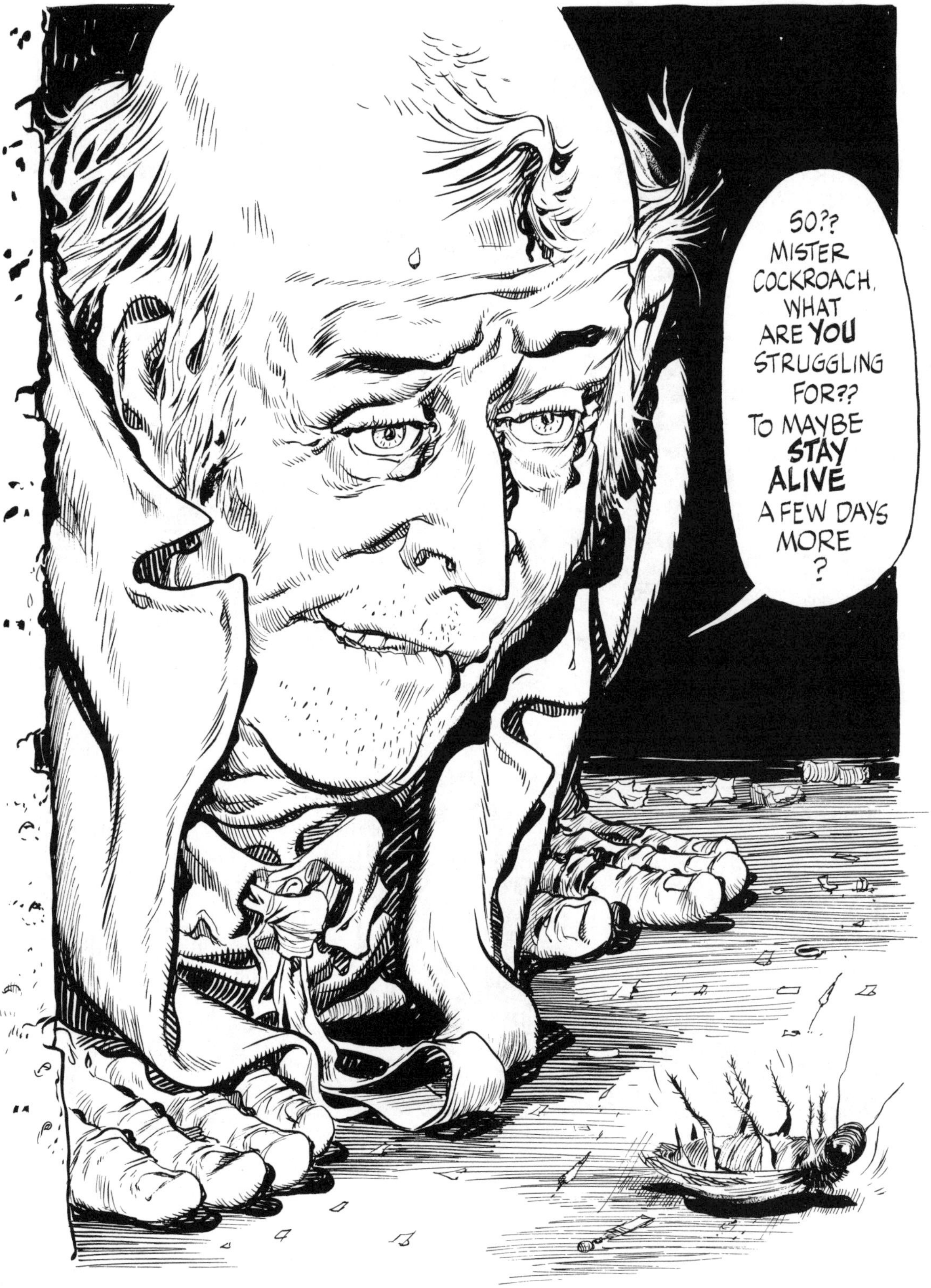
SO?? MISTER COCKROACH. WHAT ARE **YOU** STRUGGLING FOR?? TO MAYBE **STAY ALIVE** A FEW DAYS MORE ?

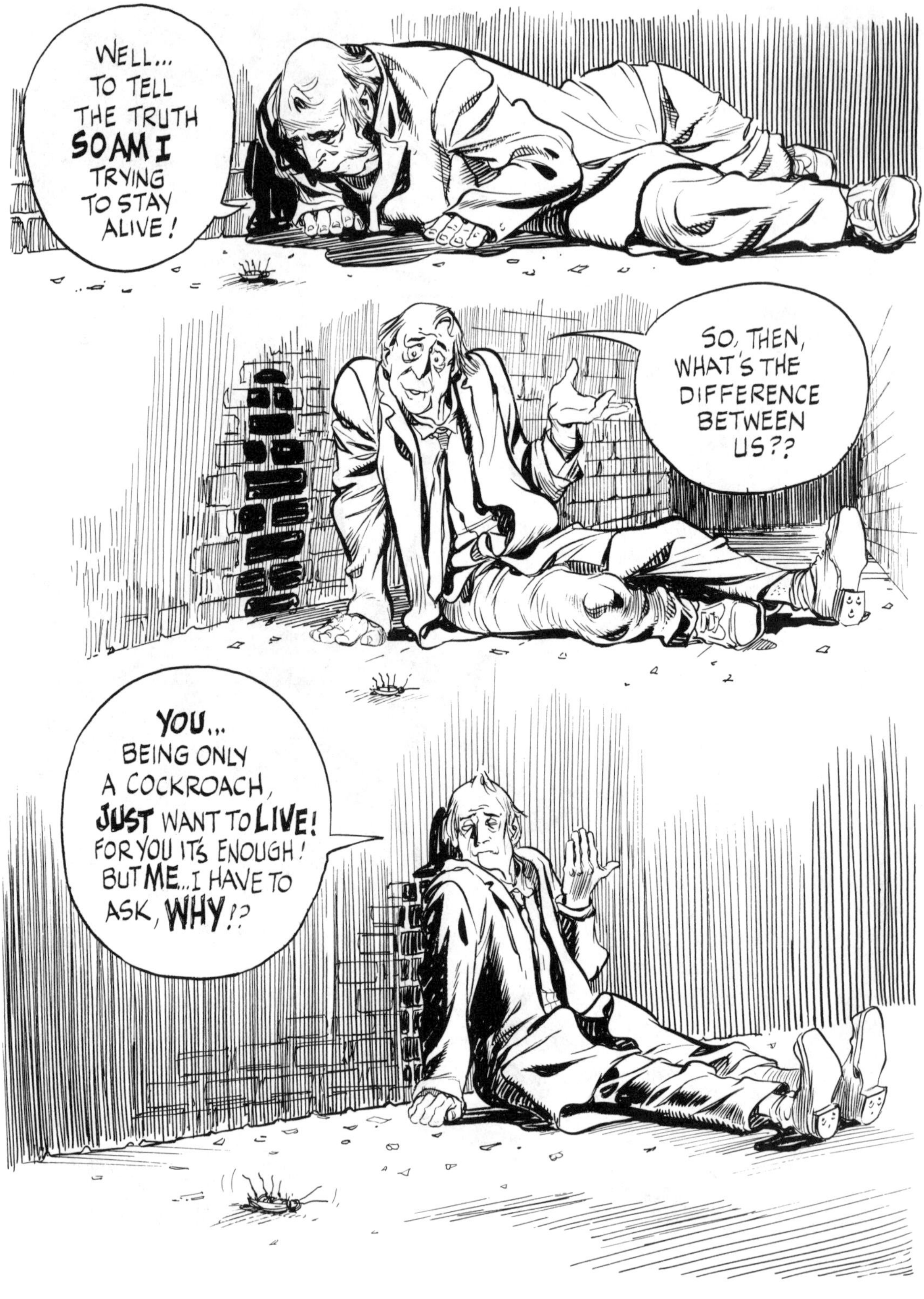
WELL... TO TELL THE TRUTH SO AM I TRYING TO STAY ALIVE!
SO, THEN, WHAT'S THE DIFFERENCE BETWEEN US??
YOU... BEING ONLY A COCKROACH, JUST WANT TO LIVE! FOR YOU IT'S ENOUGH! BUT ME...I HAVE TO ASK, WHY!?

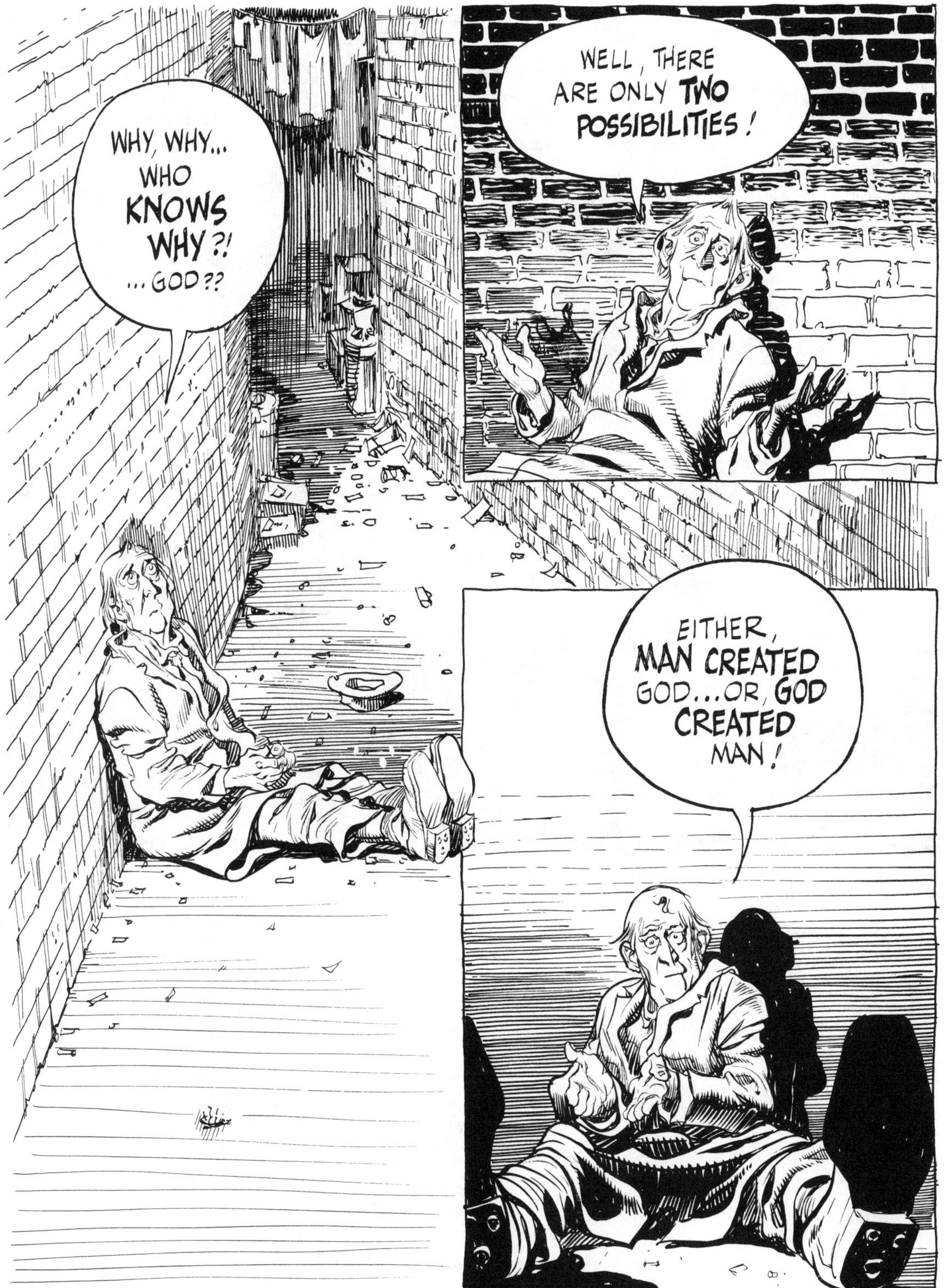
WHY, WHY... WHO KNOWS WHY?! ...GOD??
WELL, THERE ARE ONLY TWO POSSIBILITIES!
EITHER, MAN CREATED GOD...OR, GOD CREATED MAN!

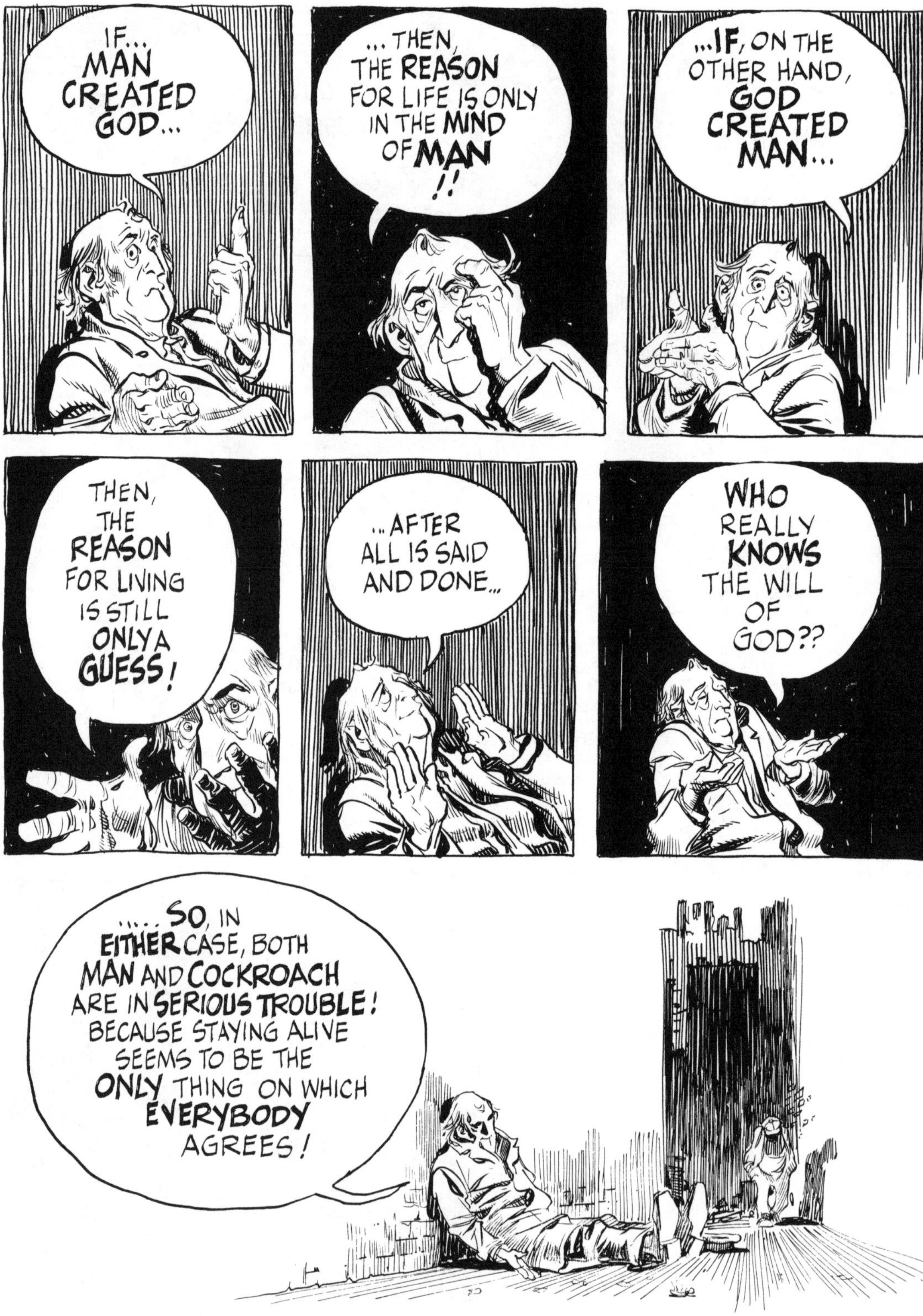
IF... MAN CREATED GOD...
...THEN, THE REASON FOR LIFE IS ONLY IN THE MIND OF MAN !!
...IF, ON THE OTHER HAND, GOD CREATED MAN...
THEN, THE REASON FOR LIVING IS STILL ONLY A GUESS!
...AFTER ALL IS SAID AND DONE...
WHO REALLY KNOWS THE WILL OF GOD??
.....SO, IN EITHER CASE, BOTH MAN AND COCKROACH ARE IN SERIOUS TROUBLE! BECAUSE STAYING ALIVE SEEMS TO BE THE ONLY THING ON WHICH EVERYBODY AGREES!

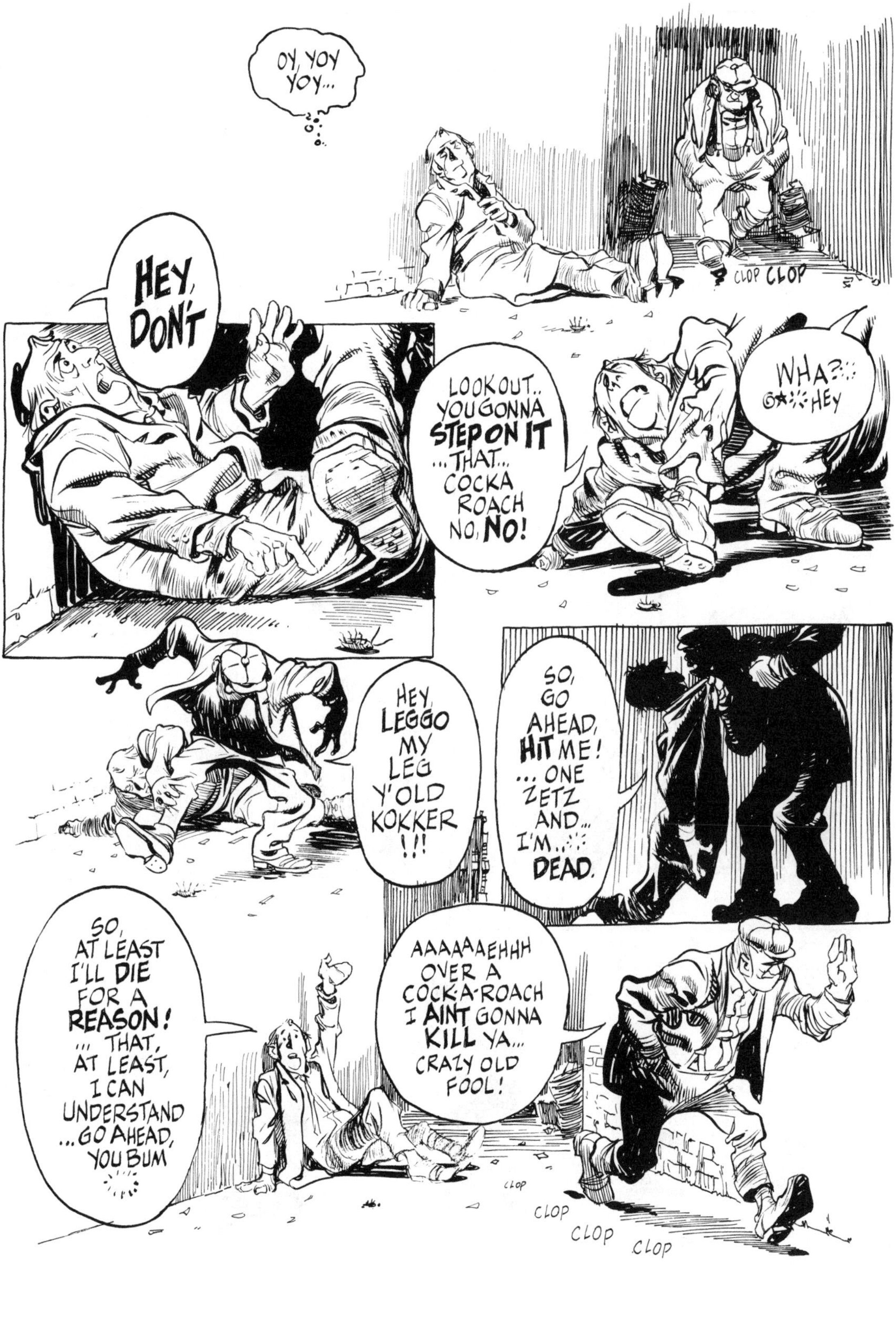
OY, YOY
YOY...
CLOP CLOP
HEY, DON'T
LOOKOUT.. YOU GONNA STEP ON IT ...THAT... COCKA ROACH NO, NO!
WHA? HEY
HEY, LEGGO MY LEG Y'OLD KOKKER !!!
SO, GO AHEAD, HIT ME! ... ONE ZETZ AND... I'M... DEAD.
SO, AT LEAST I'LL DIE FOR A REASON! ... THAT, AT LEAST, I CAN UNDERSTAND ...GO AHEAD, YOU BUM
AAAAAEHHH OVER A COCK-A-ROACH I AINT GONNA KILL YA... CRAZY OLD FOOL!
CLOP
CLOP
CLOP
CLOP

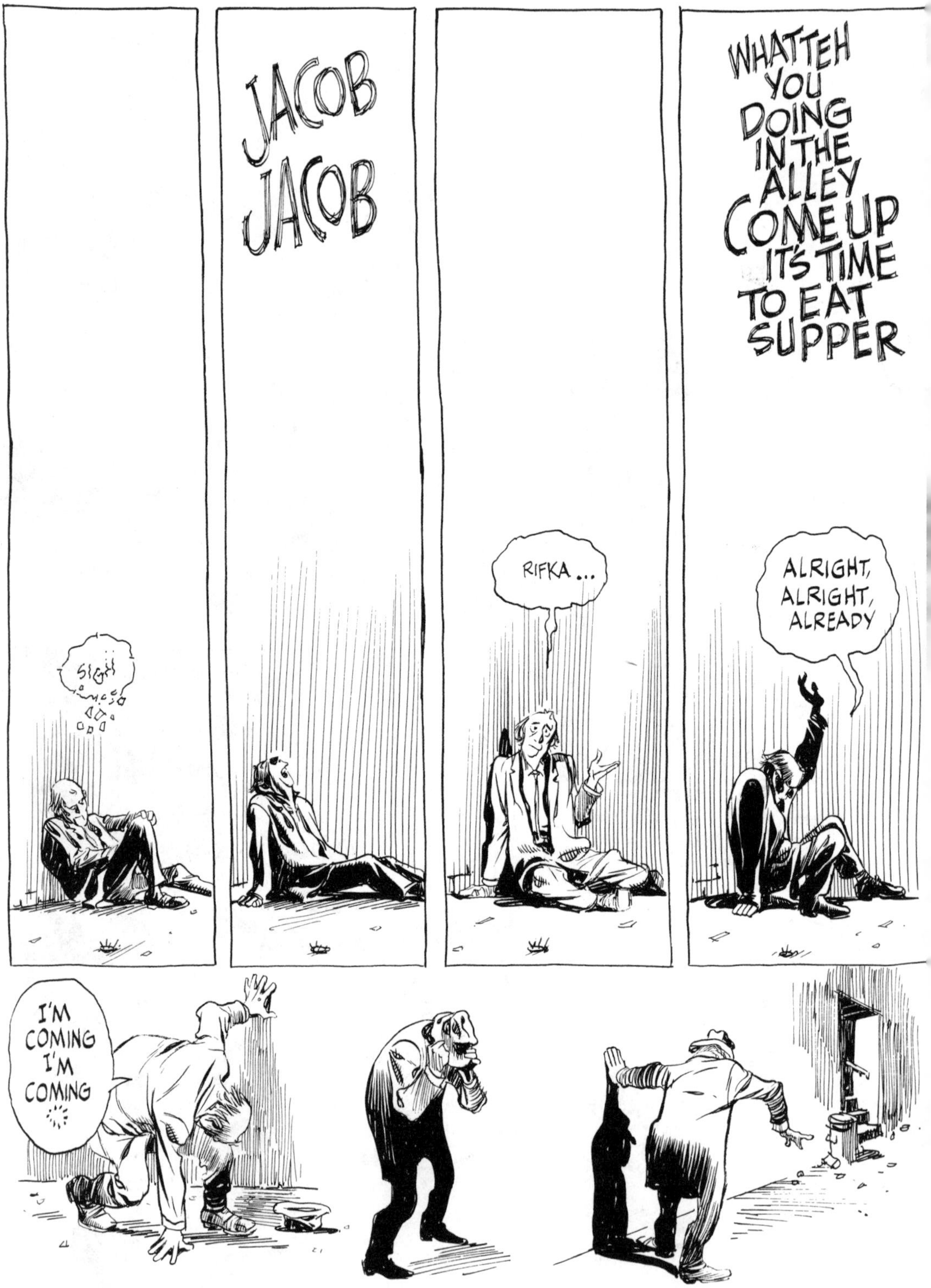
SIGH
JACOB
JACOB
RIFKA ...
WHATTEH YOU DOING IN THE ALLEY COME UP IT'S TIME TO EAT SUPPER
ALRIGHT, ALRIGHT, ALREADY
I'M COMING I'M COMING

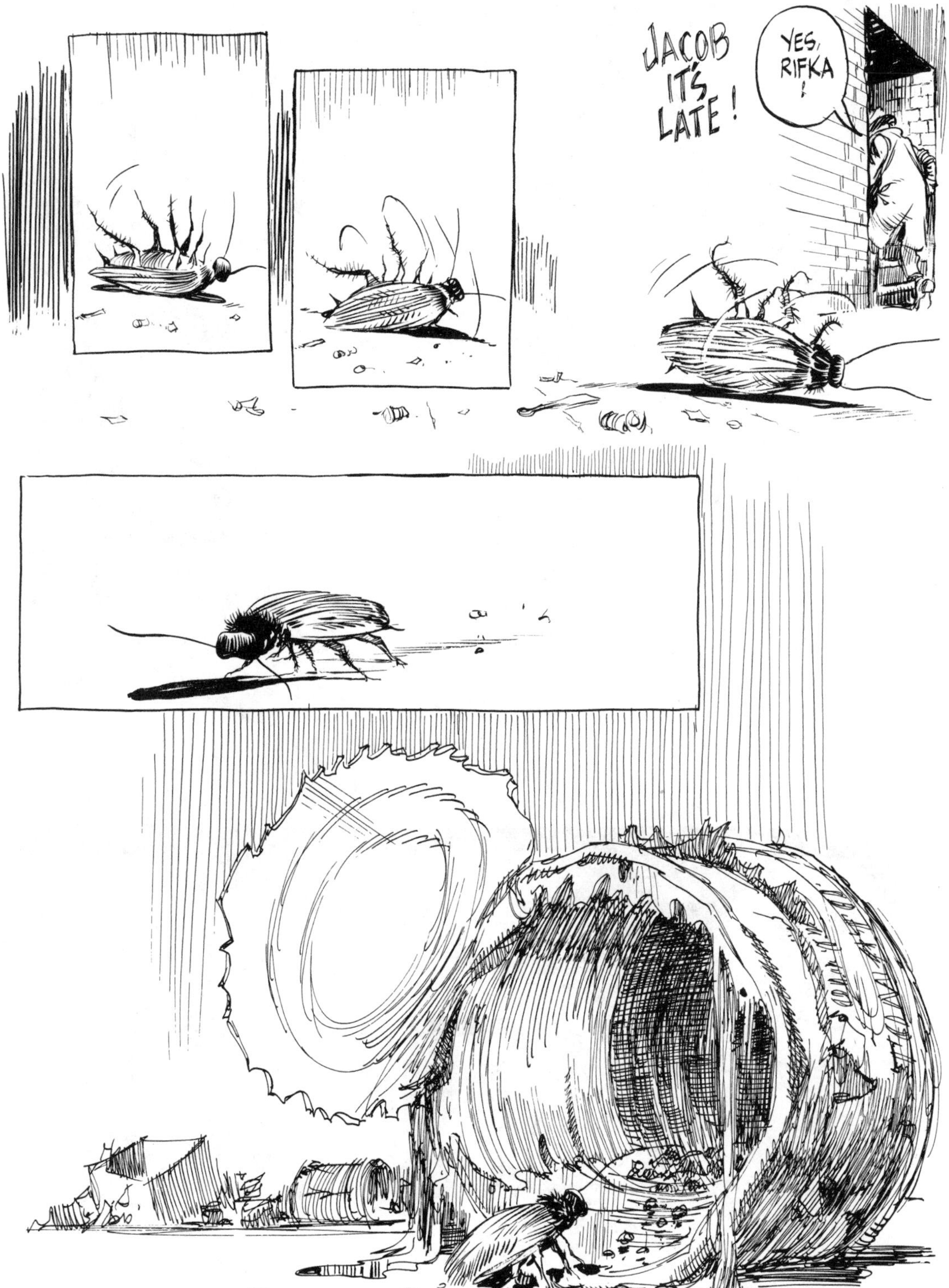
JACOB IT'S LATE!
YES, RIFKA!

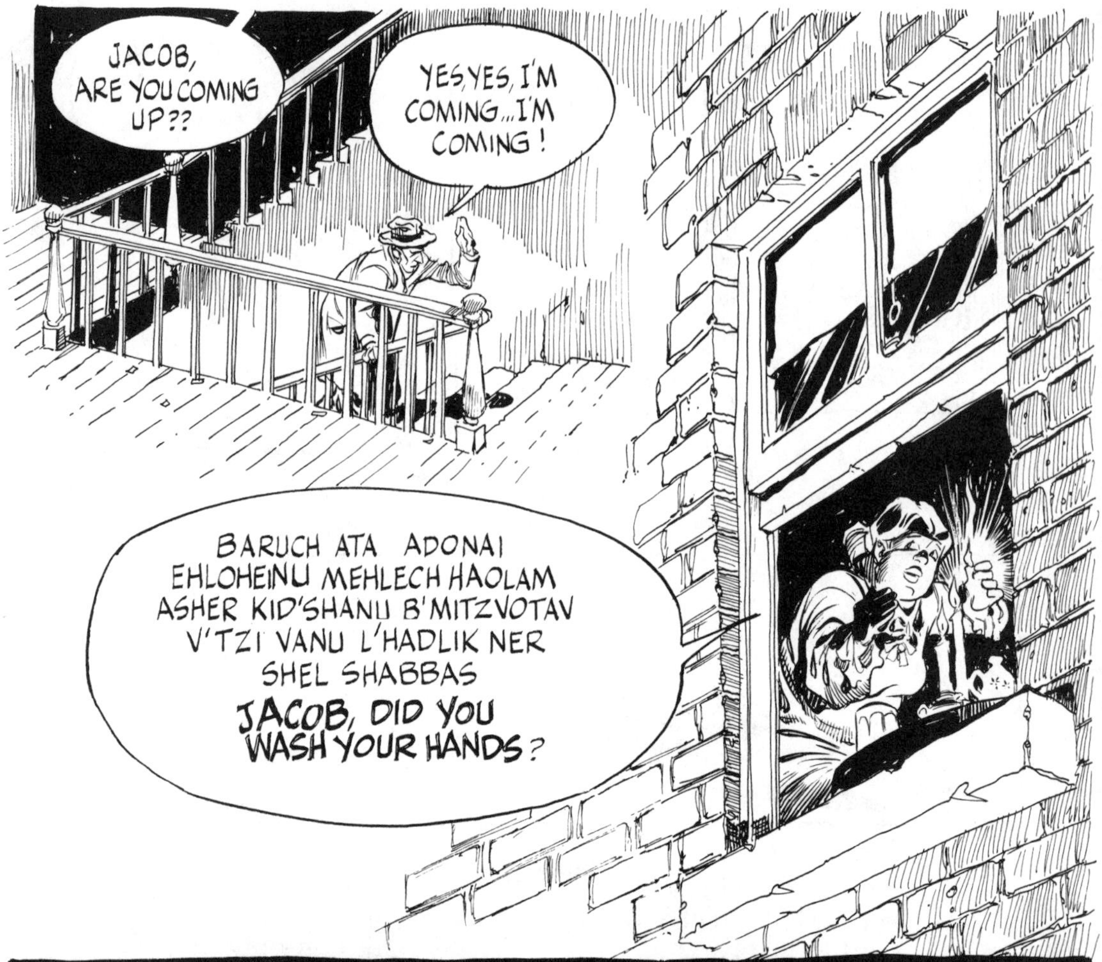
JACOB, ARE YOU COMING UP??
YES, YES, I'M COMING... I'M COMING!
BARUCH ATA ADONAI EHLOHEINU MEHLECH HAOLAM ASHER KID'SHANU B'MITZVOTAV V'TZI VANU L'HADLIK NER SHEL SHABBAS
JACOB, DID YOU WASH YOUR HANDS?

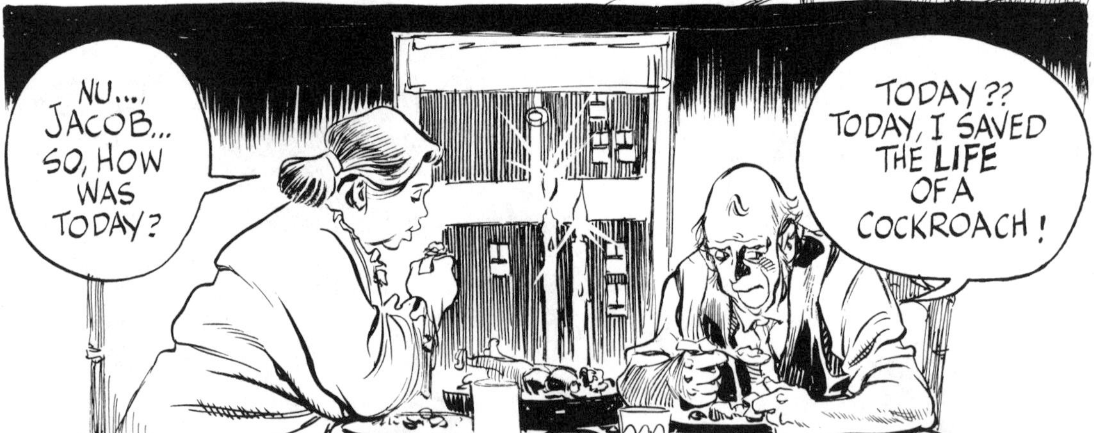
NU..., JACOB... SO, HOW WAS TODAY?
TODAY?? TODAY, I SAVED THE LIFE OF A COCKROACH!

CHAPTER 2
ESCAPEE

SOUTH, SOUTHWEST- ACROSS THE HARLEM RIVER
WHERE THE BRONX ENDS, IS MANHATTAN ISLAND.
THERE...IS THE LAND OF PROMISE.

DANIEL, SON OF JACOB,
MADE IT FROM DROPSIE AVENUE.
VIA NIGHT SCHOOL,
MEDICAL SCHOOL BY DAY
(DRIVING A TAXI BY NIGHT)
AND FINALLY
AN INTERN
AT MT. HEBRON HOSPITAL
MANHATTAN EAST SIDE.
DANIEL HAD **ESCAPED**...
INTO THE MAINSTREAM.

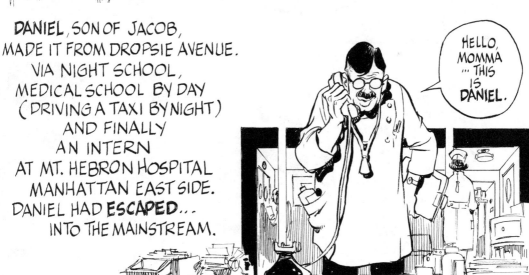

HELLO, MOMMA ... THIS IS DANIEL.

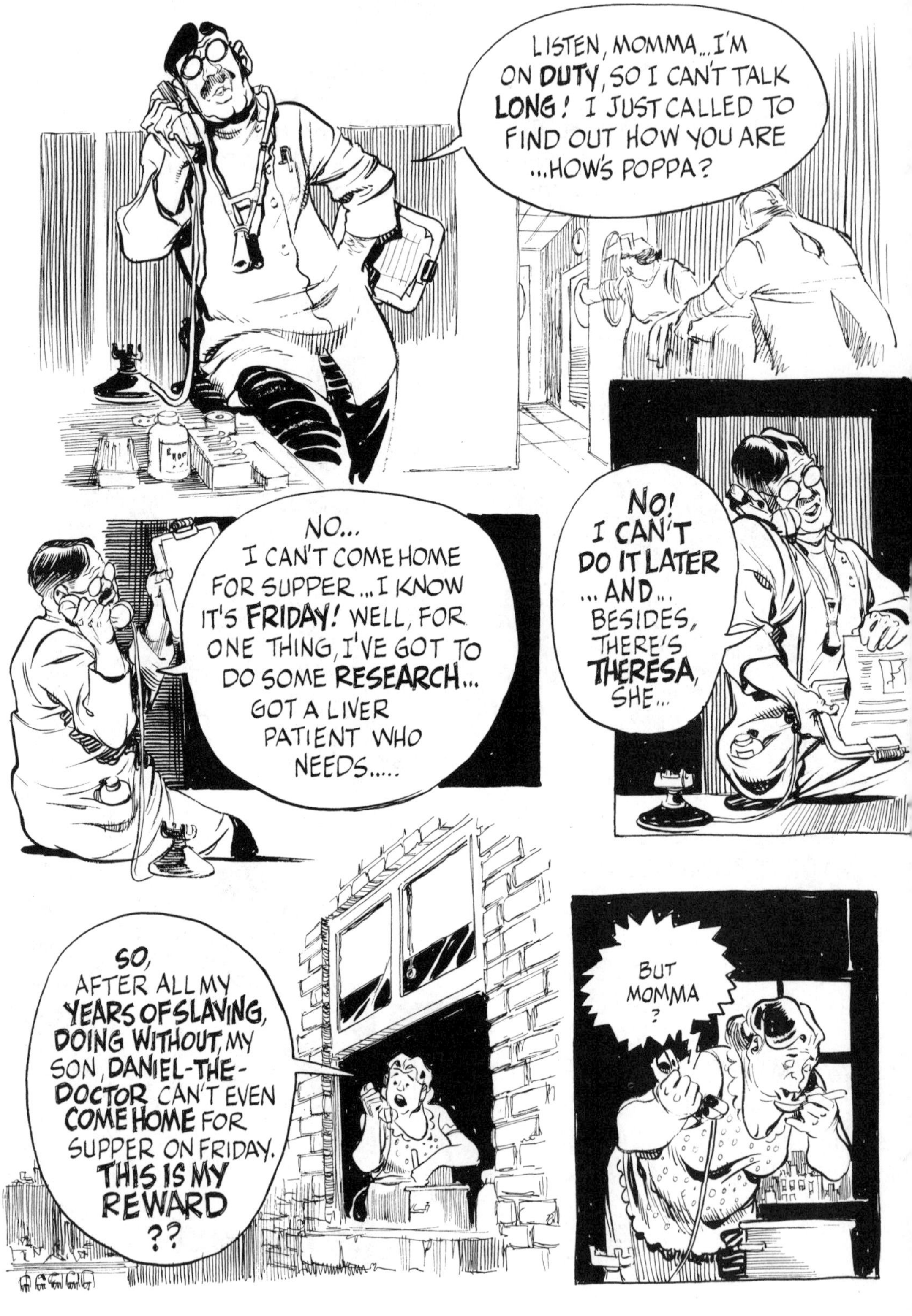
LISTEN, MOMMA... I'M ON DUTY, SO I CAN'T TALK LONG! I JUST CALLED TO FIND OUT HOW YOU ARE ...HOW'S POPPA?
NO... I CAN'T COME HOME FOR SUPPER ... I KNOW IT'S FRIDAY! WELL, FOR ONE THING, I'VE GOT TO DO SOME RESEARCH... GOT A LIVER PATIENT WHO NEEDS.....
NO! I CAN'T DO IT LATER ... AND... BESIDES, THERE'S THERESA, SHE...
SO, AFTER ALL MY YEARS OF SLAVING, DOING WITHOUT, MY SON, DANIEL-THE-DOCTOR CAN'T EVEN COME HOME FOR SUPPER ON FRIDAY. THIS IS MY REWARD ??
BUT MOMMA ?

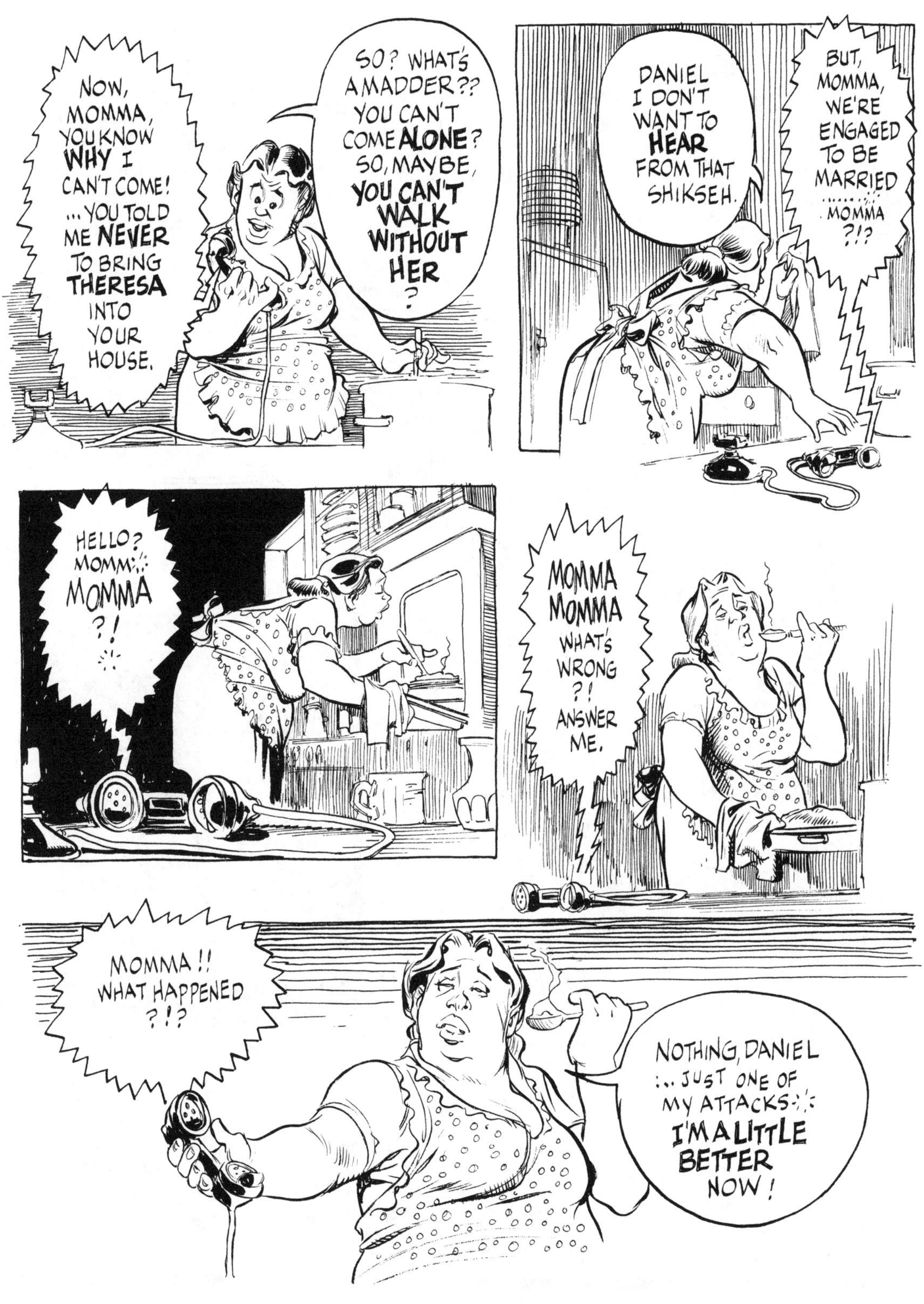
NOW, MOMMA, YOU KNOW WHY I CAN'T COME! ...YOU TOLD ME NEVER TO BRING THERESA INTO YOUR HOUSE.
SO? WHAT'S AMADDER?? YOU CAN'T COME ALONE? SO, MAYBE, YOU CAN'T WALK WITHOUT HER ?
DANIEL I DON'T WANT TO HEAR FROM THAT SHIKSEH.
BUT, MOMMA, WE'RE ENGAGED TO BE MARRIED .... MOMMA ?!?
HELLO? MOMM... MOMMA ?!
MOMMA MOMMA WHAT'S WRONG ?! ANSWER ME.
MOMMA!! WHAT HAPPENED ?!?
NOTHING, DANIEL ... JUST ONE OF MY ATTACKS... I'M A LITTLE BETTER NOW!

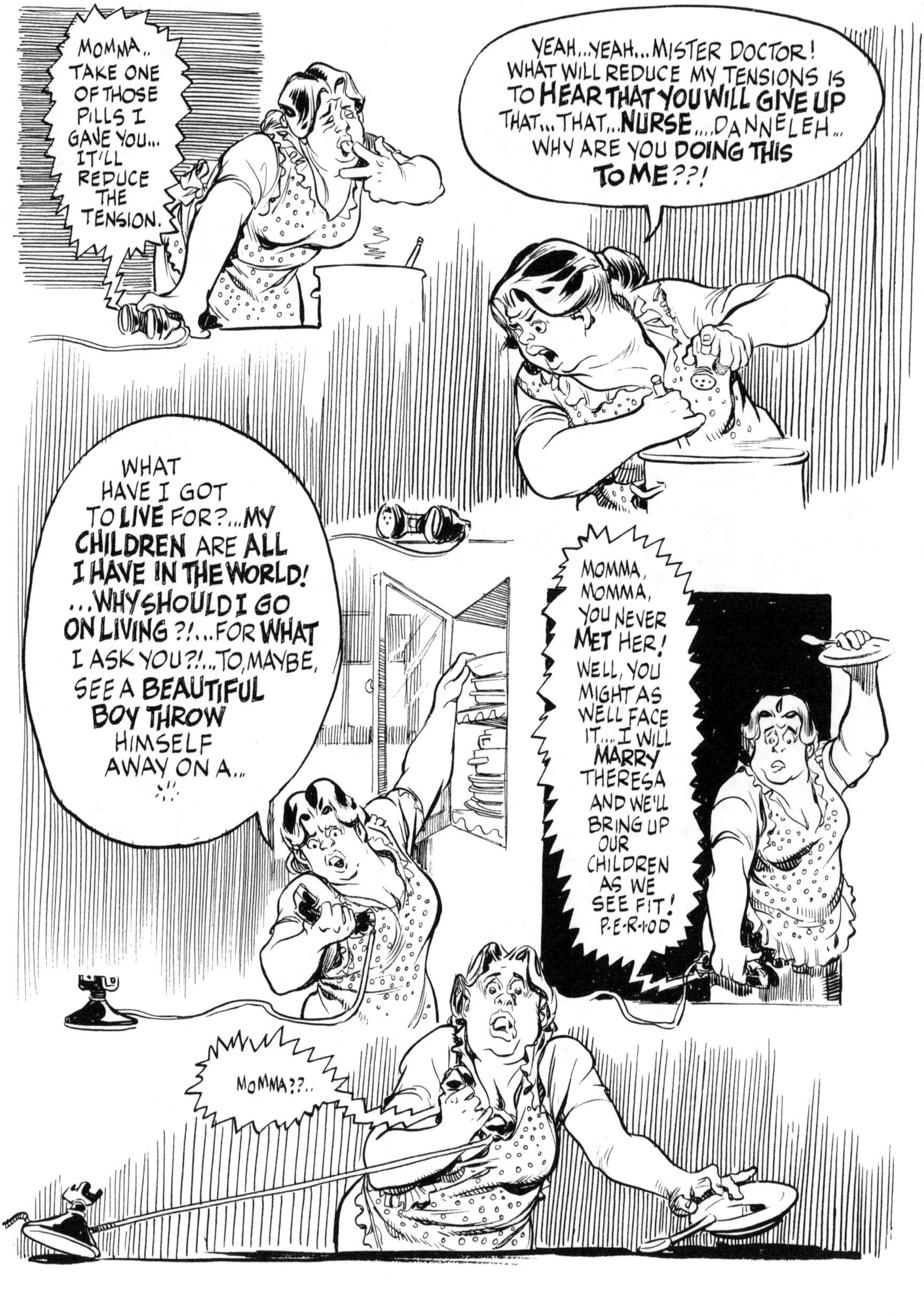
MOMMA.. TAKE ONE OF THOSE PILLS I GAVE YOU... IT'LL REDUCE THE TENSION.
YEAH...YEAH...MISTER DOCTOR! WHAT WILL REDUCE MY TENSIONS IS TO HEAR THAT YOU WILL GIVE UP THAT... THAT... NURSE.... DANNELEH... WHY ARE YOU DOING THIS TO ME??!
WHAT HAVE I GOT TO LIVE FOR?...MY CHILDREN ARE ALL I HAVE IN THE WORLD! ...WHY SHOULD I GO ON LIVING?!...FOR WHAT I ASK YOU?!...TO, MAYBE, SEE A BEAUTIFUL BOY THROW HIMSELF AWAY ON A...
MOMMA, MOMMA, YOU NEVER MET HER! WELL, YOU MIGHT AS WELL FACE IT... I WILL MARRY THERESA AND WE'LL BRING UP OUR CHILDREN AS WE SEE FIT! P-E-R-I-OD
MOMMA??..

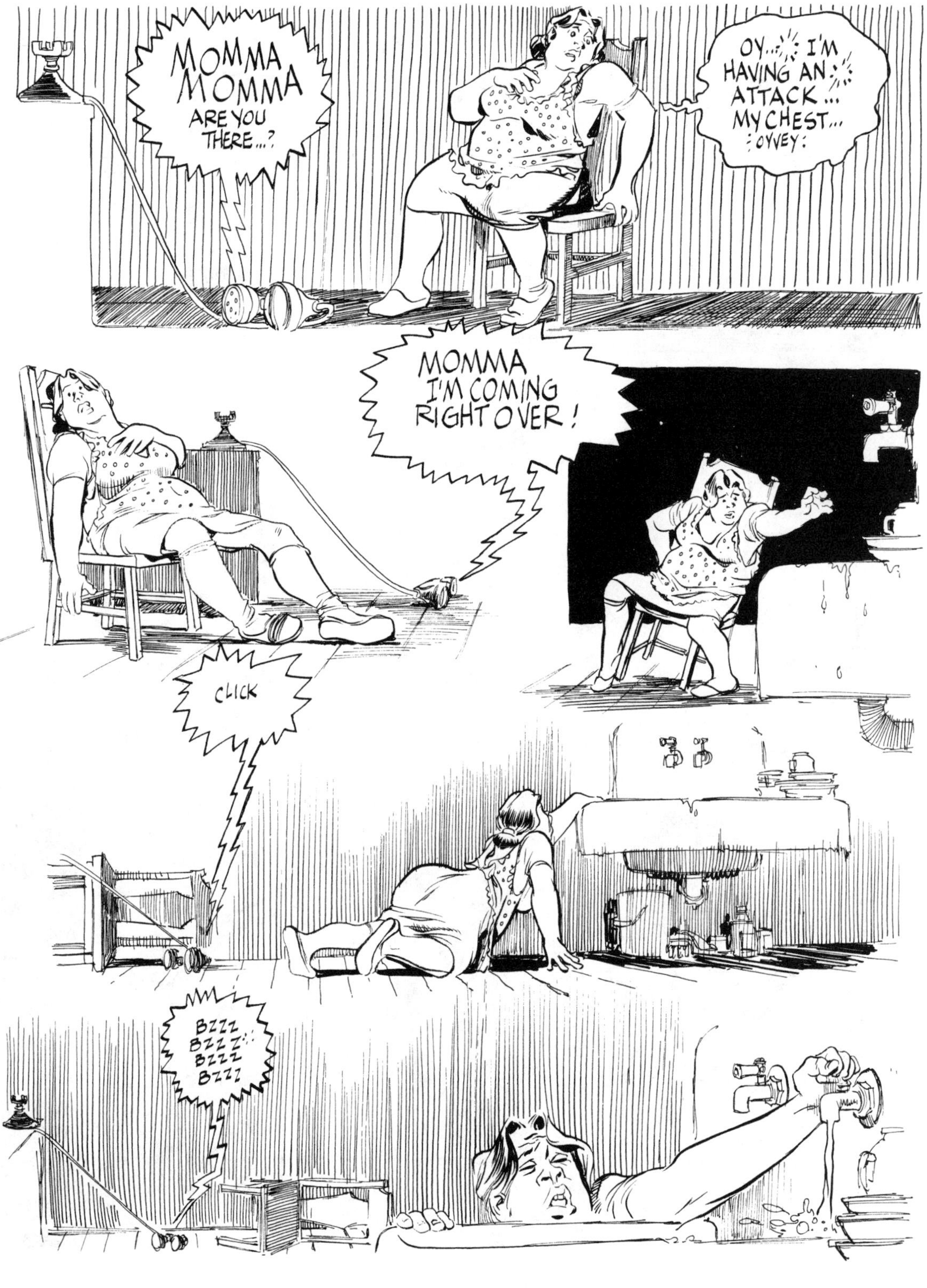
MOMMA MOMMA ARE YOU THERE...?
OY...!! I'M HAVING AN ATTACK... MY CHEST... OYVEY
MOMMA I'M COMING RIGHT OVER!
CLICK
BZZZ BZZZ BZZZ BZZZ

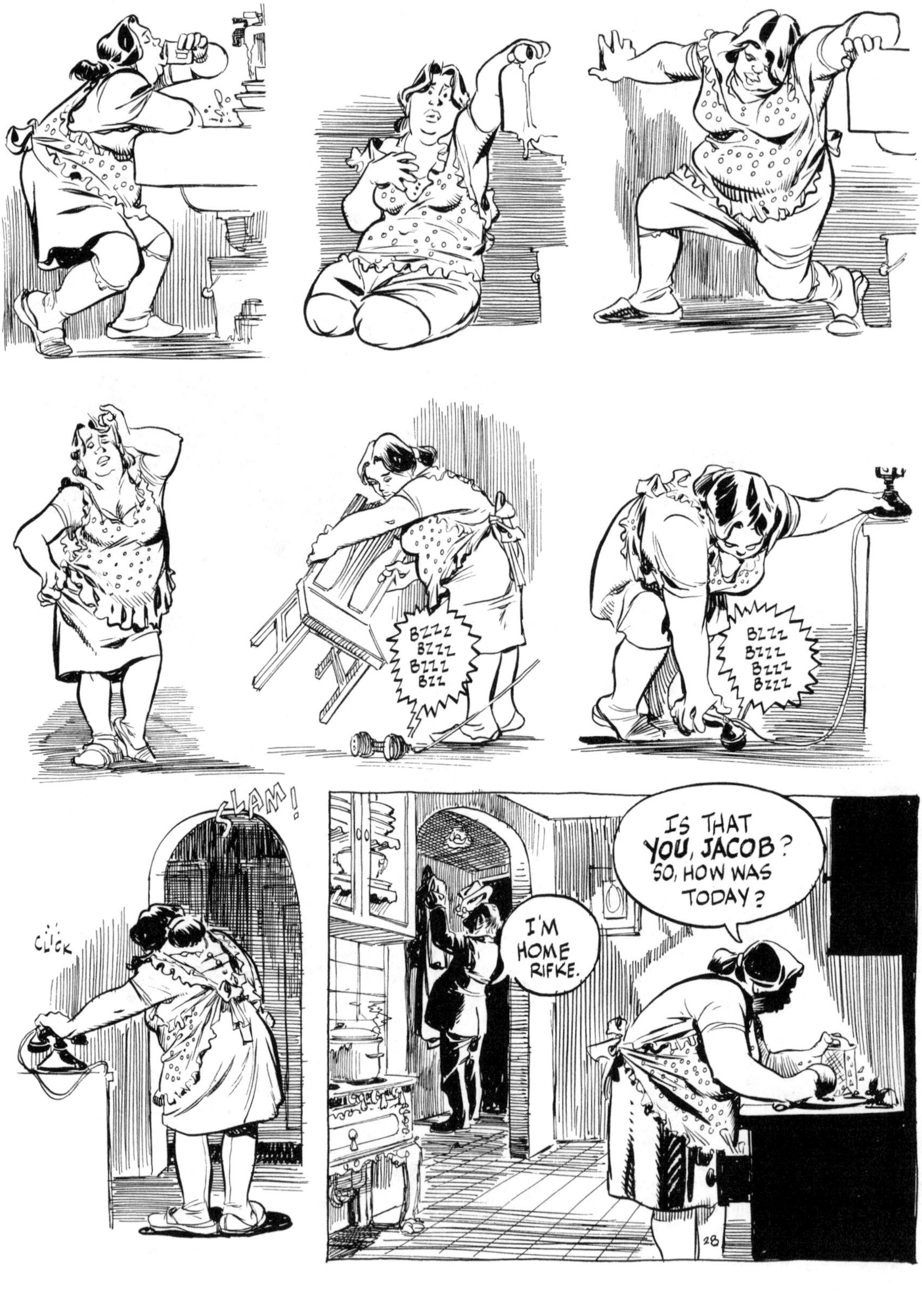
BZZZ BZZZ BZZZ BZZ
BZZZ BZZZ BZZZ BZZZ
SLAM!
CLICK
I'M HOME RIFKE.
IS THAT YOU, JACOB? SO, HOW WAS TODAY?
28

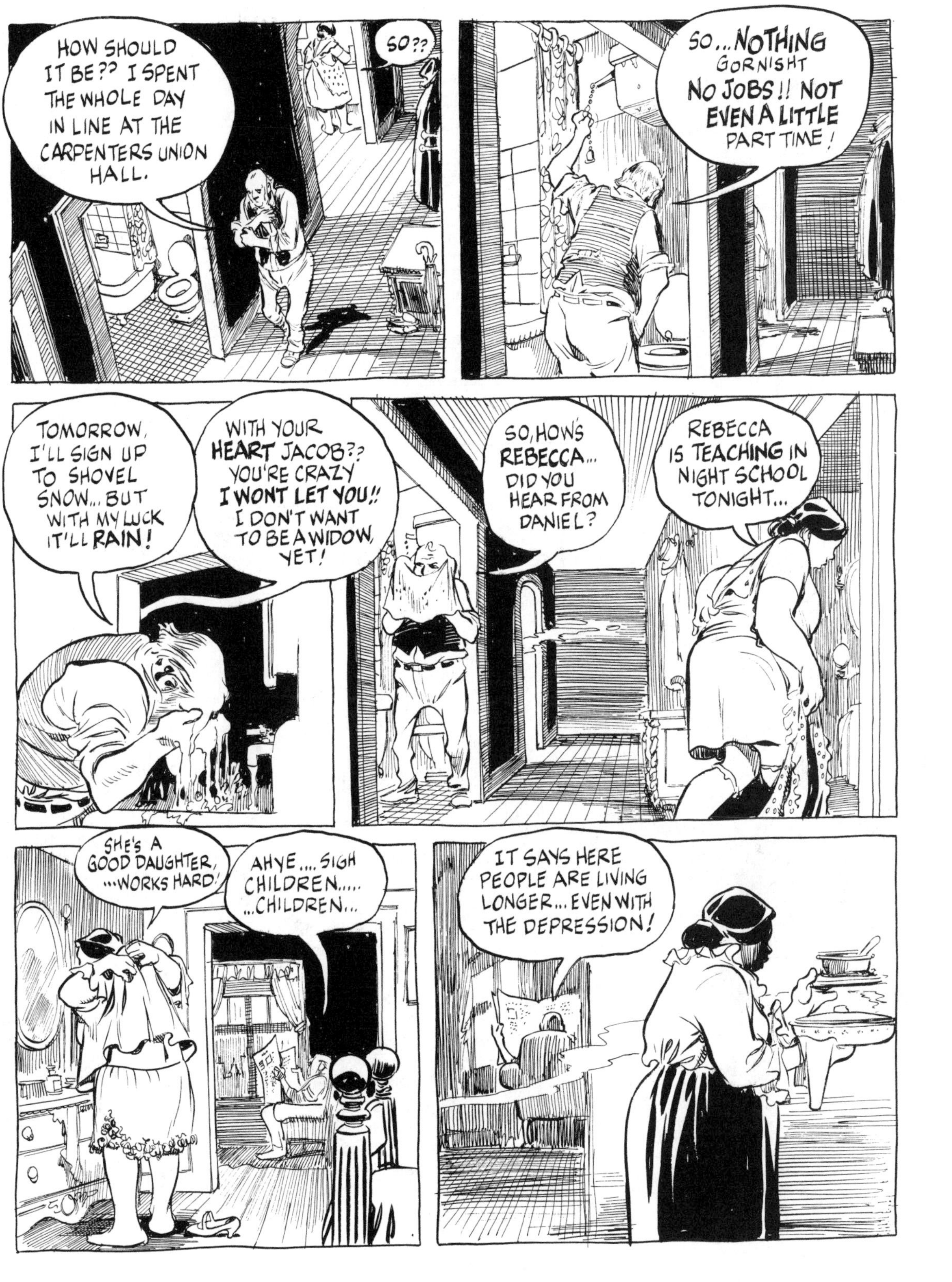
HOW SHOULD IT BE?? I SPENT THE WHOLE DAY IN LINE AT THE CARPENTERS UNION HALL.
SO??
SO...NOTHING GORNISHT NO JOBS!! NOT EVEN A LITTLE PART TIME!
TOMORROW, I'LL SIGN UP TO SHOVEL SNOW... BUT WITH MY LUCK IT'LL RAIN!
WITH YOUR HEART JACOB?? YOU'RE CRAZY I WONT LET YOU!! I DON'T WANT TO BE A WIDOW, YET!
SO, HOW'S REBECCA... DID YOU HEAR FROM DANIEL?
REBECCA IS TEACHING IN NIGHT SCHOOL TONIGHT...
SHE'S A GOOD DAUGHTER, ...WORKS HARD!
AHYE.... SIGH CHILDREN..... ...CHILDREN...
IT SAYS HERE PEOPLE ARE LIVING LONGER... EVEN WITH THE DEPRESSION!

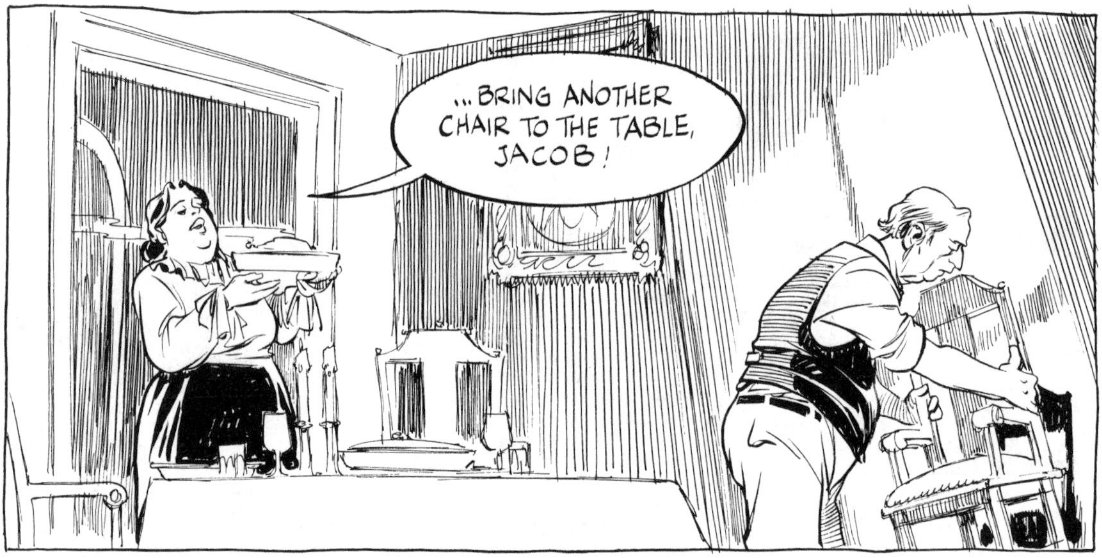
...BRING ANOTHER CHAIR TO THE TABLE, JACOB!

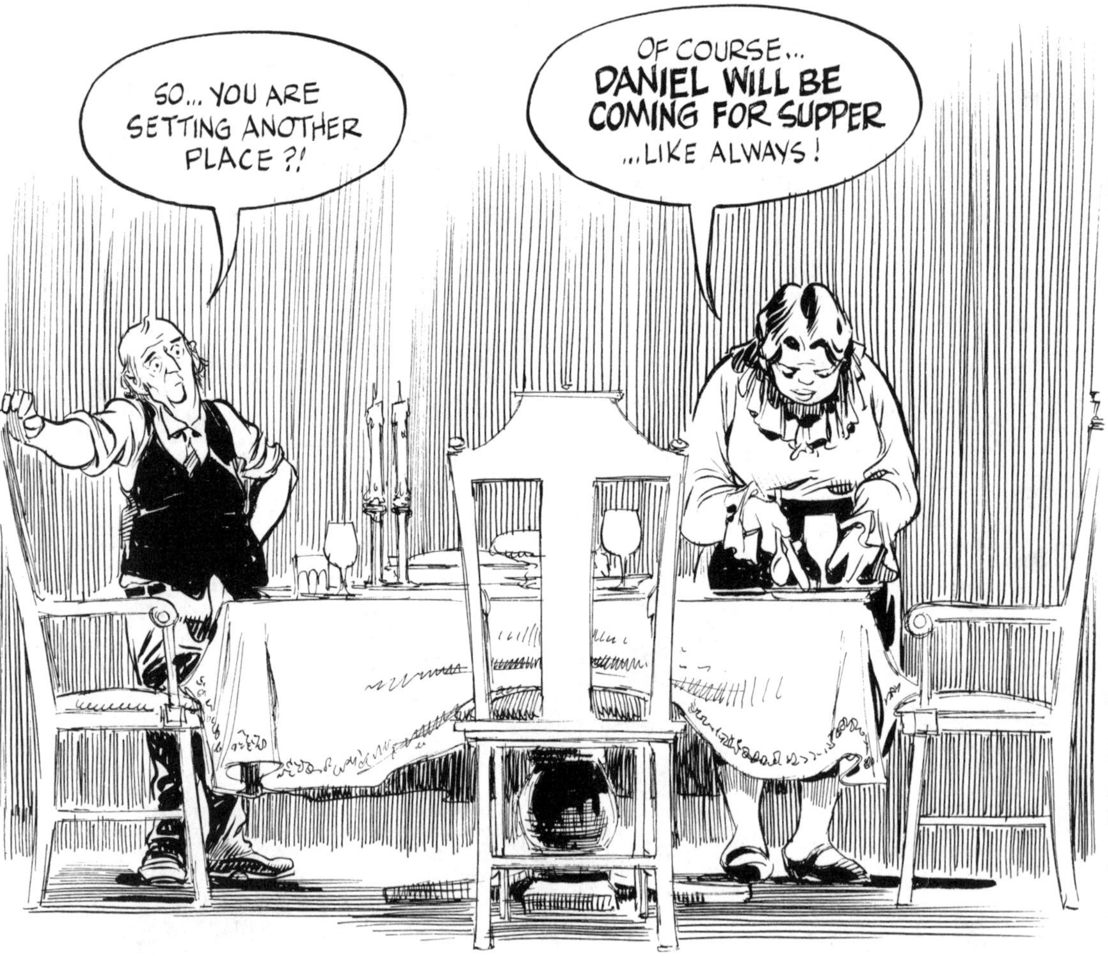
SO... YOU ARE SETTING ANOTHER PLACE ?!
OF COURSE... DANIEL WILL BE COMING FOR SUPPER ...LIKE ALWAYS!

CHAPTER 3

ON THE TOP FLOOR, BACK, LIVED GOD

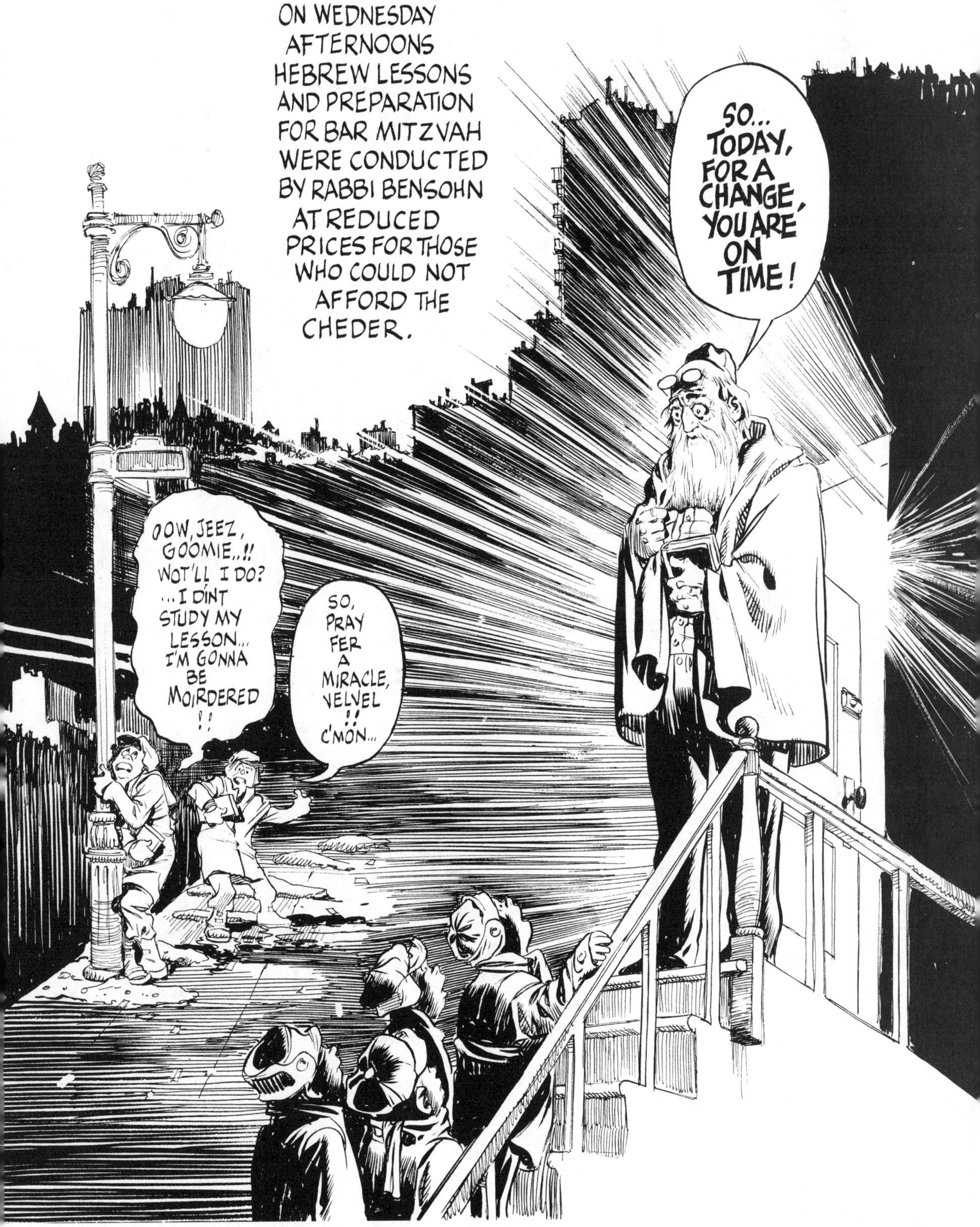
ON WEDNESDAY AFTERNOONS HEBREW LESSONS AND PREPARATION FOR BAR MITZVAH WERE CONDUCTED BY RABBI BENSOHN AT REDUCED PRICES FOR THOSE WHO COULD NOT AFFORD THE CHEDER.
SO... TODAY, FOR A CHANGE, YOU ARE ON TIME!
OOW, JEEZ, GOOMIE..!! WOT'LL I DO? ...I DINT STUDY MY LESSON... I'M GONNA BE MOIRDERED !!
SO, PRAY FER A MIRACLE, VELVEL !! C'MON...

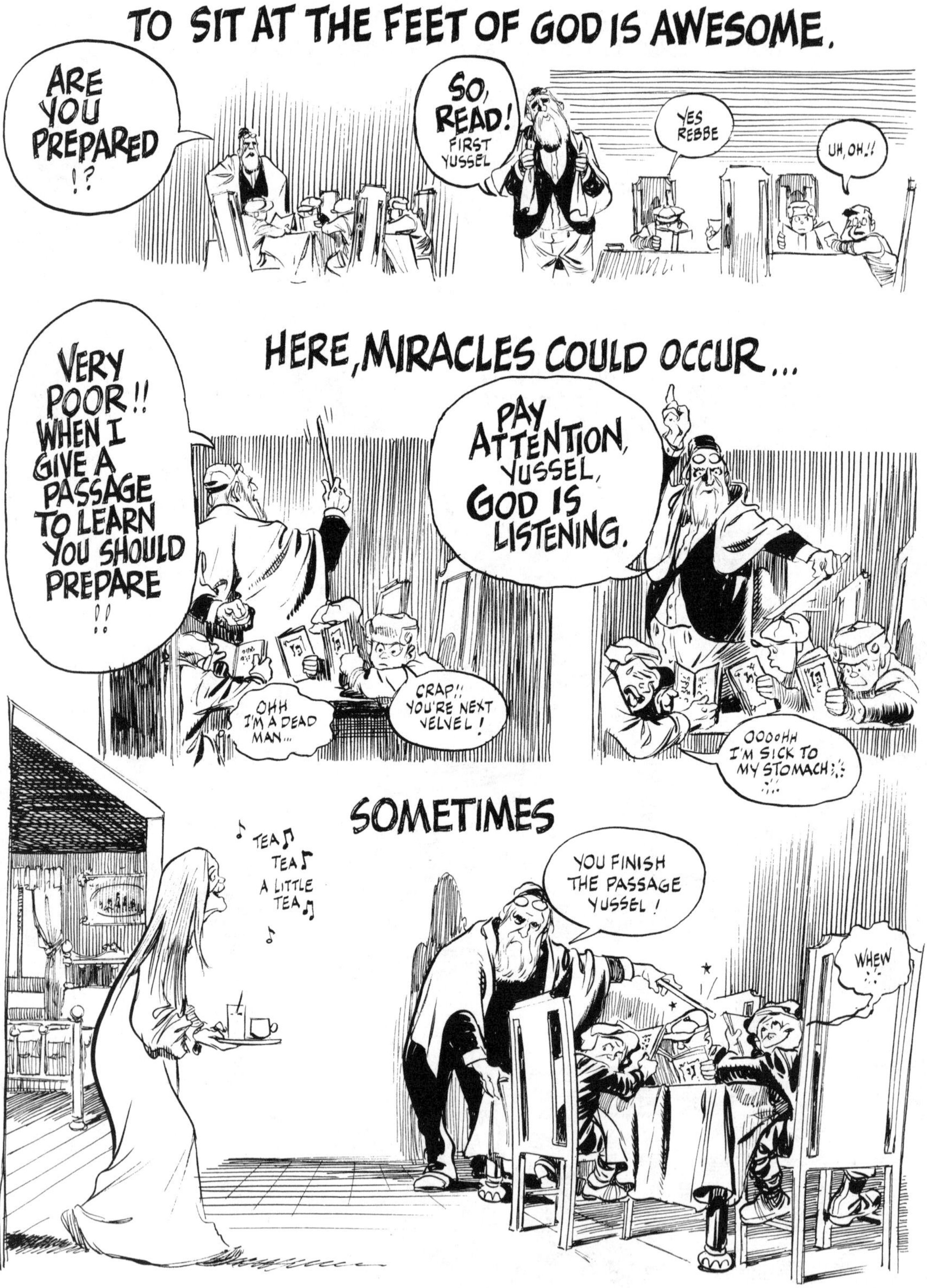
TO SIT AT THE FEET OF GOD IS AWESOME.
ARE YOU PREPARED !?
SO, READ! FIRST YUSSEL
YES REBBE
UH, OH.!!
HERE, MIRACLES COULD OCCUR...
VERY POOR!! WHEN I GIVE A PASSAGE TO LEARN YOU SHOULD PREPARE !!
OHH I'M A DEAD MAN...
CRAP!! YOU'RE NEXT VELVEL!
PAY ATTENTION, YUSSEL, GOD IS LISTENING.
OOOoHH I'M SICK TO MY STOMACH
SOMETIMES
TEA TEA A LITTLE TEA
YOU FINISH THE PASSAGE YUSSEL!
WHEW

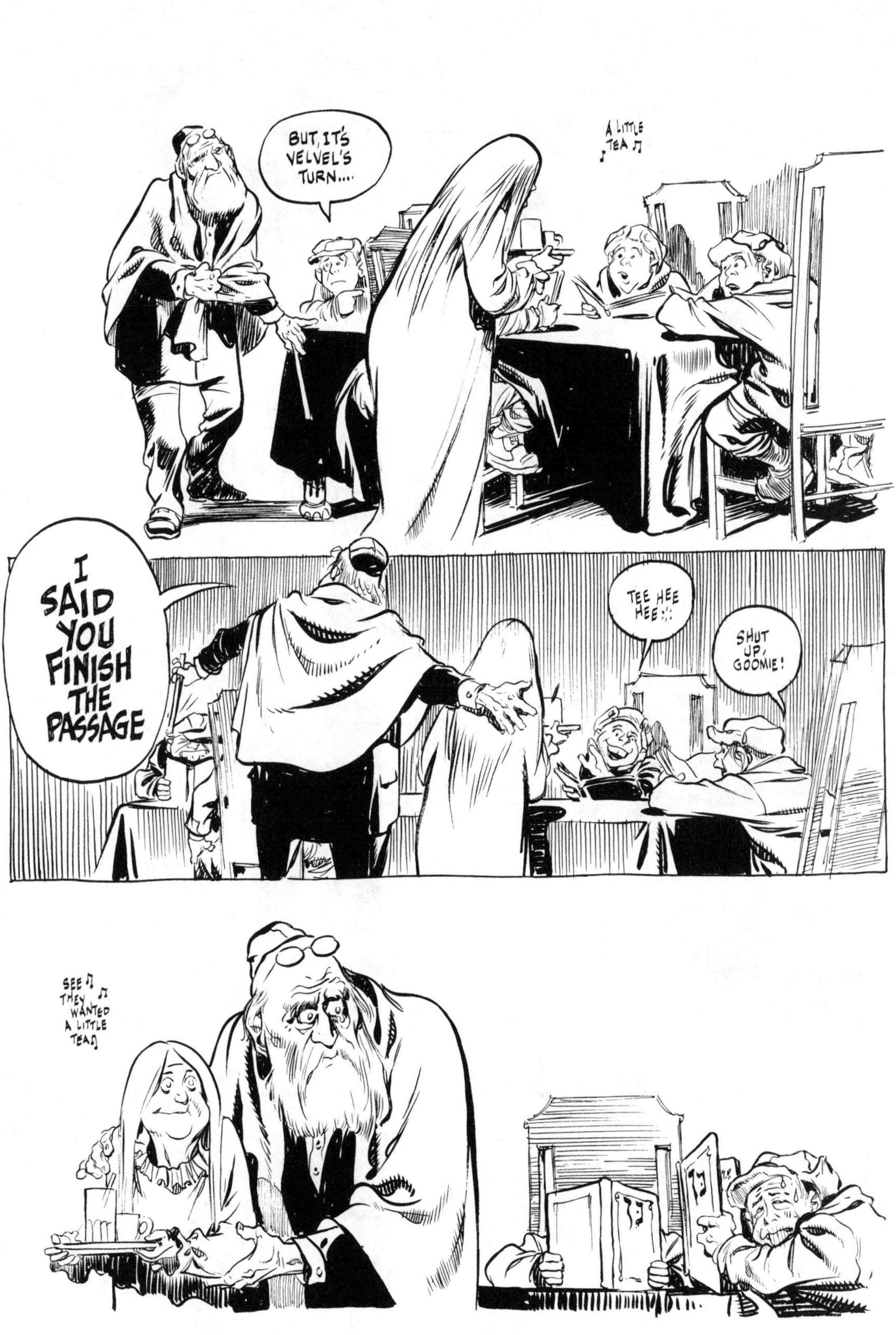
BUT, IT'S VELVEL'S TURN....
A LITTLE TEA ♫
I SAID YOU FINISH THE PASSAGE
TEE HEE HEE
SHUT UP, GOOMIE!
SEE ♫ THEY ♫ WANTED A LITTLE TEA ♫

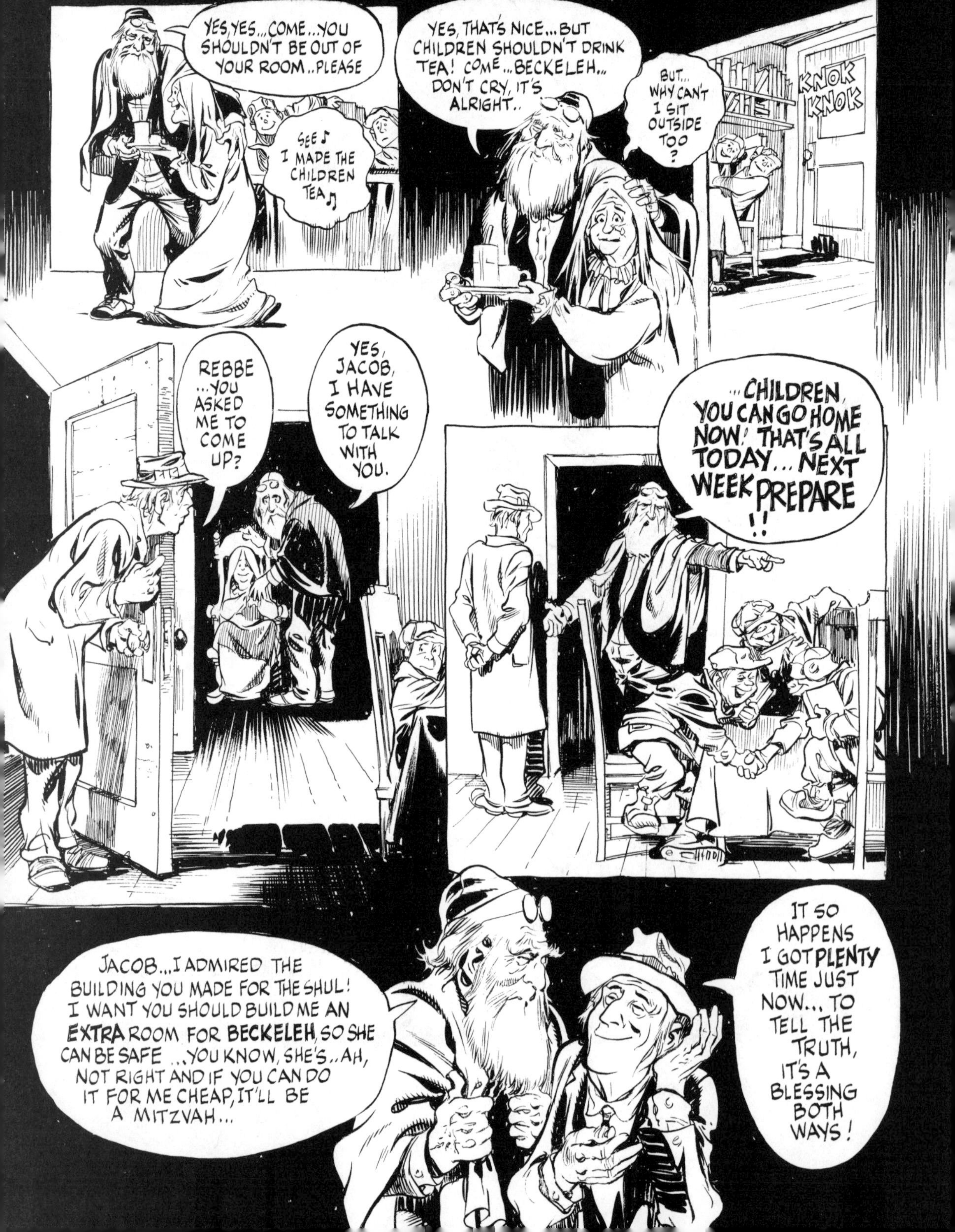
YES, YES... COME... YOU SHOULDN'T BE OUT OF YOUR ROOM.. PLEASE
SEE ♪ I MADE THE CHILDREN TEA ♫
YES, THAT'S NICE... BUT CHILDREN SHOULDN'T DRINK TEA! COME... BECKELEH... DON'T CRY, IT'S ALRIGHT..
BUT... WHY CAN'T I SIT OUTSIDE TOO?
KNOK KNOK
REBBE ...YOU ASKED ME TO COME UP?
YES, JACOB, I HAVE SOMETHING TO TALK WITH YOU.
...CHILDREN, YOU CAN GO HOME NOW! THAT'S ALL TODAY... NEXT WEEK PREPARE!!
JACOB... I ADMIRED THE BUILDING YOU MADE FOR THE SHUL! I WANT YOU SHOULD BUILD ME AN EXTRA ROOM FOR BECKELEH, SO SHE CAN BE SAFE ...YOU KNOW, SHE'S.. AH, NOT RIGHT AND IF YOU CAN DO IT FOR ME CHEAP, IT'LL BE A MITZVAH...
IT SO HAPPENS I GOT PLENTY TIME JUST NOW..., TO TELL THE TRUTH, IT'S A BLESSING BOTH WAYS!

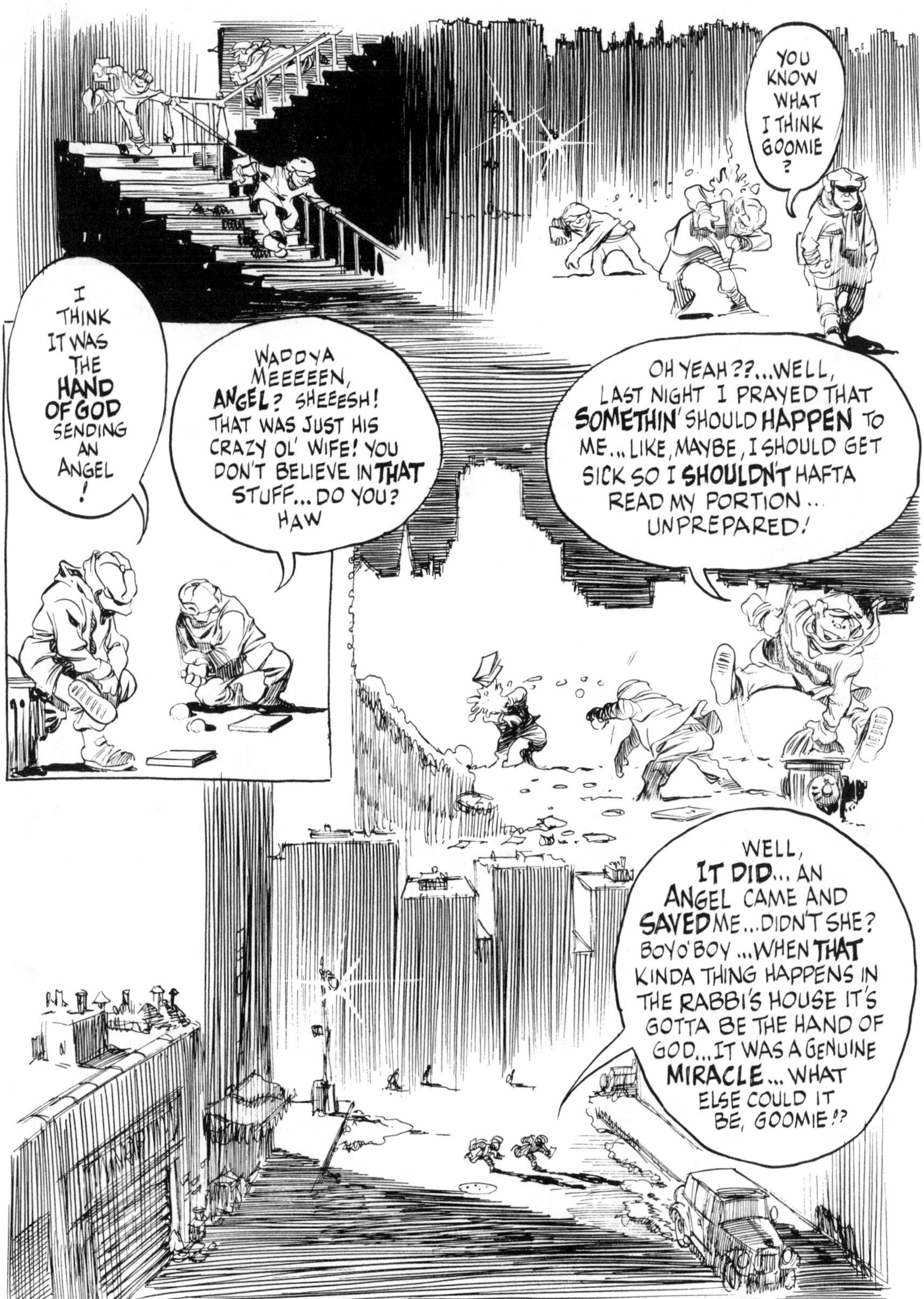
YOU KNOW WHAT I THINK GOOMIE ?
I THINK IT WAS THE HAND OF GOD SENDING AN ANGEL !
WADDYA MEEEEEN, ANGEL? SHEEESH! THAT WAS JUST HIS CRAZY OL' WIFE! YOU DON'T BELIEVE IN THAT STUFF... DO YOU? HAW
OH YEAH??...WELL, LAST NIGHT I PRAYED THAT SOMETHIN' SHOULD HAPPEN TO ME... LIKE, MAYBE, I SHOULD GET SICK SO I SHOULDN'T HAFTA READ MY PORTION... UNPREPARED!
WELL, IT DID... AN ANGEL CAME AND SAVED ME... DIDN'T SHE? BOYO'BOY ...WHEN THAT KINDA THING HAPPENS IN THE RABBI'S HOUSE IT'S GOTTA BE THE HAND OF GOD... IT WAS A GENUINE MIRACLE... WHAT ELSE COULD IT BE, GOOMIE!?

HOWEVER MANKIND DEALT WITH ITS SURVIVAL, THERE REMAINED YET ANOTHER FORCE, MIGHTY AND IMPLACABLE... THE WEATHER!

JANUARY, 1934, ARRIVED TO A SLUSHY NEW YORK. It began mildly. A warm wave thawed the accumulation of snow that was deposited on the city in the month before. Firemen had to be called out to deal with floods caused by suddenly-thawed sprinklers in over 200 buildings. Meanwhile, 40,000 were given work to clear the snow. In the New York Harbor, fog, resulting from the sudden warmth, delayed ship traffic.

JANUARY ENDED IN SUDDEN COLD! The mercury dropped 52 degrees in one day and the thermometers of the city stood at 5 degrees above zero with icy winds and snow flurries swirling around the buildings.

FEBRUARY BEGAN AFTER THREE DAYS OF BITTER COLD. Warm winds brought relief, just briefly, for a heavy snowfall buried the city! While 2000 worked at shovelling streets and 20,000 out-of-work people eagerly awaited a chance for a job, bad news came from the Bronx! At the Bronx Zoo the groundhogs failed to come out! Those who counted on these creatures to predict spring were bitterly disappointed. Then the temperature dropped to 15 degrees and a pile-up of 9.6 inches of snow, giving employment to the 20,000 jobless at snow removal.

ON FEBRUARY 2, THERE WAS OTHER GOOD NEWS! Up in the Bronx Zoo the groundhog finally came out, saw his shadow, and promptly scurried back to his nest. It was clearly a portent of an early spring. But by the day's end the mercury dropped to 4 degrees . . . a record for this date.

ON FEBRUARY 3RD ICE FLOES RAMPANT ON THE HUDSON RIVER! Propelled by the currents they dragged three ships for twenty blocks from their anchorage.

ON FEBRUARY 13 THE CITY WAS LASHED BY A BITTER GALE FOLLOWED BY A HEAVY SNOWFALL! Within eleven hours the mercury dropped 20 degrees. On the rivers the Coast Guard struggled to save men on barges adrift on the icy waters. But the snowfall gave work to 6000 jobless men hired to clean streets.

ON FEBRUARY 15, N.Y. BRACED FOR ANOTHER COLD. The New York Times reported that a cold wave was coming from the Rocky Mountains and that an unemployed man was found dead of the cold alongside a bunkmate who was unconscious. The following day the paper reported that the first half of February was the coldest in the 63 years of the New York City Weather Bureau's records.

ON FEBRUARY 20, THE CITY WAS HIT AGAIN! After almost a week of wavering the mercury dropped to 9 degrees above zero and a 9-inch snowfall immobilized the city. For hours the suburbs were cut off. Suburbanites in snow shoes and skis were also using horses and sleds to get around.

ON FEBRUARY 22, N.Y. WAS PINIONED BY SNOW! The city's newspapers carried stories of milk being delivered to the suburbs by plane. In the city itself 50,000 people were at work digging out. Slowly, commuters were able to get back to work. In the New York Times an expert, Mr. Raubenheimer, called the storm ". . . a carbon copy of the Blizzard of 1888."

BY FEBRUARY 27, THE CITY TRIED TO FREE ITSELF! After a day or two of rising and falling temperature which caused icy streets that were soon covered by a 9-inch snowfall, the papers carried reports that some Long Island and New Jersey communities were cut off from the city. In Manhattan hotels were jammed with snowbound commuters. Only the busses were running. Nine storm-related injuries were reported. The following day the total fatalities related to the thermometer rose to 14. Stores announced that skis and earmuffs sold out! The mercury dropped to 9 degrees above zero but the city somehow averted a coal and food shortage and fed its park animals, while in Westchester County the roads were cleared.

MARCH CAME IN LIKE A LAMB THIS YEAR. With a 15 degree rise in temperature which caused a thaw that melted the accumulated ice, water flooded the streets of the city.

ON APRIL 24, THE CITY FELT THE FIRST THUNDERSTORM OF THE YEAR!

BY MAY 21, THE CITY SWELTERED! A record heat of 88 degrees Fahrenheit roasted the city and left one heat prostration case. This was followed by hail, rain and lightning which caused damage and resulted in 3 prostrations within 72 hours.

JULY ARRIVED WITH THE MERCURY AT 91 DEGREES. Within the next three days 13 more heat prostrations and 5 deaths were reported in the press before a rainstorm finally brought a short relief. But the mercury hovered at over 92 degrees for the next eight days leaving about 12 overcome and 3 dead.

ST. SWITHEN'S DAY WAS SULTRY and ended in showers.

JULY ENDED WITH THE MERCURY AT 89 DEGREES. A count of the heat-related casualties which the New York Times reported for the month came to 29 prostrations and 11 deaths. Two heat records were set, they said.

AUGUST BEGAN, RECORDING THE COOLEST AUGUST 6 IN HISTORY. At the end of the month, after zooming up to 95 degrees, the month ended with the coolest day in August's history.

FINALLY, BY DECEMBER   New York returned to a seasonal norm and a light snow powdered the rooftops.

* * * *

NEVERTHELESS, THE COCKROACHES IN THE TENEMENTS ON DROPSIE AVENUE, RESPONDING TO A LIFE FORCE EQUAL TO THE ENVIRONMENT, CONTINUED THEIR PROLIFERATION AS THEY HAD FOR OVER FOUR MILLION YEARS!

CHAPTER 4

SHABBASGOY

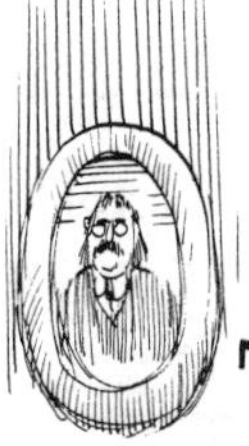

THE SHAFTSBURYS EMIGRATED TO NEW ENGLAND IN 1850. THERE THEY FOUNDED AN AXE-HANDLE FACTORY WHICH FLOURISHED. IT REMAINED IN THE FAMILY'S HANDS UNTIL THE DEATH OF ELTON JOSIAH SHAFTSBURY AROUND 1927.

HIS SON, ELTON SHAFTSBURY II, HIS ONLY HEIR, THEN TOOK OVER THE OPERATION OF THE SHAFTSBURY WOOD PRODUCTS COMPANY.

ACTUALLY, YOUNG ELTON HAD LITTLE INTEREST IN RUNNING A BUSINESS. HE HAD BEEN REARED IN COMFORT AND SECURITY. WITH AN UNQUESTIONED CONFIDENCE IN HIS SURVIVAL THAT CAME FROM THE CERTAINTY OF HIS SOCIAL POSITION, HE EXPECTED HIS WORLD TO GO ON, AS IT WAS, FOREVER. HIS SKILLS WERE MAINLY CENTERED IN THE ART OF BEING ACCEPTED AND THE MAINTENANCE OF THE SHALLOW RELATIONSHIPS THAT WERE NORMAL FOR HIS SET.

WHAT ELTON SHAFTSBURY II REALLY WANTED WAS FREEDOM TO PURSUE HIS SOCIAL LIFE.

SO, UPON THE DEATH OF HIS FATHER, ELTON SOLD THE FACTORY AND PUT THE PROCEEDS INTO THE STOCK MARKET.

THIS ENABLED HIM TO ENGAGE IN A MORE 'GENTLEMANLY' VOCATION. HE JOINED A MAIN-LINE WALL STREET BROKERAGE HOUSE AND OCCUPIED HIMSELF WITH BEING A 'CUSTOMER'S-MAN'. HERE HIS SOCIAL CONTACTS AND RICH FRIENDS WERE AN ASSET THAT ALLOWED HIM TO MAKE MONEY IN A 'NICE WAY'!

IN THE FALL OF 1929, THE STOCK MARKET COLLAPSED, AND WITHIN MONTHS HIS HOLDINGS WERE WIPED OUT. THE BROKERAGE HOUSE, LIKE SO MANY OTHERS, COLLAPSED AND HIS CIRCLE OF FRIENDS SUFFERED SIMILARLY... THEY SOON DISPERSED.

ELTON'S LAST SAVINGS WERE DEMOLISHED IN THE FAILURE OF THE NOTORIOUS BANK OF U.S.

BY THE WINTER OF 1933 ELTON SHAFTSBURY II, BROKE AND UNEMPLOYED, WAS REDUCED TO SELLING APPLES ON THE CORNER OF WALL AND WILLIAM STREETS.

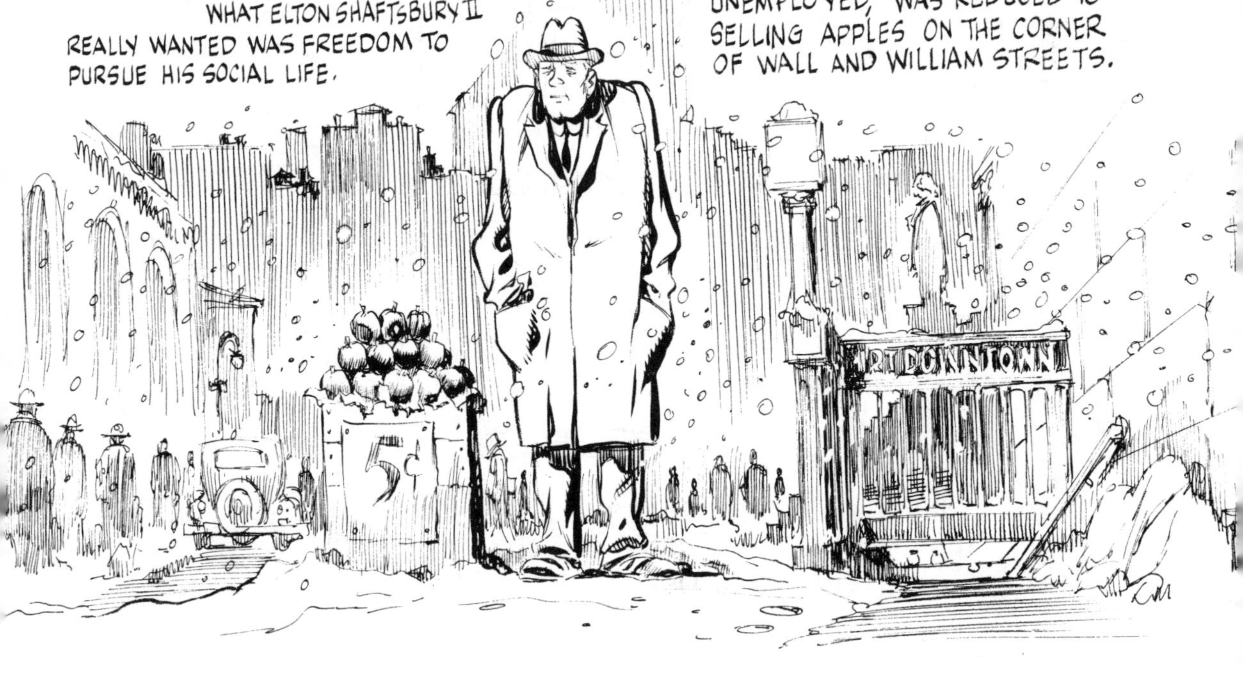
RT DOWNTOWN
5¢

1929

BYRD IN SAFE FLIGHT OVER SOUTH POLE

The N.Y. Times on Nov. 30 reported that Admiral Byrd, the first to conquer the North Pole, succeeded in flying over the South Pole as well.

President Herbert Hoover sent the aviator and his crew a congratulatory message that said in part ". . . we are glad of proof that the spirit of great adventure still lives."

Mayor Jimmy Walker, of New York said, ". . . the American flag will look great down there."

SOCIAL NOTE

BERLIN, OCT. 29

Fritz Von Opel, the first man to fly a rocket plane, revealed today, he would wed Frau Selnik who is one of Germany's six women pilots. They will come to New York in November.

STOCK MARKET DROPS 15 BILLION OCT. 29 SELL OFF WORST IN HISTORY 16,410,030 SHARES TRADED

EMBEZZLER GIVES UP $47,000 NAVY LOOT

BURIED IN D.C. CHICKEN YARD

OCT. 30, 1929

Lt. Charles Musil, U.S. Navy Paymaster surrendered to the authorities and led them to the cache in a chicken yard. However, $6,100 is still missing and the embezzler admits that he bought some stock before he became penitent and gave up.

BANKS OPTIMISTIC BUT SUPPORT FAILS

On Wednesday, Oct. 30, the New York press reported a major sell off of panic proportions on the previous day. By the end of trading, however, leading issues recovered as much as 14 points in 15 minutes to momentarily, at least, assuage the pall of gloom that overhung the financial centers.

RALLY BRIEF

Organized support from the leading financial houses is gathering to help offset the "mob psychology" that is blamed for the plunge.

1930

MURDER OF GAMBLER STILL UNSOLVED

FEB. 4, 1930

The New York Times in a special report revealed that the killing of Arnold Rothstein on Nov. 4, 1928 has precipitated an inquiry into the affairs of the city's magistrates courts, police department, and possibly fire department. Governor Franklin D. Roosevelt, when asked whether he would or would not veto an investigation, laughed, and said he would wait until he saw the legislation before deciding.

LINDBERGH SETS RECORD CROSSES U.S. IN 14½ HRS.

APRIL 20, 1930

Col. Charles A. Lindbergh added another first to his laurels by flying coast to coast, 14,000 feet at 180 mph. His wife served as navigator.

UNEMPLOYMENT ATTACKED IN SENATE

DEMOCRATS BLAME HOOVER'S POLICIES

MARCH 3, 1930

A major New York paper in an exclusive article reported that the Senate's Democratic leaders accused the Hoover Administration of diverting attention from the increase in unemployment. He questioned administration statistics.

"RECOVERY NEAR" DEPRESSION PEAK OVER SAYS HOOVER

"STOCK MARKET CRASH DUE TO SPECULATION ORGY BY PUBLIC"

MAY 1930

President Herbert Hoover in a statement to the press, said today that the programs he instituted succeeded in maintaining courage and confidence. The worst is over, he feels.

CONDITIONS GROWING DAILY WORSE SAYS SENATOR LA FOLLETTE.

The Republican Senator from Wisconsin denounced attempts to label demonstrations by the unemployed as a movement by "The Reds." Another Republican guessed that unemployment stood at 6 million despite the questionably lower statistics from federal agencies.

300 N.Y. UNION LOCALS MEET IN MOVE TO COMBAT ACUTE UNEMPLOYMENT

MARCH 8, 1930

A meeting of major union locals in New York's Beethoven Hall will be held on March 19th.

1931

STOCK MARKET UP

FEB. 17, 1931

The Stock Market rose 2-8 points yesterday on accumulating evidence of a business pickup. This followed a flurry of buying activity the week earlier when on Feb. 11, a rally from public buying sent the list up.

HOOVER WILL VETO BONUS BILL DESPITE SENATE PASSAGE

FEB. 20, 1931

The President, despite a vote in the Senate of 72-2 in favor of a loan bill for veterans' payments, warned that it would cause a weakening of the government's financial structure.

400,000 DEPOSITORS OF NY BANK OF U.S. FATE NOW IN DOUBT

REAL VALUE OF BANK'S ASSETS UNACCOUNTED

FEB. 2, 1931

The NY State Banking Dept. report issued yesterday was without a satisfactory account of the actual condition of the failed bank's assets. After weeks of liquidation, the books of the bank remain as cloudy as they were on the day it closed.

$75,000,000 of the closed bank's assets are apparently lost or at least cannot be accounted for.

HUNGER RIOTS FAIL AS BRONX MARCH IS BROKEN UP BY COPS

JANUARY 9, 1931

In a demonstration that was reportedly staged by Communists in Manhattan, Brooklyn and the Bronx, police succeeded in easily dispersing what was termed as a "sparse" turnout.

At the Salvation Army's bread line on the Bowery at 4th Street, Manhattan, a policeman's jaw was broken.

HOUSEPAINTERS MAY USE NARROWER BRUSH TO CREATE MORE JOBS

FEB. 20, 1931

The New York Times carried a story today of a threat by the Painters Union of Long Island to go from the normal 6-inch paint brush to a smaller 3-inch brush so as to double the employment of housepainters in the city.

1932

F.D. ROOSEVELT WINS IN A LANDSLIDE
ANTI-PROHIBITION CONGRESS NOW IN
O'BRIEN BECOMES NEW YORK'S MAYOR

DEMOCRATS CONTROL CONGRESS IN RECORD NATIONAL VOTE

N.Y. CITY ASKS BANKS AID MAY DEFAULT CITY WAGE CUT $20,000,000

DEC. 7, 1932

The city faced an inevitable default on its obligations. Local bankers called on to rescue New York said that the cut in city payrolls was not enough and urged that another $25,000,000 be cut in city spending before credit could be restored to permit their loan.

Meanwhile, members of the Patrolmen's Benevolent Assn. launched a drive to enlist public support against their pay cut.

SWARMS OF MOTHS BLANKET THE BRONX

JULY 9, 1932

By midnight last night, a blizzard of fluttering moths engulfed the Bronx and then headed on to include Manhattan, Queens and Brooklyn. According to the New York Times, these were a gypsy moth specie and in such great numbers that they halted auto traffic on Jerome Avenue and Pelham Parkway. The police, deluged with phone calls, said that they were at a loss as to just what they were expected to do about it.

ONLY SIX STATES VOTED FOR HERBERT HOOVER

NOV. 9, 1932

In his lead article in the New York Times, Arthur Krock said ". . . a political cataclysm unprecedented in the nation's history and produced by three years of Depression" elected Franklin Delano Roosevelt, President of the United States.

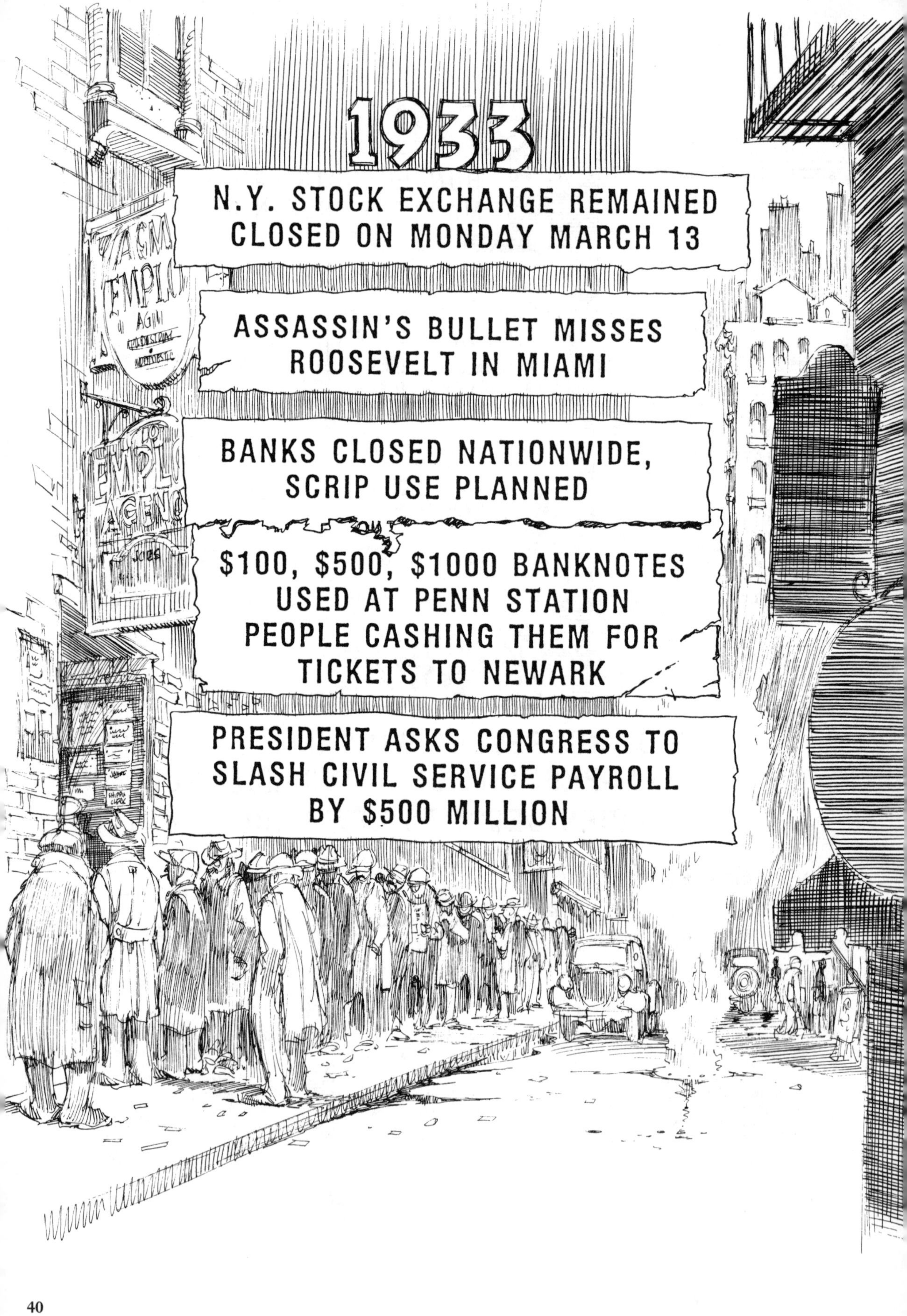
1933
N.Y. STOCK EXCHANGE REMAINED CLOSED ON MONDAY MARCH 13
ASSASSIN'S BULLET MISSES ROOSEVELT IN MIAMI
BANKS CLOSED NATIONWIDE, SCRIP USE PLANNED
$100, $500, $1000 BANKNOTES USED AT PENN STATION PEOPLE CASHING THEM FOR TICKETS TO NEWARK
PRESIDENT ASKS CONGRESS TO SLASH CIVIL SERVICE PAYROLL BY $500 MILLION

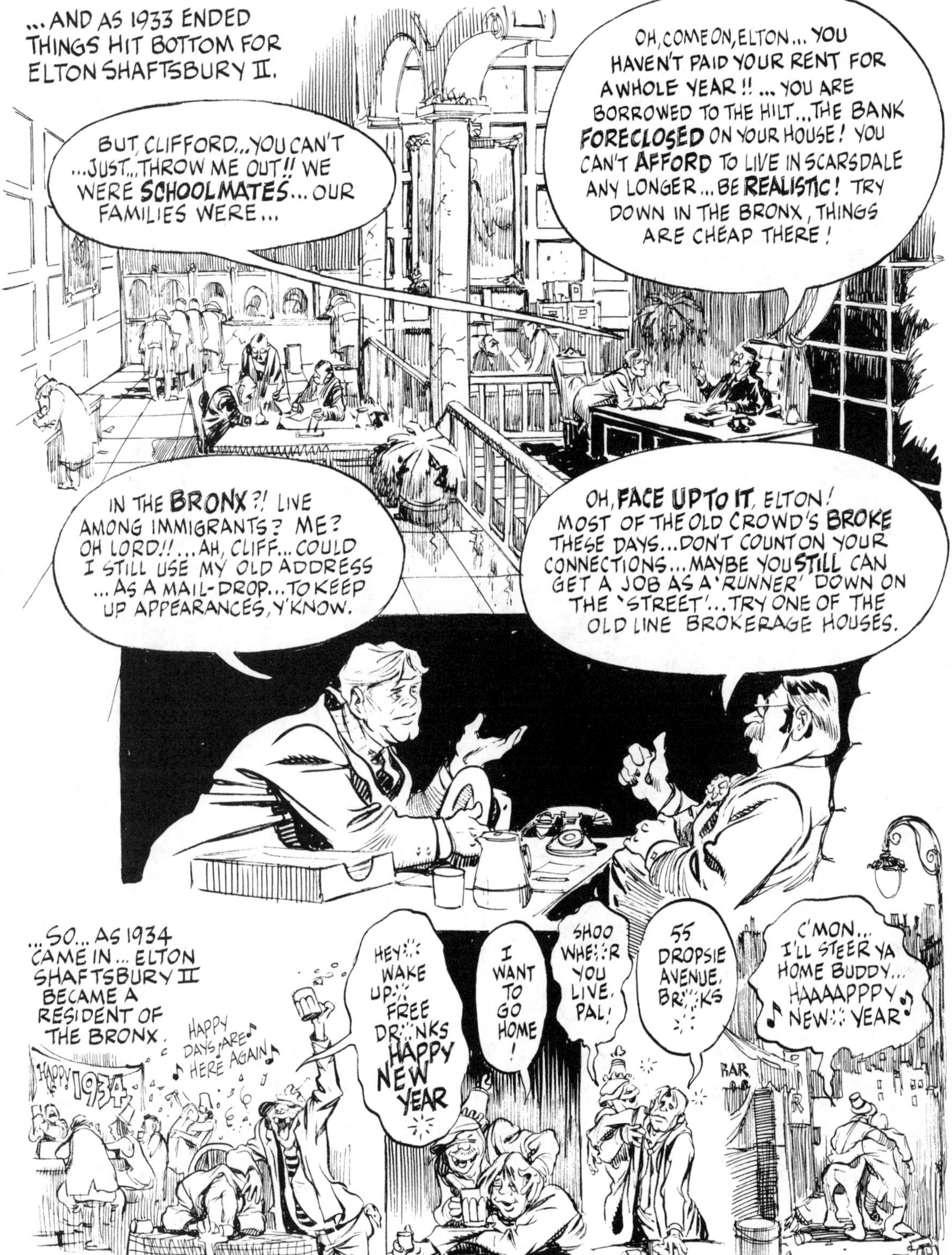
...AND AS 1933 ENDED THINGS HIT BOTTOM FOR ELTON SHAFTSBURY II.
BUT, CLIFFORD...YOU CAN'T ...JUST...THROW ME OUT!! WE WERE SCHOOLMATES...OUR FAMILIES WERE...
OH, COME ON, ELTON... YOU HAVEN'T PAID YOUR RENT FOR A WHOLE YEAR!! ... YOU ARE BORROWED TO THE HILT...THE BANK FORECLOSED ON YOUR HOUSE! YOU CAN'T AFFORD TO LIVE IN SCARSDALE ANY LONGER...BE REALISTIC! TRY DOWN IN THE BRONX, THINGS ARE CHEAP THERE!
IN THE BRONX?! LIVE AMONG IMMIGRANTS? ME? OH LORD!!...AH, CLIFF...COULD I STILL USE MY OLD ADDRESS ...AS A MAIL-DROP...TO KEEP UP APPEARANCES, Y'KNOW.
OH, FACE UP TO IT, ELTON! MOST OF THE OLD CROWD'S BROKE THESE DAYS...DON'T COUNT ON YOUR CONNECTIONS...MAYBE YOU STILL CAN GET A JOB AS A 'RUNNER' DOWN ON THE 'STREET'...TRY ONE OF THE OLD LINE BROKERAGE HOUSES.
...SO...AS 1934 CAME IN...ELTON SHAFTSBURY II BECAME A RESIDENT OF THE BRONX.
HAPPY 1934
HAPPY DAYS ARE HERE AGAIN
HEY WAKE UP FREE DR NKS HAPPY NEW YEAR
I WANT TO GO HOME!
SHOO WHE R YOU LIVE, PAL!
55 DROPSIE AVENUE, BR KS
BAR
C'MON... I'LL STEER YA HOME BUDDY... HAAAAPPPY NEW YEAR

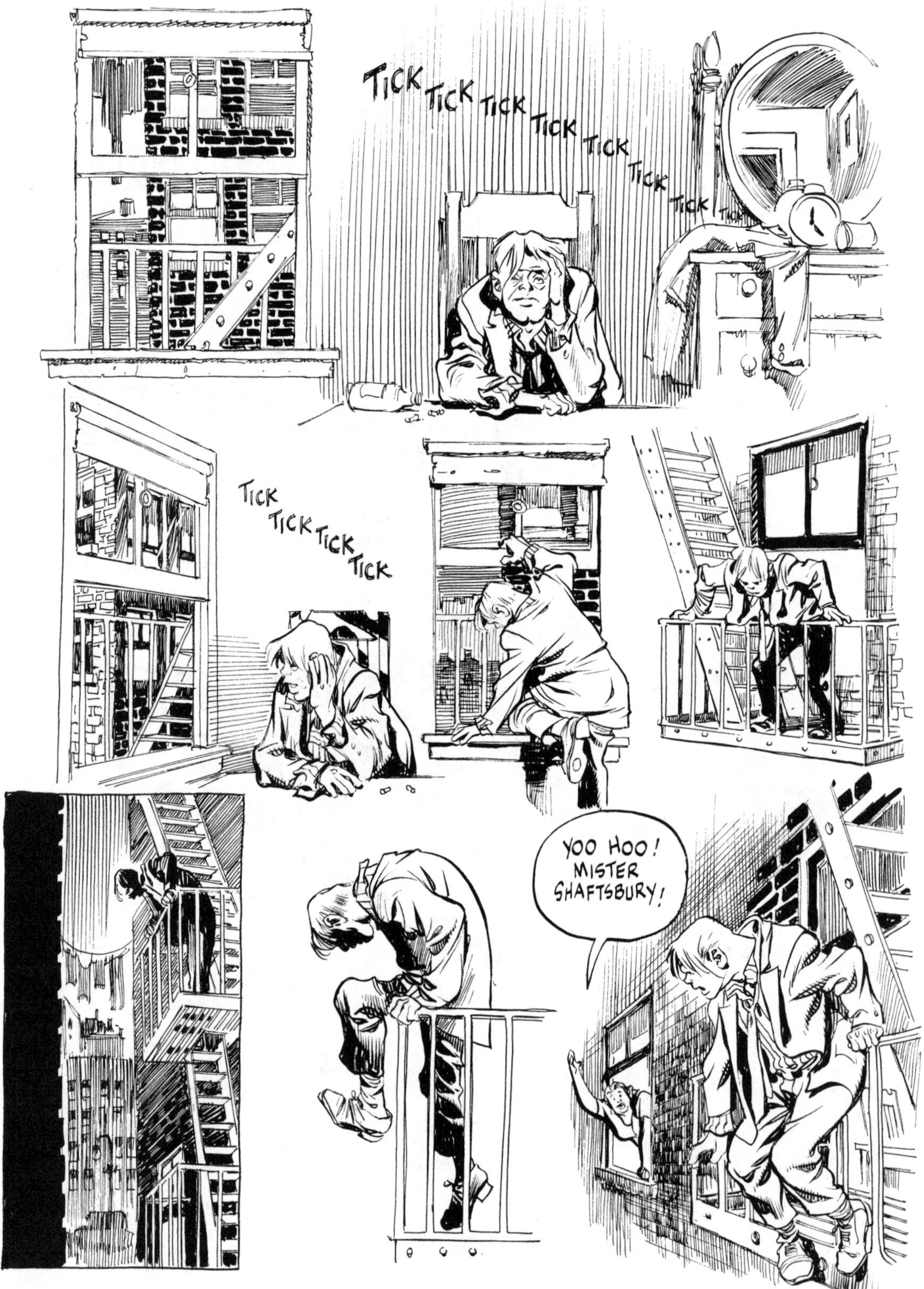
TICK TICK TICK TICK TICK TICK TICK TICK
TICK TICK TICK TICK
YOO HOO! MISTER SHAFTSBURY!

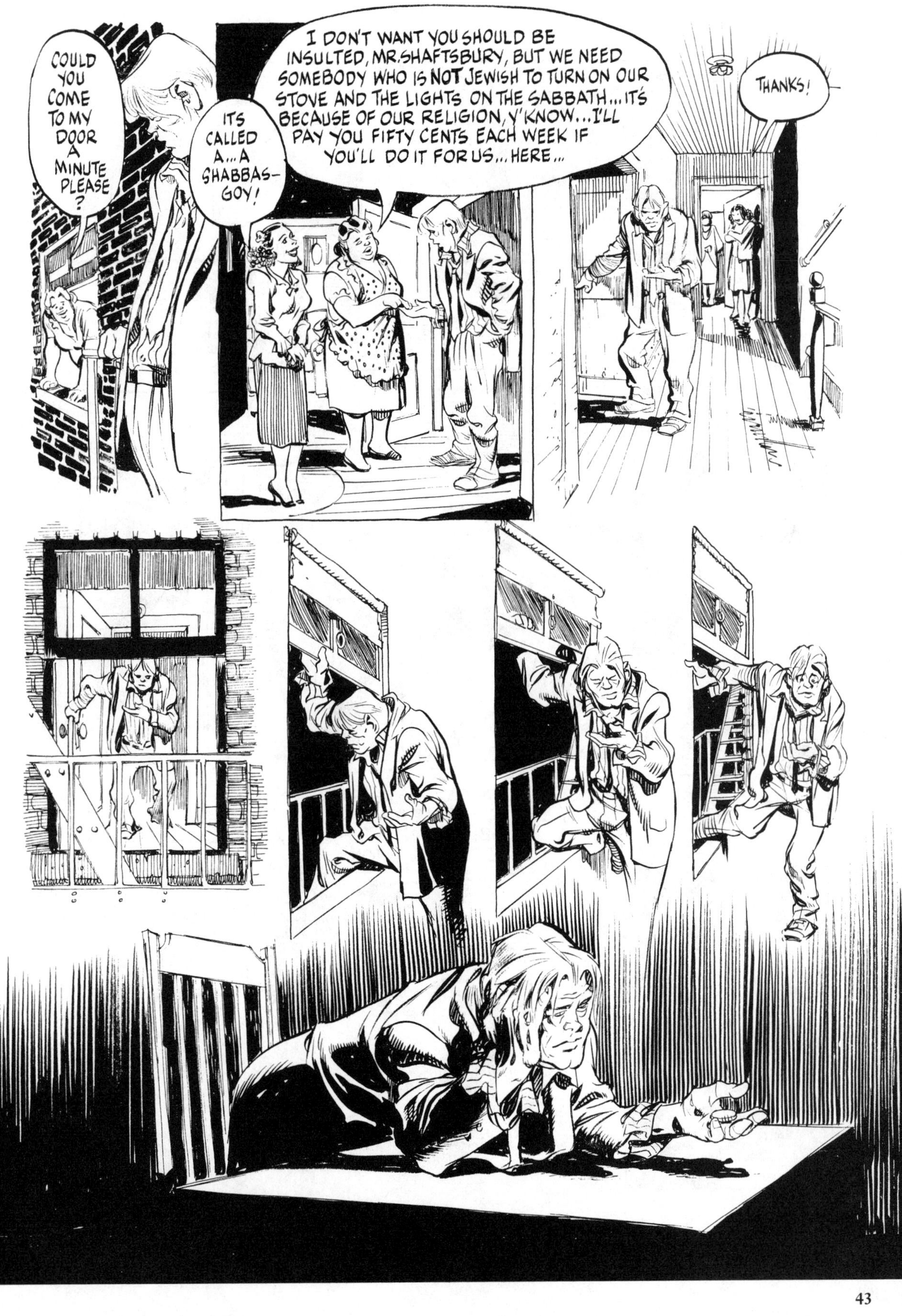
COULD YOU COME TO MY DOOR A MINUTE PLEASE?
ITS CALLED A...A SHABBAS-GOY!
I DON'T WANT YOU SHOULD BE INSULTED, MR. SHAFTSBURY, BUT WE NEED SOMEBODY WHO IS NOT JEWISH TO TURN ON OUR STOVE AND THE LIGHTS ON THE SABBATH... IT'S BECAUSE OF OUR RELIGION, Y'KNOW... I'LL PAY YOU FIFTY CENTS EACH WEEK IF YOU'LL DO IT FOR US... HERE...
THANKS!

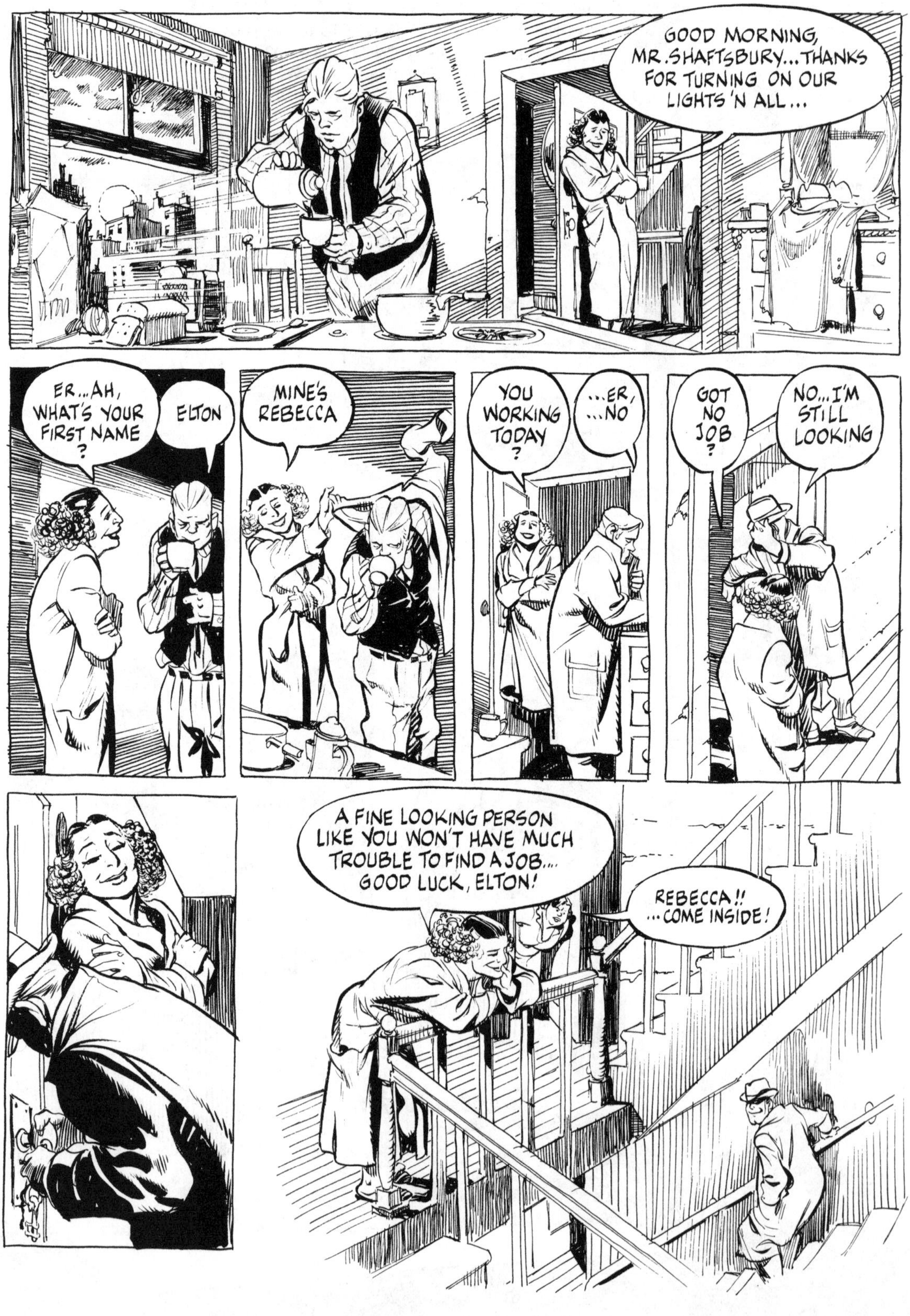
GOOD MORNING, MR. SHAFTSBURY... THANKS FOR TURNING ON OUR LIGHTS 'N ALL...
ER...AH, WHAT'S YOUR FIRST NAME ?
ELTON
MINE'S REBECCA
YOU WORKING TODAY ?
...ER, ...NO
GOT NO JOB ?
NO...I'M STILL LOOKING
A FINE LOOKING PERSON LIKE YOU WON'T HAVE MUCH TROUBLE TO FIND A JOB... GOOD LUCK, ELTON!
REBECCA!! ...COME INSIDE!

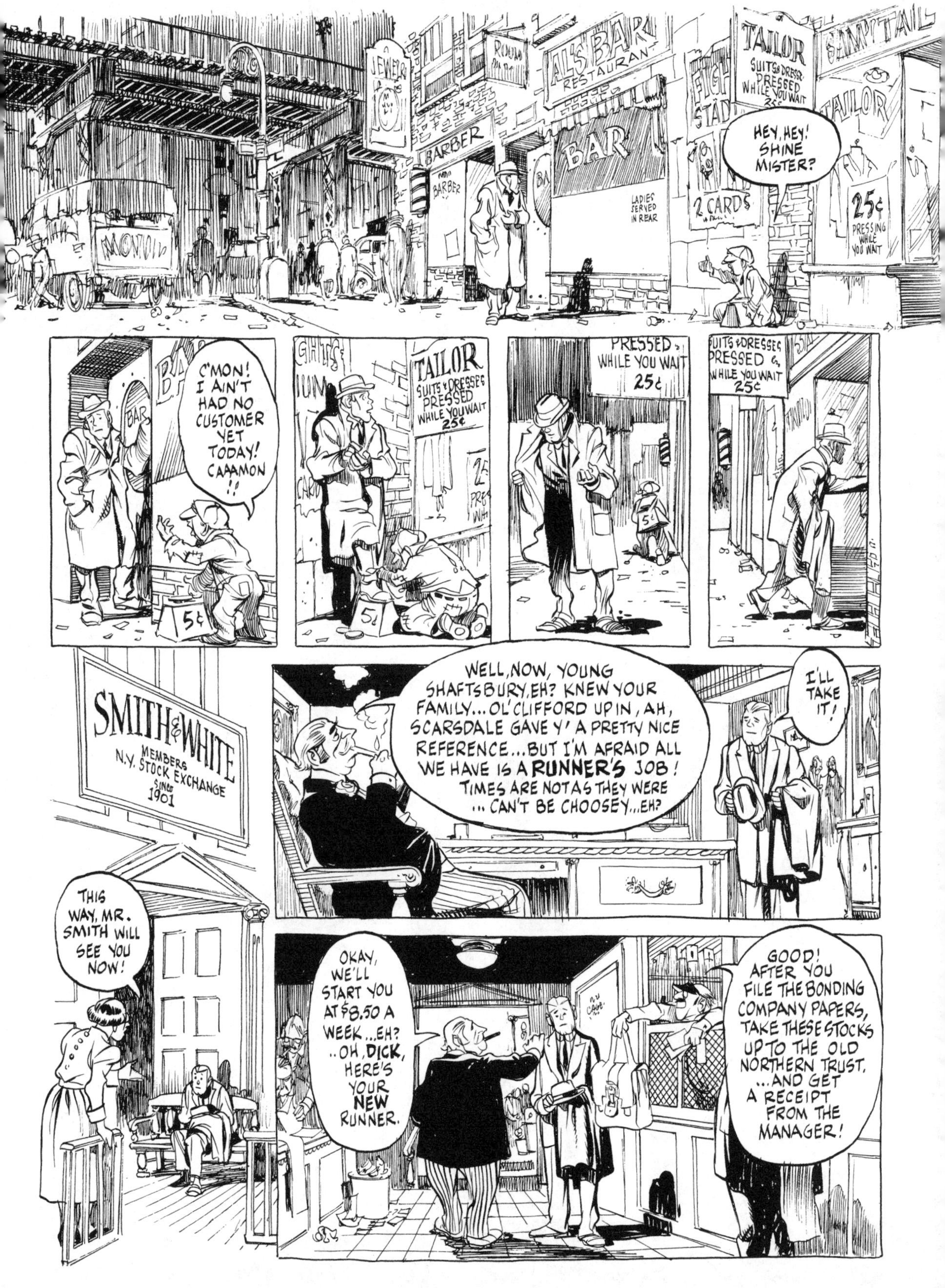
AL'S BAR RESTAURANT
TAILOR SUITS & DRESSES PRESSED WHILE YOU WAIT
BARBER
BARBER
BAR
LADIES SERVED IN REAR
2 CARDS
TAILOR
25¢ PRESSING WHILE YOU WAIT
HEY, HEY! SHINE MISTER?
BAR
C'MON! I AIN'T HAD NO CUSTOMER YET TODAY! CAAAMON !!
5¢
TAILOR SUITS & DRESSES PRESSED WHILE YOU WAIT 25¢
5¢
PRESSED WHILE YOU WAIT 25¢
SUITS & DRESSES PRESSED WHILE YOU WAIT 25¢
SMITH & WHITE
MEMBERS N.Y. STOCK EXCHANGE SINCE 1901
THIS WAY, MR. SMITH WILL SEE YOU NOW!
WELL, NOW, YOUNG SHAFTSBURY, EH? KNEW YOUR FAMILY... OL' CLIFFORD UP IN, AH, SCARSDALE GAVE Y' A PRETTY NICE REFERENCE... BUT I'M AFRAID ALL WE HAVE IS A **RUNNER'S** JOB! TIMES ARE NOT AS THEY WERE ... CAN'T BE CHOOSEY... EH?
I'LL TAKE IT!
OKAY, WE'LL START YOU AT $8.50 A WEEK... EH? ..OH, **DICK**, HERE'S YOUR **NEW** RUNNER.
GOOD! AFTER YOU FILE THE BONDING COMPANY PAPERS, TAKE THESE STOCKS UP TO THE OLD NORTHERN TRUST, ...AND GET A RECEIPT FROM THE MANAGER!

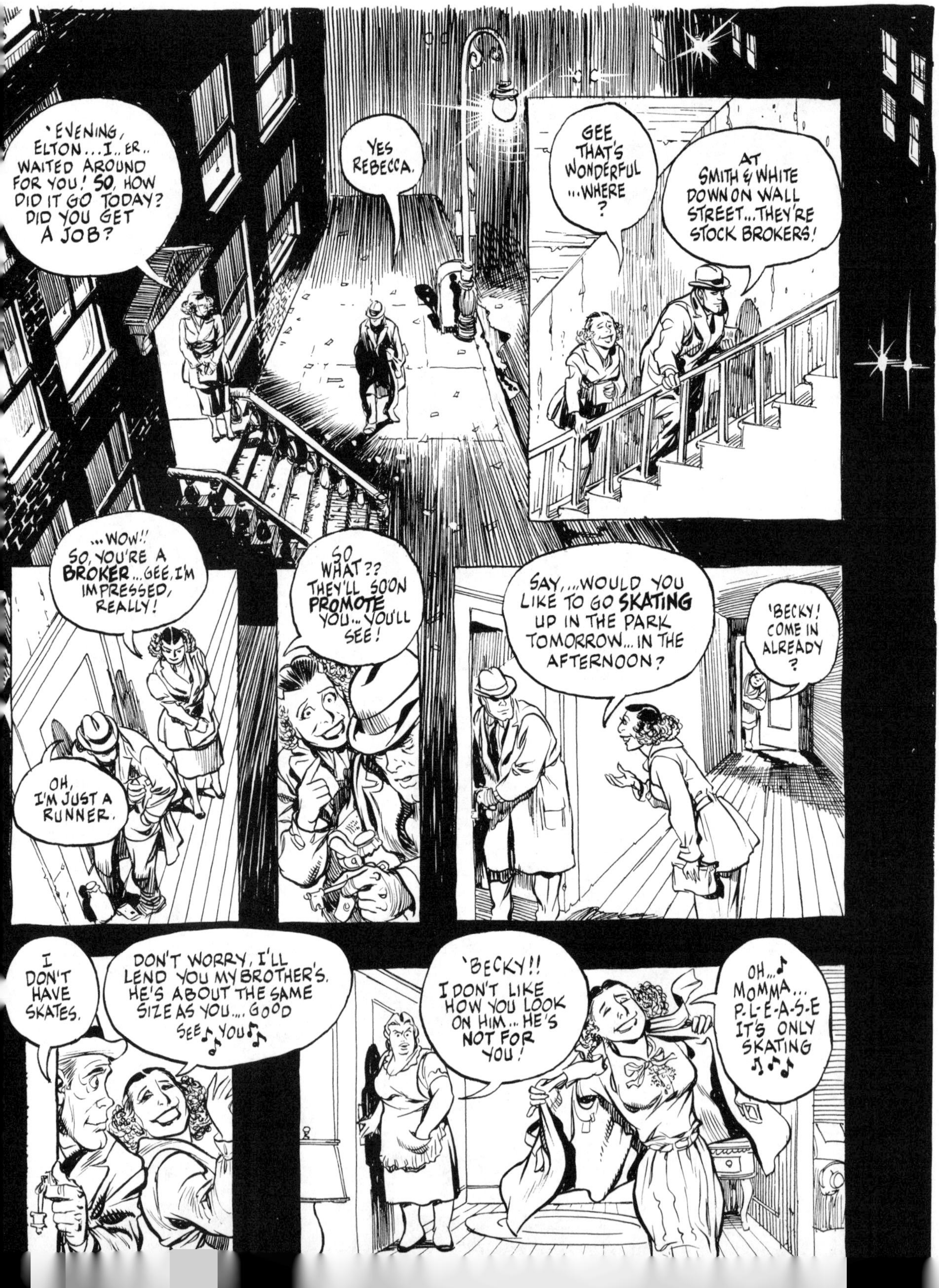
'EVENING, ELTON...I..ER.. WAITED AROUND FOR YOU! SO, HOW DID IT GO TODAY? DID YOU GET A JOB?
YES REBECCA.
GEE THAT'S WONDERFUL ...WHERE ?
AT SMITH & WHITE DOWN ON WALL STREET...THEY'RE STOCK BROKERS!
...WOW!! SO, YOU'RE A BROKER...GEE, I'M IMPRESSED, REALLY!
OH, I'M JUST A RUNNER.
SO WHAT?? THEY'LL SOON PROMOTE YOU...YOU'LL SEE!
SAY,...WOULD YOU LIKE TO GO SKATING UP IN THE PARK TOMORROW...IN THE AFTERNOON?
'BECKY! COME IN ALREADY ?
I DON'T HAVE SKATES.
DON'T WORRY, I'LL LEND YOU MY BROTHER'S. HE'S ABOUT THE SAME SIZE AS YOU....GOOD SEE♪ YOU♪
'BECKY!! I DON'T LIKE HOW YOU LOOK ON HIM...HE'S NOT FOR YOU!
OH...♪ MOMMA... P-L-E-A-S-E IT'S ONLY SKATING ♪♪♪

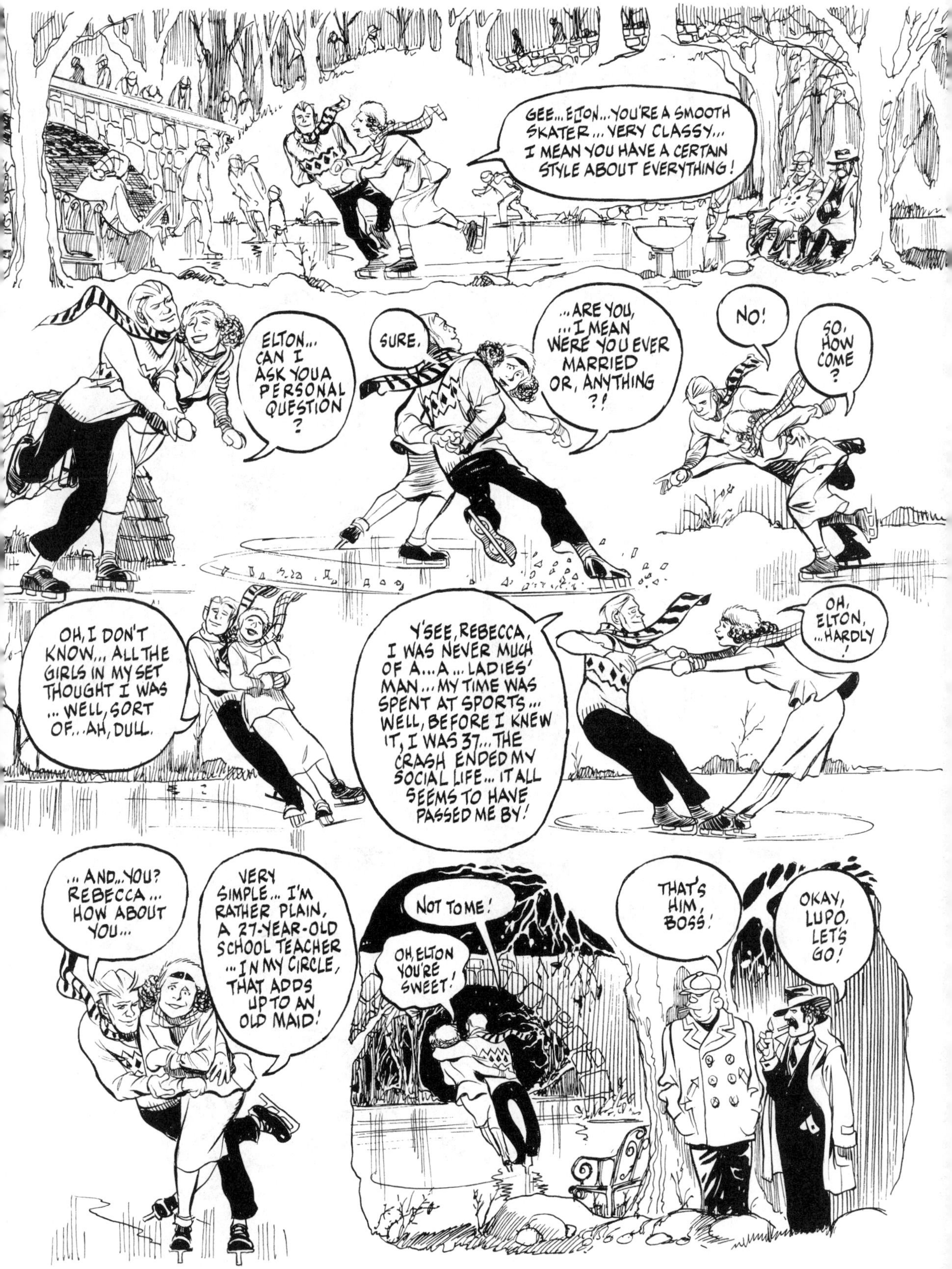
GEE... ELTON... YOU'RE A SMOOTH SKATER... VERY CLASSY... I MEAN YOU HAVE A CERTAIN STYLE ABOUT EVERYTHING!
ELTON... CAN I ASK YOU A PERSONAL QUESTION?
SURE.
...ARE YOU, ...I MEAN WERE YOU EVER MARRIED OR, ANYTHING?!
NO!
SO, HOW COME?
OH, I DON'T KNOW... ALL THE GIRLS IN MY SET THOUGHT I WAS ...WELL, SORT OF... AH, DULL.
Y'SEE, REBECCA, I WAS NEVER MUCH OF A... A... LADIES' MAN... MY TIME WAS SPENT AT SPORTS... WELL, BEFORE I KNEW IT, I WAS 37... THE CRASH ENDED MY SOCIAL LIFE... IT ALL SEEMS TO HAVE PASSED ME BY!
OH, ELTON, ...HARDLY!
...AND... YOU? REBECCA... HOW ABOUT YOU...
VERY SIMPLE... I'M RATHER PLAIN, A 27-YEAR-OLD SCHOOL TEACHER ...IN MY CIRCLE, THAT ADDS UP TO AN OLD MAID!
NOT TO ME!
OH, ELTON YOU'RE SWEET!
THAT'S HIM, BOSS!
OKAY, LUPO, LET'S GO!

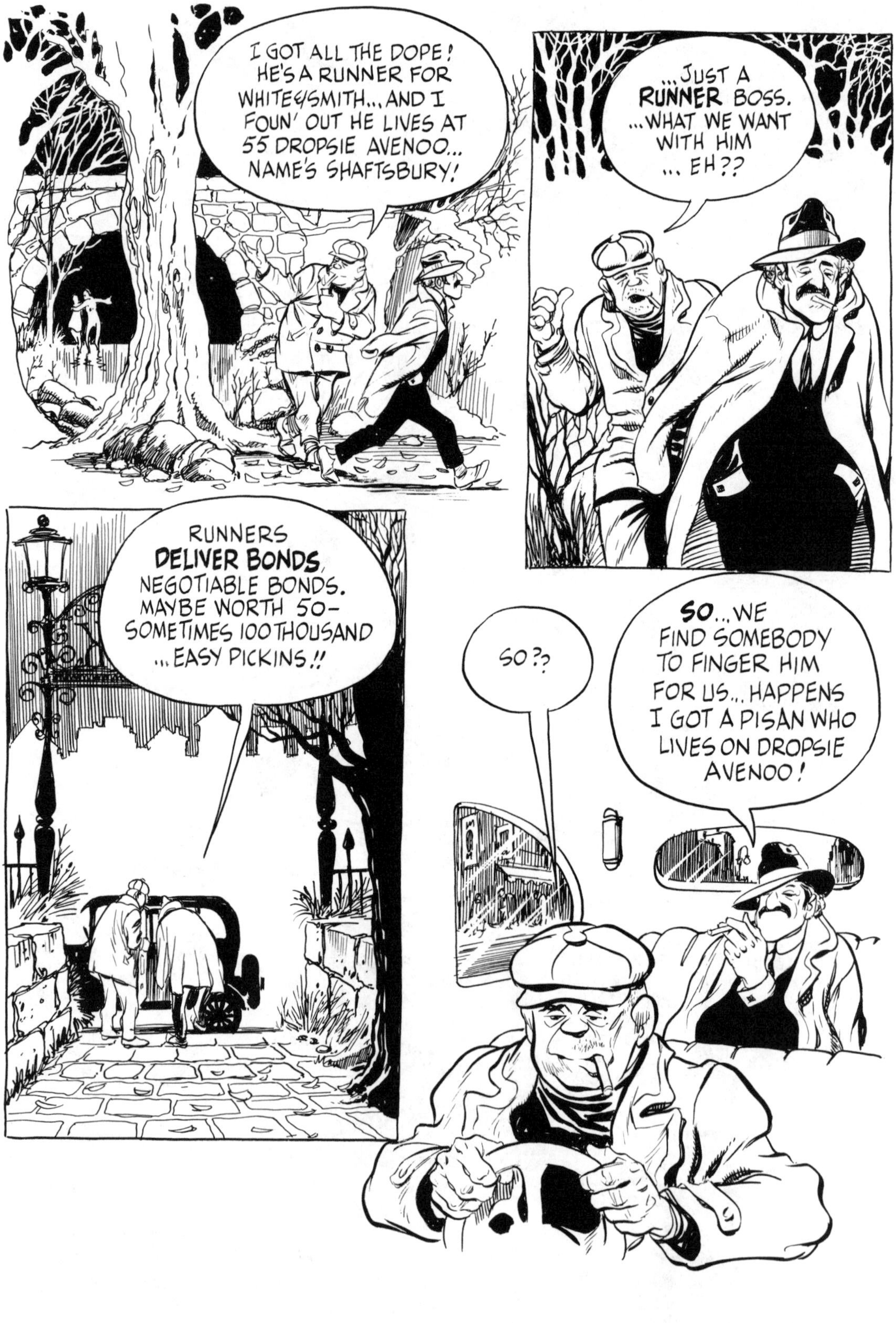
I GOT ALL THE DOPE! HE'S A RUNNER FOR WHITE&SMITH... AND I FOUN' OUT HE LIVES AT 55 DROPSIE AVENOO... NAME'S SHAFTSBURY!
...JUST A RUNNER BOSS. ...WHAT WE WANT WITH HIM ... EH??
RUNNERS DELIVER BONDS, NEGOTIABLE BONDS. MAYBE WORTH 50- SOMETIMES 100 THOUSAND ...EASY PICKINS!!
SO??
SO... WE FIND SOMEBODY TO FINGER HIM FOR US... HAPPENS I GOT A PISAN WHO LIVES ON DROPSIE AVENOO!

CHAPTER 5

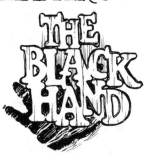

THE BLACK HAND

BETWEEN 1861 AND 1934 THE POPULATION OF ITALY HAD A NATURAL INCREASE OF ABOUT 400,000 A YEAR. THE DENSITY OF ITS POPULATION AVERAGED ABOUT 359 PERSONS PER SQUARE MILE.

DURING THE YEARS AFTER WORLD WAR I, THE ECONOMY, ESPECIALLY IN SOUTHERN ITALY AND SICILY, COULD BARELY SUPPORT ITS POPULATION. EMPLOYMENT WAS SO SCARCE THAT ONLY 150 DAYS OF WORK PER YEAR WAS THE AVERAGE. IN THE SOUTHERN FARM LANDS, MALARIA AND OTHER POVERTY-RELATED DISEASES KEPT PRODUCTIVITY LOW.

THE STRONG CENTRAL GOVERNMENT SET UP IN 1870 HAD LONG BEEN BESET BY LOCAL GROUPS THAT GREW OUT OF STRONG 'FAMILIES' WHO CONTROLLED REGIONS. SMUGGLING, PETTY CRIME AND CORRUPTION WAS RIFE. LOYALTY TO A 'FAMILY' OR A SECRET SOCIETY WAS A WAY OF LIFE.

SO, BETWEEN 1919 AND 1924 EMIGRATION SOARED... WITH AMERICA AS THE FAVORED DESTINATION.

IN 1920, ALONE, OVER 300,000 ITALIAN IMMIGRANTS ENTERED THE UNITED STATES.

FINALLY, IN 1924, THE U.S. IMMIGRATION ACT CUT THE TORRENT AND ESTABLISHED A QUOTA OF ONLY 3,845 ITALIAN IMMIGRANTS PER YEAR.

THEREAFTER, ABETTED BY THE POLICIES OF THE FASCIST GOVERNMENT, IMMIGRATION TO THE U.S. DWINDLED TO A TRICKLE. NOW, GETTING TO AMERICA BECAME A MATTER OF SOME SKILL AND CONNECTION.

HERE, THE OLD WORLD 'FAMILY' GROUPS AND SECRET SOCIETIES CAME INTO IMPORTANCE. FOR A FEE, THEY WANGLED VISAS, BRIBED OFFICIALS... OR ACTUALLY SMUGGLED MANY IMMIGRANTS INTO THE COUNTRY.

ONCE HERE, THEY WERE OFTEN INDENTURED TO THE SMUGGLING 'FAMILIES'... OR AT LEAST IN HEAVY DEBT FOR THEIR PASSAGE FEE. THESE FEES WERE INVARIABLY COLLECTED.

ONE OF THE GROUPS, WITH SICILIAN ROOTS WAS **THE BLACK HAND**. THEY, LIKE THE MAFIA, WERE OLD HANDS AT DISCIPLINE AND ENFORCEMENT.

A BLACK HAND IMPRINT ON ONE'S DOOR OR ON A LETTER WAS A NOTICE THAT WAS NOT TAKEN LIGHTLY.

HEY, KID!! THIS 55 DROPSIE AVENOO ??
YUP!

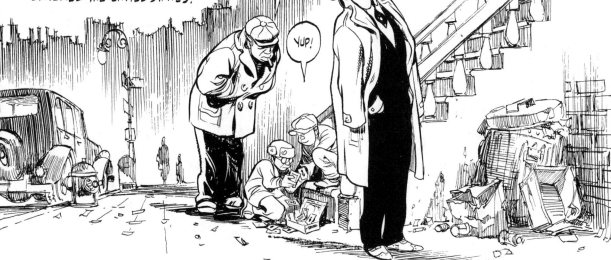

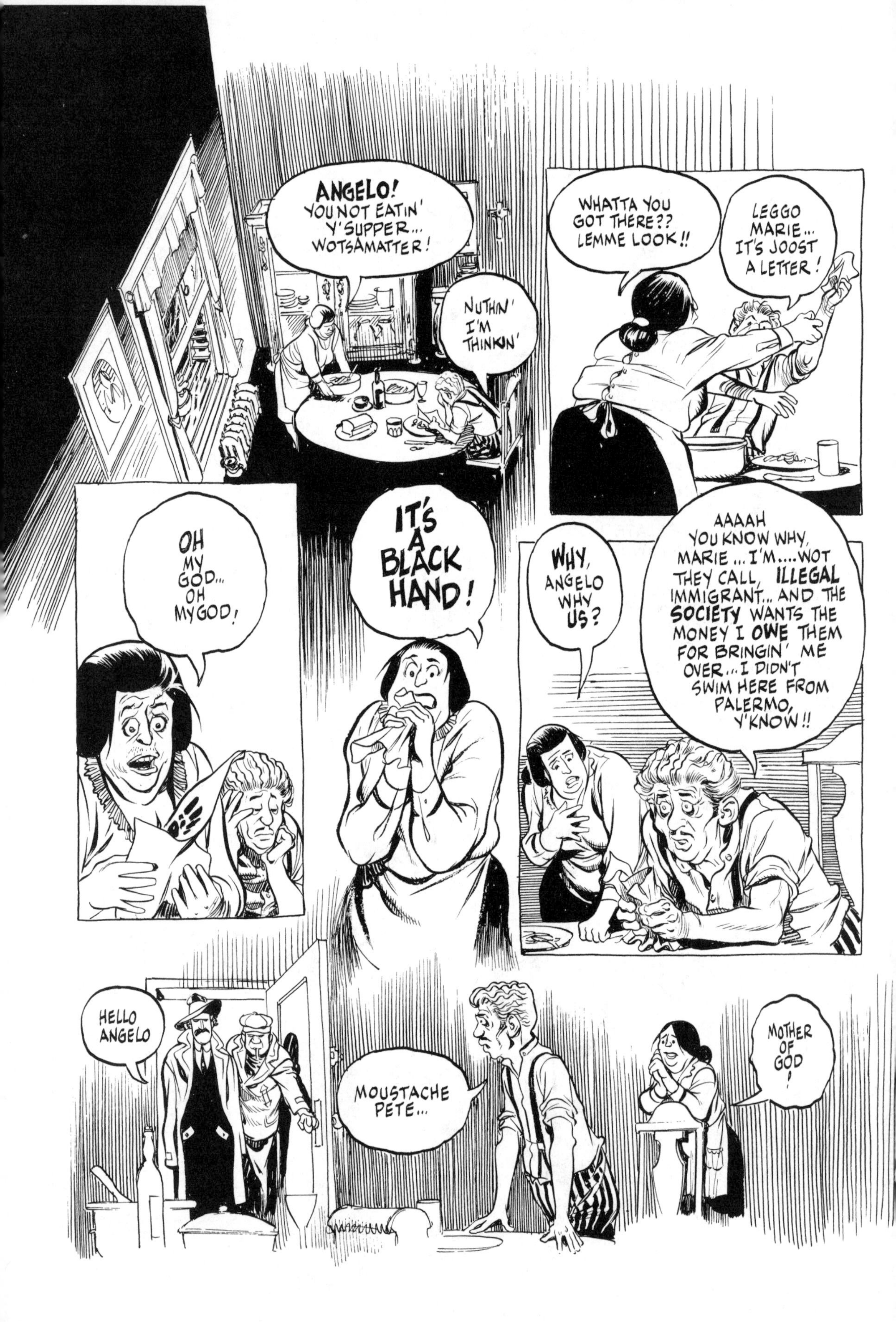
ANGELO! YOU NOT EATIN' Y'SUPPER... WOTSAMATTER!
NUTHIN' I'M THINKIN'
WHATTA YOU GOT THERE?? LEMME LOOK!!
LEGGO MARIE... IT'S JOOST A LETTER!
OH MY GOD... OH MY GOD!
IT'S A BLACK HAND!
WHY, ANGELO WHY US?
AAAAH YOU KNOW WHY, MARIE... I'M.... WOT THEY CALL, ILLEGAL IMMIGRANT... AND THE SOCIETY WANTS THE MONEY I OWE THEM FOR BRINGIN' ME OVER... I DIDN'T SWIM HERE FROM PALERMO, Y'KNOW!!
HELLO ANGELO
MOUSTACHE PETE...
MOTHER OF GOD!

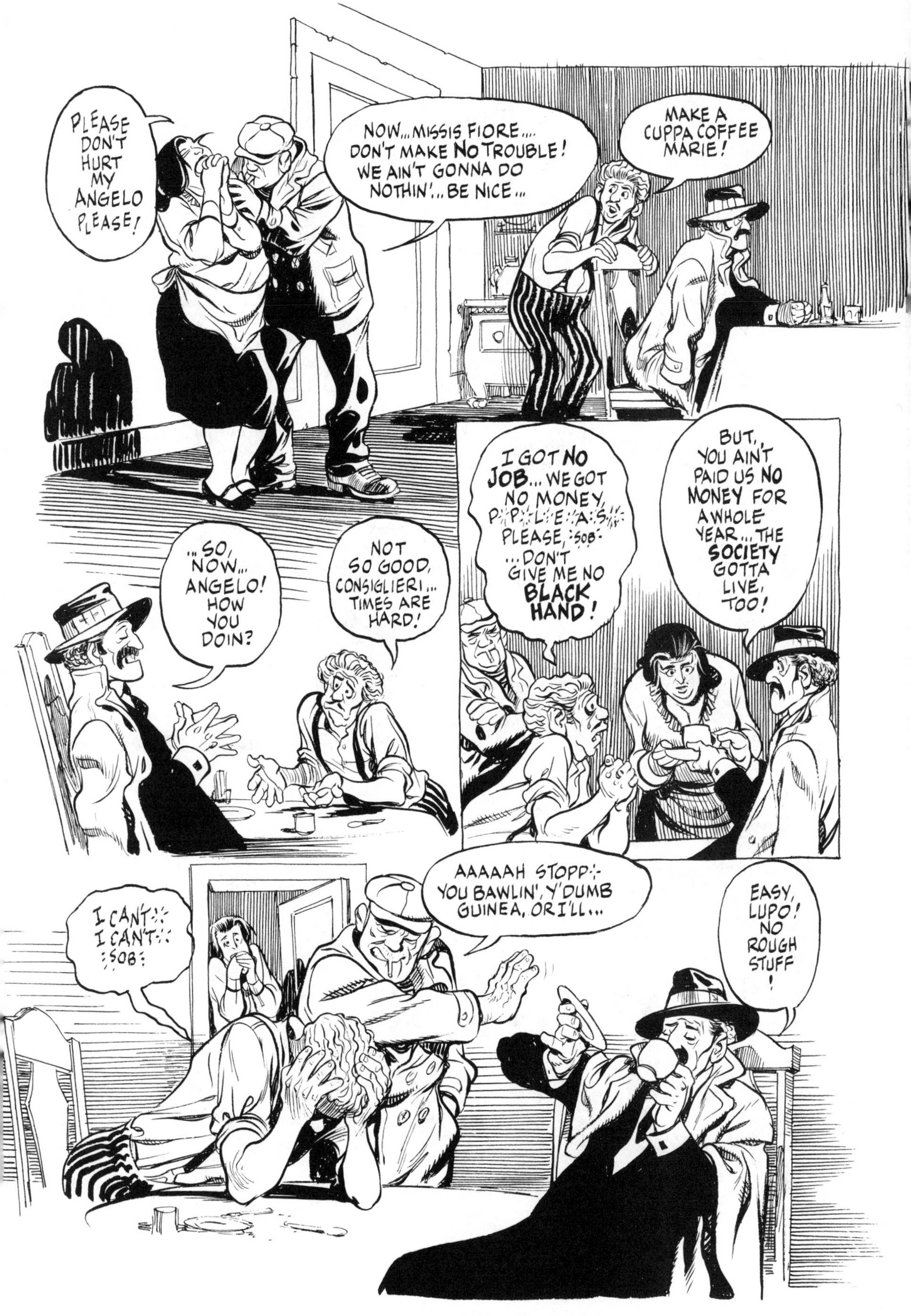
PLEASE DON'T HURT MY ANGELO PLEASE!
NOW... MISSIS FIORE.... DON'T MAKE NO TROUBLE! WE AIN'T GONNA DO NOTHIN'... BE NICE...
MAKE A CUPPA COFFEE MARIE!
...SO, NOW... ANGELO! HOW YOU DOIN?
NOT SO GOOD, CONSIGLIERI... TIMES ARE HARD!
I GOT NO JOB... WE GOT NO MONEY, P-P-L-E-A-S- PLEASE, -SOB- ...DON'T GIVE ME NO BLACK HAND!
BUT,, YOU AIN'T PAID US NO MONEY FOR A WHOLE YEAR... THE SOCIETY GOTTA LIVE, TOO!
I CAN'T I CAN'T SOB
AAAAAH STOPP- YOU BAWLIN', Y'DUMB GUINEA, OR I'LL...
EASY, LUPO! NO ROUGH STUFF!

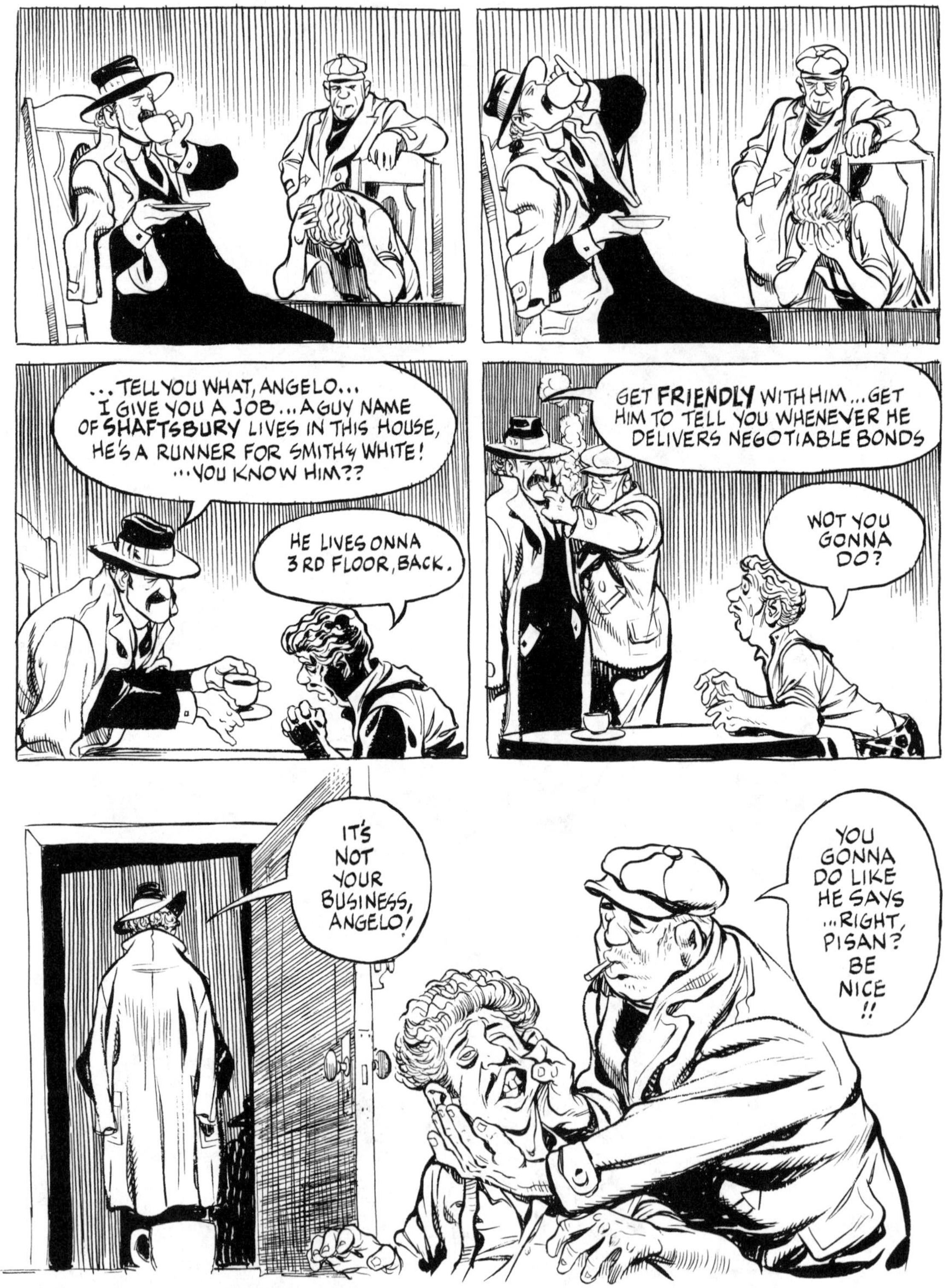
...TELL YOU WHAT, ANGELO... I GIVE YOU A JOB... A GUY NAME OF SHAFTSBURY LIVES IN THIS HOUSE, HE'S A RUNNER FOR SMITH & WHITE! ...YOU KNOW HIM??
HE LIVES ONNA 3RD FLOOR, BACK.
GET FRIENDLY WITH HIM... GET HIM TO TELL YOU WHENEVER HE DELIVERS NEGOTIABLE BONDS
WOT YOU GONNA DO?
IT'S NOT YOUR BUSINESS, ANGELO!
YOU GONNA DO LIKE HE SAYS ...RIGHT, PISAN? BE NICE !!

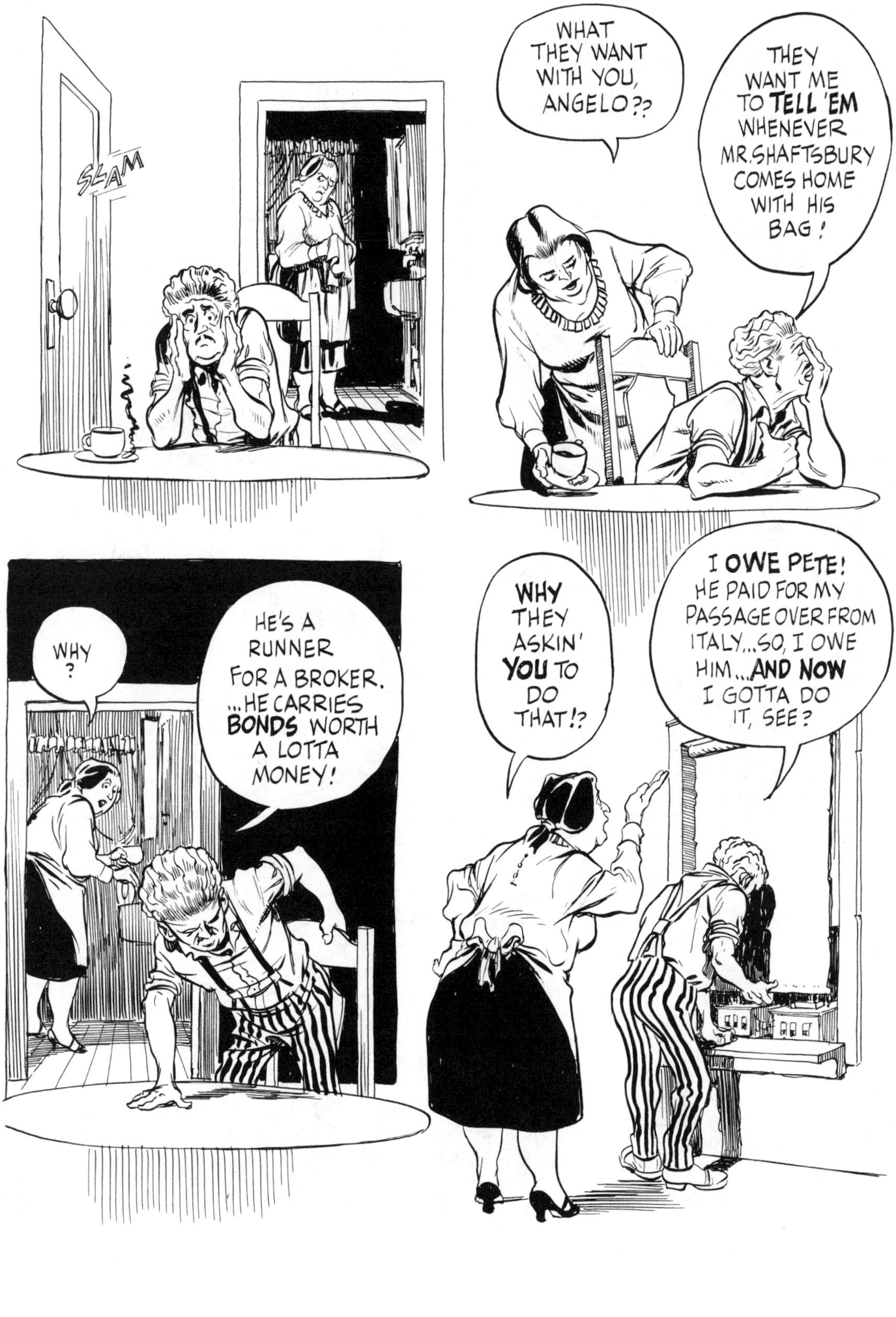
SLAM
WHAT THEY WANT WITH YOU, ANGELO??
THEY WANT ME TO TELL 'EM WHENEVER MR. SHAFTSBURY COMES HOME WITH HIS BAG!
WHY?
HE'S A RUNNER FOR A BROKER. ...HE CARRIES BONDS WORTH A LOTTA MONEY!
WHY THEY ASKIN' YOU TO DO THAT!?
I OWE PETE! HE PAID FOR MY PASSAGE OVER FROM ITALY...SO, I OWE HIM...AND NOW I GOTTA DO IT, SEE?

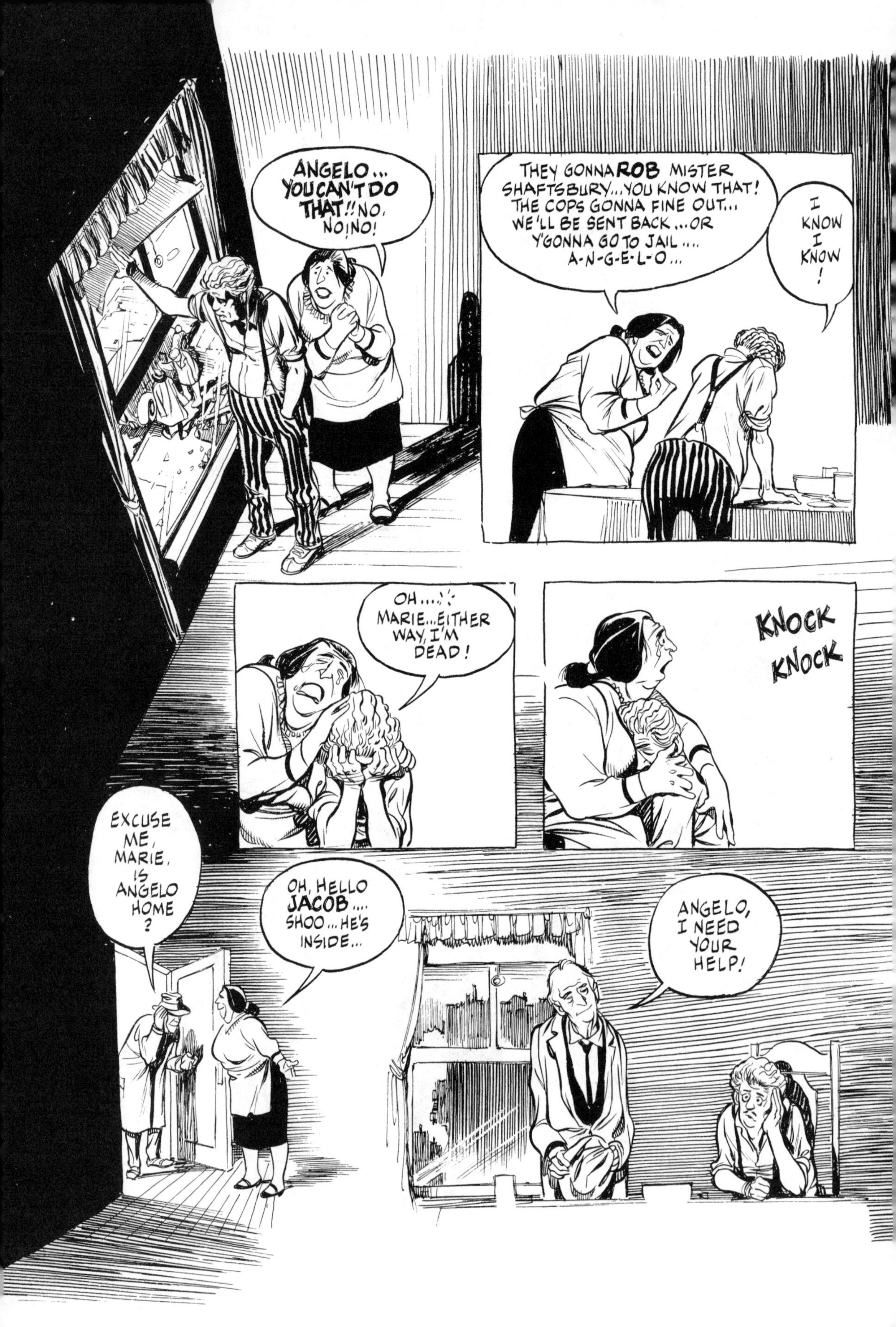
ANGELO... YOU CAN'T DO THAT!! NO, NO, NO!
THEY GONNA ROB MISTER SHAFTSBURY... YOU KNOW THAT! THE COPS GONNA FINE OUT... WE'LL BE SENT BACK... OR Y'GONNA GO TO JAIL.... A-N-G-E-L-O...
I KNOW I KNOW!
OH...! MARIE... EITHER WAY, I'M DEAD!
KNOCK KNOCK
EXCUSE ME, MARIE, IS ANGELO HOME?
OH, HELLO JACOB.... SHOO... HE'S INSIDE...
ANGELO, I NEED YOUR HELP!

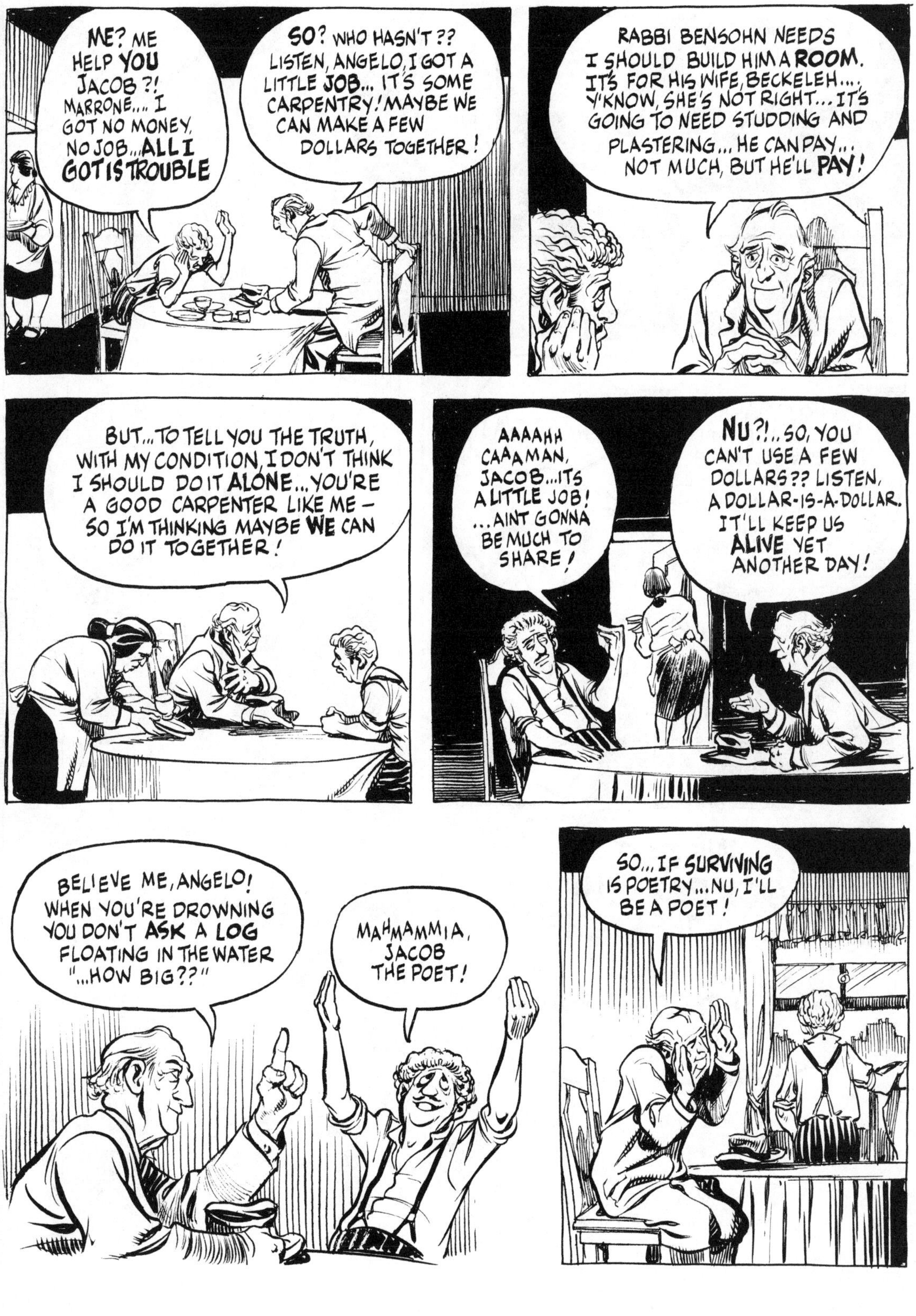
ME? ME HELP YOU JACOB?! MARRONE... I GOT NO MONEY, NO JOB... ALL I GOT IS TROUBLE
SO? WHO HASN'T?? LISTEN, ANGELO, I GOT A LITTLE JOB... IT'S SOME CARPENTRY! MAYBE WE CAN MAKE A FEW DOLLARS TOGETHER!
RABBI BENSOHN NEEDS I SHOULD BUILD HIM A ROOM. IT'S FOR HIS WIFE, BECKELEH..., Y'KNOW, SHE'S NOT RIGHT... IT'S GOING TO NEED STUDDING AND PLASTERING... HE CAN PAY... NOT MUCH, BUT HE'LL PAY!
BUT... TO TELL YOU THE TRUTH, WITH MY CONDITION, I DON'T THINK I SHOULD DO IT ALONE... YOU'RE A GOOD CARPENTER LIKE ME – SO I'M THINKING MAYBE WE CAN DO IT TOGETHER!
AAAAHH CAAAMAN, JACOB... ITS A LITTLE JOB! ...AINT GONNA BE MUCH TO SHARE!
NU?!.. SO, YOU CAN'T USE A FEW DOLLARS?? LISTEN, A DOLLAR-IS-A-DOLLAR. IT'LL KEEP US ALIVE YET ANOTHER DAY!
BELIEVE ME, ANGELO! WHEN YOU'RE DROWNING YOU DON'T ASK A LOG FLOATING IN THE WATER "...HOW BIG??"
MAHMAMMIA, JACOB THE POET!
SO... IF SURVIVING IS POETRY... NU, I'LL BE A POET!

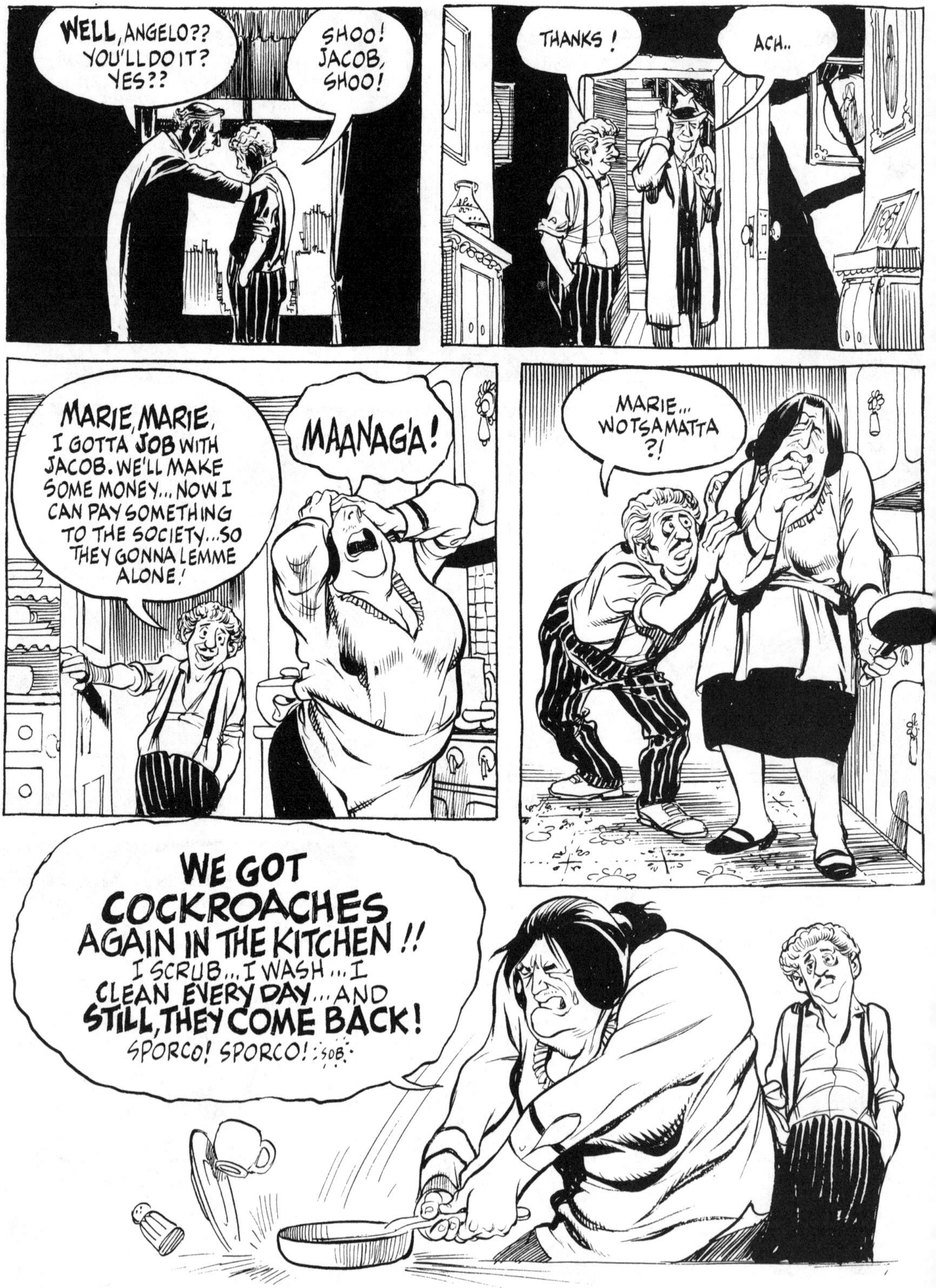
WELL, ANGELO?? YOU'LL DO IT? YES??
SHOO! JACOB, SHOO!
THANKS!
ACH..
MARIE, MARIE, I GOTTA JOB WITH JACOB. WE'LL MAKE SOME MONEY... NOW I CAN PAY SOMETHING TO THE SOCIETY... SO THEY GONNA LEMME ALONE!
MAANAGA'A!
MARIE... WOTSAMATTA ?!
WE GOT COCKROACHES AGAIN IN THE KITCHEN!! I SCRUB... I WASH... I CLEAN EVERY DAY... AND STILL, THEY COME BACK! SPORCO! SPORCO! SOB

CHAPTER 6

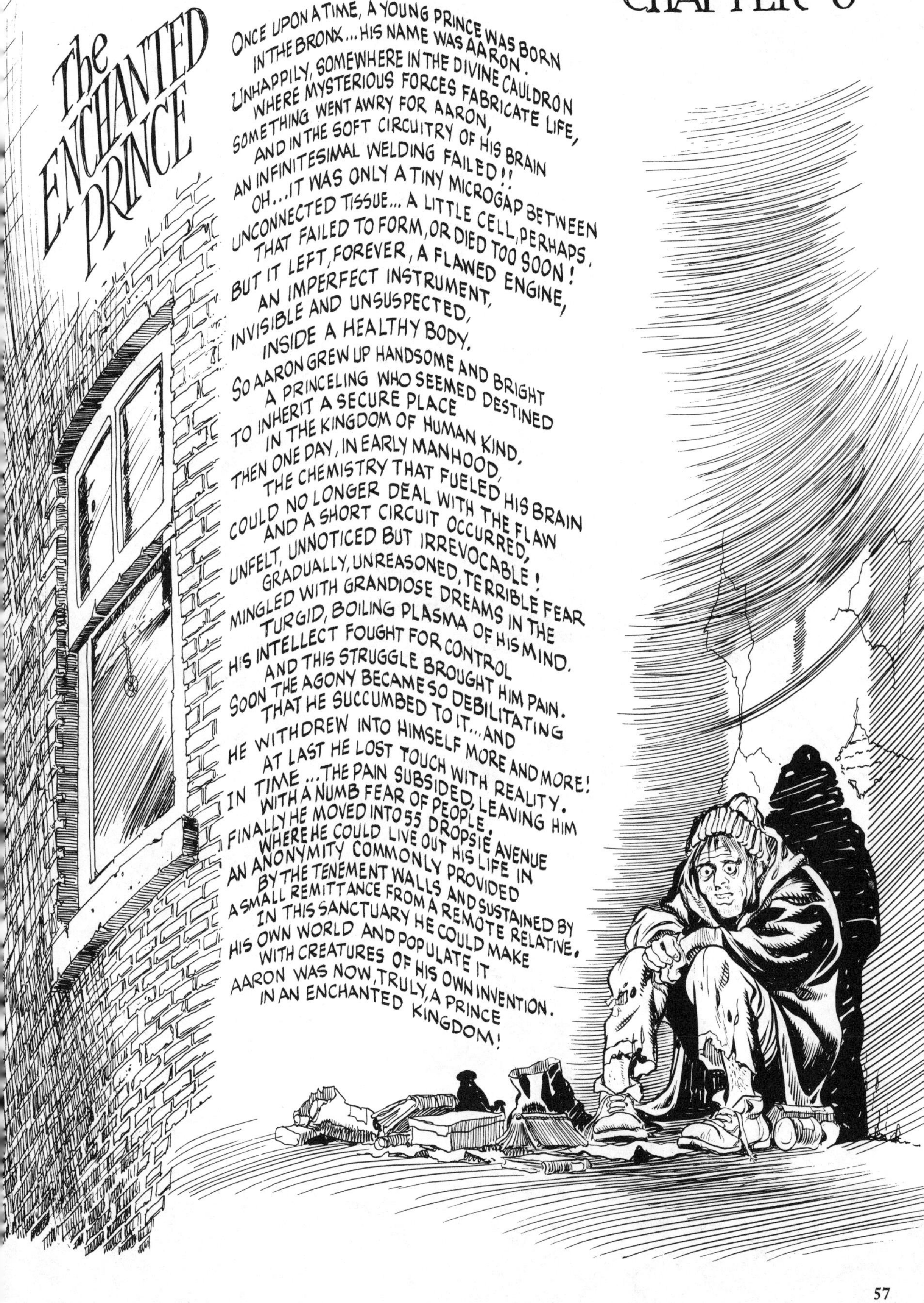
The ENCHANTED PRINCE
ONCE UPON A TIME, A YOUNG PRINCE WAS BORN IN THE BRONX... HIS NAME WAS AARON.
UNHAPPILY, SOMEWHERE IN THE DIVINE CAULDRON WHERE MYSTERIOUS FORCES FABRICATE LIFE, SOMETHING WENT AWRY FOR AARON, AND IN THE SOFT CIRCUITRY OF HIS BRAIN AN INFINITESIMAL WELDING FAILED!!
OH... IT WAS ONLY A TINY MICROGAP BETWEEN UNCONNECTED TISSUE... A LITTLE CELL, PERHAPS, THAT FAILED TO FORM, OR DIED TOO SOON!
BUT IT LEFT, FOREVER, A FLAWED ENGINE, AN IMPERFECT INSTRUMENT, INVISIBLE AND UNSUSPECTED, INSIDE A HEALTHY BODY.
SO AARON GREW UP HANDSOME AND BRIGHT A PRINCELING WHO SEEMED DESTINED TO INHERIT A SECURE PLACE IN THE KINGDOM OF HUMAN KIND.
THEN ONE DAY, IN EARLY MANHOOD, THE CHEMISTRY THAT FUELED HIS BRAIN COULD NO LONGER DEAL WITH THE FLAW AND A SHORT CIRCUIT OCCURRED, UNFELT, UNNOTICED BUT IRREVOCABLE!
GRADUALLY, UNREASONED, TERRIBLE FEAR MINGLED WITH GRANDIOSE DREAMS IN THE TURGID, BOILING PLASMA OF HIS MIND.
HIS INTELLECT FOUGHT FOR CONTROL AND THIS STRUGGLE BROUGHT HIM PAIN.
SOON THE AGONY BECAME SO DEBILITATING THAT HE SUCCUMBED TO IT... AND HE WITHDREW INTO HIMSELF MORE AND MORE!
AT LAST HE LOST TOUCH WITH REALITY.
IN TIME... THE PAIN SUBSIDED, LEAVING HIM WITH A NUMB FEAR OF PEOPLE.
FINALLY HE MOVED INTO 55 DROPSIE AVENUE WHERE HE COULD LIVE OUT HIS LIFE IN AN ANONYMITY COMMONLY PROVIDED BY THE TENEMENT WALLS AND SUSTAINED BY A SMALL REMITTANCE FROM A REMOTE RELATIVE.
IN THIS SANCTUARY HE COULD MAKE HIS OWN WORLD AND POPULATE IT WITH CREATURES OF HIS OWN INVENTION.
AARON WAS NOW, TRULY, A PRINCE IN AN ENCHANTED KINGDOM!

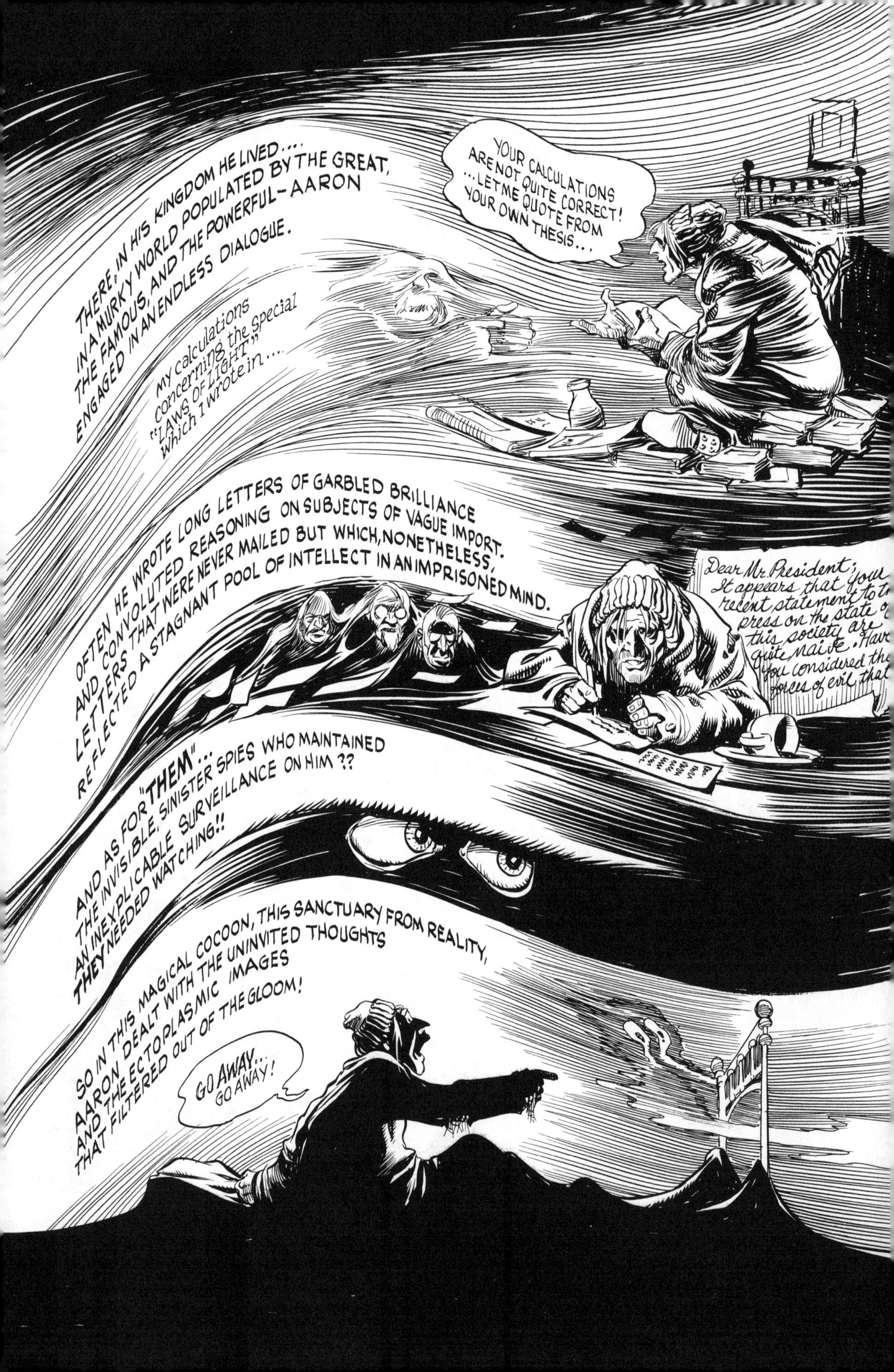
THERE, IN HIS KINGDOM HE LIVED.... IN A MURKY WORLD POPULATED BY THE GREAT, THE FAMOUS, AND THE POWERFUL- AARON ENGAGED IN AN ENDLESS DIALOGUE.
YOUR CALCULATIONS ARE NOT QUITE CORRECT! ...LET ME QUOTE FROM YOUR OWN THESIS...
My calculations concerning the special "LAWS OF LIGHT" which I wrote in....
OFTEN HE WROTE LONG LETTERS OF GARBLED BRILLIANCE AND CONVOLUTED REASONING ON SUBJECTS OF VAGUE IMPORT. LETTERS THAT WERE NEVER MAILED BUT WHICH, NONETHELESS, REFLECTED A STAGNANT POOL OF INTELLECT IN AN IMPRISONED MIND.
Dear Mr. President; It appears that you recent statement to th press on the state o this society are quite naive. Hav you considered th forces of evil that
AND AS FOR "THEM"... THE INVISIBLE, SINISTER SPIES WHO MAINTAINED AN INEXPLICABLE SURVEILLANCE ON HIM ?? THEY NEEDED WATCHING!!
SO IN THIS MAGICAL COCOON, THIS SANCTUARY FROM REALITY, AARON DEALT WITH THE UNINVITED THOUGHTS AND THE ECTOPLASMIC IMAGES THAT FILTERED OUT OF THE GLOOM!
GO AWAY... GO AWAY!

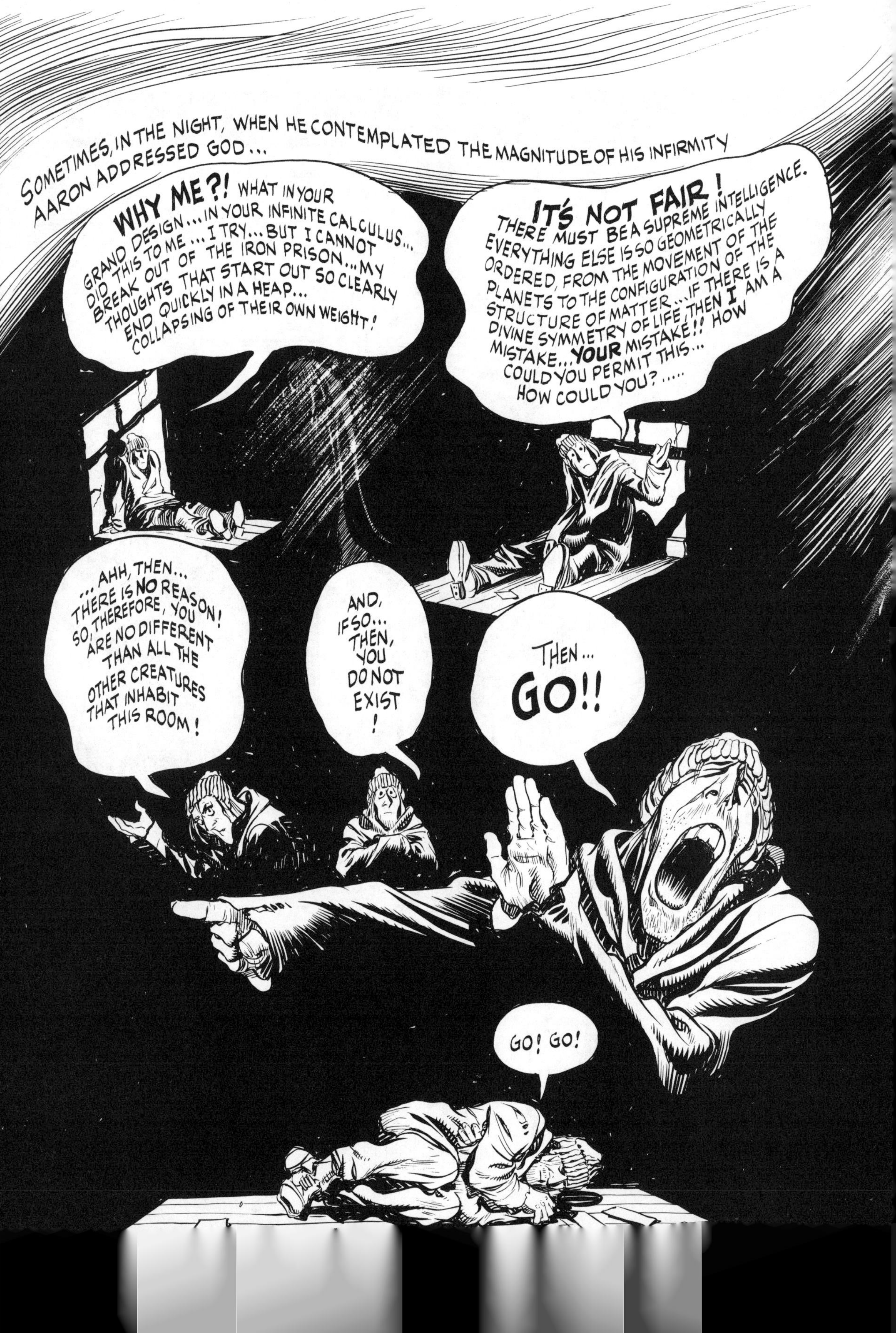
SOMETIMES, IN THE NIGHT, WHEN HE CONTEMPLATED THE MAGNITUDE OF HIS INFIRMITY AARON ADDRESSED GOD...
WHY ME?! WHAT IN YOUR GRAND DESIGN... IN YOUR INFINITE CALCULUS... DID THIS TO ME... I TRY... BUT I CANNOT BREAK OUT OF THE IRON PRISON... MY THOUGHTS THAT START OUT SO CLEARLY END QUICKLY IN A HEAP... COLLAPSING OF THEIR OWN WEIGHT!
IT'S NOT FAIR! THERE MUST BE A SUPREME INTELLIGENCE. EVERYTHING ELSE IS SO GEOMETRICALLY ORDERED, FROM THE MOVEMENT OF THE PLANETS TO THE CONFIGURATION OF THE STRUCTURE OF MATTER... IF THERE IS A DIVINE SYMMETRY OF LIFE, THEN I AM A MISTAKE... YOUR MISTAKE!! HOW COULD YOU PERMIT THIS... HOW COULD YOU?.....
... AHH, THEN... ... THERE IS NO REASON! SO, THEREFORE, YOU ARE NO DIFFERENT THAN ALL THE OTHER CREATURES THAT INHABIT THIS ROOM!
AND, IF SO... THEN, YOU DO NOT EXIST!
THEN... GO!!
GO! GO!

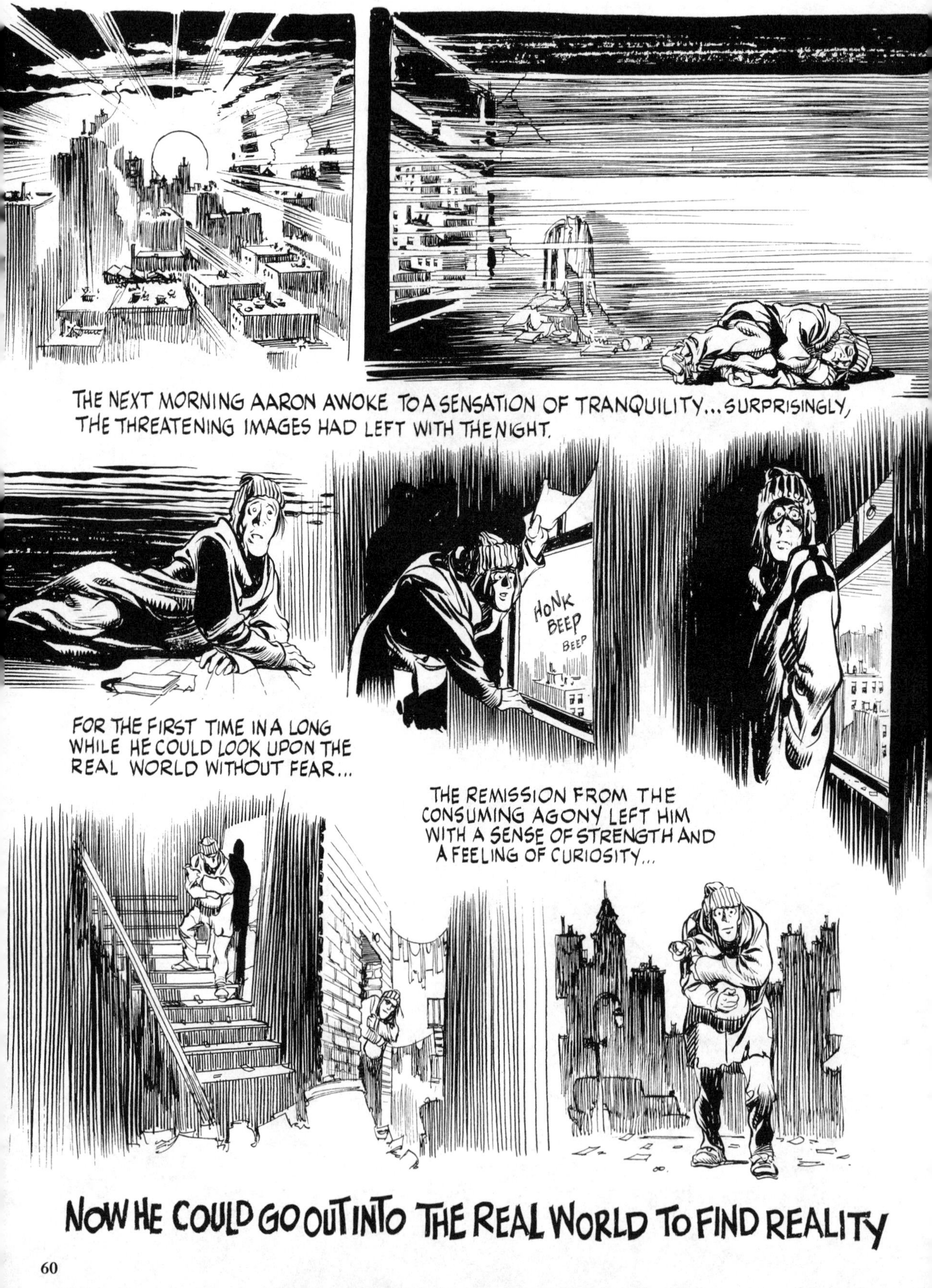
THE NEXT MORNING AARON AWOKE TO A SENSATION OF TRANQUILITY... SURPRISINGLY, THE THREATENING IMAGES HAD LEFT WITH THE NIGHT.
HONK
BEEP
BEEP
FOR THE FIRST TIME IN A LONG WHILE HE COULD LOOK UPON THE REAL WORLD WITHOUT FEAR...
THE REMISSION FROM THE CONSUMING AGONY LEFT HIM WITH A SENSE OF STRENGTH AND A FEELING OF CURIOSITY...
NOW HE COULD GO OUT INTO THE REAL WORLD TO FIND REALITY

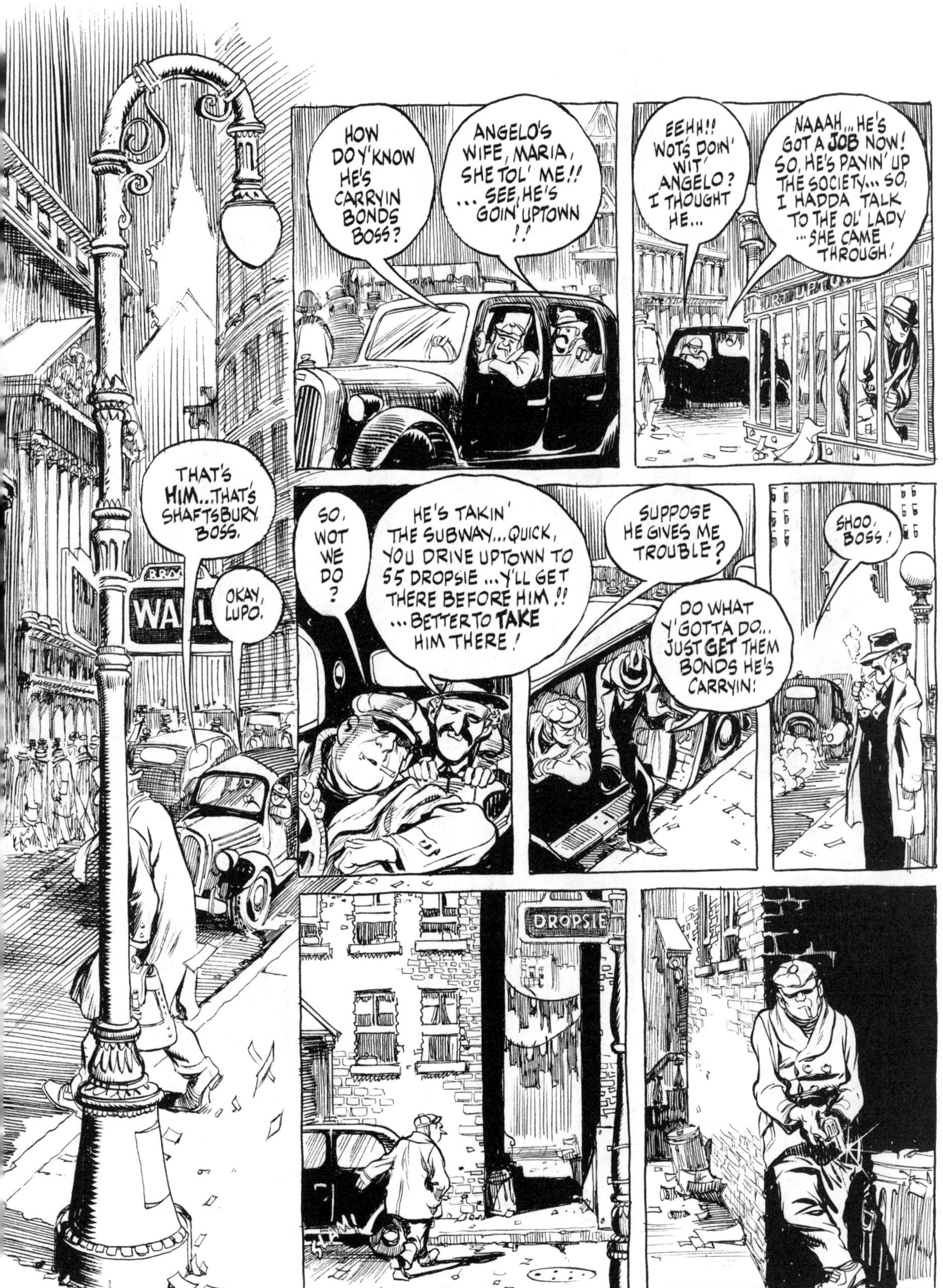
HOW DO Y'KNOW HE'S CARRYIN BONDS BOSS?
ANGELO'S WIFE, MARIA, SHE TOL' ME!! ... SEE, HE'S GOIN' UPTOWN !!
EEHH!! WOT'S DOIN' WIT' ANGELO? I THOUGHT HE...
NAAAH... HE'S GOT A JOB NOW! SO, HE'S PAYIN' UP THE SOCIETY... SO, I HADDA TALK TO THE OL' LADY ... SHE CAME THROUGH!
THAT'S HIM... THAT'S SHAFTSBURY, BOSS.
OKAY, LUPO.
WALL
SO, WOT WE DO?
HE'S TAKIN' THE SUBWAY... QUICK, YOU DRIVE UPTOWN TO 55 DROPSIE ... Y'LL GET THERE BEFORE HIM!! ... BETTER TO TAKE HIM THERE!
SUPPOSE HE GIVES ME TROUBLE?
DO WHAT Y'GOTTA DO... JUST GET THEM BONDS HE'S CARRYIN!
SHOO, BOSS!
DROPSIE

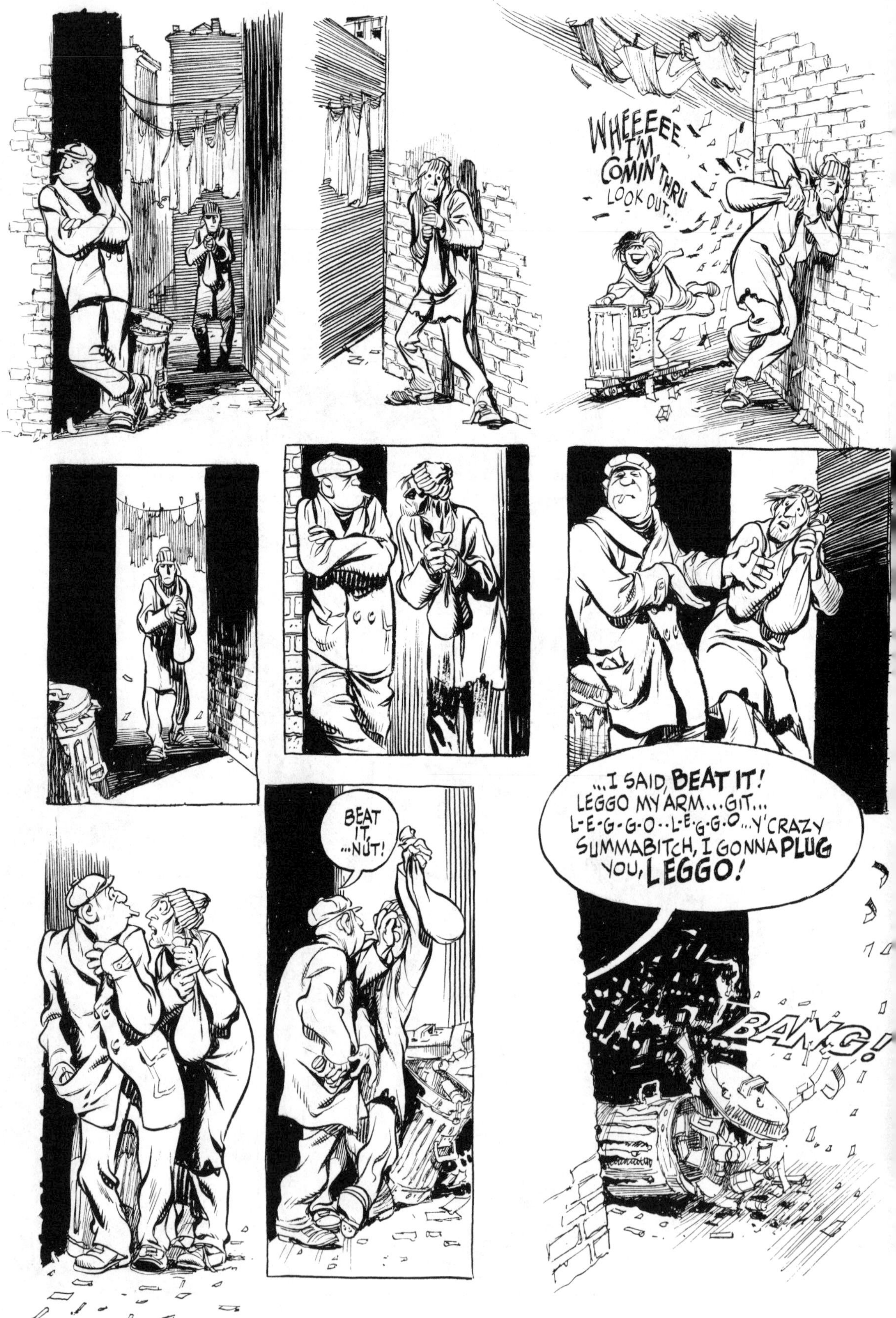
WHEEEEE I'M COMIN' THRU LOOK OUT...
BEAT IT ...NUT!
...I SAID, BEAT IT! LEGGO MY ARM...GIT... L-E-G-G-O...L-E-G-G-O...Y'CRAZY SUMMABITCH, I GONNA PLUG YOU, LEGGO!
BANG!

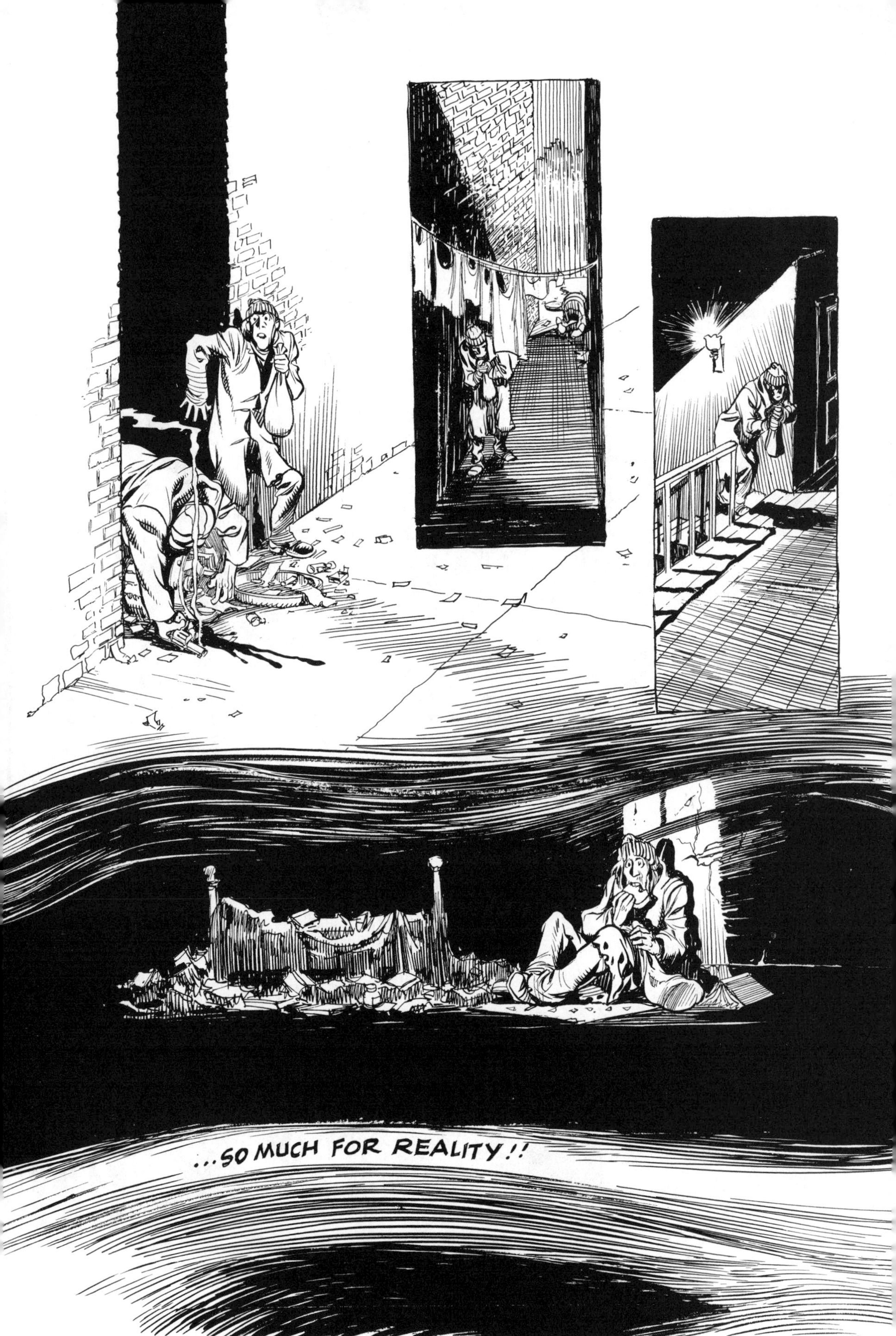
...SO MUCH FOR REALITY!!

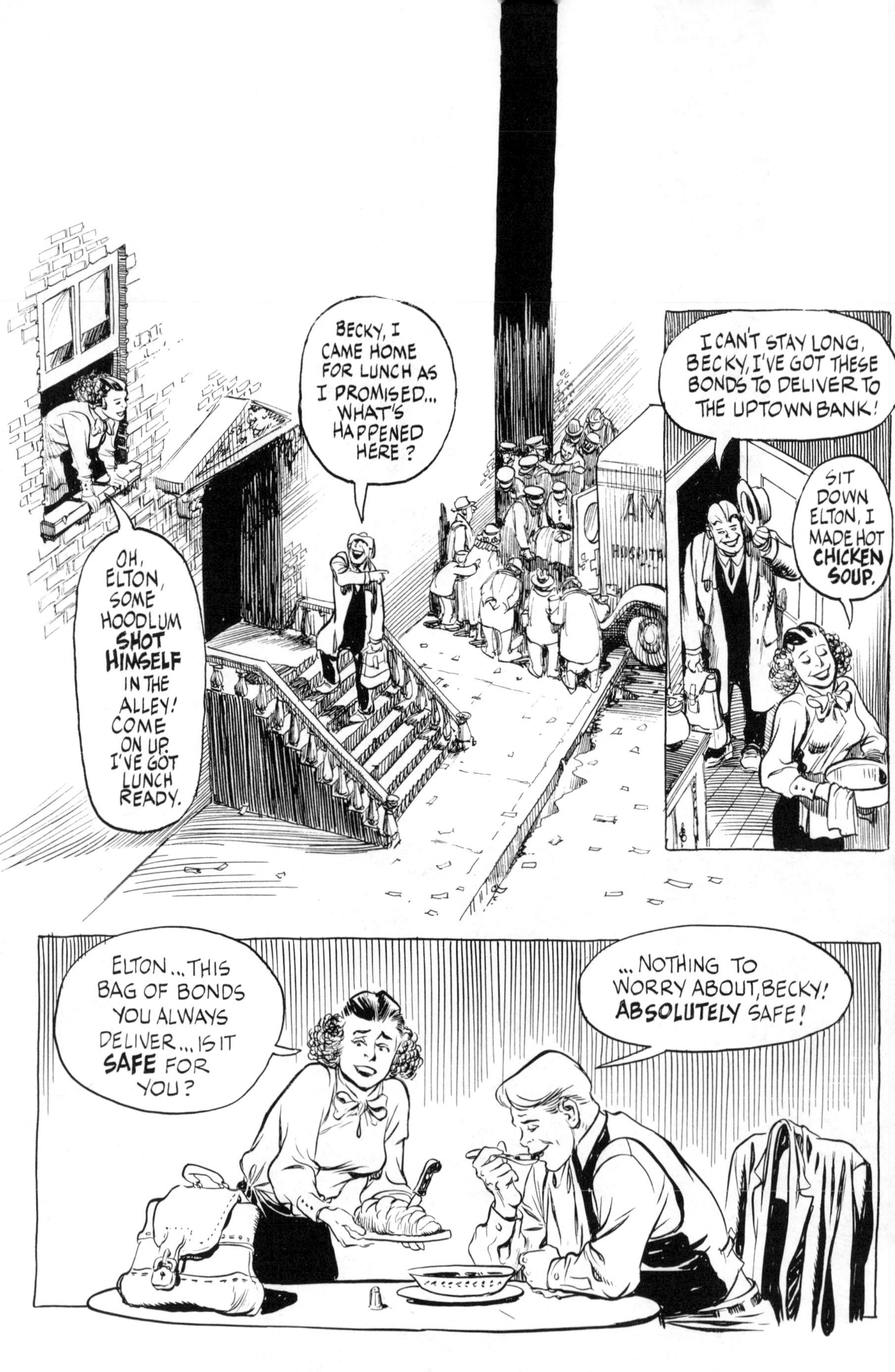
BECKY, I CAME HOME FOR LUNCH AS I PROMISED... WHAT'S HAPPENED HERE ?
OH, ELTON, SOME HOODLUM **SHOT HIMSELF** IN THE ALLEY! COME ON UP. I'VE GOT LUNCH READY.
I CAN'T STAY LONG, BECKY, I'VE GOT THESE BONDS TO DELIVER TO THE UPTOWN BANK!
SIT DOWN ELTON, I MADE HOT **CHICKEN SOUP.**
ELTON... THIS BAG OF BONDS YOU ALWAYS DELIVER... IS IT **SAFE** FOR YOU?
... NOTHING TO WORRY ABOUT, BECKY! **ABSOLUTELY** SAFE!

CHAPTER 7
THE REVOLUTIONARY

IN 1934 THE WINDS OF CHANGE
SWIRLED AROUND
55 DROPSIE AVENUE, THE BRONX.

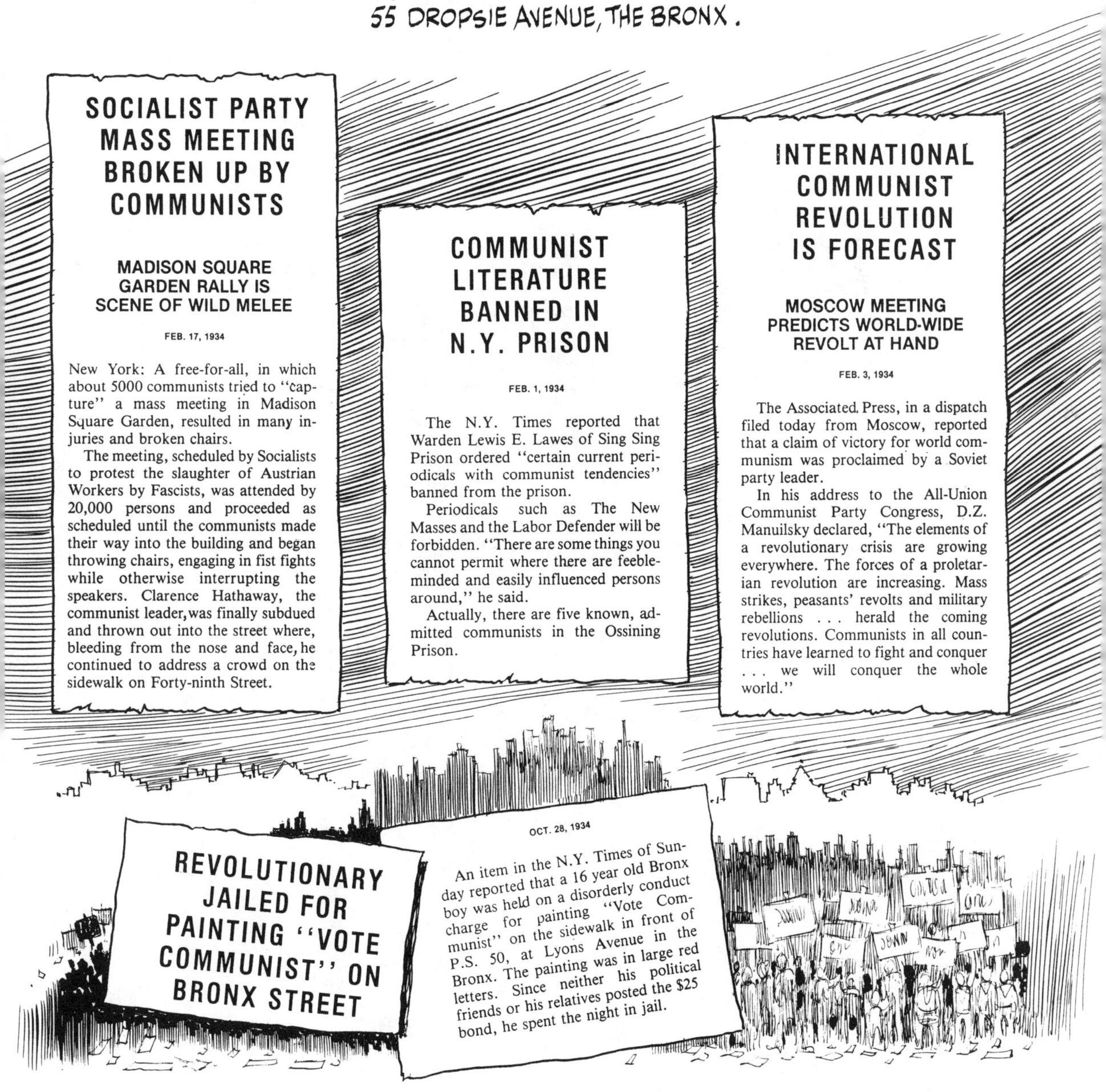
SOCIALIST PARTY MASS MEETING BROKEN UP BY COMMUNISTS
MADISON SQUARE GARDEN RALLY IS SCENE OF WILD MELEE
FEB. 17, 1934
New York: A free-for-all, in which about 5000 communists tried to "capture" a mass meeting in Madison Square Garden, resulted in many injuries and broken chairs.
The meeting, scheduled by Socialists to protest the slaughter of Austrian Workers by Fascists, was attended by 20,000 persons and proceeded as scheduled until the communists made their way into the building and began throwing chairs, engaging in fist fights while otherwise interrupting the speakers. Clarence Hathaway, the communist leader, was finally subdued and thrown out into the street where, bleeding from the nose and face, he continued to address a crowd on the sidewalk on Forty-ninth Street.
COMMUNIST LITERATURE BANNED IN N.Y. PRISON
FEB. 1, 1934
The N.Y. Times reported that Warden Lewis E. Lawes of Sing Sing Prison ordered "certain current periodicals with communist tendencies" banned from the prison.
Periodicals such as The New Masses and the Labor Defender will be forbidden. "There are some things you cannot permit where there are feeble-minded and easily influenced persons around," he said.
Actually, there are five known, admitted communists in the Ossining Prison.
INTERNATIONAL COMMUNIST REVOLUTION IS FORECAST
MOSCOW MEETING PREDICTS WORLD-WIDE REVOLT AT HAND
FEB. 3, 1934
The Associated Press, in a dispatch filed today from Moscow, reported that a claim of victory for world communism was proclaimed by a Soviet party leader.
In his address to the All-Union Communist Party Congress, D.Z. Manuilsky declared, "The elements of a revolutionary crisis are growing everywhere. The forces of a proletarian revolution are increasing. Mass strikes, peasants' revolts and military rebellions ... herald the coming revolutions. Communists in all countries have learned to fight and conquer ... we will conquer the whole world."
REVOLUTIONARY JAILED FOR PAINTING "VOTE COMMUNIST" ON BRONX STREET
OCT. 28, 1934
An item in the N.Y. Times of Sunday reported that a 16 year old Bronx boy was held on a disorderly conduct charge for painting "Vote Communist" on the sidewalk in front of P.S. 50, at Lyons Avenue in the Bronx. The painting was in large red letters. Since neither his political friends or his relatives posted the $25 bond, he spent the night in jail.

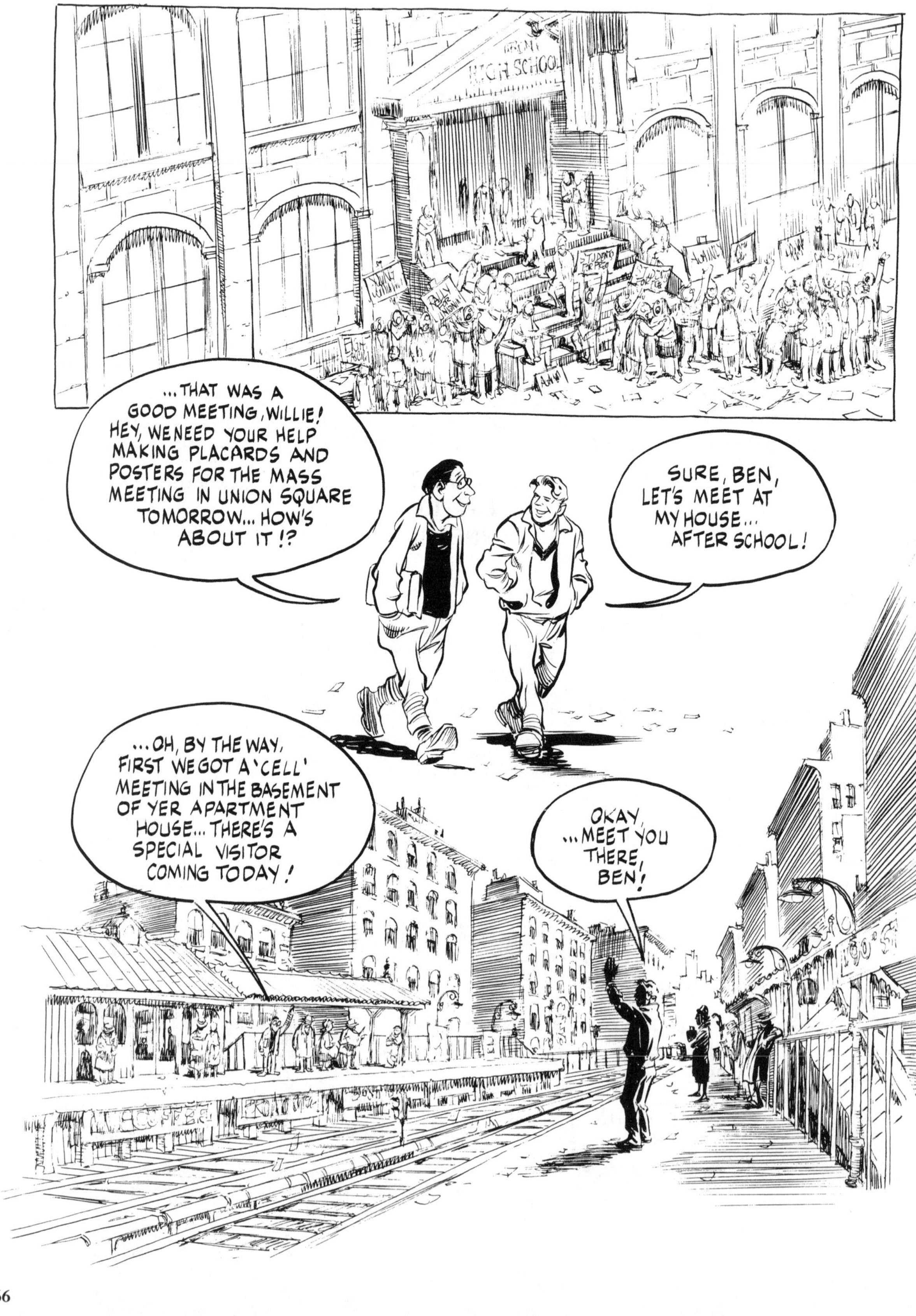
HIGH SCHOOL
...THAT WAS A GOOD MEETING, WILLIE! HEY, WE NEED YOUR HELP MAKING PLACARDS AND POSTERS FOR THE MASS MEETING IN UNION SQUARE TOMORROW... HOW'S ABOUT IT!?
SURE, BEN, LET'S MEET AT MY HOUSE... AFTER SCHOOL!
...OH, BY THE WAY, FIRST WE GOT A 'CELL' MEETING IN THE BASEMENT OF YER APARTMENT HOUSE... THERE'S A SPECIAL VISITOR COMING TODAY!
OKAY, ...MEET YOU THERE, BEN!

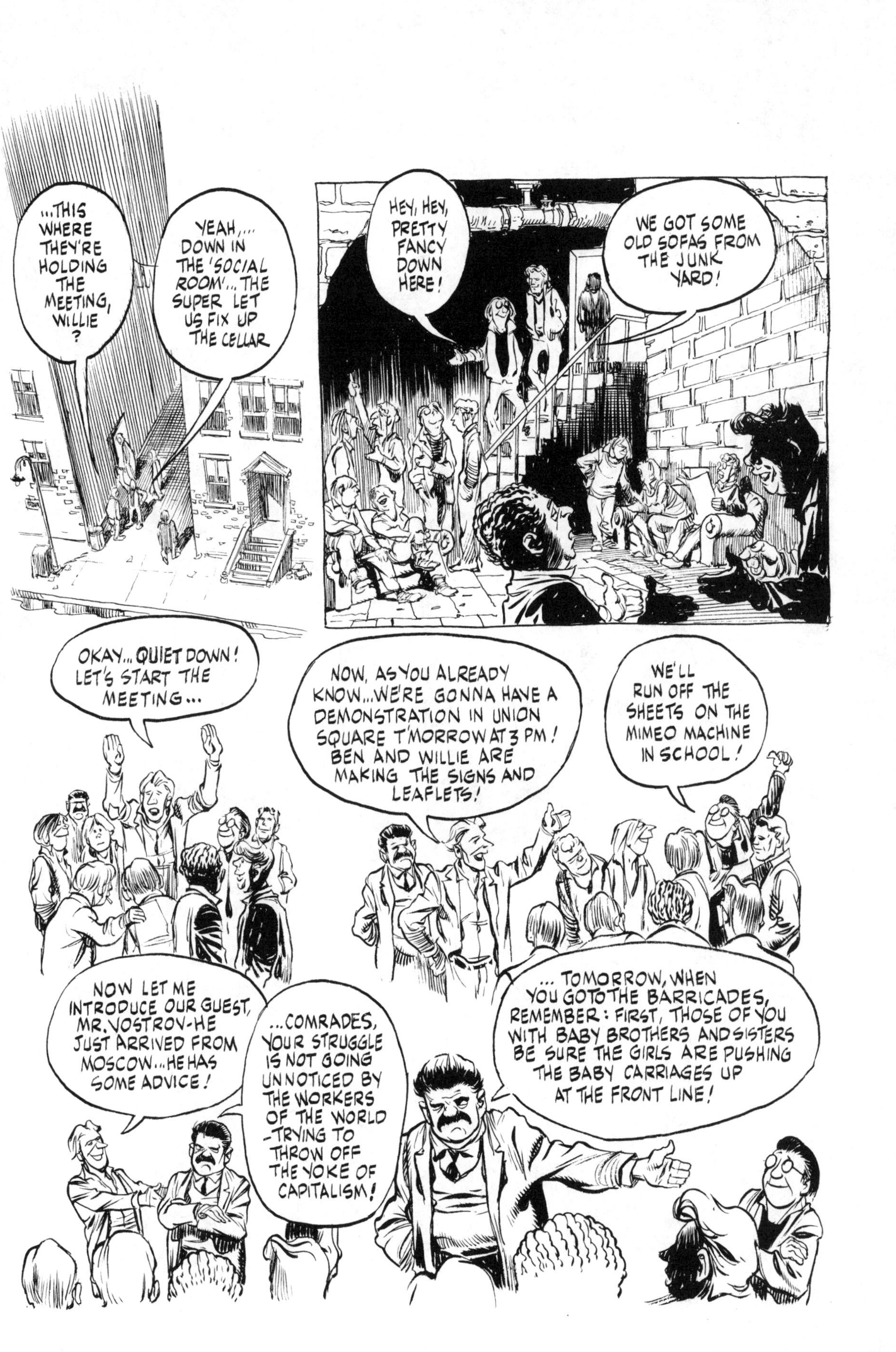
...THIS WHERE THEY'RE HOLDING THE MEETING, WILLIE ?
YEAH,... DOWN IN THE 'SOCIAL ROOM'... THE SUPER LET US FIX UP THE CELLAR
HEY, HEY, PRETTY FANCY DOWN HERE!
WE GOT SOME OLD SOFAS FROM THE JUNK YARD!
OKAY... QUIET DOWN! LET'S START THE MEETING...
NOW, AS YOU ALREADY KNOW... WE'RE GONNA HAVE A DEMONSTRATION IN UNION SQUARE T'MORROW AT 3 PM! BEN AND WILLIE ARE MAKING THE SIGNS AND LEAFLETS!
WE'LL RUN OFF THE SHEETS ON THE MIMEO MACHINE IN SCHOOL!
NOW LET ME INTRODUCE OUR GUEST, MR. VOSTROV-HE JUST ARRIVED FROM MOSCOW... HE HAS SOME ADVICE!
...COMRADES, YOUR STRUGGLE IS NOT GOING UNNOTICED BY THE WORKERS OF THE WORLD -TRYING TO THROW OFF THE YOKE OF CAPITALISM!
... TOMORROW, WHEN YOU GO TO THE BARRICADES, REMEMBER: FIRST, THOSE OF YOU WITH BABY BROTHERS AND SISTERS BE SURE THE GIRLS ARE PUSHING THE BABY CARRIAGES UP AT THE FRONT LINE!

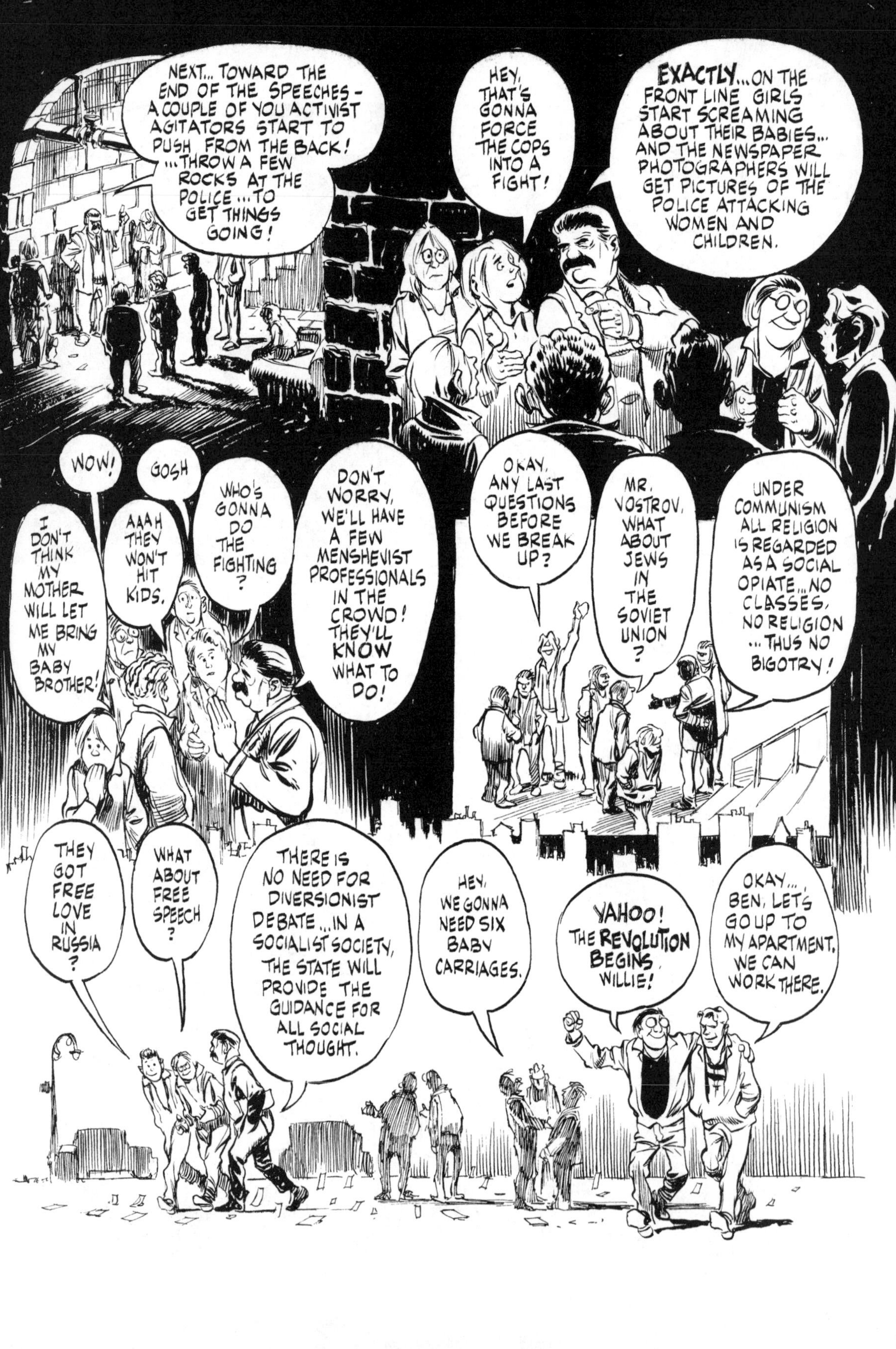
NEXT... TOWARD THE END OF THE SPEECHES - A COUPLE OF YOU ACTIVIST AGITATORS START TO PUSH FROM THE BACK! ...THROW A FEW ROCKS AT THE POLICE ... TO GET THINGS GOING!
HEY, THAT'S GONNA FORCE THE COPS INTO A FIGHT!
EXACTLY... ON THE FRONT LINE GIRLS START SCREAMING ABOUT THEIR BABIES... AND THE NEWSPAPER PHOTOGRAPHERS WILL GET PICTURES OF THE POLICE ATTACKING WOMEN AND CHILDREN.
WOW!
I DON'T THINK MY MOTHER WILL LET ME BRING MY BABY BROTHER!
GOSH
AAAH THEY WON'T HIT KIDS.
WHO'S GONNA DO THE FIGHTING?
DON'T WORRY, WE'LL HAVE A FEW MENSHEVIST PROFESSIONALS IN THE CROWD! THEY'LL KNOW WHAT TO DO!
OKAY, ANY LAST QUESTIONS BEFORE WE BREAK UP?
MR. VOSTROV, WHAT ABOUT JEWS IN THE SOVIET UNION?
UNDER COMMUNISM ALL RELIGION IS REGARDED AS A SOCIAL OPIATE... NO CLASSES, NO RELIGION ... THUS NO BIGOTRY!
THEY GOT FREE LOVE IN RUSSIA?
WHAT ABOUT FREE SPEECH?
THERE IS NO NEED FOR DIVERSIONIST DEBATE... IN A SOCIALIST SOCIETY, THE STATE WILL PROVIDE THE GUIDANCE FOR ALL SOCIAL THOUGHT.
HEY, WE GONNA NEED SIX BABY CARRIAGES.
YAHOO! THE REVOLUTION BEGINS, WILLIE!
OKAY... BEN, LET'S GO UP TO MY APARTMENT, WE CAN WORK THERE.

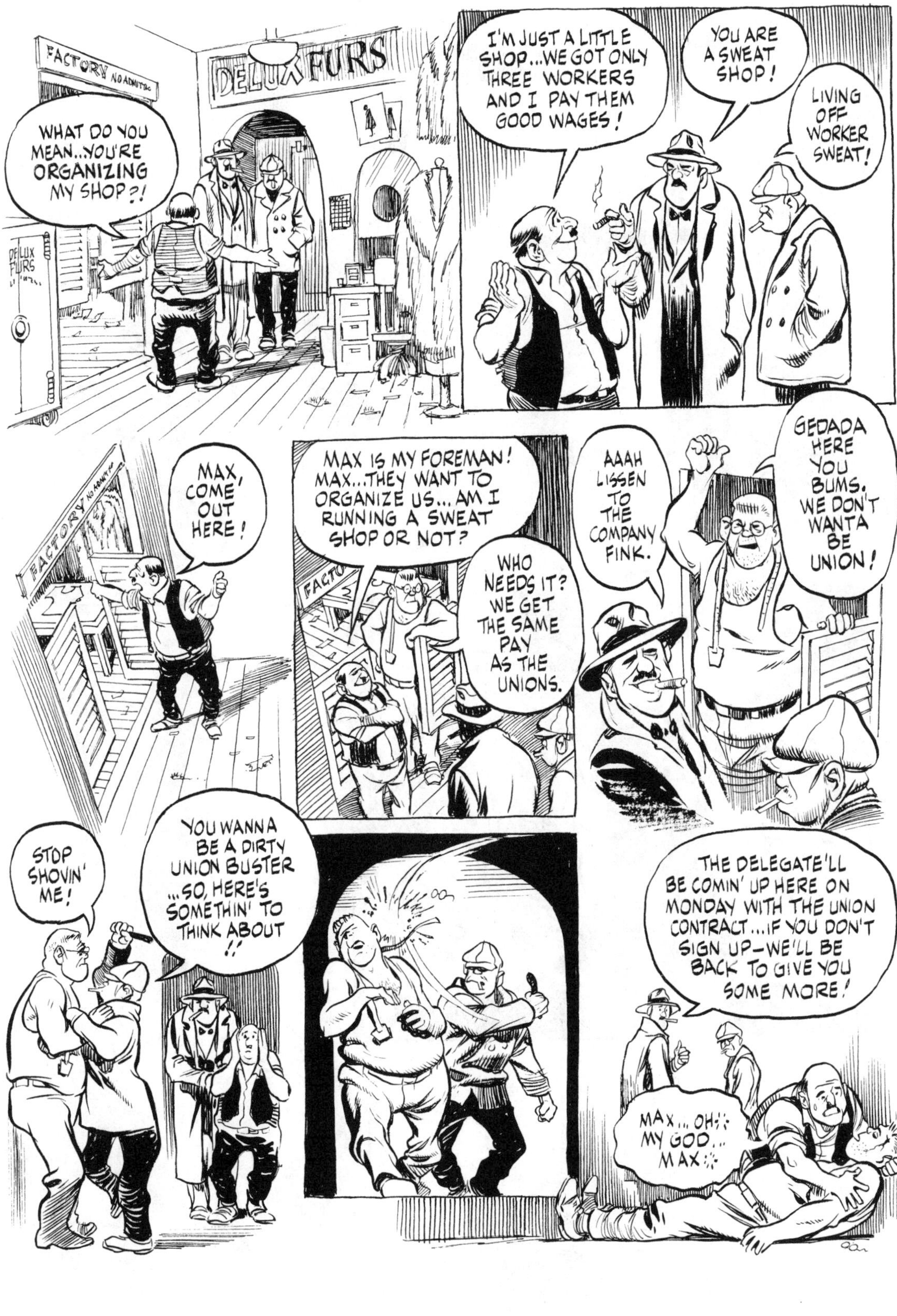
FACTORY NO ADMITTANCE
DELUX FURS
WHAT DO YOU MEAN...YOU'RE ORGANIZING MY SHOP?!
I'M JUST A LITTLE SHOP...WE GOT ONLY THREE WORKERS AND I PAY THEM GOOD WAGES!
YOU ARE A SWEAT SHOP!
LIVING OFF WORKER SWEAT!
MAX, COME OUT HERE!
MAX IS MY FOREMAN! MAX...THEY WANT TO ORGANIZE US...AM I RUNNING A SWEAT SHOP OR NOT?
WHO NEEDS IT? WE GET THE SAME PAY AS THE UNIONS.
AAAH LISSEN TO THE COMPANY FINK.
GEDADA HERE YOU BUMS. WE DON'T WANTA BE UNION!
STOP SHOVIN' ME!
YOU WANNA BE A DIRTY UNION BUSTER ...SO, HERE'S SOMETHIN' TO THINK ABOUT!!
THE DELEGATE'LL BE COMIN' UP HERE ON MONDAY WITH THE UNION CONTRACT...IF YOU DON'T SIGN UP–WE'LL BE BACK TO GIVE YOU SOME MORE!
MAX... OH... MY GOD... MAX...

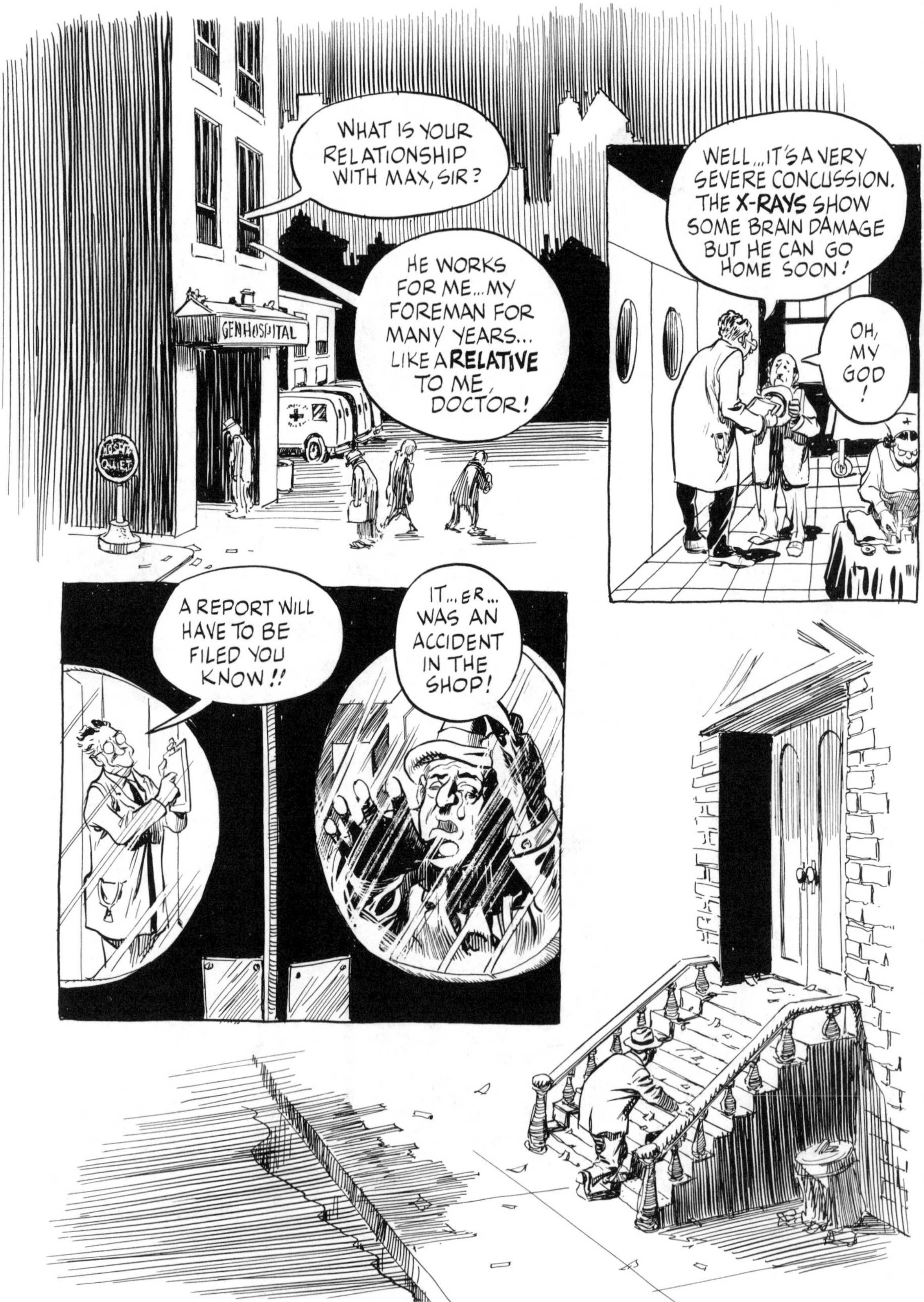
GEN HOSPITAL
WHAT IS YOUR RELATIONSHIP WITH MAX, SIR?
HE WORKS FOR ME...MY FOREMAN FOR MANY YEARS... LIKE A **RELATIVE** TO ME, DOCTOR!
WELL...IT'S A VERY SEVERE CONCUSSION. THE **X-RAYS** SHOW SOME BRAIN DAMAGE BUT HE CAN GO HOME SOON!
OH, MY GOD!
A REPORT WILL HAVE TO BE FILED YOU KNOW!!
IT...ER... WAS AN ACCIDENT IN THE SHOP!

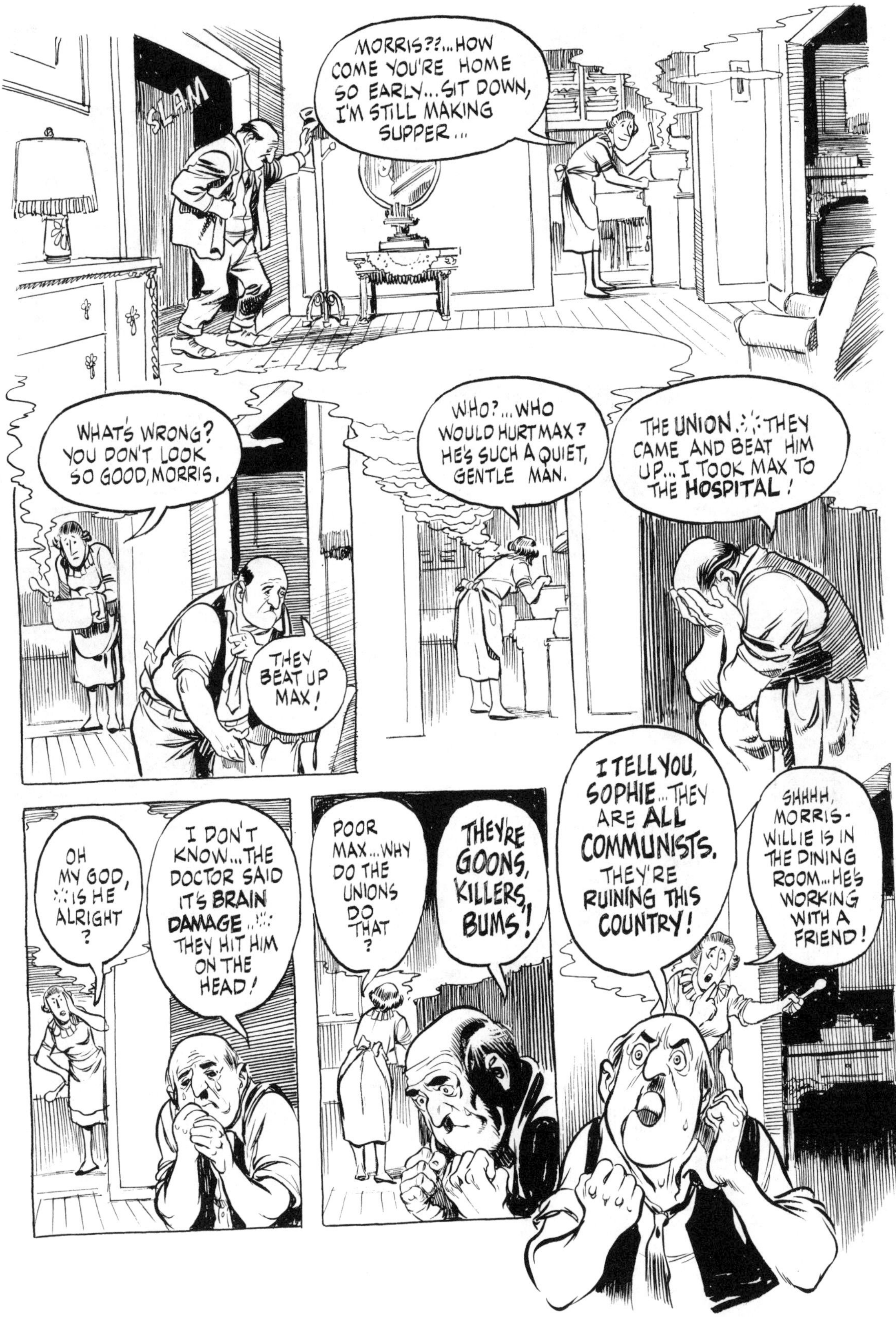
SLAM
MORRIS??... HOW COME YOU'RE HOME SO EARLY... SIT DOWN, I'M STILL MAKING SUPPER...
WHAT'S WRONG? YOU DON'T LOOK SO GOOD, MORRIS.
THEY BEAT UP MAX!
WHO?... WHO WOULD HURT MAX? HE'S SUCH A QUIET, GENTLE MAN.
THE UNION... THEY CAME AND BEAT HIM UP... I TOOK MAX TO THE HOSPITAL!
OH MY GOD, IS HE ALRIGHT?
I DON'T KNOW... THE DOCTOR SAID IT'S BRAIN DAMAGE... THEY HIT HIM ON THE HEAD!
POOR MAX... WHY DO THE UNIONS DO THAT?
THEY'RE GOONS, KILLERS, BUMS!
I TELL YOU, SOPHIE... THEY ARE ALL COMMUNISTS. THEY'RE RUINING THIS COUNTRY!
SHHHH, MORRIS- WILLIE IS IN THE DINING ROOM... HE'S WORKING WITH A FRIEND!

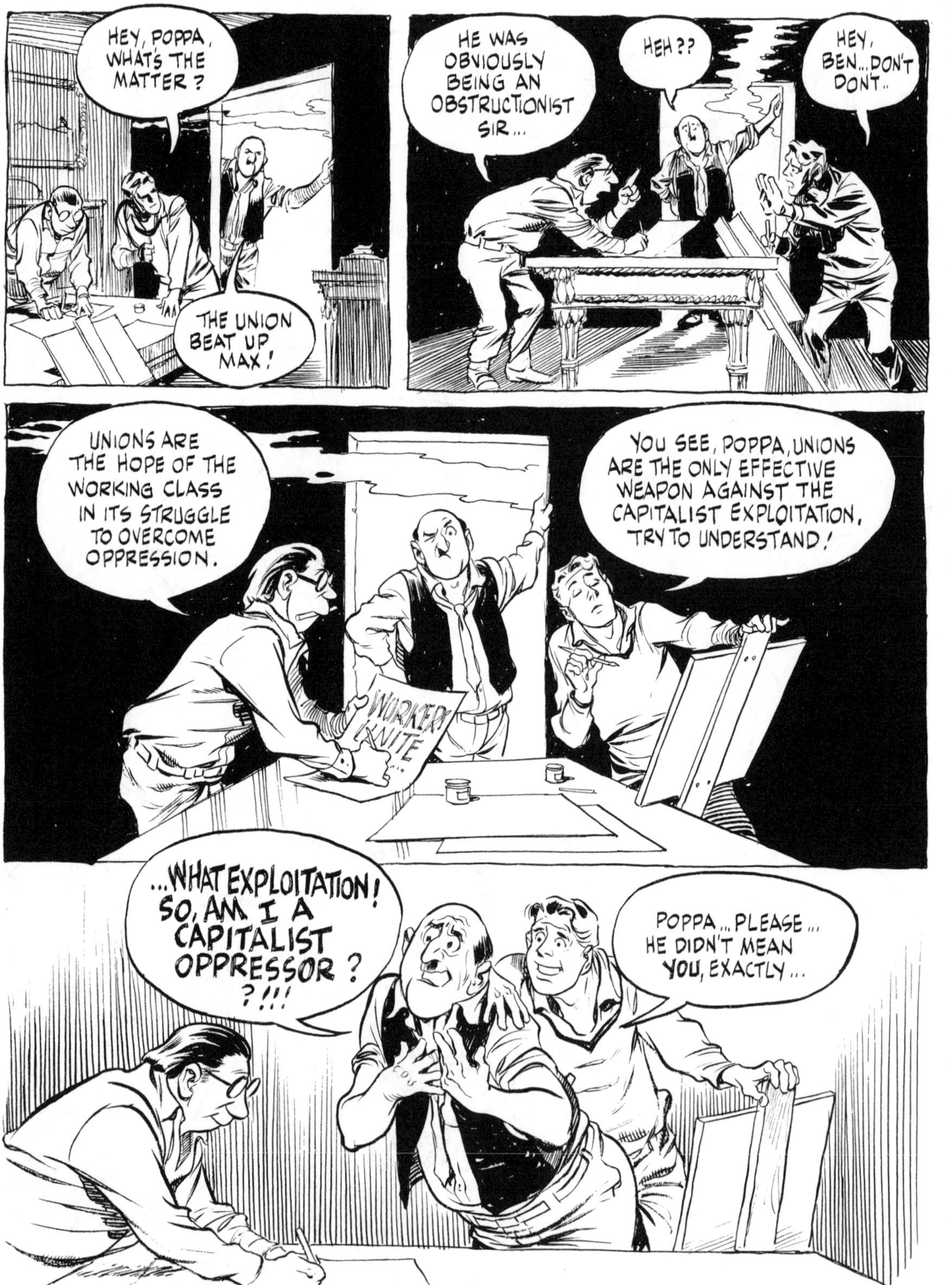
HEY, POPPA, WHAT'S THE MATTER?
THE UNION BEAT UP MAX!
HE WAS OBVIOUSLY BEING AN OBSTRUCTIONIST SIR...
HEH??
HEY, BEN... DON'T DON'T..
UNIONS ARE THE HOPE OF THE WORKING CLASS IN ITS STRUGGLE TO OVERCOME OPPRESSION.
YOU SEE, POPPA, UNIONS ARE THE ONLY EFFECTIVE WEAPON AGAINST THE CAPITALIST EXPLOITATION, TRY TO UNDERSTAND!
WORKERS UNITE
...WHAT EXPLOITATION! SO, AM I A CAPITALIST OPPRESSOR? ?!!!
POPPA... PLEASE... HE DIDN'T MEAN YOU, EXACTLY...

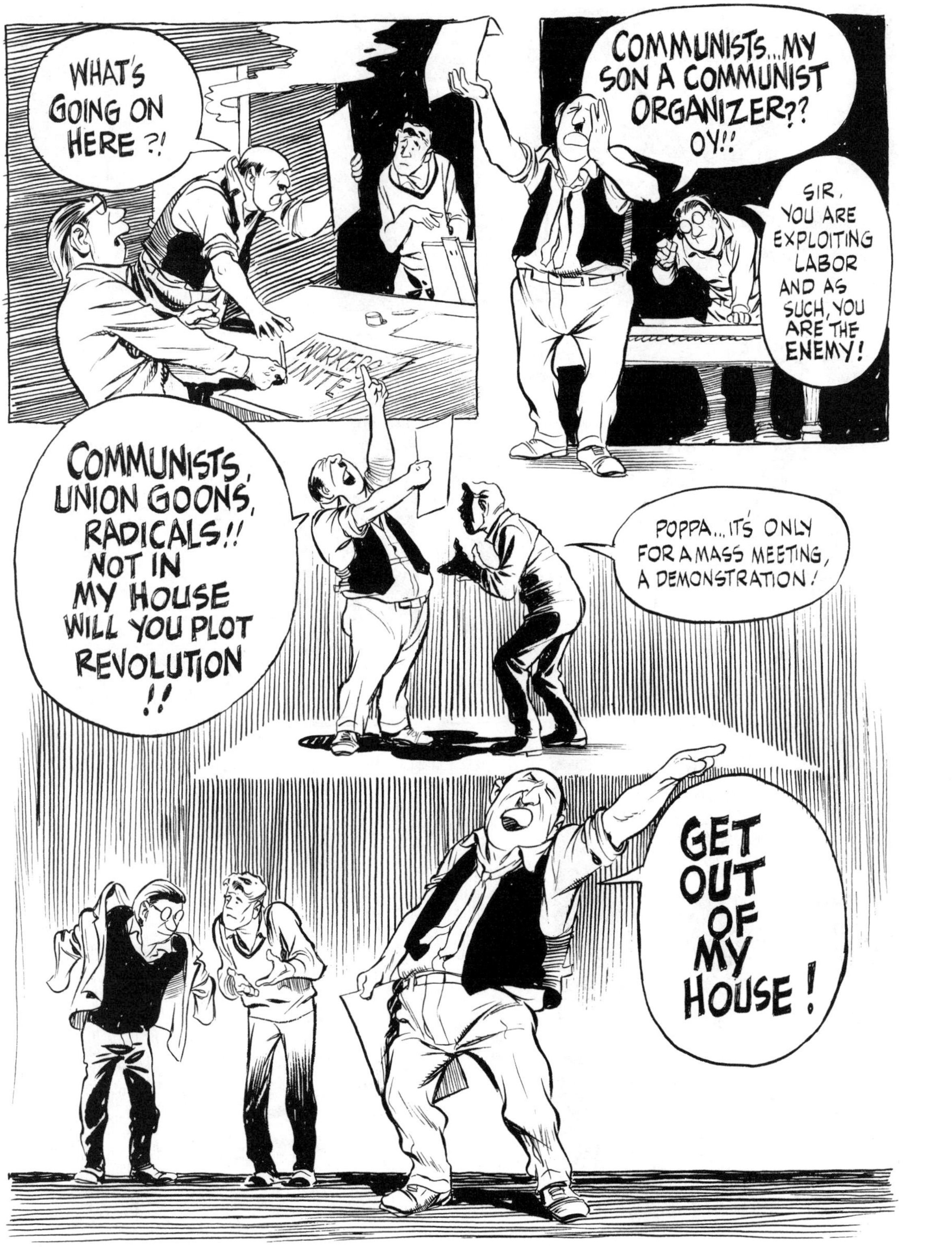
WHAT'S GOING ON HERE ?!
WORKERS UNITE
COMMUNISTS...MY SON A COMMUNIST ORGANIZER?? OY!!
SIR, YOU ARE EXPLOITING LABOR AND AS SUCH, YOU ARE THE ENEMY!
COMMUNISTS, UNION GOONS, RADICALS!! NOT IN MY HOUSE WILL YOU PLOT REVOLUTION !!
POPPA... IT'S ONLY FOR A MASS MEETING, A DEMONSTRATION!
GET OUT OF MY HOUSE!

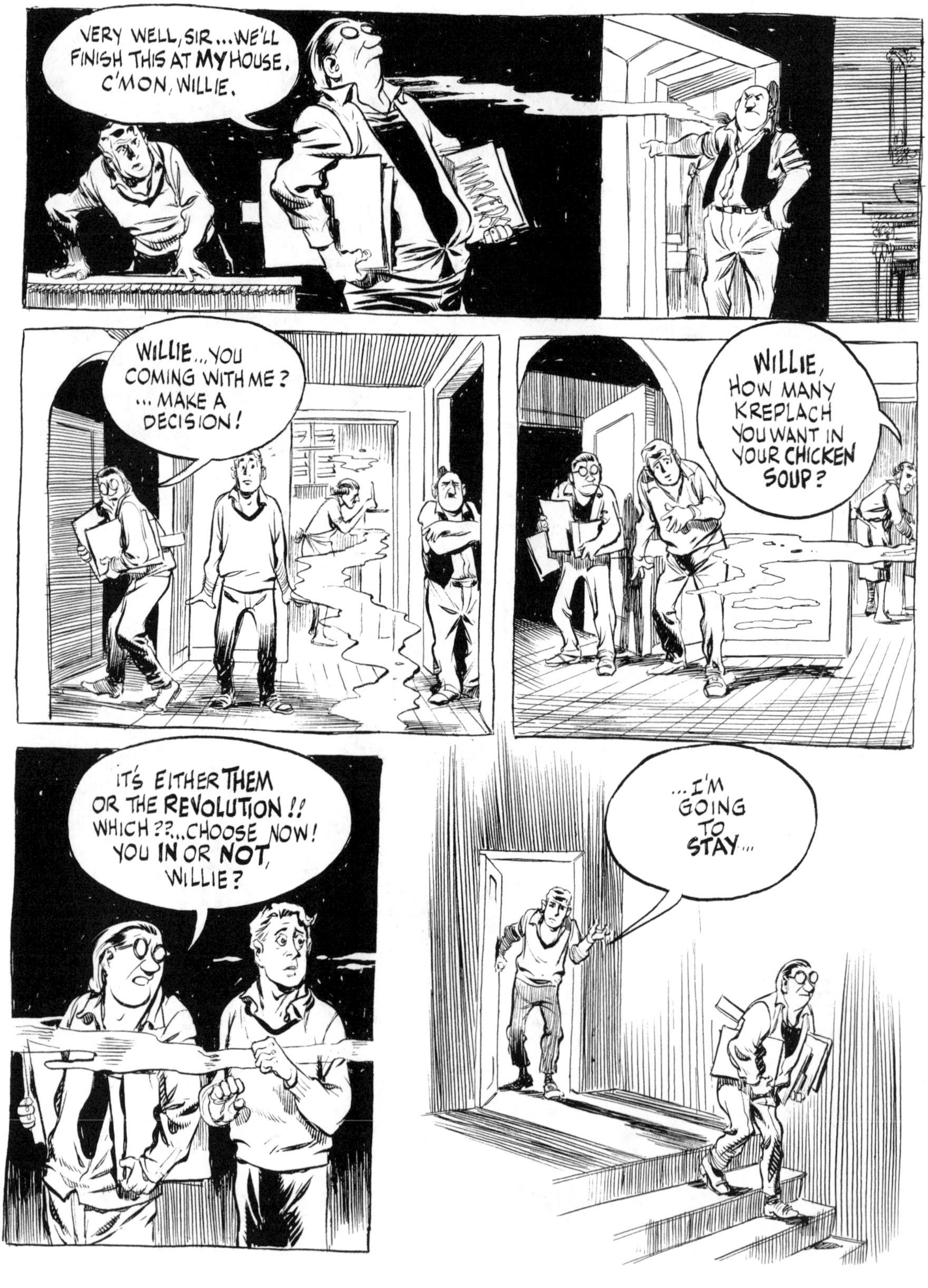
VERY WELL, SIR...WE'LL FINISH THIS AT MY HOUSE. C'MON, WILLIE.
WORKERS
WILLIE...YOU COMING WITH ME? ...MAKE A DECISION!
WILLIE, HOW MANY KREPLACH YOU WANT IN YOUR CHICKEN SOUP?
IT'S EITHER THEM OR THE REVOLUTION!! WHICH??...CHOOSE NOW! YOU IN OR NOT, WILLIE?
...I'M GOING TO STAY...

CHAPTER 8

UPTURN

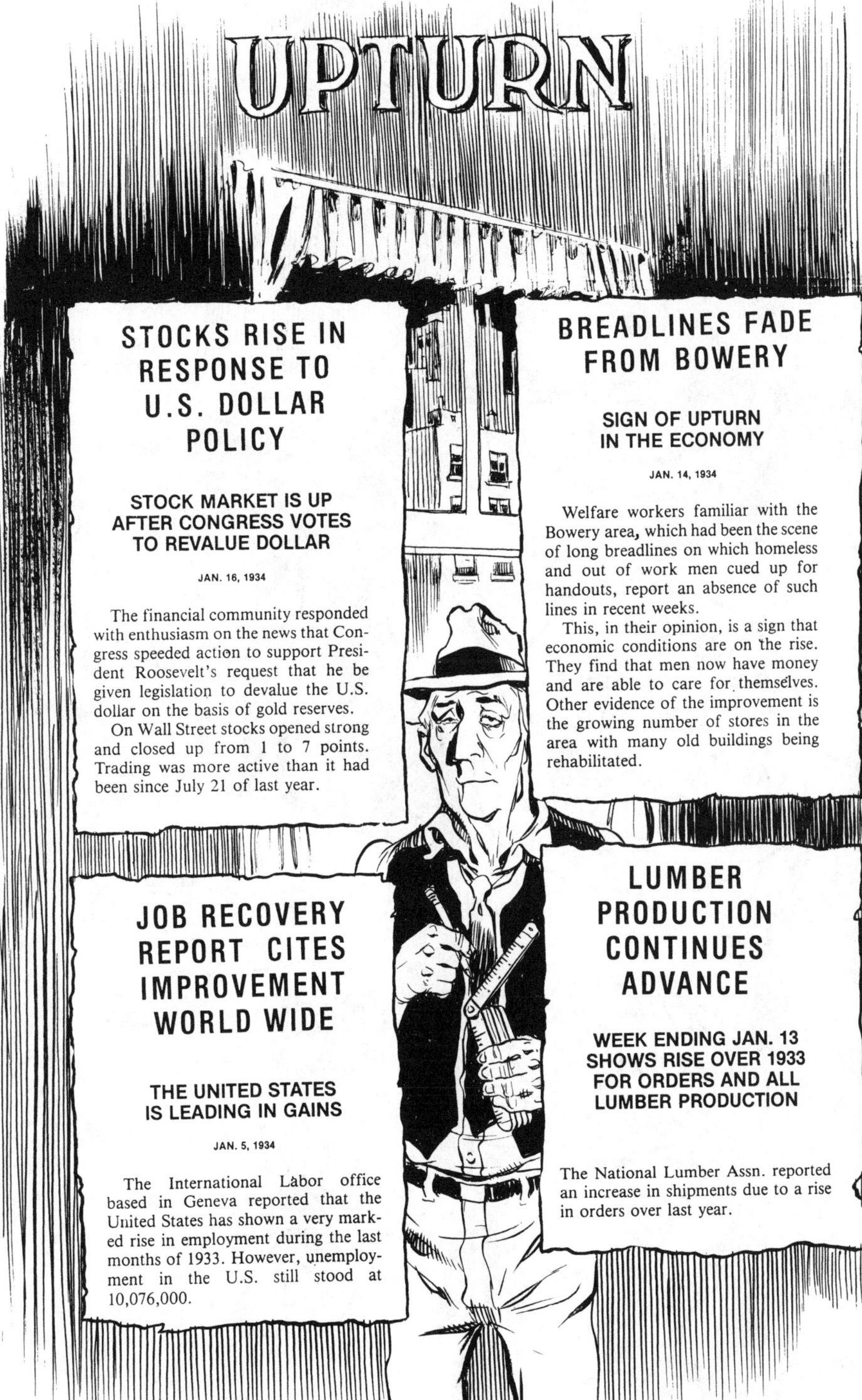

STOCKS RISE IN RESPONSE TO U.S. DOLLAR POLICY

STOCK MARKET IS UP AFTER CONGRESS VOTES TO REVALUE DOLLAR

JAN. 16, 1934

The financial community responded with enthusiasm on the news that Congress speeded action to support President Roosevelt's request that he be given legislation to devalue the U.S. dollar on the basis of gold reserves.

On Wall Street stocks opened strong and closed up from 1 to 7 points. Trading was more active than it had been since July 21 of last year.

BREADLINES FADE FROM BOWERY

SIGN OF UPTURN IN THE ECONOMY

JAN. 14, 1934

Welfare workers familiar with the Bowery area, which had been the scene of long breadlines on which homeless and out of work men cued up for handouts, report an absence of such lines in recent weeks.

This, in their opinion, is a sign that economic conditions are on the rise. They find that men now have money and are able to care for. themselves. Other evidence of the improvement is the growing number of stores in the area with many old buildings being rehabilitated.

JOB RECOVERY REPORT CITES IMPROVEMENT WORLD WIDE

THE UNITED STATES IS LEADING IN GAINS

JAN. 5, 1934

The International Labor office based in Geneva reported that the United States has shown a very marked rise in employment during the last months of 1933. However, unemployment in the U.S. still stood at 10,076,000.

LUMBER PRODUCTION CONTINUES ADVANCE

WEEK ENDING JAN. 13 SHOWS RISE OVER 1933 FOR ORDERS AND ALL LUMBER PRODUCTION

The National Lumber Assn. reported an increase in shipments due to a rise in orders over last year.

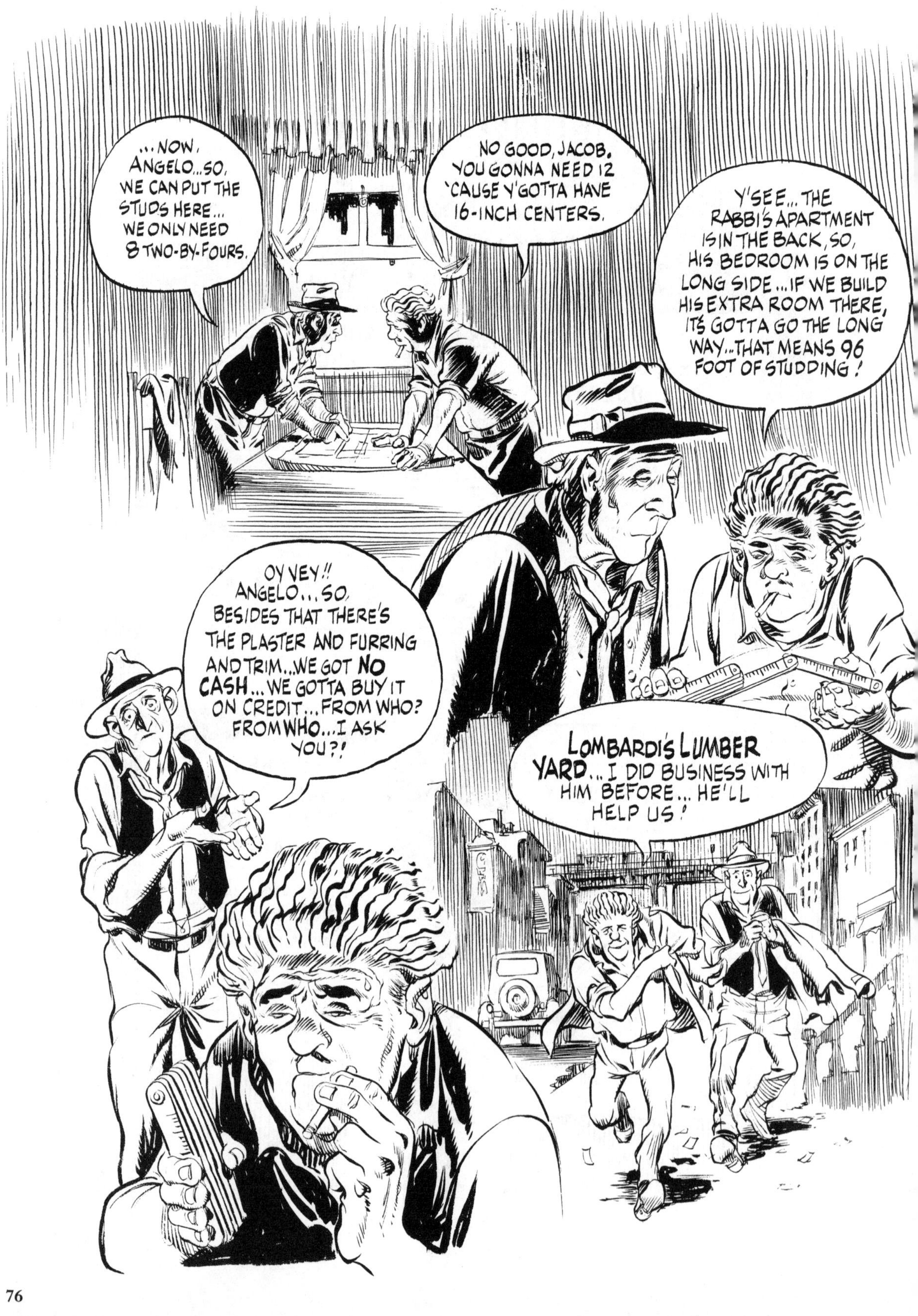
...NOW, ANGELO...SO, WE CAN PUT THE STUDS HERE... WE ONLY NEED 8 TWO-BY-FOURS.
NO GOOD, JACOB. YOU GONNA NEED 12 'CAUSE Y'GOTTA HAVE 16-INCH CENTERS.
Y'SEE... THE RABBI'S APARTMENT IS IN THE BACK, SO, HIS BEDROOM IS ON THE LONG SIDE... IF WE BUILD HIS EXTRA ROOM THERE, IT'S GOTTA GO THE LONG WAY... THAT MEANS 96 FOOT OF STUDDING!
OY VEY!! ANGELO... SO, BESIDES THAT THERE'S THE PLASTER AND FURRING AND TRIM... WE GOT NO CASH... WE GOTTA BUY IT ON CREDIT... FROM WHO? FROM WHO... I ASK YOU?!
LOMBARDI'S LUMBER YARD... I DID BUSINESS WITH HIM BEFORE... HE'LL HELP US!

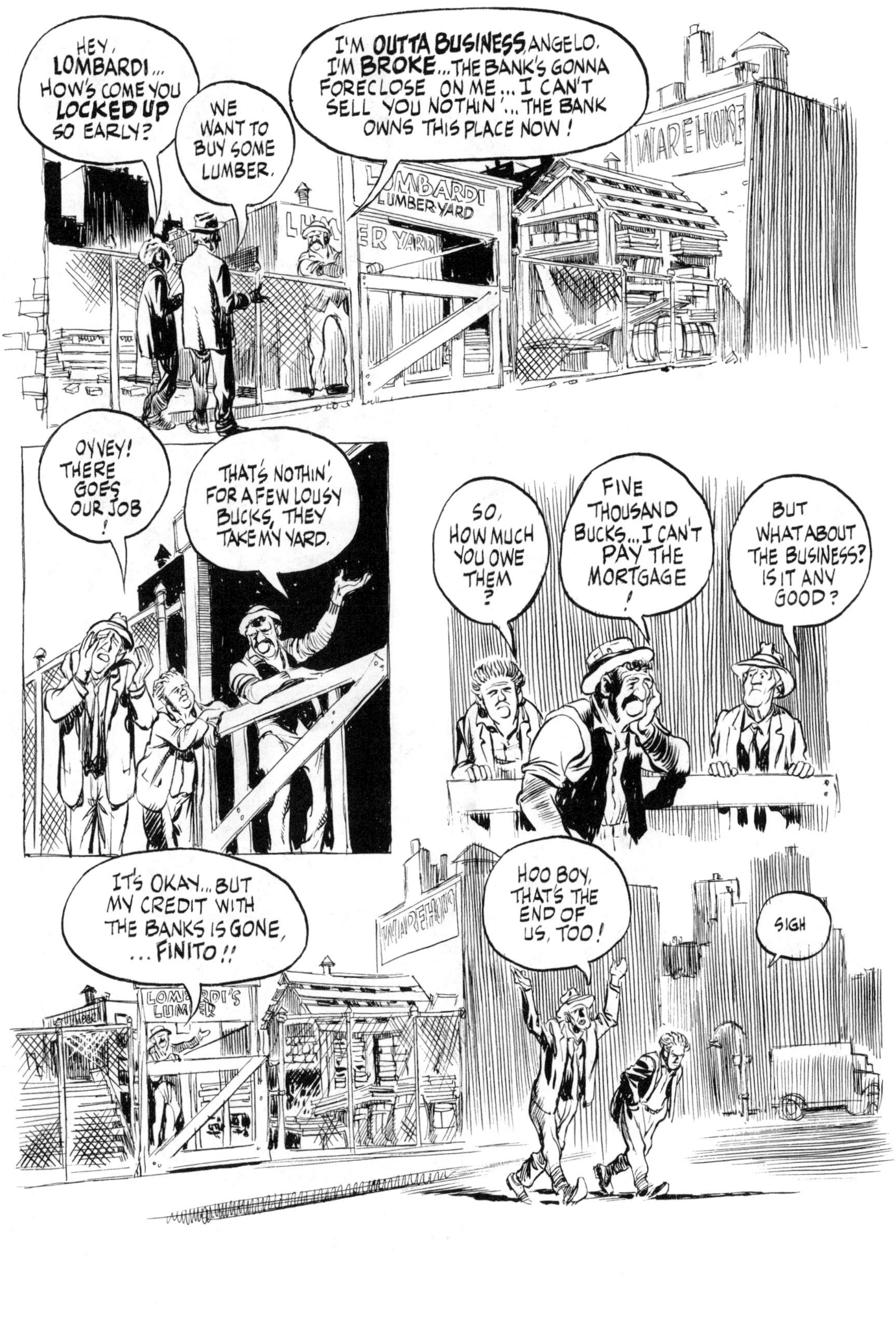
HEY, LOMBARDI... HOW'S COME YOU LOCKED UP SO EARLY?
WE WANT TO BUY SOME LUMBER.
I'M OUTTA BUSINESS ANGELO. I'M BROKE... THE BANK'S GONNA FORECLOSE ON ME... I CAN'T SELL YOU NOTHIN'... THE BANK OWNS THIS PLACE NOW!
WAREHOUSE
LOMBARDI LUMBER YARD
OY VEY! THERE GOES OUR JOB!
THAT'S NOTHIN', FOR A FEW LOUSY BUCKS, THEY TAKE MY YARD.
SO, HOW MUCH YOU OWE THEM?
FIVE THOUSAND BUCKS... I CAN'T PAY THE MORTGAGE!
BUT WHAT ABOUT THE BUSINESS? IS IT ANY GOOD?
IT'S OKAY... BUT MY CREDIT WITH THE BANKS IS GONE, ...FINITO!!
LOMBARDI'S LUMBER
HOO BOY, THAT'S THE END OF US, TOO!
SIGH

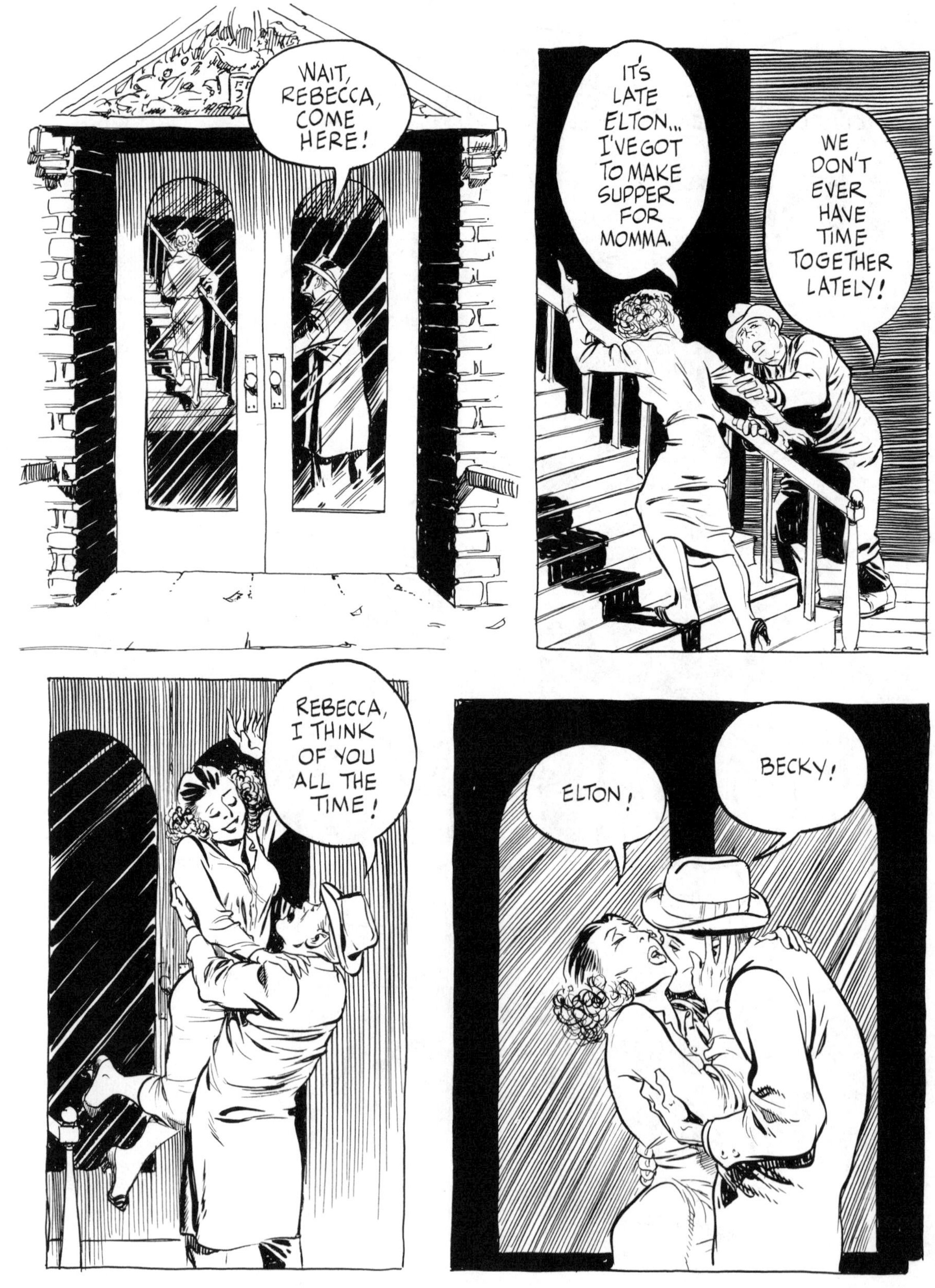
WAIT, REBECCA, COME HERE!
IT'S LATE ELTON... I'VE GOT TO MAKE SUPPER FOR MOMMA.
WE DON'T EVER HAVE TIME TOGETHER LATELY!
REBECCA, I THINK OF YOU ALL THE TIME!
ELTON!
BECKY!

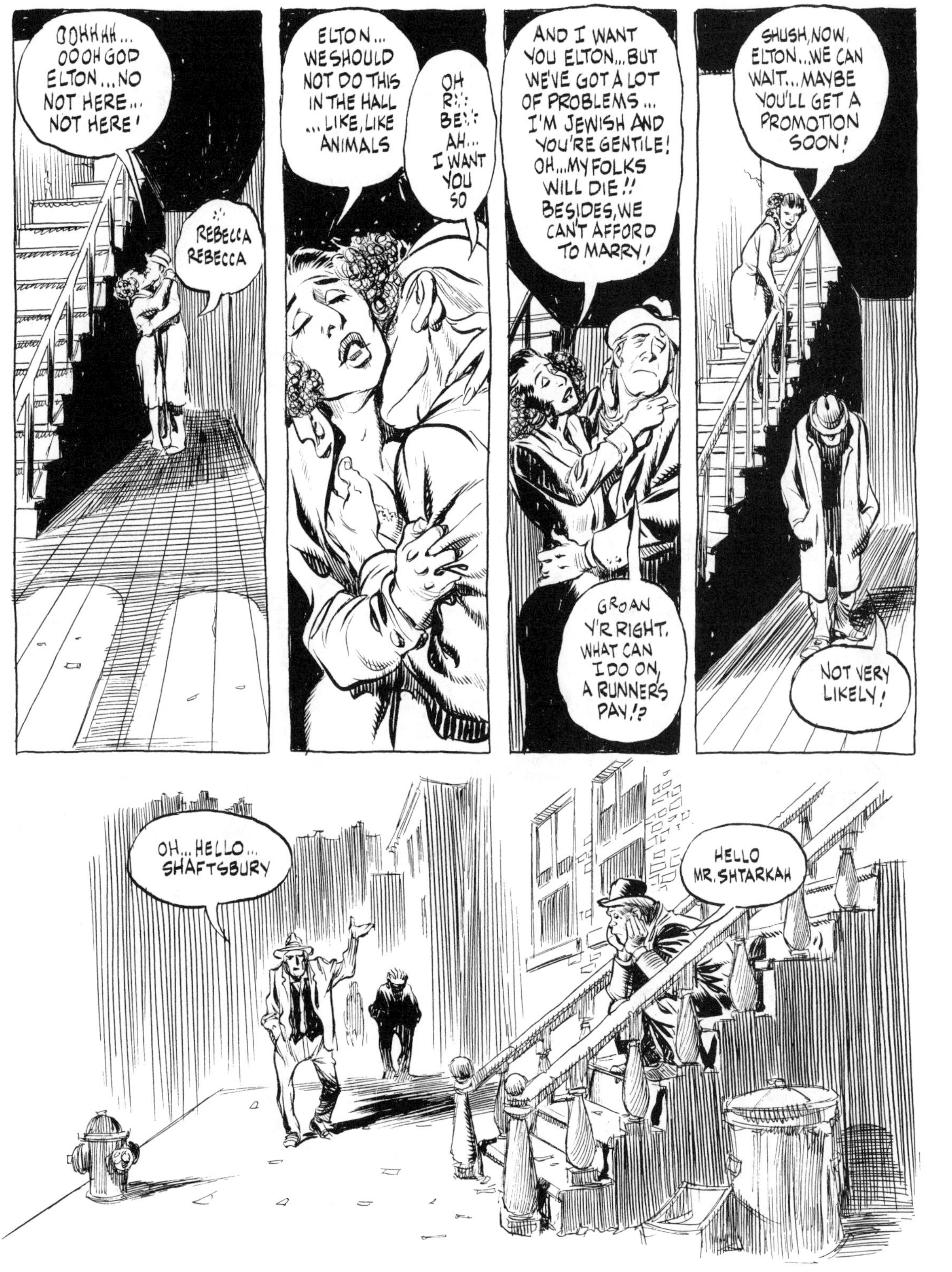
OOHHHH... OOOH GOD ELTON...NO NOT HERE... NOT HERE!
REBECCA REBECCA
ELTON... WE SHOULD NOT DO THIS IN THE HALL ...LIKE, LIKE ANIMALS
OH R... BE... AH... I WANT YOU SO
AND I WANT YOU ELTON...BUT WE'VE GOT A LOT OF PROBLEMS... I'M JEWISH AND YOU'RE GENTILE! OH...MY FOLKS WILL DIE!! BESIDES, WE CAN'T AFFORD TO MARRY!
GROAN
Y'R RIGHT. WHAT CAN I DO ON, A RUNNER'S PAY!?
SHUSH, NOW, ELTON...WE CAN WAIT...MAYBE YOU'LL GET A PROMOTION SOON!
NOT VERY LIKELY!
OH...HELLO... SHAFTSBURY
HELLO MR. SHTARKAH

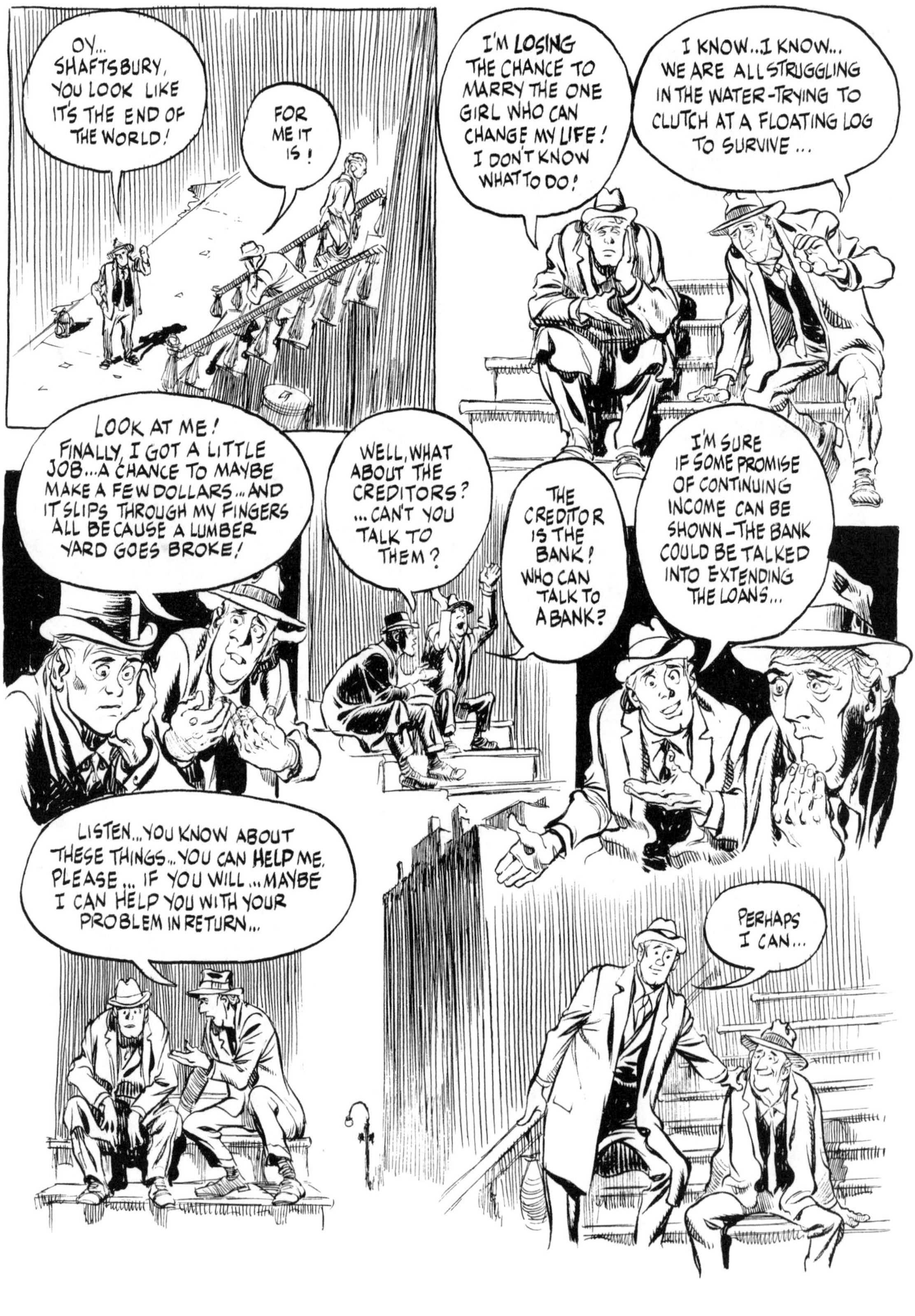
OY... SHAFTSBURY, YOU LOOK LIKE IT'S THE END OF THE WORLD!
FOR ME IT IS!
I'M LOSING THE CHANCE TO MARRY THE ONE GIRL WHO CAN CHANGE MY LIFE! I DON'T KNOW WHAT TO DO!
I KNOW...I KNOW... WE ARE ALL STRUGGLING IN THE WATER-TRYING TO CLUTCH AT A FLOATING LOG TO SURVIVE...
LOOK AT ME! FINALLY, I GOT A LITTLE JOB...A CHANCE TO MAYBE MAKE A FEW DOLLARS...AND IT SLIPS THROUGH MY FINGERS ALL BECAUSE A LUMBER YARD GOES BROKE!
WELL, WHAT ABOUT THE CREDITORS? ...CAN'T YOU TALK TO THEM?
THE CREDITOR IS THE BANK! WHO CAN TALK TO A BANK?
I'M SURE IF SOME PROMISE OF CONTINUING INCOME CAN BE SHOWN-THE BANK COULD BE TALKED INTO EXTENDING THE LOANS...
LISTEN...YOU KNOW ABOUT THESE THINGS...YOU CAN HELP ME. PLEASE... IF YOU WILL...MAYBE I CAN HELP YOU WITH YOUR PROBLEM IN RETURN...
PERHAPS I CAN...

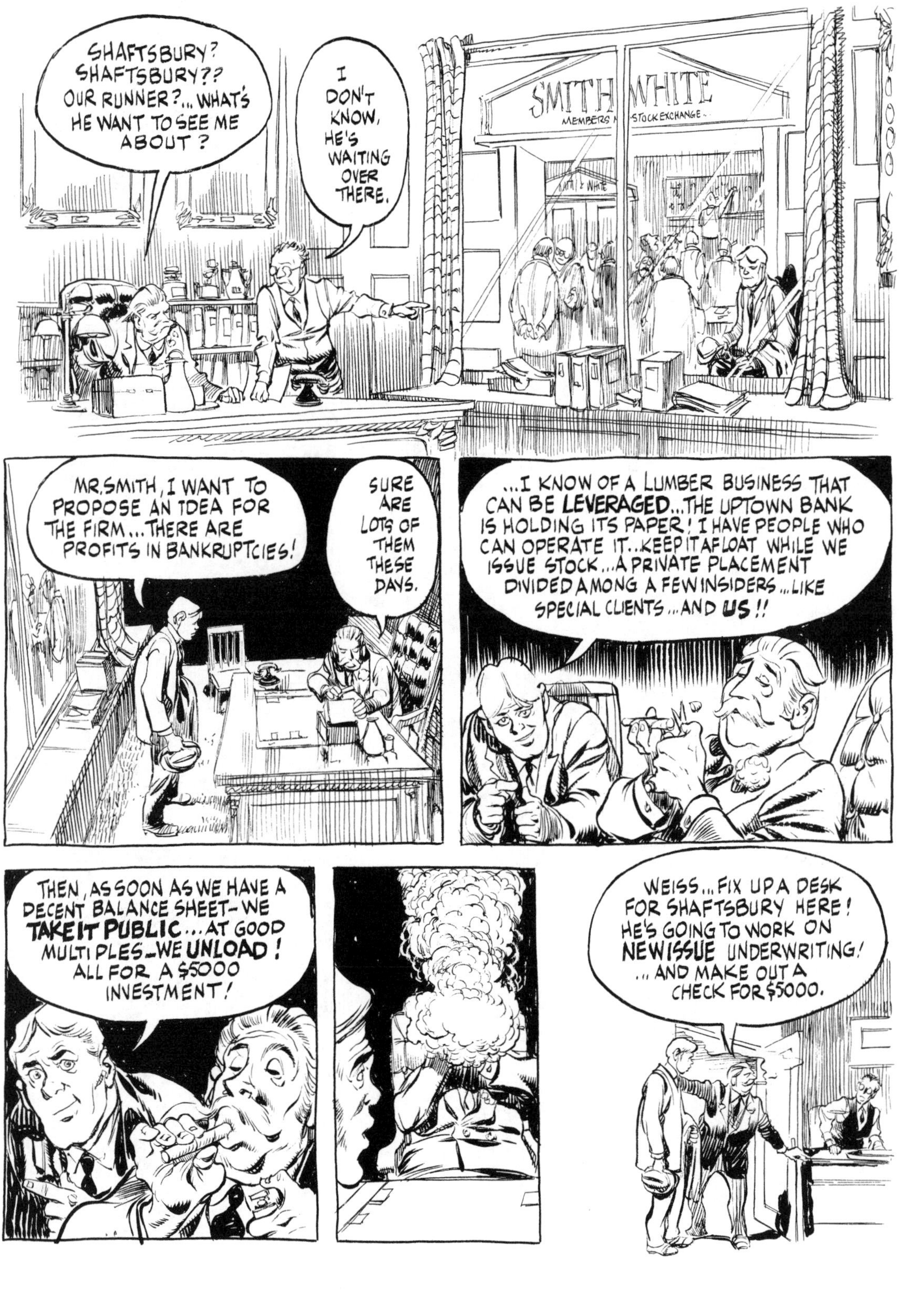
SHAFTSBURY? SHAFTSBURY?? OUR RUNNER?... WHAT'S HE WANT TO SEE ME ABOUT?
I DON'T KNOW, HE'S WAITING OVER THERE.
SMITH WHITE
MEMBERS STOCK EXCHANGE
MR. SMITH, I WANT TO PROPOSE AN IDEA FOR THE FIRM... THERE ARE PROFITS IN BANKRUPTCIES!
SURE ARE LOTS OF THEM THESE DAYS.
...I KNOW OF A LUMBER BUSINESS THAT CAN BE **LEVERAGED**... THE UPTOWN BANK IS HOLDING ITS PAPER! I HAVE PEOPLE WHO CAN OPERATE IT... KEEP IT AFLOAT WHILE WE ISSUE STOCK... A PRIVATE PLACEMENT DIVIDED AMONG A FEW INSIDERS... LIKE SPECIAL CLIENTS... AND **US**!!
THEN, AS SOON AS WE HAVE A DECENT BALANCE SHEET- WE **TAKE IT PUBLIC**... AT GOOD MULTIPLES- WE **UNLOAD**! ALL FOR A $5000 INVESTMENT!
WEISS... FIX UP A DESK FOR SHAFTSBURY HERE! HE'S GOING TO WORK ON **NEW ISSUE** UNDERWRITING! ... AND MAKE OUT A CHECK FOR $5000.

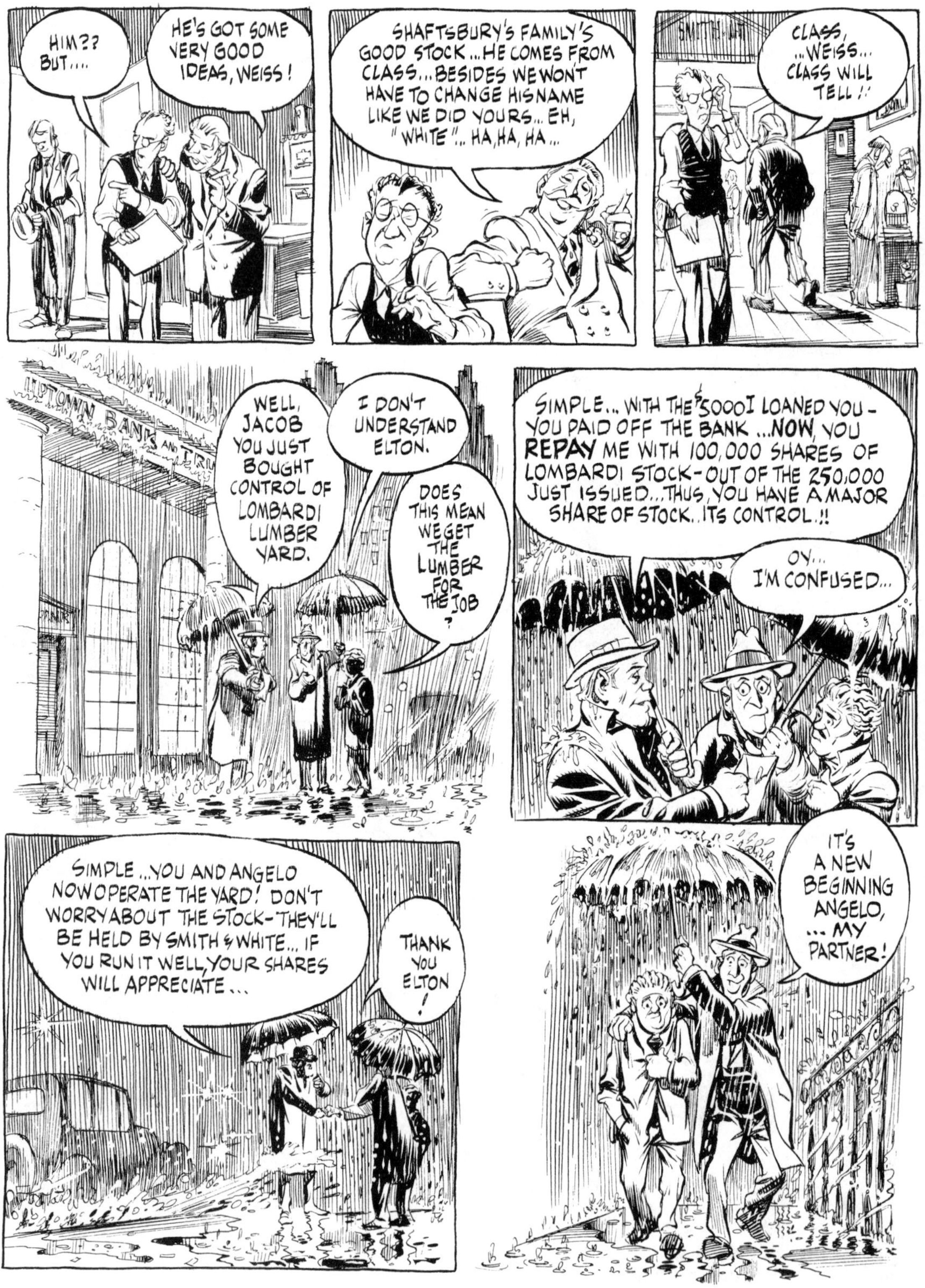
HIM?? BUT....
HE'S GOT SOME VERY GOOD IDEAS, WEISS!
SHAFTSBURY'S FAMILY'S GOOD STOCK... HE COMES FROM CLASS... BESIDES WE WON'T HAVE TO CHANGE HIS NAME LIKE WE DID YOURS... EH, "WHITE".. HA, HA, HA...
CLASS, ...WEISS... CLASS WILL TELL!!
WELL, JACOB YOU JUST BOUGHT CONTROL OF LOMBARDI LUMBER YARD.
I DON'T UNDERSTAND ELTON.
DOES THIS MEAN WE GET THE LUMBER FOR THE JOB?
SIMPLE... WITH THE $5000 I LOANED YOU - YOU PAID OFF THE BANK ...NOW, YOU REPAY ME WITH 100,000 SHARES OF LOMBARDI STOCK - OUT OF THE 250,000 JUST ISSUED... THUS, YOU HAVE A MAJOR SHARE OF STOCK.. ITS CONTROL.!!
OY... I'M CONFUSED...
SIMPLE ...YOU AND ANGELO NOW OPERATE THE YARD! DON'T WORRY ABOUT THE STOCK - THEY'LL BE HELD BY SMITH & WHITE... IF YOU RUN IT WELL, YOUR SHARES WILL APPRECIATE...
THANK YOU ELTON!
IT'S A NEW BEGINNING ANGELO, ... MY PARTNER!

CHAPTER 9
SANCTUARY

GERMANY RESTRICTS EMIGRATION & TRAVEL

JUNE 28, 1934

In a decree, the German government has restricted travellers to 50 marks in silver — a sum virtually worthless on the foreign exchange. In a second decree it reduced the amount emigrants may take with them to 2000 marks, equal to about $650 . . . U.S. currency. In the case of Jews who want to go to Palestine, they may take out a little more — enough to meet the British Mandate regulations. They could also get a little more if they agree to buy German goods when in Palestine.

This, according to a N.Y. Times correspondent, has the effect of stopping all travel outside of Germany for those without funds abroad.

GOEBBELS PUBLISHES CALL TO DISMISS ALL JEWS IN EXPORT FIELD

URGES REPLACEMENT OF "NON-ARYANS" BY MEN OF "GERMAN RACE"

JAN. 15, 1934

The Nazi anti-semitic program was pushed farther by Dr. Joseph Goebbels, Minister of Propaganda in his newspaper, "Der Angriff." The article said, "It seems intolerable to us that German firms still permit Jews to represent them abroad." He added that those concerned know this and will now make the necessary changes.

REICH TAKES ACTION TO DISCOURAGE ALL MIXED MARRIAGES

MARCH 26, 1934

Berlin: Aryans who married "non-Aryans" after the Nazi revolution may not use the divorce courts. The journal, German Justice, announced today that unless those who seek to annul such marriages by legal proceedings may do so only if they file during a six month period under the new law. It said, "All those who contracted mixed-marriages after their condemnation by National Socialism placed themselves in opposition to public opinion and will have to bear the consequences of their acts."

NAZIS NOW BAN JEWISH ACTORS

MARCH 7, 1934

Berlin: Anti-Jewish boycotts are now being encouraged officially in Germany. The Nazi organ, "Der Deutsche" has called on all places of entertainment to bar Jewish performers. This follows an order by Dr. Joseph Goebbels to remove all "non-Aryans" from the German stage. S.A. (Storm Troopers) have been stationed at cabaret entrances to enforce the boycott.

U.S. SECRETARY OF LABOR SAYS INCREASED IMMIGRATION NOW WOULD COMPLICATE U.S. UNEMPLOYMENT PROBLEMS

JAN. 30, 1934

Frances Perkins, Secretary of Labor, said in a speech today that her Department has been making efforts to "humanize the immigration service." She added that she perceived no sentiment in the country to increase present immigration.

THE N.J. STATE JEWISH WAR VETERANS ASSN. ASKS U.S. TO LOWER IMMIGRATION BARRIERS FOR ALL REFUGEES

MAR. 12, 1934

In a resolution at its annual convention, today, the group called on the United States to permit more German refugees to enter the country.

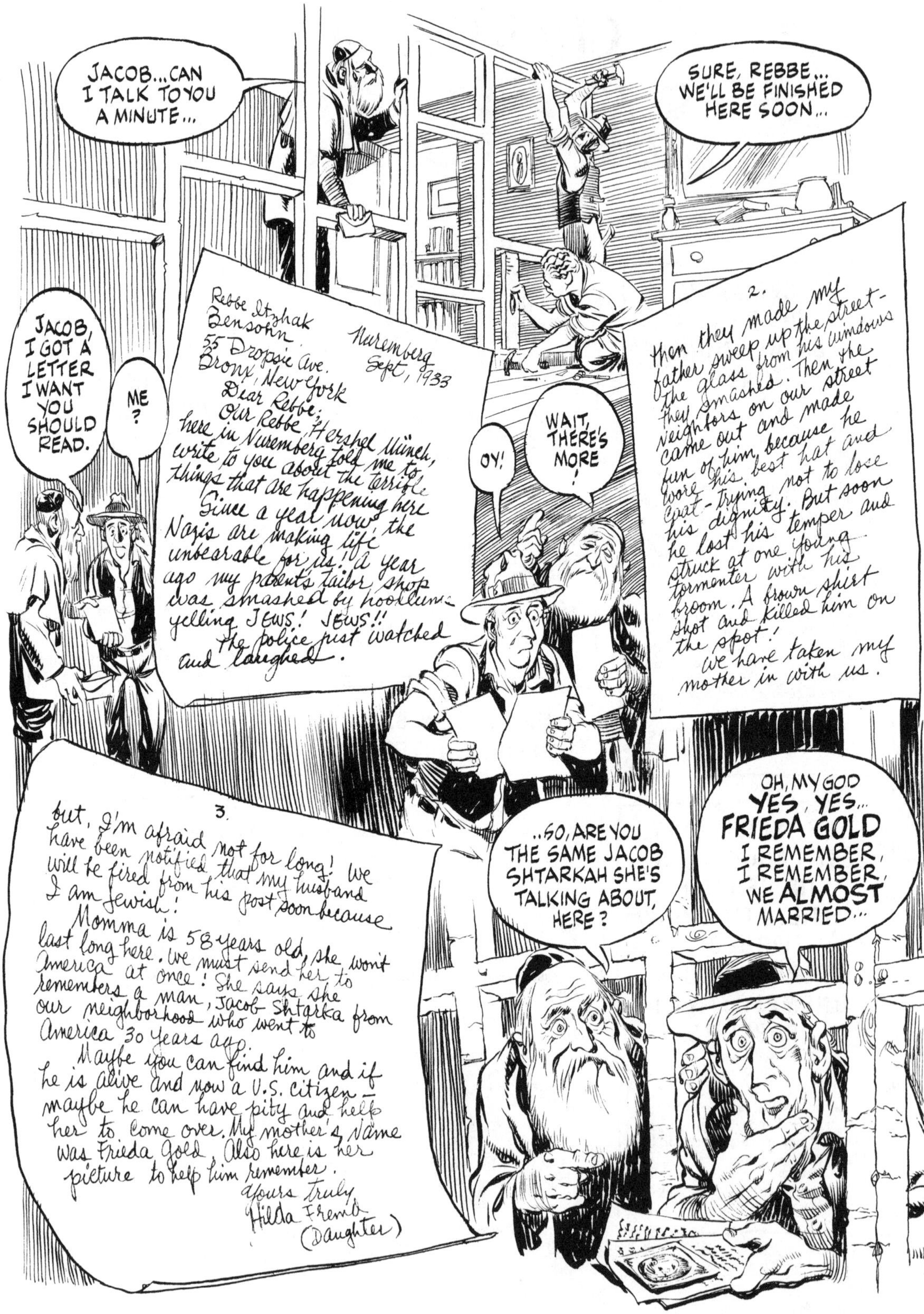
JACOB...CAN I TALK TO YOU A MINUTE...
SURE, REBBE... WE'LL BE FINISHED HERE SOON...
JACOB, I GOT A LETTER I WANT YOU SHOULD READ.
ME?
Rebbe Itzhak Bensohn
55 Dropsie Ave.
Bronx, New York
Nuremberg Sept, 1933
Dear Rebbe,
Our Rebbe, Hershel Münch, here in Nuremberg told me to write to you about the terrible things that are happening here.
Since a year now the Nazis are making life unbearable for us! A year ago my parent's tailor shop was smashed by hoodlums yelling JEWS! JEWS!!
The police just watched and laughed.
OY!
WAIT, THERE'S MORE!
2.
then they made my father sweep up the street the glass from his windows they smashed. Then the neighbors on our street came out and made fun of him because he wore his best hat and coat - trying not to lose his dignity. But soon he lost his temper and struck at one young tormenter with his broom. A brown shirt shot and killed him on the spot!
We have taken my mother in with us.
3.
but, I'm afraid not for long! We have been notified that my husband will be fired from his post soon because I am Jewish!
Momma is 58 years old, she won't last long here. We must send her to America at once! She says she remembers a man, Jacob Shtarka from our neighborhood who went to America 30 years ago.
Maybe you can find him and if he is alive and now a U.S. citizen — maybe he can have pity and help her to come over. My mother's name was Frieda Gold. Also here is her picture to help him remember.
Yours truly
Hilda Fremd
(Daughter)
..SO, ARE YOU THE SAME JACOB SHTARKAH SHE'S TALKING ABOUT, HERE?
OH, MY GOD YES, YES... FRIEDA GOLD I REMEMBER, I REMEMBER, WE ALMOST MARRIED...

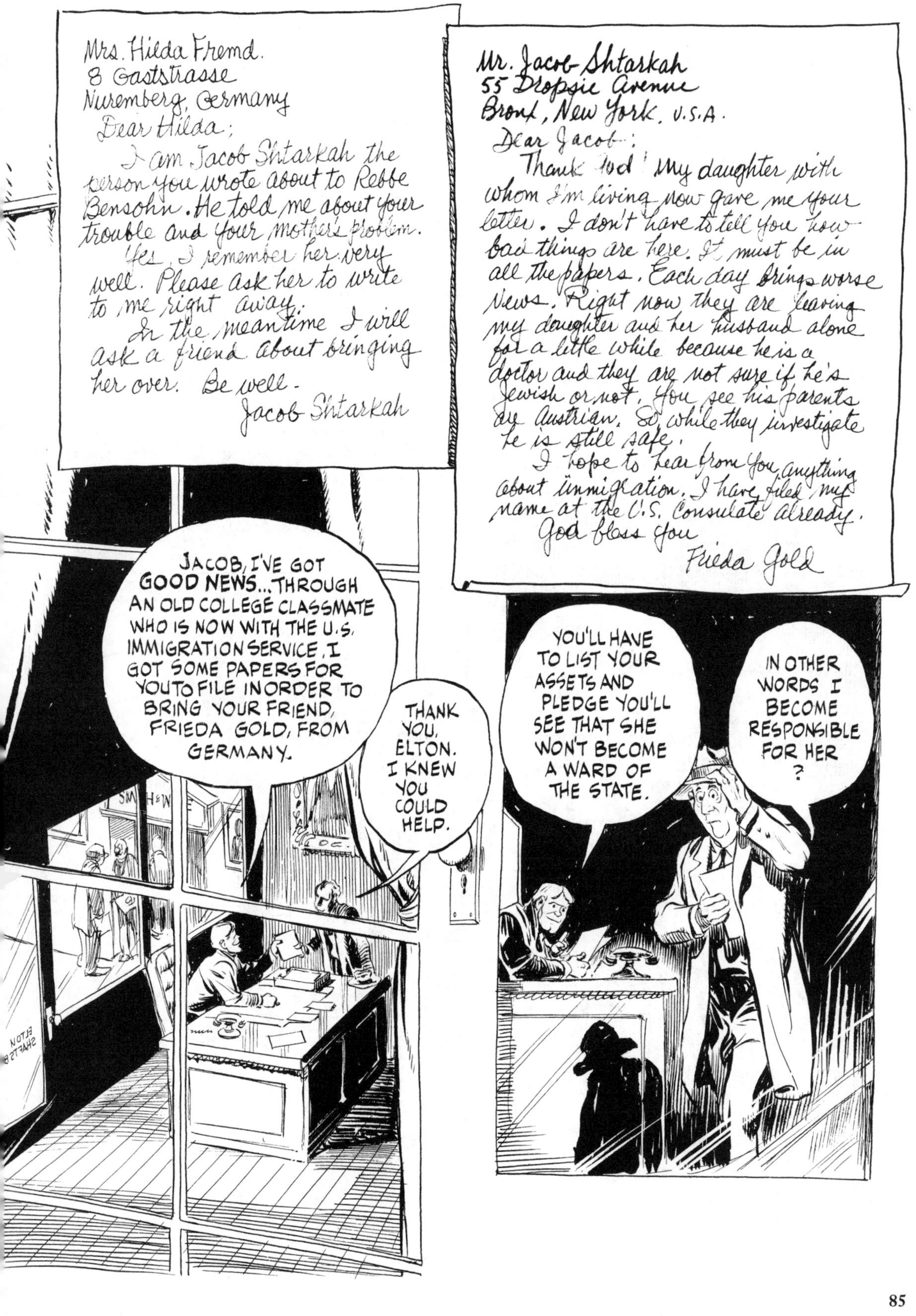
Mrs. Hilda Fremd.
8 Gaststrasse
Nuremberg, Germany
Dear Hilda;
I am Jacob Shtarkah the person you wrote about to Rebbe Bensohn. He told me about your trouble and your mother's problem.
Yes, I remember her very well. Please ask her to write to me right away.
In the meantime I will ask a friend about bringing her over. Be well.
Jacob Shtarkah
Mr. Jacob Shtarkah
55 Dropsie Avenue
Bronx, New York. U.S.A.
Dear Jacob:
Thank God! My daughter with whom I'm living now gave me your letter. I don't have to tell you how bad things are here. It must be in all the papers. Each day brings worse News. Right now they are leaving my daughter and her husband alone for a little while because he is a doctor and they are not sure if he's Jewish or not. You see his parents are Austrian. So while they investigate he is still safe.
I hope to hear from you anything about immigration. I have filed my name at the U.S. Consulate already.
God bless you
Frieda Gold
JACOB, I'VE GOT GOOD NEWS... THROUGH AN OLD COLLEGE CLASSMATE WHO IS NOW WITH THE U.S. IMMIGRATION SERVICE, I GOT SOME PAPERS FOR YOU TO FILE IN ORDER TO BRING YOUR FRIEND, FRIEDA GOLD, FROM GERMANY.
THANK YOU, ELTON. I KNEW YOU COULD HELP.
YOU'LL HAVE TO LIST YOUR ASSETS AND PLEDGE YOU'LL SEE THAT SHE WON'T BECOME A WARD OF THE STATE.
IN OTHER WORDS I BECOME RESPONSIBLE FOR HER ?

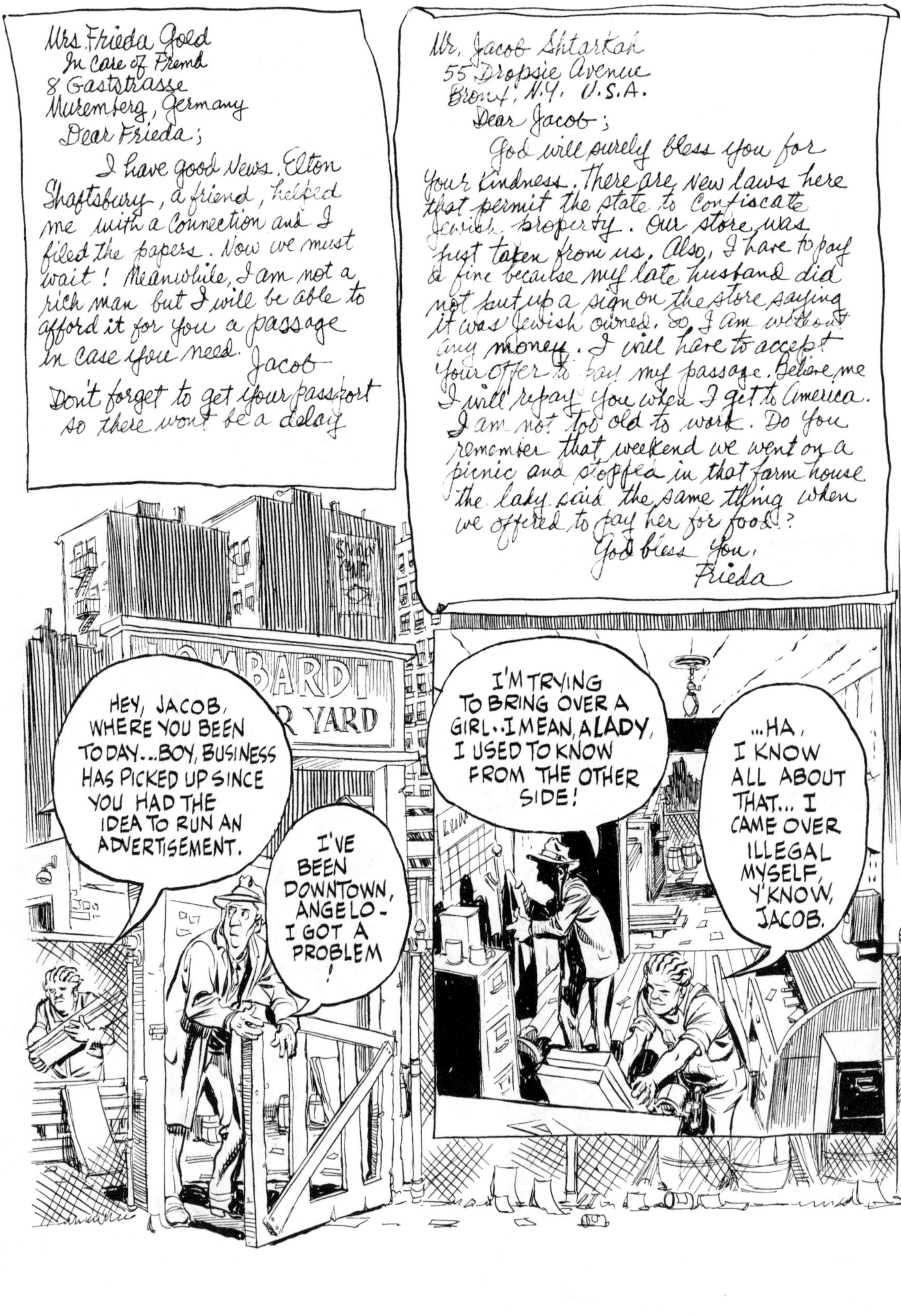
Mrs. Frieda Gold
In care of Fremd
8 Gaststrasse
Nuremberg, Germany
Dear Frieda;
I have good News. Elton Shaftsbury, a friend, helped me with a Connection and I filed the papers. Now we must wait! Meanwhile, I am not a rich man but I will be able to afford it for you a passage in case you need.
Jacob
Don't forget to get your passport so there wont be a delay
Mr. Jacob Shtarkah
55 Dropsie Avenue
Bronx, N.Y. U.S.A.
Dear Jacob;
God will surely bless you for your kindness. There are new laws here that permit the state to confiscate Jewish property. Our store was just taken from us. Also, I have to pay a fine because my late husband did not put up a sign on the store saying it was Jewish owned. So, I am without any money. I will have to accept your offer to pay my passage. Believe me I will repay you when I get to America. I am not too old to work. Do you remember that weekend we went on a picnic and stopped in that farm house the lady said the same thing when we offered to pay her for food?
God bless You,
Frieda
HEY, JACOB, WHERE YOU BEEN TODAY... BOY, BUSINESS HAS PICKED UP SINCE YOU HAD THE IDEA TO RUN AN ADVERTISEMENT.
I'VE BEEN DOWNTOWN, ANGELO - I GOT A PROBLEM!
I'M TRYING TO BRING OVER A GIRL.. I MEAN, A LADY, I USED TO KNOW FROM THE OTHER SIDE!
...HA, I KNOW ALL ABOUT THAT... I CAME OVER ILLEGAL MYSELF, Y'KNOW, JACOB.

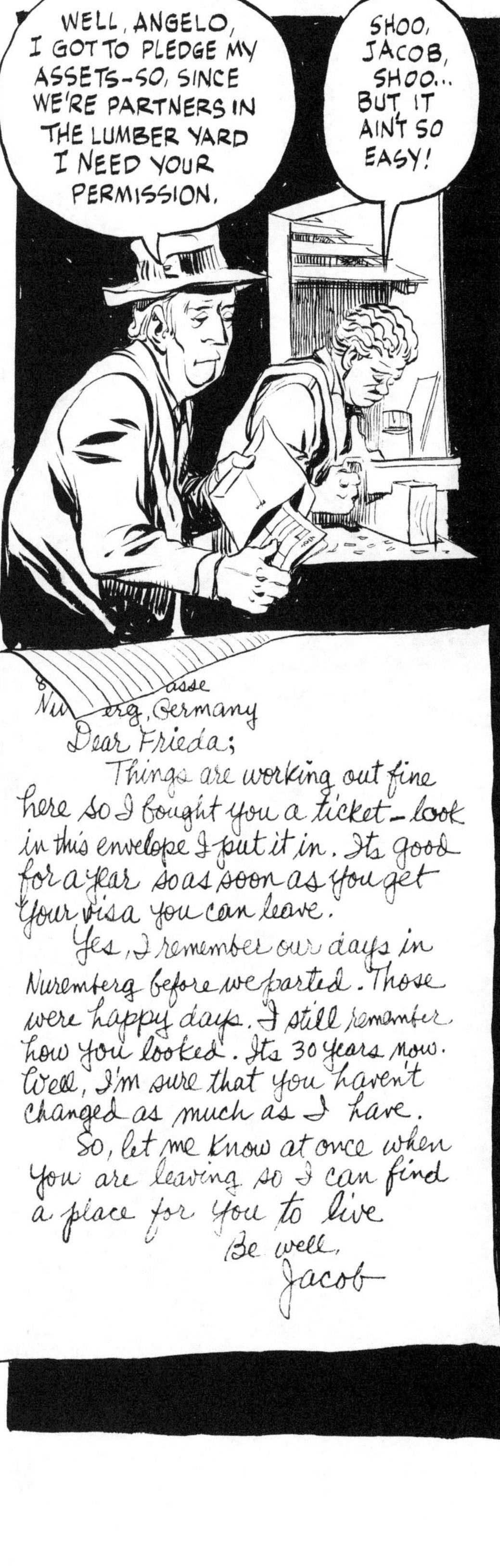
WELL, ANGELO, I GOT TO PLEDGE MY ASSETS-SO, SINCE WE'RE PARTNERS IN THE LUMBER YARD I NEED YOUR PERMISSION.
SHOO, JACOB, SHOO... BUT IT AIN'T SO EASY!
asse
erg, Germany
Dear Frieda;
Things are working out fine here so I bought you a ticket - look in this envelope I put it in. Its good for a year so as soon as you get your visa you can leave.
Yes, I remember our days in Nuremberg before we parted. Those were happy days. I still remember how you looked. Its 30 years now. Well, I'm sure that you haven't changed as much as I have.
So, let me know at once when you are leaving so I can find a place for you to live
Be well,
Jacob

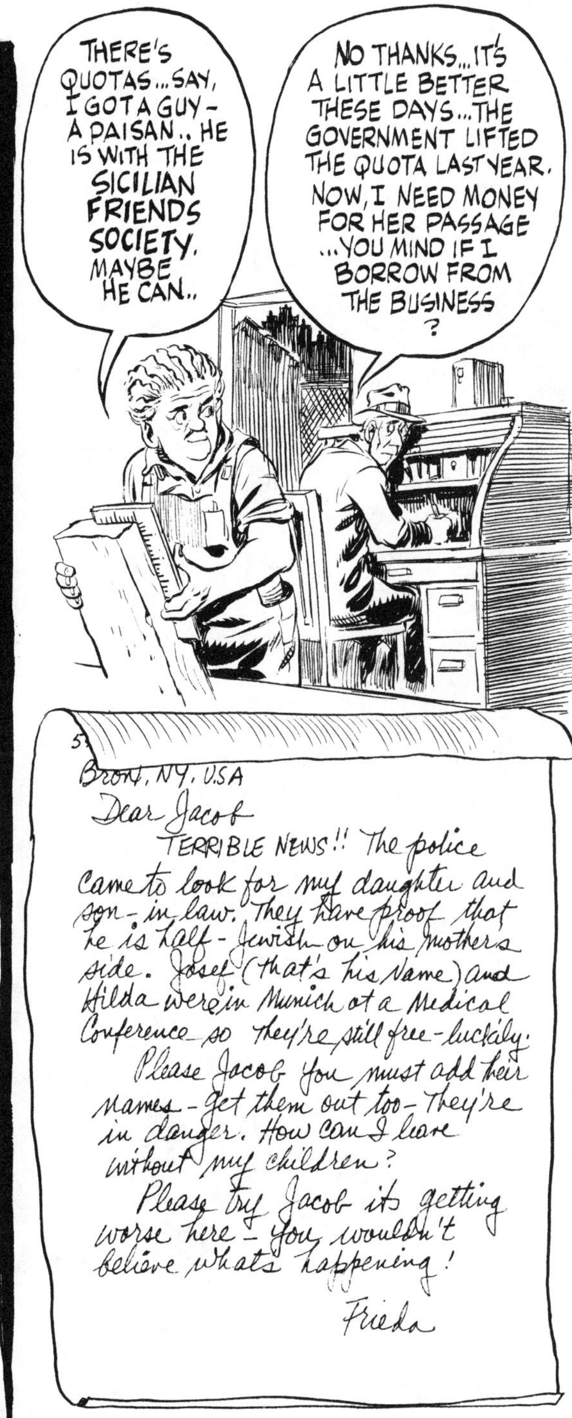
THERE'S QUOTAS...SAY, I GOT A GUY - A PAISAN.. HE IS WITH THE SICILIAN FRIENDS SOCIETY. MAYBE HE CAN..
NO THANKS...IT'S A LITTLE BETTER THESE DAYS...THE GOVERNMENT LIFTED THE QUOTA LAST YEAR. NOW, I NEED MONEY FOR HER PASSAGE ...YOU MIND IF I BORROW FROM THE BUSINESS ?
Bron, NY. USA
Dear Jacob
TERRIBLE NEWS!! The police came to look for my daughter and son-in law. They have proof that he is half-Jewish on his mother's side. Josef (that's his name) and Hilda were in Munich at a Medical Conference so they're still free-luckily.
Please Jacob you must add heir names - get them out too - they're in danger. How can I leave without my children?
Please try Jacob its getting worse here - you wouldn't believe whats happening!
Frieda

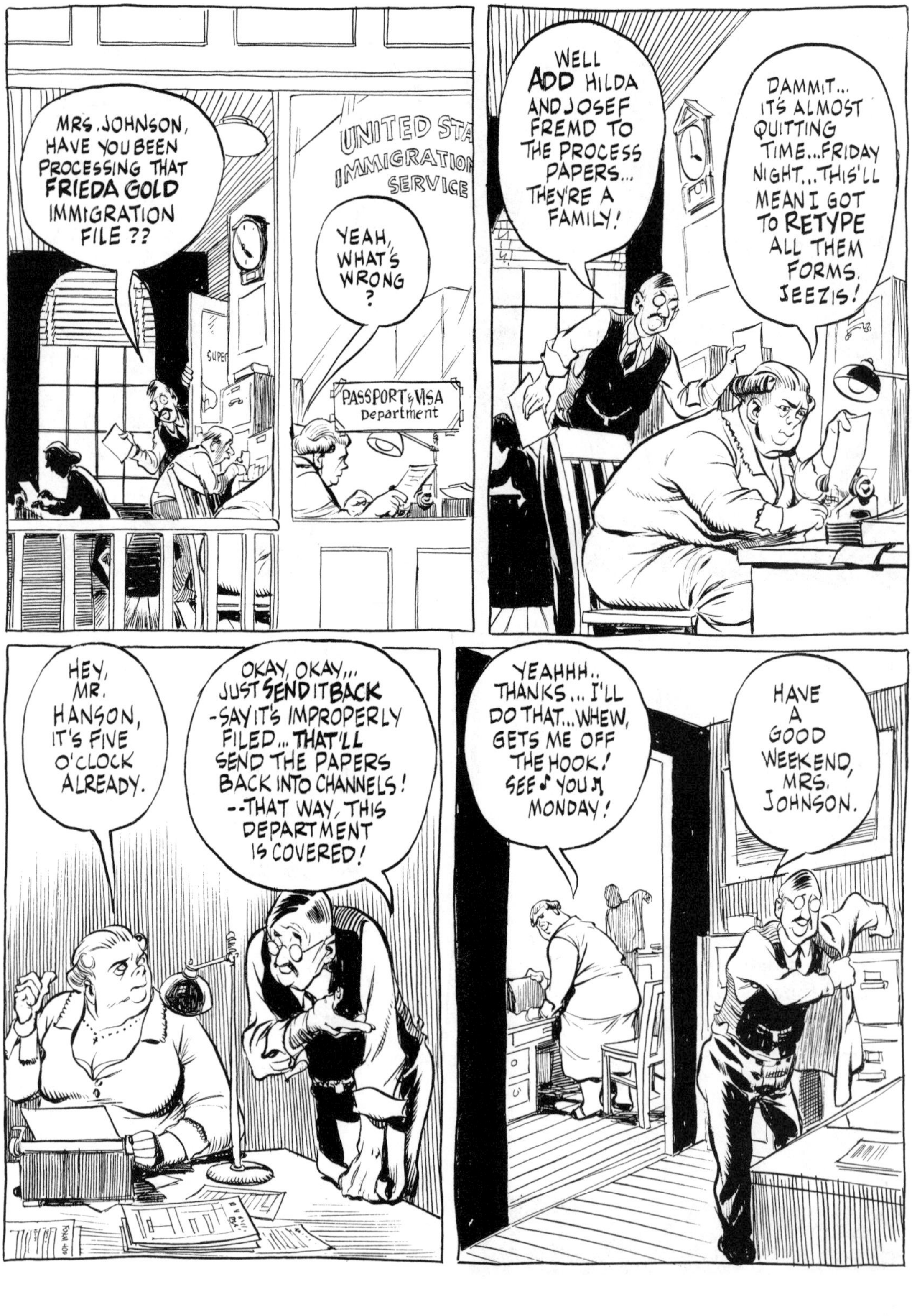
MRS. JOHNSON, HAVE YOU BEEN PROCESSING THAT **FRIEDA GOLD** IMMIGRATION FILE??
UNITED STA
IMMIGRATION SERVICE
YEAH, WHAT'S WRONG?
PASSPORT & VISA Department
WELL **ADD** HILDA AND JOSEF FREMD TO THE PROCESS PAPERS... THEY'RE A FAMILY!
DAMMIT... IT'S ALMOST QUITTING TIME... FRIDAY NIGHT... THIS'LL MEAN I GOT TO **RETYPE** ALL THEM FORMS. JEEZIS!
HEY, MR. HANSON, IT'S FIVE O'CLOCK ALREADY.
OKAY, OKAY,,, JUST **SEND** IT **BACK** -SAY IT'S IMPROPERLY FILED... **THAT'LL** SEND THE PAPERS BACK INTO CHANNELS! --THAT WAY, THIS DEPARTMENT IS COVERED!
YEAHHH.. THANKS... I'LL DO THAT... WHEW, GETS ME OFF THE HOOK! SEE ♪ YOU ♫ MONDAY!
HAVE A GOOD WEEKEND, MRS. JOHNSON.

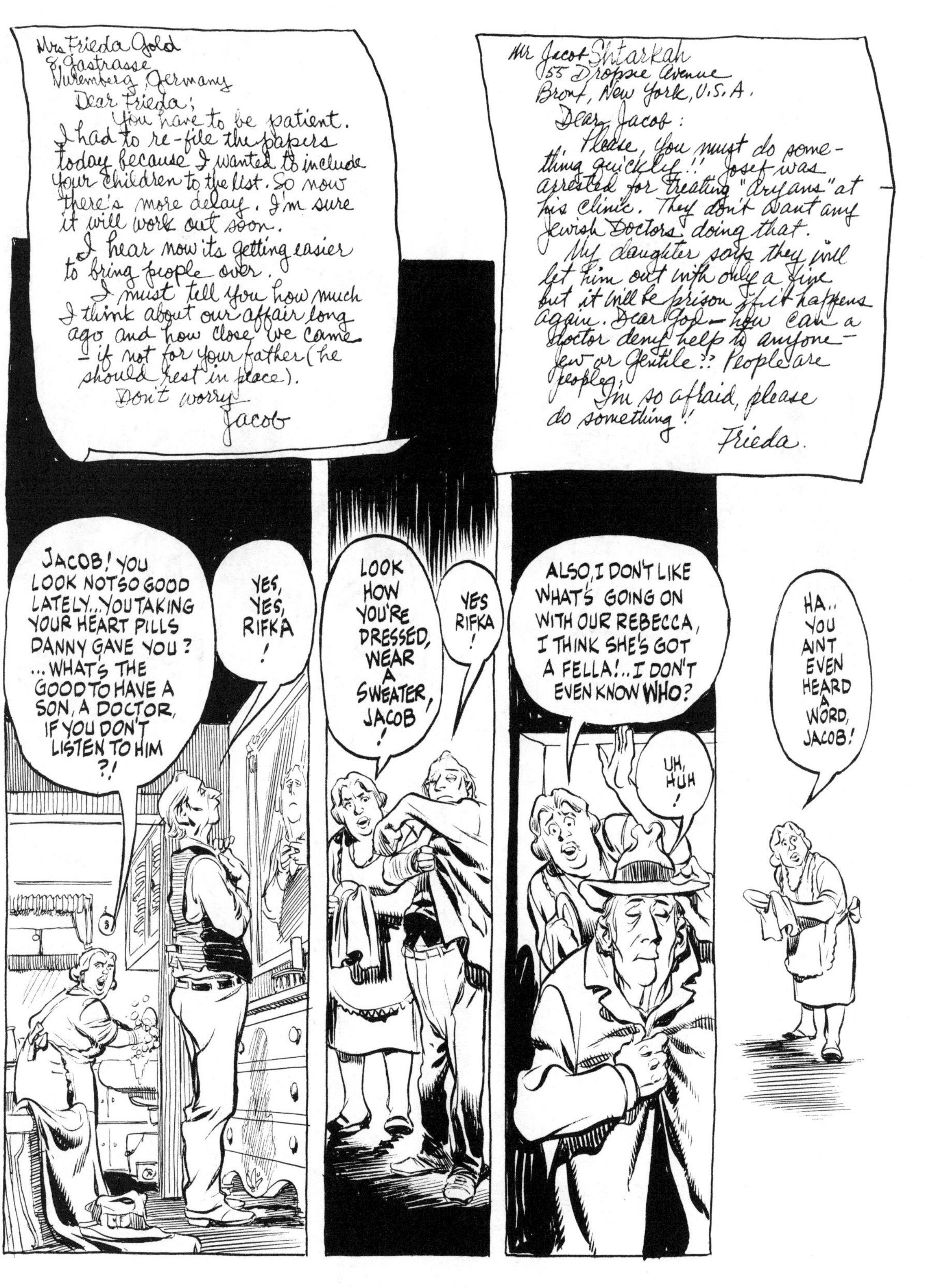
Mrs Frieda Gold
8 Gastrasse
Nuremberg, Germany
Dear Frieda:
You have to be patient. I had to re-file the papers today because I wanted to include your children to the list. So now there's more delay. I'm sure it will work out soon.
I hear now its getting easier to bring people over.
I must tell you how much I think about our affair long ago and how close we came - if not for your father (he should rest in peace).
Don't worry
Jacob
Mr Jacob Shtarkah
55 Dropsie Avenue
Bronx, New York, U.S.A.
Dear Jacob:
Please, you must do something quickly!! Josef was arrested for treating "Aryans" at his clinic. They don't want any Jewish Doctors doing that.
My daughter says they will let him out with only a fine but it will be prison if it happens again. Dear God - how can a doctor deny help to anyone - Jew or Gentile?? People are people.
I'm so afraid, please do something!!
Frieda.
JACOB! YOU LOOK NOT SO GOOD LATELY... YOU TAKING YOUR HEART PILLS DANNY GAVE YOU? ... WHAT'S THE GOOD TO HAVE A SON, A DOCTOR, IF YOU DON'T LISTEN TO HIM ?!
YES, YES, RIFKA !
LOOK HOW YOU'RE DRESSED, WEAR A SWEATER, JACOB !
YES RIFKA !
ALSO, I DON'T LIKE WHAT'S GOING ON WITH OUR REBECCA, I THINK SHE'S GOT A FELLA!... I DON'T EVEN KNOW WHO?
UH, HUH !
HA.. YOU AINT EVEN HEARD A WORD, JACOB!

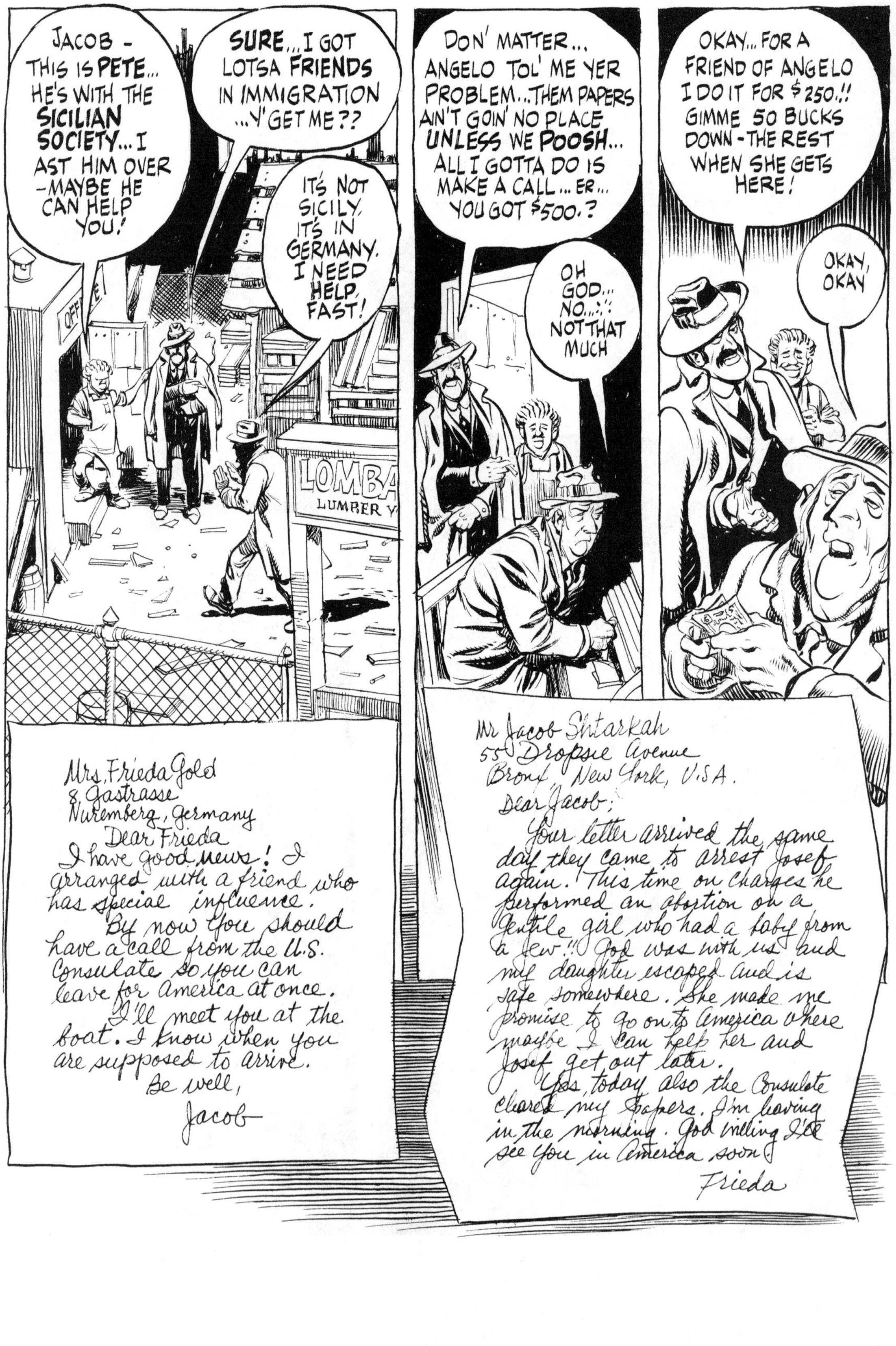
JACOB - THIS IS PETE... HE'S WITH THE SICILIAN SOCIETY... I AST HIM OVER -MAYBE HE CAN HELP YOU!
SURE... I GOT LOTSA FRIENDS IN IMMIGRATION ...Y' GET ME??
IT'S NOT SICILY, IT'S IN GERMANY. I NEED HELP, FAST!
LOMBA
LUMBER Y
DON' MATTER... ANGELO TOL' ME YER PROBLEM... THEM PAPERS AIN'T GOIN' NO PLACE UNLESS WE POOSH... ALL I GOTTA DO IS MAKE A CALL... ER... YOU GOT $500.?
OH GOD... NO... NOT THAT MUCH
OKAY... FOR A FRIEND OF ANGELO I DO IT FOR $250.!! GIMME 50 BUCKS DOWN - THE REST WHEN SHE GETS HERE!
OKAY, OKAY
Mrs. Frieda Gold
8 Gastrasse
Nuremberg, Germany
Dear Frieda
I have good news! I arranged with a friend who has special influence.
By now you should have a call from the U.S. Consulate so you can leave for America at once.
I'll meet you at the boat. I know when you are supposed to arrive.
Be well,
Jacob
Mr Jacob Shtarkah
55 Dropsie Avenue
Bronx, New York, U.S.A.
Dear Jacob;
Your letter arrived the same day they came to arrest Josef again. This time on charges he performed an abortion on a Gentile girl who had a baby from a Jew!! God was with us and my daughter escaped and is safe somewhere. She made me promise to go on to America where maybe I can help her and Josef get out later.
Yes, today also the Consulate cleared my papers. I'm leaving in the morning. God willing I'll see you in America soon.
Frieda

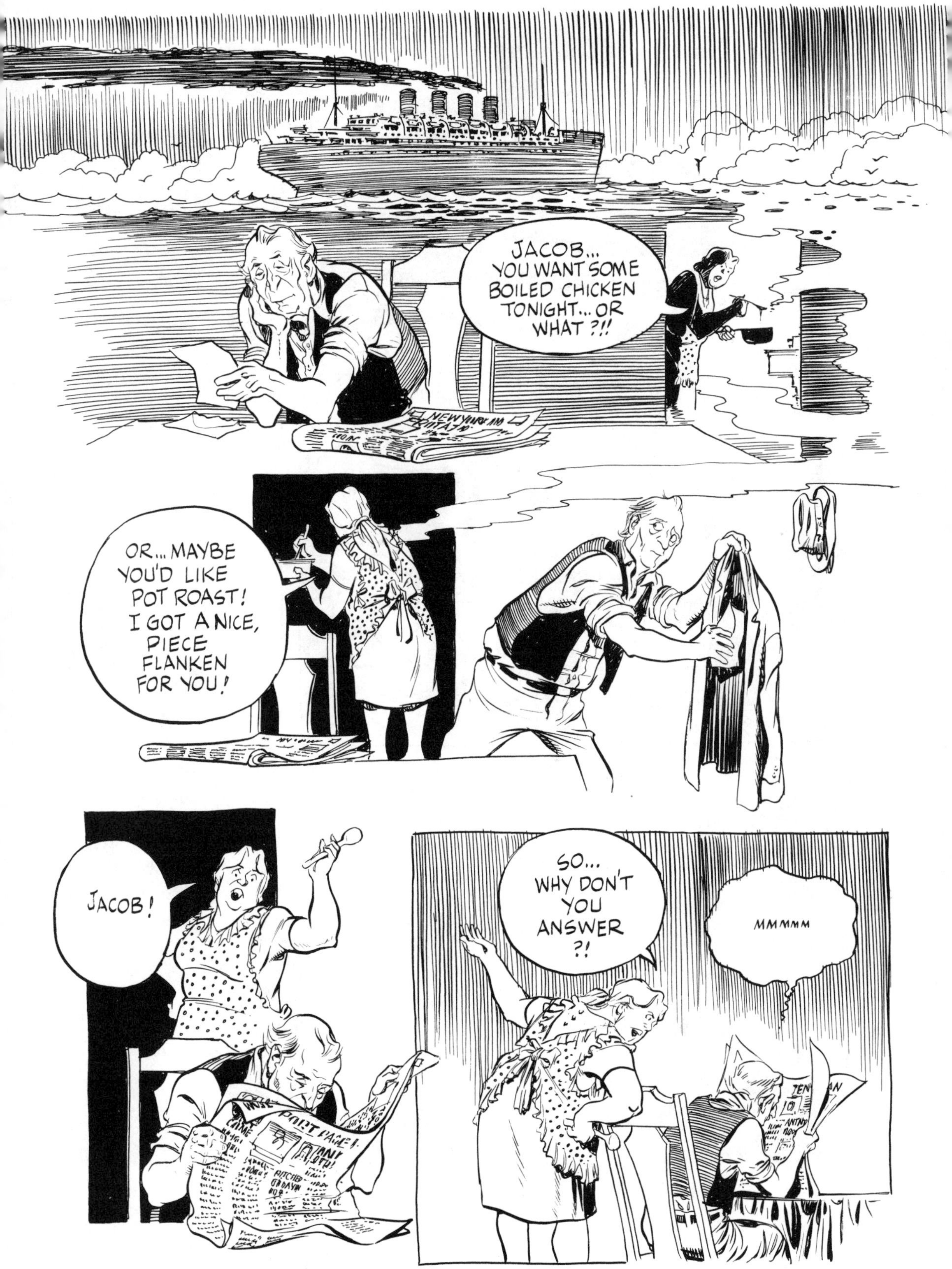
JACOB... YOU WANT SOME BOILED CHICKEN TONIGHT... OR WHAT ?!!
OR... MAYBE YOU'D LIKE POT ROAST! I GOT A NICE, PIECE FLANKEN FOR YOU!
JACOB!
SO... WHY DON'T YOU ANSWER ?!
MMMMM

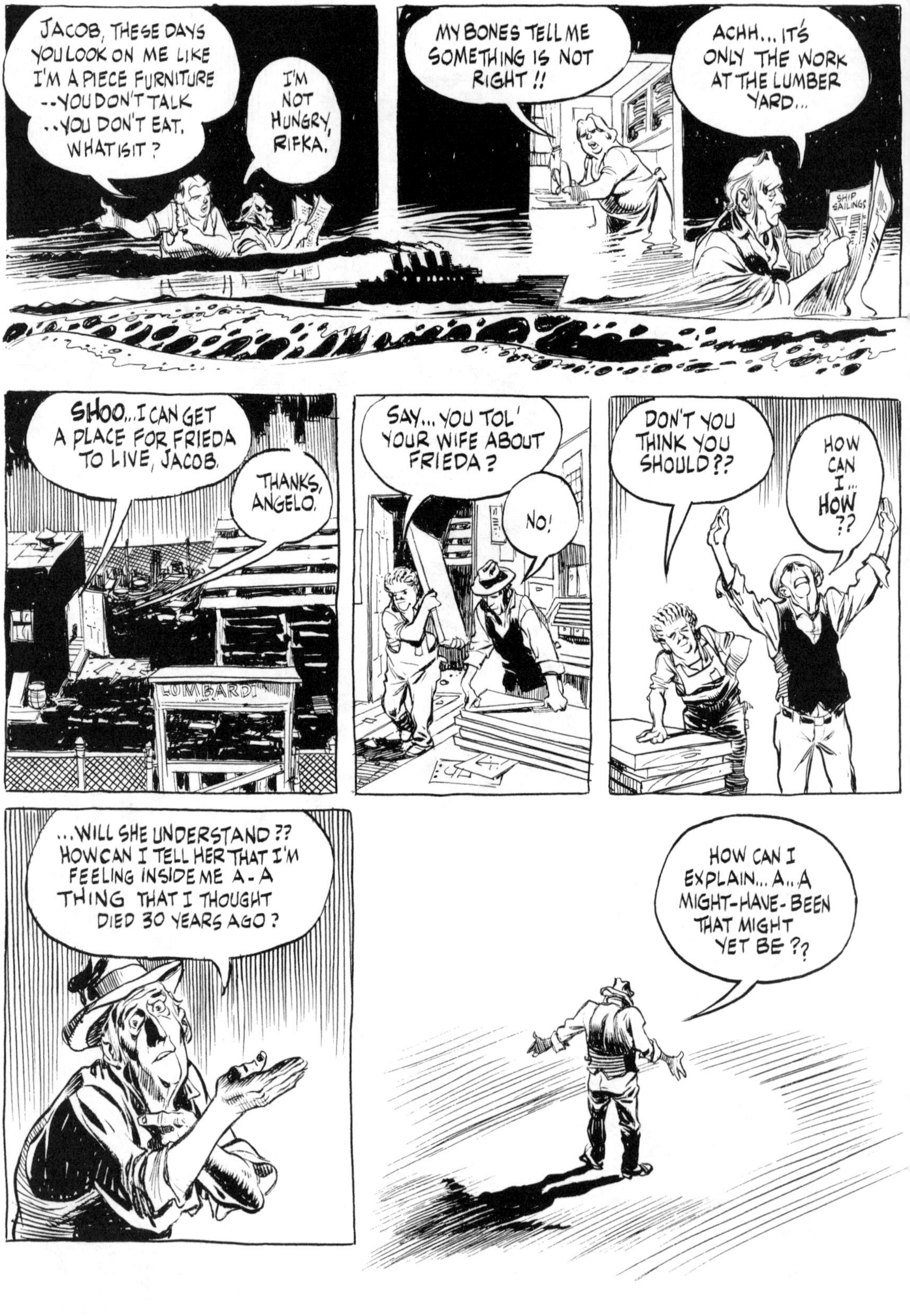
JACOB, THESE DAYS YOU LOOK ON ME LIKE I'M A PIECE FURNITURE --YOU DON'T TALK ..YOU DON'T EAT. WHAT IS IT?
I'M NOT HUNGRY, RIFKA.
MY BONES TELL ME SOMETHING IS NOT RIGHT!!
ACHH... IT'S ONLY THE WORK AT THE LUMBER YARD...
SHIP SAILINGS
SHOO... I CAN GET A PLACE FOR FRIEDA TO LIVE, JACOB.
THANKS, ANGELO.
LOMBARDI
SAY... YOU TOL' YOUR WIFE ABOUT FRIEDA?
NO!
DON'T YOU THINK YOU SHOULD??
HOW CAN I... HOW??
...WILL SHE UNDERSTAND?? HOW CAN I TELL HER THAT I'M FEELING INSIDE ME A-A THING THAT I THOUGHT DIED 30 YEARS AGO?
HOW CAN I EXPLAIN... A.. A MIGHT-HAVE-BEEN THAT MIGHT YET BE??

CHAPTER 10
AMERICA, AMERICA

JEWISH REFUGEES GET LOCAL HELP

JUNE 15, 1934

The New York Times reported that 259 refugees of the 430 Jews who arrived in New York during May had fled from Nazi Germany. Of these a few came from other countries in Europe where they had fled earlier.

AMERICAN GROUP ASKS U.S. HAVEN FOR NAZI VICTIMS

PRESIDENT ROOSEVELT ASKED TO EASE CURB ON IMMIGRATION

MARCH 19, 1934

Mrs. Carrie Chapman Catt, chairman of a committee of outstanding American women, appealed to President Roosevelt for relief from an executive order issued by former President Herbert Hoover restricting immigration. Due to the rigid enforcement of the rules under Hoover beginning in 1930, definite proof that an alien applying for an immigration visa would not become a public charge was very strictly applied. The appeal pointed out that while legal German immigration quotas were 25,959, fewer than 600 had been admitted here in the period from July 1933 to date.

FEWER IMMIGRANTS AT ELLIS ISLAND NOW

JULY 8, 1934

Immigrants arriving in Ellis Island have dwindled in number from 5000 a day to only about 25 in the past 25 years. According to officials this reduced use of the depot is a result of the restrictions on immigration and that most of the aliens coming to settle here pass their technical requirements at the port of embarkation. This permits them to land at piers in this port with other passengers.

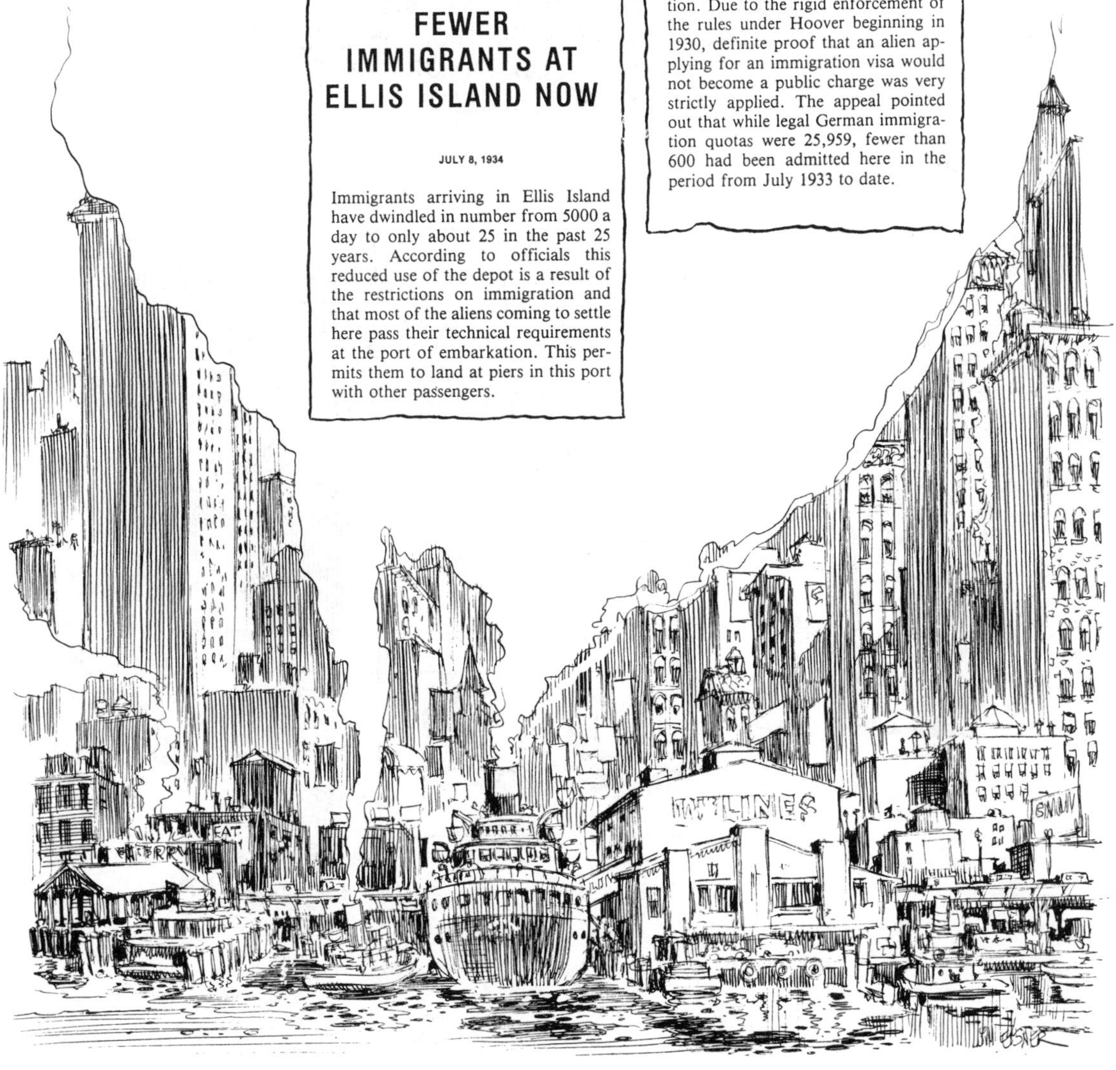

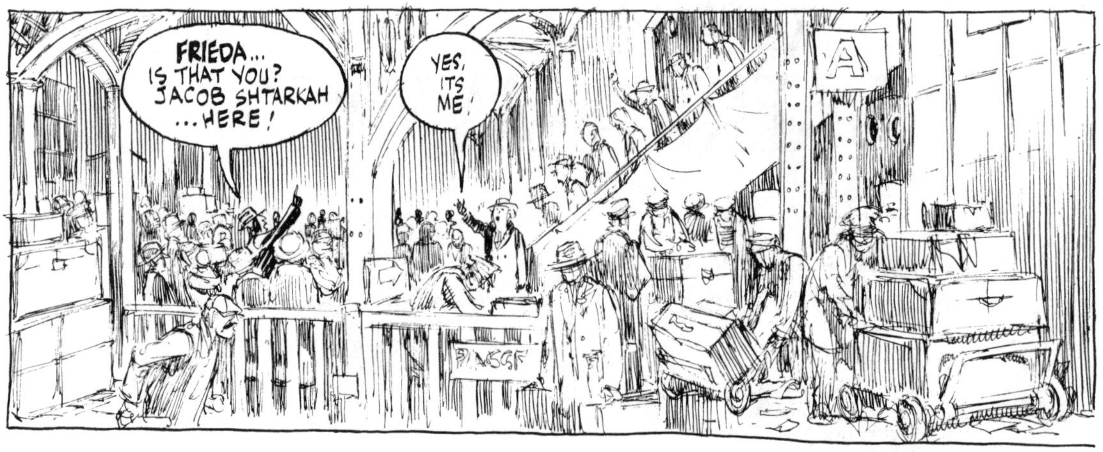
FRIEDA... IS THAT YOU? JACOB SHTARKAH ...HERE!
YES, ITS ME!
A

AT LONG LAST,
FRIEDA GOLD ARRIVED IN AMERICA.
BEHIND HER WERE THE ASHES OF
A ONCE-SECURE MIDDLE CLASS LIFE
WHERE SHE HAD TAKEN FOR GRANTED...
THE COMFORT OF BELONGING.

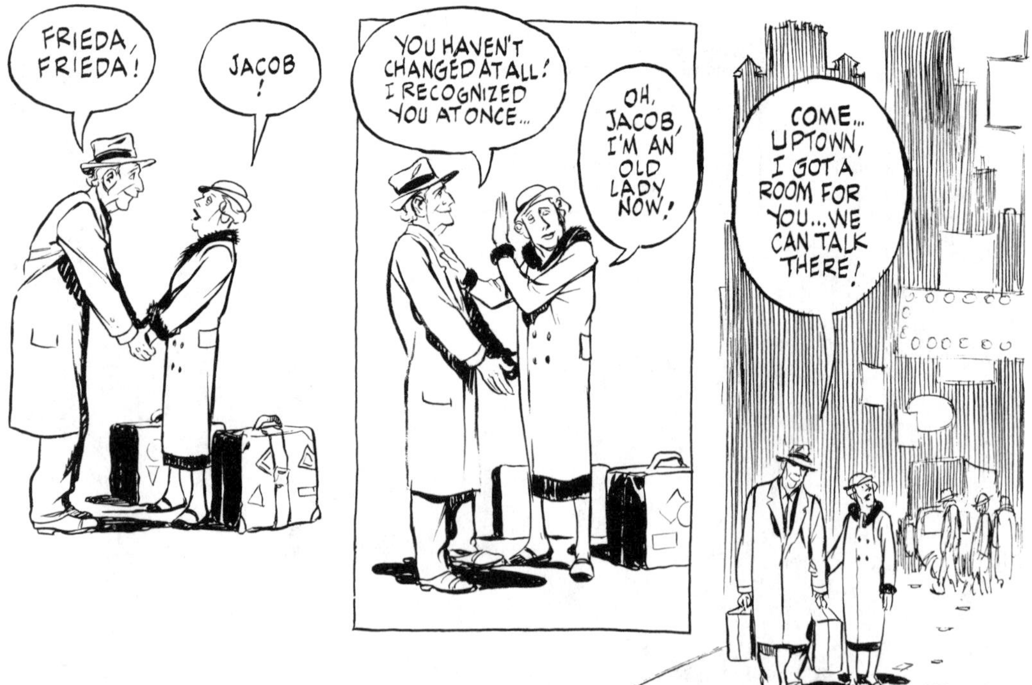
FRIEDA, FRIEDA!
JACOB!
YOU HAVEN'T CHANGED AT ALL! I RECOGNIZED YOU AT ONCE...
OH, JACOB, I'M AN OLD LADY NOW!
COME... UPTOWN, I GOT A ROOM FOR YOU...WE CAN TALK THERE!

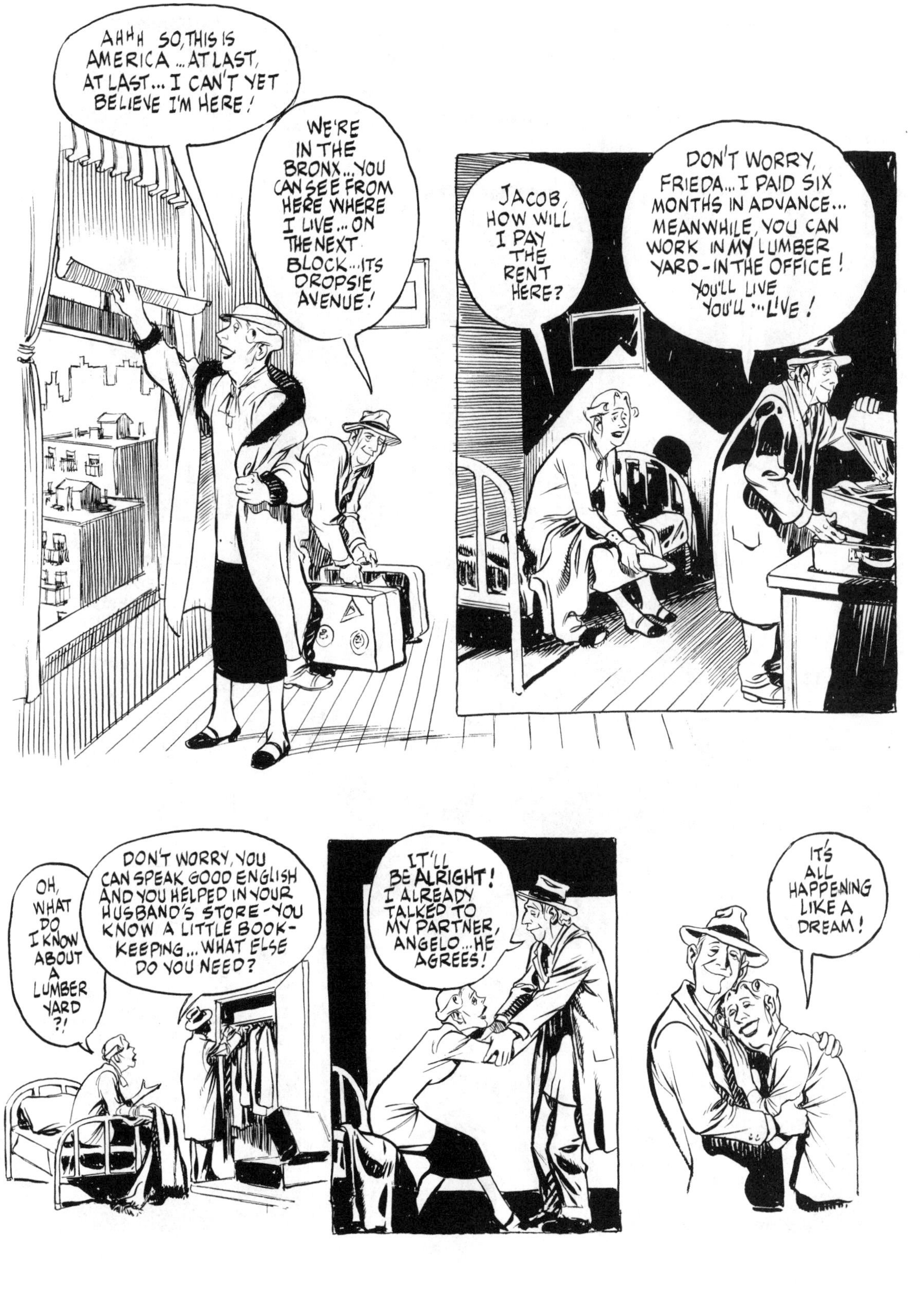
AHHH SO, THIS IS AMERICA ... AT LAST, AT LAST ... I CAN'T YET BELIEVE I'M HERE!
WE'RE IN THE BRONX ... YOU CAN SEE FROM HERE WHERE I LIVE ... ON THE NEXT BLOCK ... ITS DROPSIE AVENUE!
JACOB, HOW WILL I PAY THE RENT HERE?
DON'T WORRY, FRIEDA ... I PAID SIX MONTHS IN ADVANCE ... MEANWHILE, YOU CAN WORK IN MY LUMBER YARD - IN THE OFFICE! YOU'LL LIVE YOU'LL ... LIVE!
OH, WHAT DO I KNOW ABOUT A LUMBER YARD ?!
DON'T WORRY, YOU CAN SPEAK GOOD ENGLISH AND YOU HELPED IN YOUR HUSBAND'S STORE - YOU KNOW A LITTLE BOOK-KEEPING ... WHAT ELSE DO YOU NEED?
IT'LL BE ALRIGHT! I ALREADY TALKED TO MY PARTNER, ANGELO ... HE AGREES!
IT'S ALL HAPPENING LIKE A DREAM!

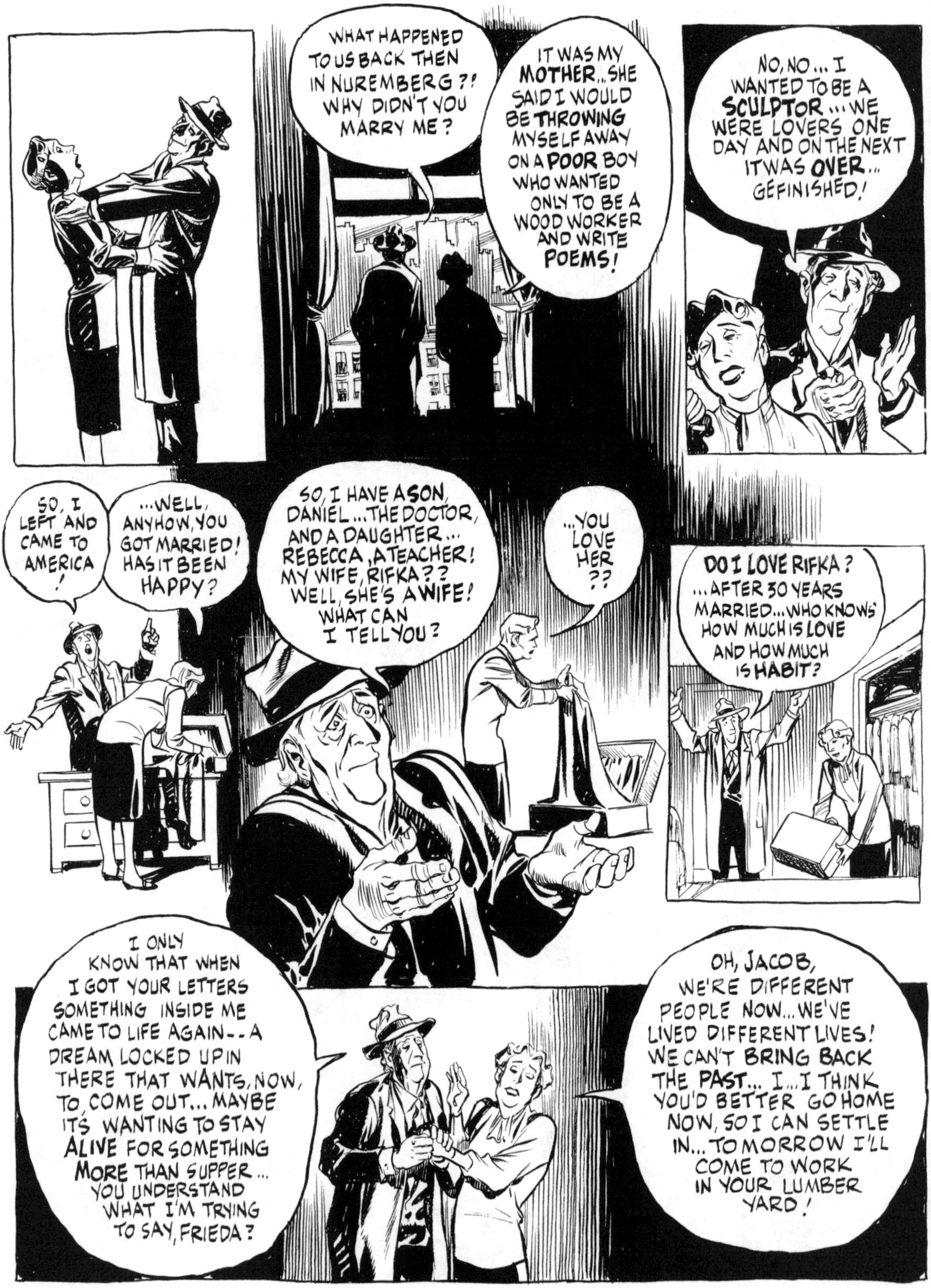

WHAT HAPPENED TO US BACK THEN IN NUREMBERG?! WHY DIDN'T YOU MARRY ME?
IT WAS MY MOTHER... SHE SAID I WOULD BE THROWING MYSELF AWAY ON A POOR BOY WHO WANTED ONLY TO BE A WOOD WORKER AND WRITE POEMS!
NO, NO... I WANTED TO BE A SCULPTOR... WE WERE LOVERS ONE DAY AND ON THE NEXT IT WAS OVER... GEFINISHED!
SO, I LEFT AND CAME TO AMERICA!
...WELL, ANYHOW, YOU GOT MARRIED! HAS IT BEEN HAPPY?
SO, I HAVE A SON, DANIEL... THE DOCTOR, AND A DAUGHTER... REBECCA, A TEACHER! MY WIFE, RIFKA?? WELL, SHE'S A WIFE! WHAT CAN I TELL YOU?
...YOU LOVE HER??
DO I LOVE RIFKA? ...AFTER 30 YEARS MARRIED... WHO KNOWS HOW MUCH IS LOVE AND HOW MUCH IS HABIT?
I ONLY KNOW THAT WHEN I GOT YOUR LETTERS SOMETHING INSIDE ME CAME TO LIFE AGAIN-- A DREAM LOCKED UP IN THERE THAT WANTS, NOW, TO COME OUT... MAYBE IT'S WANTING TO STAY ALIVE FOR SOMETHING MORE THAN SUPPER... YOU UNDERSTAND WHAT I'M TRYING TO SAY, FRIEDA?
OH, JACOB, WE'RE DIFFERENT PEOPLE NOW... WE'VE LIVED DIFFERENT LIVES! WE CAN'T BRING BACK THE PAST... I... I THINK YOU'D BETTER GO HOME NOW, SO I CAN SETTLE IN... TOMORROW I'LL COME TO WORK IN YOUR LUMBER YARD!

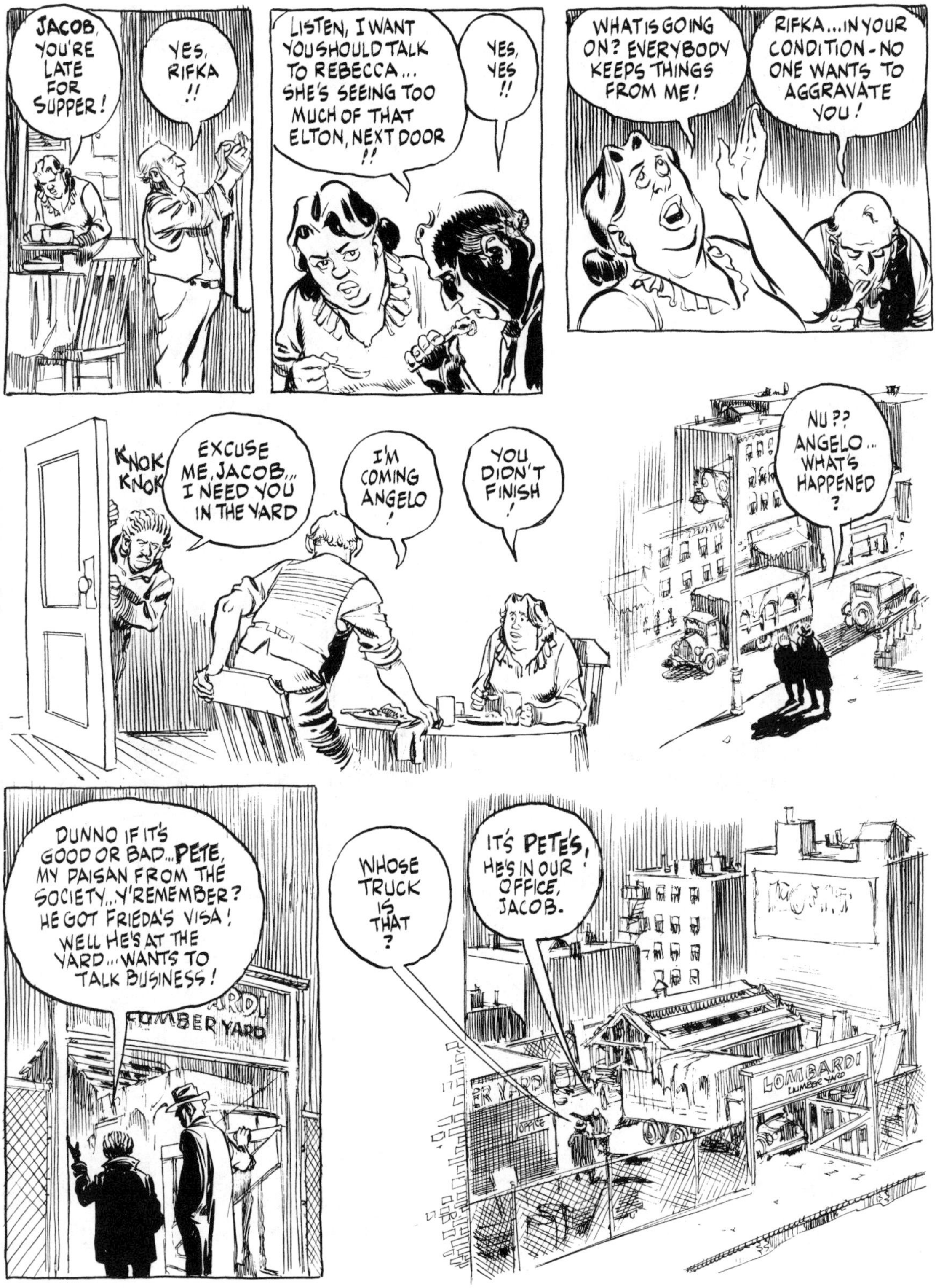

JACOB, YOU'RE LATE FOR SUPPER!
YES, RIFKA !!
LISTEN, I WANT YOU SHOULD TALK TO REBECCA... SHE'S SEEING TOO MUCH OF THAT ELTON, NEXT DOOR !!
YES, YES !!
WHAT IS GOING ON? EVERYBODY KEEPS THINGS FROM ME!
RIFKA... IN YOUR CONDITION - NO ONE WANTS TO AGGRAVATE YOU!
KNOK KNOK
EXCUSE ME, JACOB... I NEED YOU IN THE YARD
I'M COMING ANGELO!
YOU DIDN'T FINISH!
NU?? ANGELO... WHAT'S HAPPENED?
DUNNO IF IT'S GOOD OR BAD... PETE, MY PAISAN FROM THE SOCIETY... Y'REMEMBER? HE GOT FRIEDA'S VISA! WELL HE'S AT THE YARD... WANTS TO TALK BUSINESS!
LUMBER YARD
WHOSE TRUCK IS THAT?
IT'S PETE'S, HE'S IN OUR OFFICE, JACOB.
OFFICE
LOMBARDI LUMBER YARD

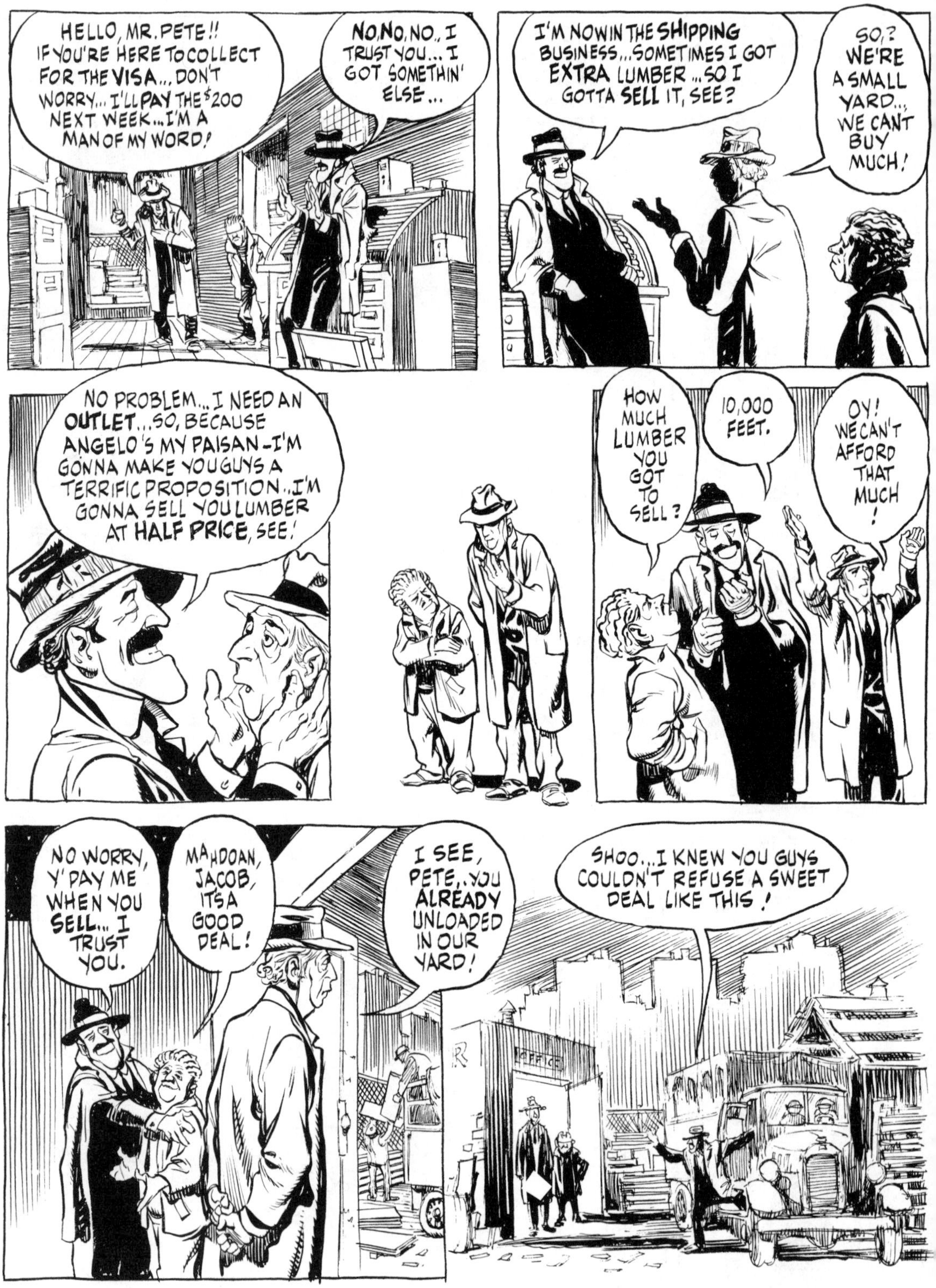
HELLO, MR. PETE!! IF YOU'RE HERE TO COLLECT FOR THE VISA... DON'T WORRY... I'LL PAY THE $200 NEXT WEEK... I'M A MAN OF MY WORD!
NO, NO, NO.. I TRUST YOU... I GOT SOMETHIN' ELSE...
I'M NOW IN THE SHIPPING BUSINESS... SOMETIMES I GOT EXTRA LUMBER... SO I GOTTA SELL IT, SEE?
SO? WE'RE A SMALL YARD.. WE CAN'T BUY MUCH!
NO PROBLEM... I NEED AN OUTLET... SO, BECAUSE ANGELO'S MY PAISAN - I'M GONNA MAKE YOU GUYS A TERRIFIC PROPOSITION.. I'M GONNA SELL YOU LUMBER AT HALF PRICE, SEE!
HOW MUCH LUMBER YOU GOT TO SELL?
10,000 FEET.
OY! WE CAN'T AFFORD THAT MUCH!
NO WORRY, Y' PAY ME WHEN YOU SELL... I TRUST YOU.
MAHDOAN, JACOB, ITS A GOOD DEAL!
I SEE, PETE.. YOU ALREADY UNLOADED IN OUR YARD!
SHOO... I KNEW YOU GUYS COULDN'T REFUSE A SWEET DEAL LIKE THIS!
OFFICE

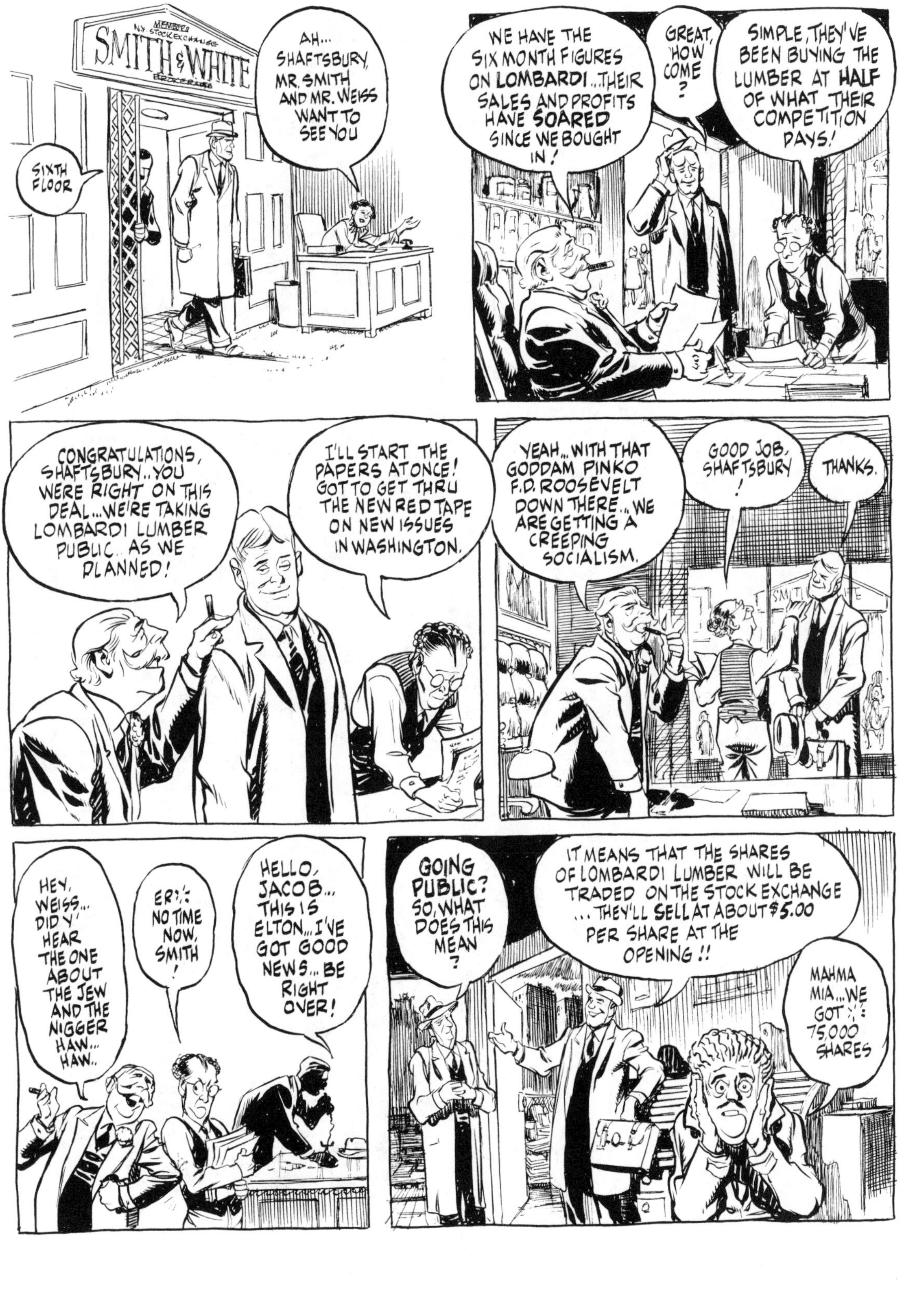
MEMBERS N.Y. STOCK EXCHANGE
SMITH & WHITE
BROKERAGE
SIXTH FLOOR
AH... SHAFTSBURY, MR. SMITH AND MR. WEISS WANT TO SEE YOU
WE HAVE THE SIX MONTH FIGURES ON LOMBARDI.. THEIR SALES AND PROFITS HAVE SOARED SINCE WE BOUGHT IN!
GREAT, HOW COME?
SIMPLE, THEY'VE BEEN BUYING THE LUMBER AT HALF OF WHAT THEIR COMPETITION PAYS!
CONGRATULATIONS, SHAFTSBURY.. YOU WERE RIGHT ON THIS DEAL... WE'RE TAKING LOMBARDI LUMBER PUBLIC.. AS WE PLANNED!
I'LL START THE PAPERS AT ONCE! GOT TO GET THRU THE NEW RED TAPE ON NEW ISSUES IN WASHINGTON.
YEAH... WITH THAT GODDAM PINKO F.D. ROOSEVELT DOWN THERE... WE ARE GETTING A CREEPING SOCIALISM.
GOOD JOB, SHAFTSBURY!
THANKS.
HEY, WEISS... DID Y' HEAR THE ONE ABOUT THE JEW AND THE NIGGER HAW... HAW..
ER?!: NO TIME NOW, SMITH!
HELLO, JACOB... THIS IS ELTON... I'VE GOT GOOD NEWS... BE RIGHT OVER!
GOING PUBLIC? SO, WHAT DOES THIS MEAN?
IT MEANS THAT THE SHARES OF LOMBARDI LUMBER WILL BE TRADED ON THE STOCK EXCHANGE ... THEY'LL SELL AT ABOUT $5.00 PER SHARE AT THE OPENING!!
MAHMA MIA... WE GOT !?! 75,000 SHARES

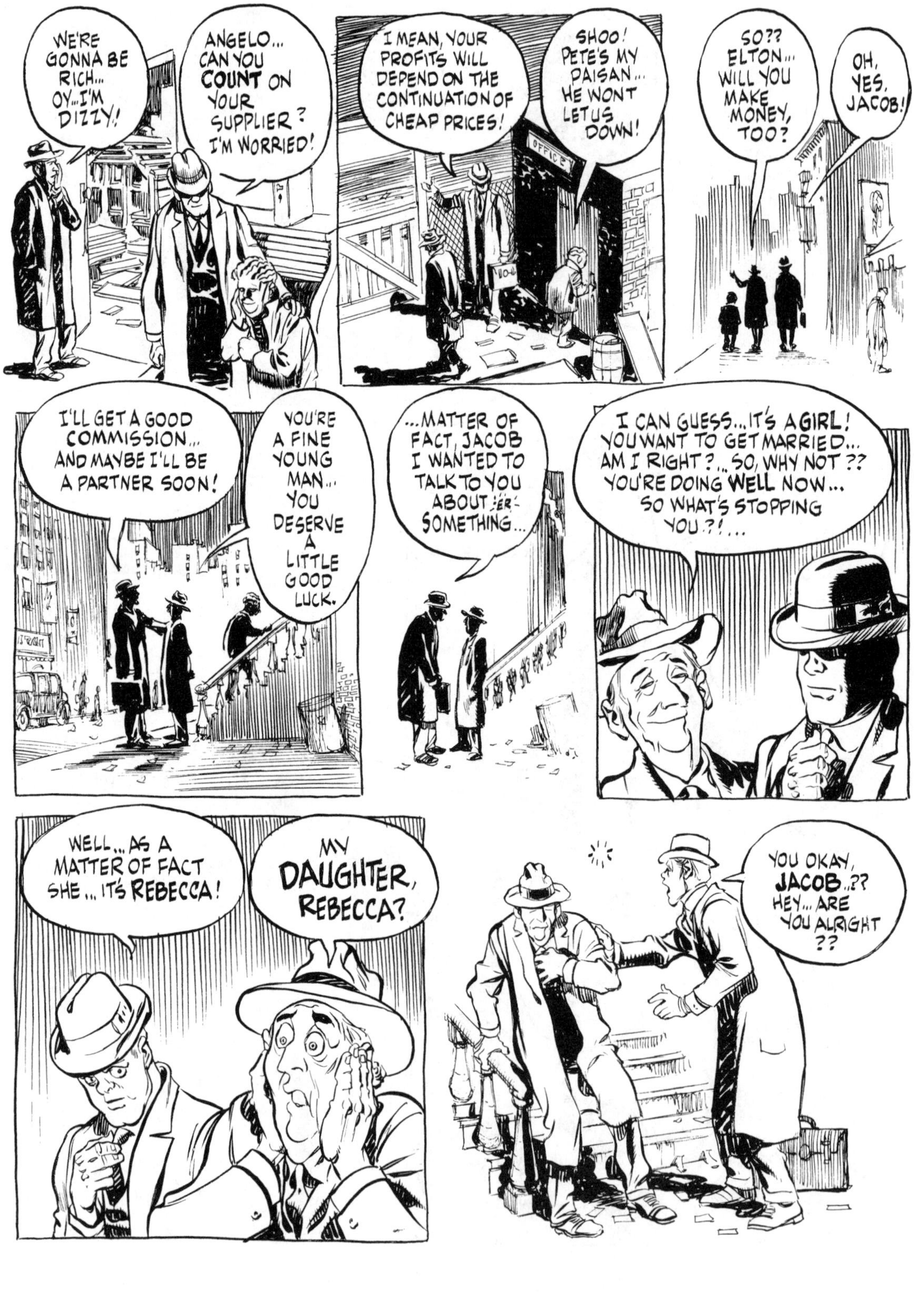
WE'RE GONNA BE RICH... OY...I'M DIZZY!
ANGELO... CAN YOU COUNT ON YOUR SUPPLIER? I'M WORRIED!
I MEAN, YOUR PROFITS WILL DEPEND ON THE CONTINUATION OF CHEAP PRICES!
SHOO! PETE'S MY PAISAN... HE WONT LET US DOWN!
OFFICE
SO?? ELTON... WILL YOU MAKE MONEY, TOO?
OH, YES, JACOB!
I'LL GET A GOOD COMMISSION... AND MAYBE I'LL BE A PARTNER SOON!
YOU'RE A FINE YOUNG MAN... YOU DESERVE A LITTLE GOOD LUCK.
...MATTER OF FACT, JACOB I WANTED TO TALK TO YOU ABOUT ...ER... SOMETHING...
I CAN GUESS... IT'S A GIRL! YOU WANT TO GET MARRIED... AM I RIGHT?.. SO, WHY NOT?? YOU'RE DOING WELL NOW... SO WHAT'S STOPPING YOU?!...
WELL... AS A MATTER OF FACT SHE... IT'S REBECCA!
MY DAUGHTER, REBECCA?
YOU OKAY, JACOB..?? HEY... ARE YOU ALRIGHT ??

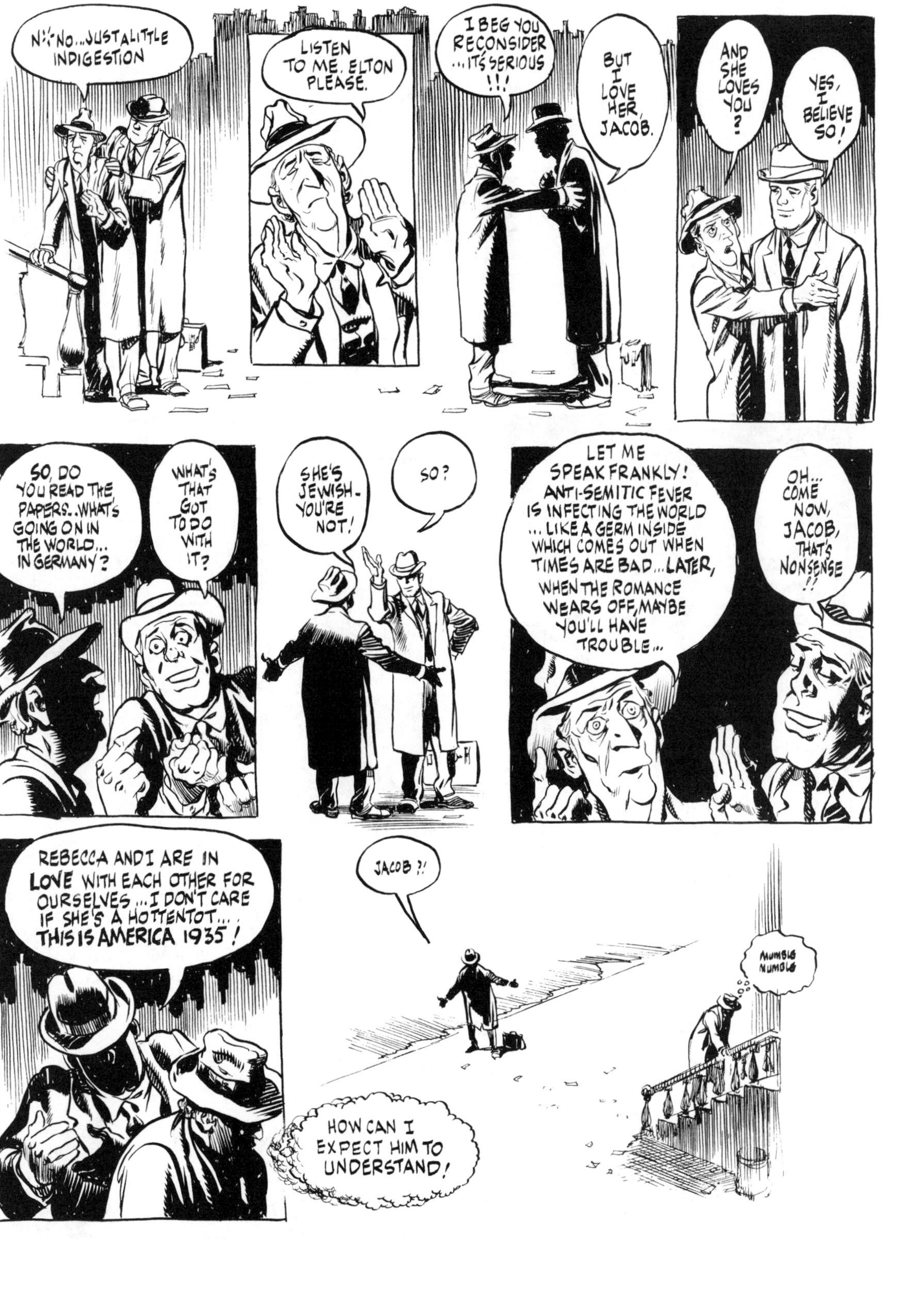
N-NO...JUST A LITTLE INDIGESTION
LISTEN TO ME. ELTON PLEASE.
I BEG YOU RECONSIDER ...IT'S SERIOUS !!!
BUT I LOVE HER, JACOB.
AND SHE LOVES YOU ?
YES, I BELIEVE SO!
SO, DO YOU READ THE PAPERS...WHAT'S GOING ON IN THE WORLD... IN GERMANY?
WHAT'S THAT GOT TO DO WITH IT?
SHE'S JEWISH - YOU'RE NOT!
SO?
LET ME SPEAK FRANKLY! ANTI-SEMITIC FEVER IS INFECTING THE WORLD ... LIKE A GERM INSIDE WHICH COMES OUT WHEN TIMES ARE BAD... LATER, WHEN THE ROMANCE WEARS OFF, MAYBE YOU'LL HAVE TROUBLE...
OH... COME NOW, JACOB, THAT'S NONSENSE !!
REBECCA AND I ARE IN LOVE WITH EACH OTHER FOR OURSELVES ... I DON'T CARE IF SHE'S A HOTTENTOT... THIS IS AMERICA 1935!
JACOB ?!
MUMBLE MUMBLE
HOW CAN I EXPECT HIM TO UNDERSTAND!

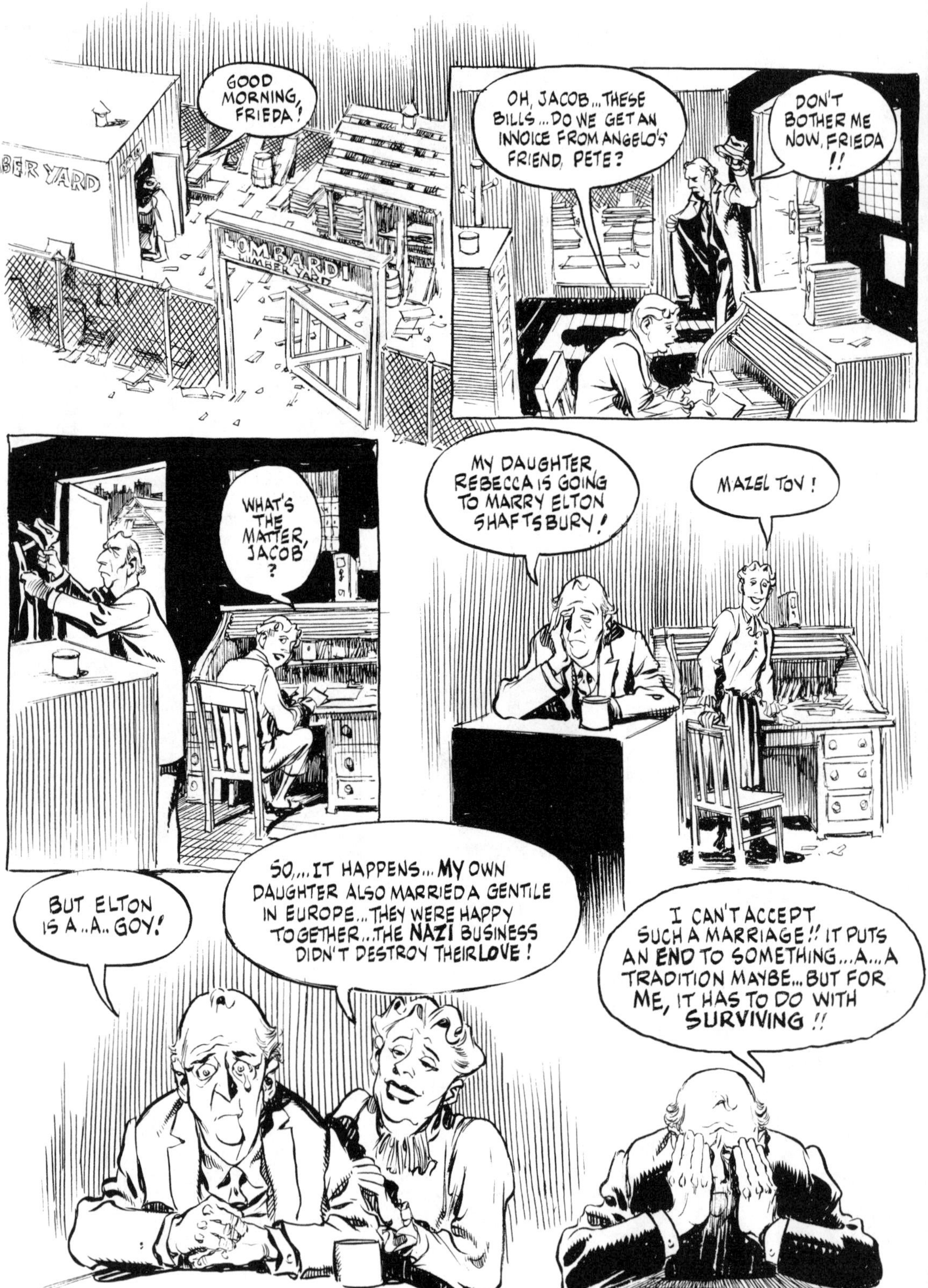
BER YARD
LOMBARDI LUMBER YARD
GOOD MORNING, FRIEDA!
OH, JACOB... THESE BILLS... DO WE GET AN INVOICE FROM ANGELO'S FRIEND, PETE?
DON'T BOTHER ME NOW, FRIEDA!!
WHAT'S THE MATTER, JACOB?
MY DAUGHTER REBECCA IS GOING TO MARRY ELTON SHAFTSBURY!
MAZEL TOV!
BUT ELTON IS A..A.. GOY!
SO,... IT HAPPENS... MY OWN DAUGHTER ALSO MARRIED A GENTILE IN EUROPE... THEY WERE HAPPY TOGETHER... THE NAZI BUSINESS DIDN'T DESTROY THEIR LOVE!
I CAN'T ACCEPT SUCH A MARRIAGE!! IT PUTS AN END TO SOMETHING... A... A TRADITION MAYBE... BUT FOR ME, IT HAS TO DO WITH SURVIVING!!

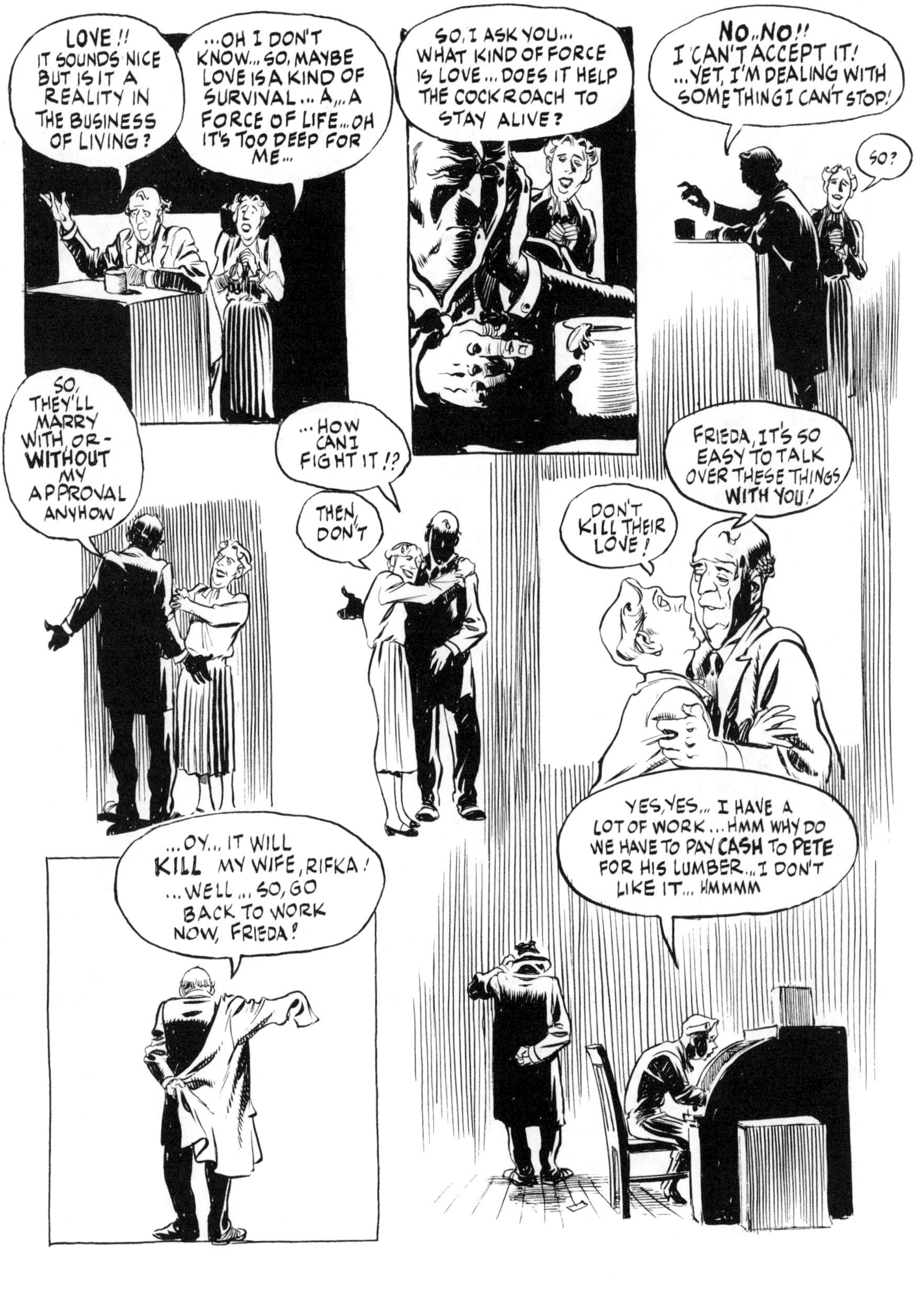
LOVE!! IT SOUNDS NICE BUT IS IT A REALITY IN THE BUSINESS OF LIVING?
...OH I DON'T KNOW... SO, MAYBE LOVE IS A KIND OF SURVIVAL... A,.. A FORCE OF LIFE... OH IT'S TOO DEEP FOR ME...
SO, I ASK YOU... WHAT KIND OF FORCE IS LOVE... DOES IT HELP THE COCKROACH TO STAY ALIVE?
NO.. NO!! I CAN'T ACCEPT IT! ...YET, I'M DEALING WITH SOMETHING I CAN'T STOP!
SO?
SO, THEY'LL MARRY WITH, OR- WITHOUT MY APPROVAL ANYHOW
...HOW CAN I FIGHT IT!?
THEN, DON'T
FRIEDA, IT'S SO EASY TO TALK OVER THESE THINGS WITH YOU!
DON'T KILL THEIR LOVE!
YES, YES... I HAVE A LOT OF WORK... HMM WHY DO WE HAVE TO PAY CASH TO PETE FOR HIS LUMBER... I DON'T LIKE IT... HMMMM
...OY... IT WILL KILL MY WIFE, RIFKA! ...WELL... SO, GO BACK TO WORK NOW, FRIEDA!

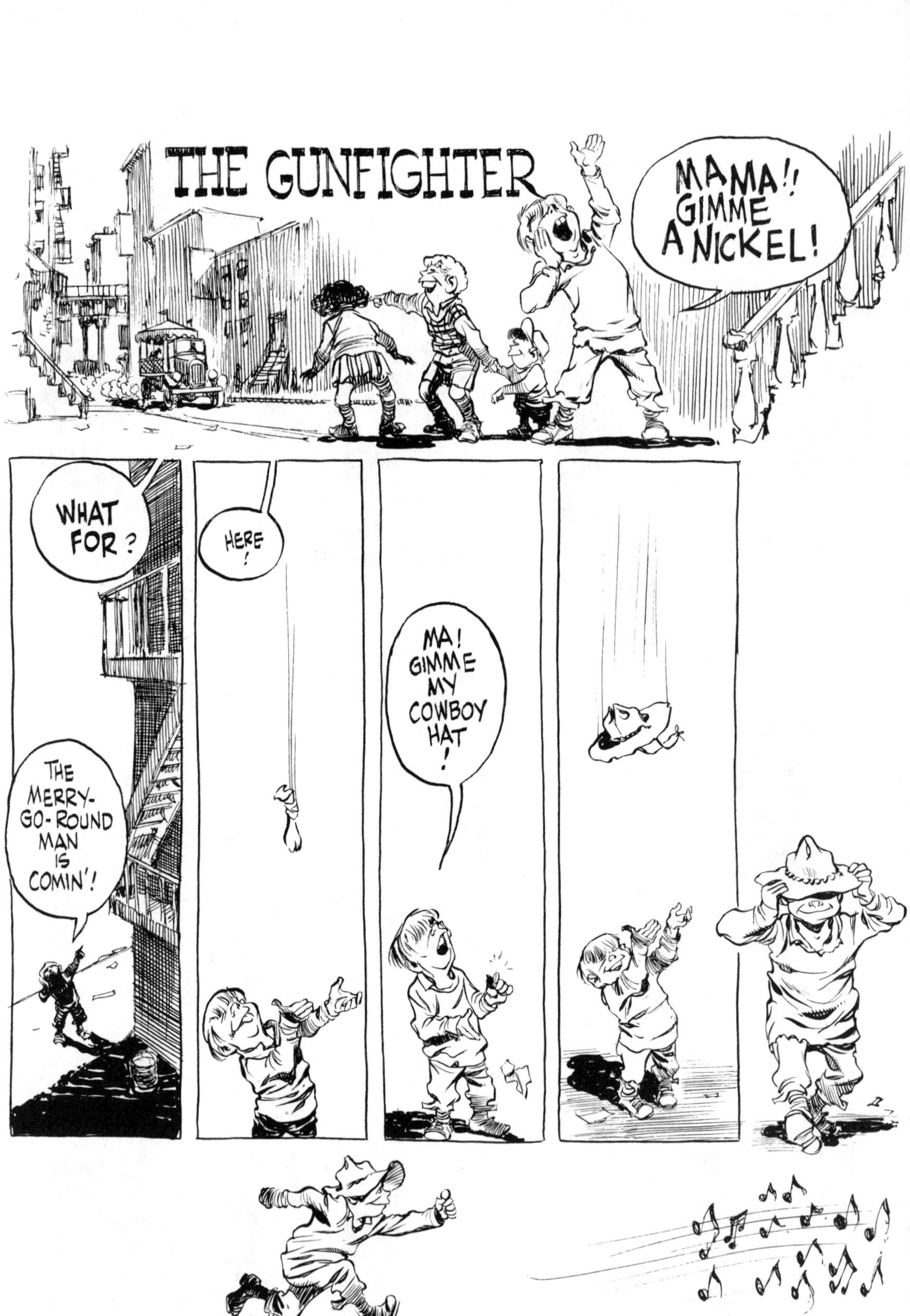
THE GUNFIGHTER
MAMA!! GIMME A NICKEL!
WHAT FOR?
THE MERRY-GO-ROUND MAN IS COMIN'!
HERE!
MA! GIMME MY COWBOY HAT!

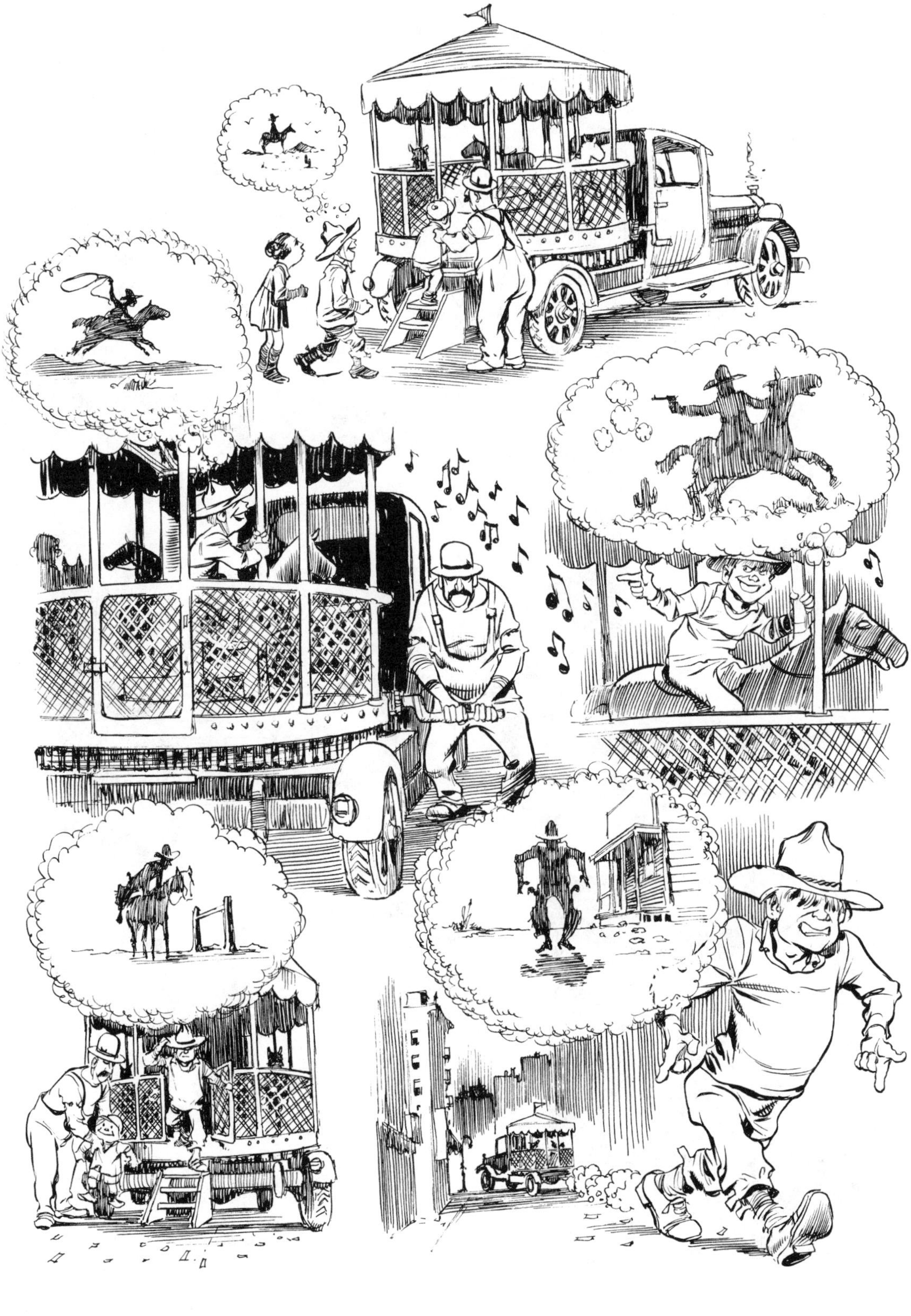

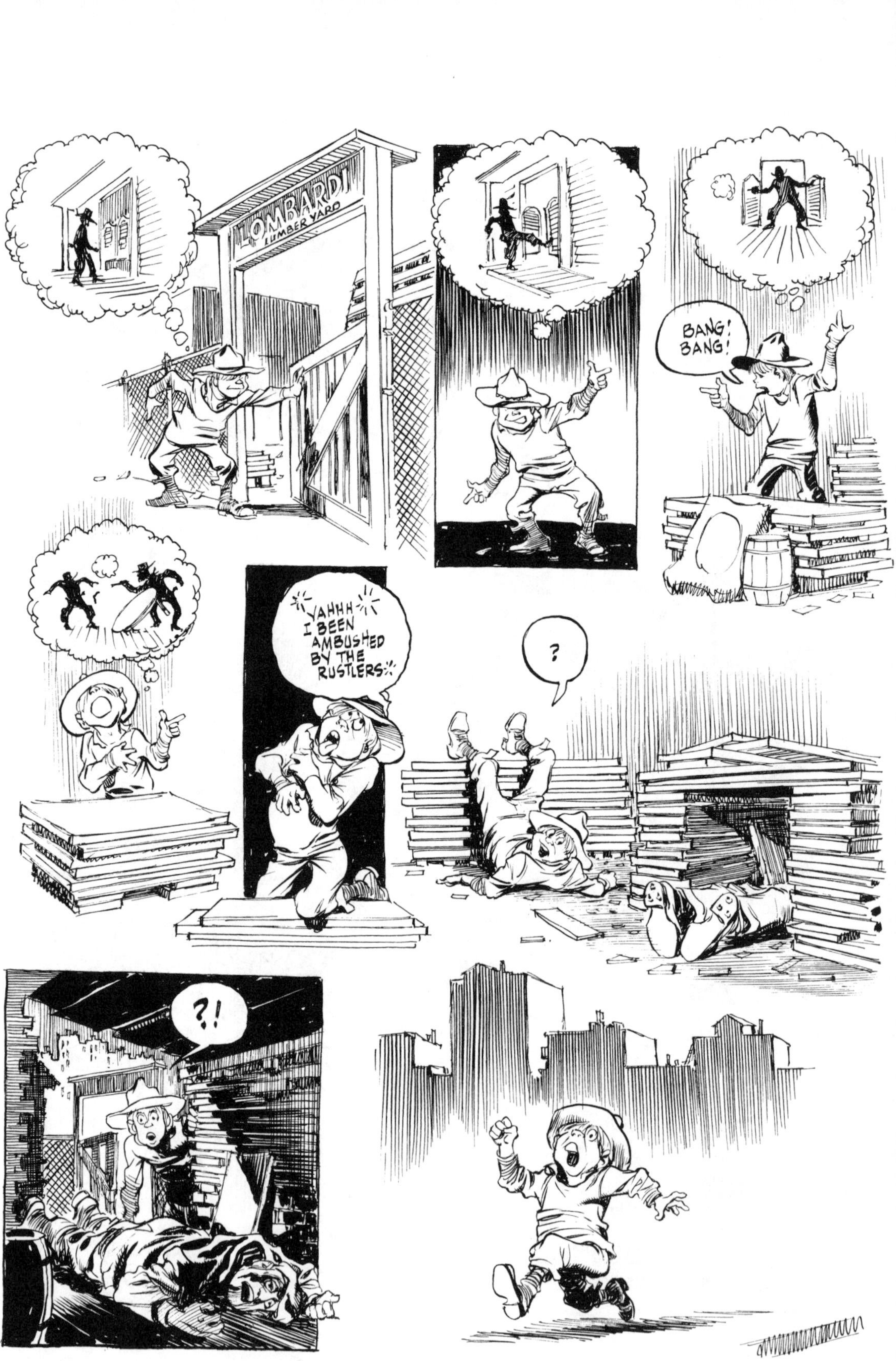
LOMBARDI
LUMBER YARD
BANG! BANG!
YAHHH I BEEN AMBUSHED BY THE RUSTLERS
?
?!

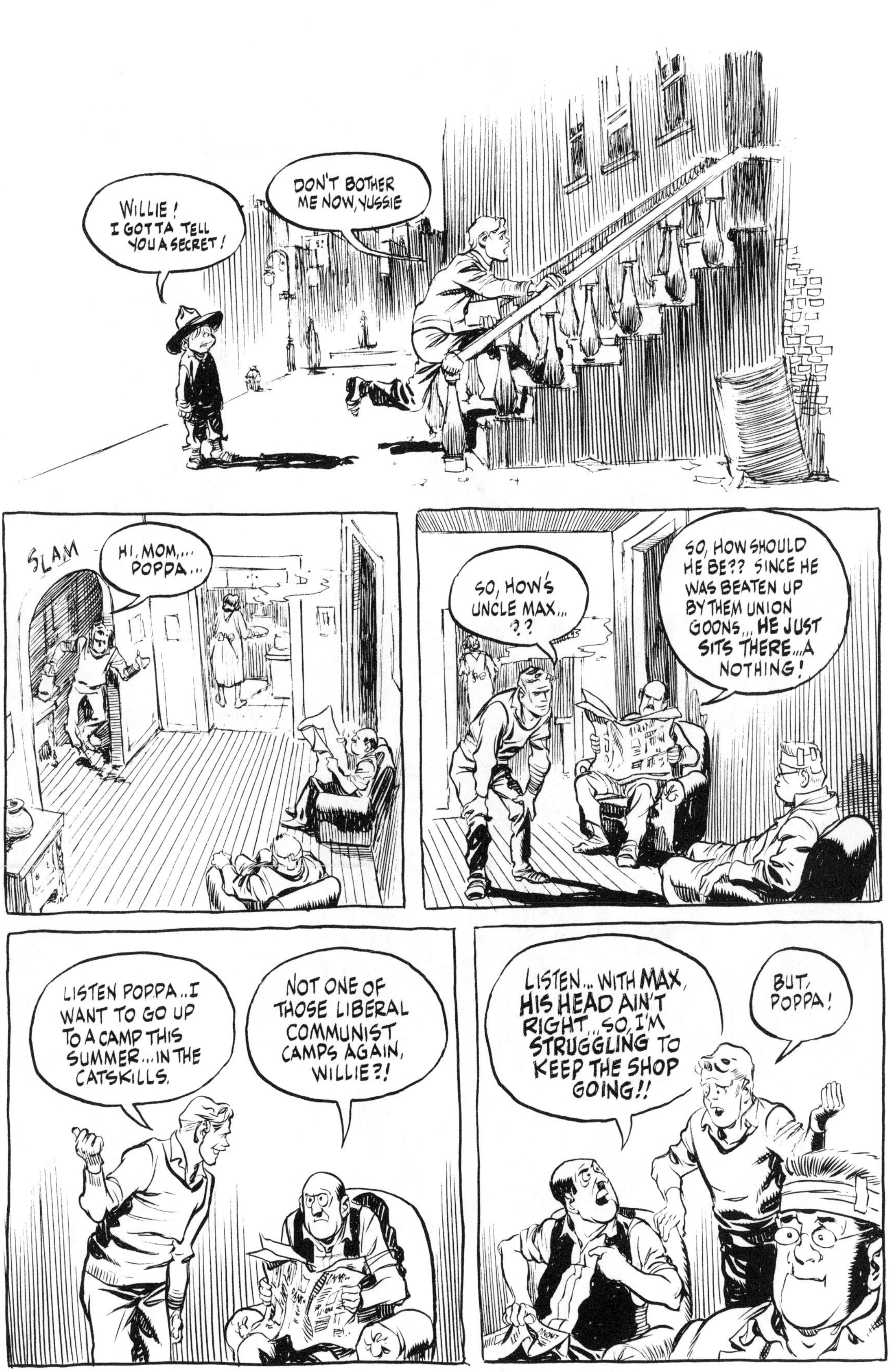
WILLIE! I GOTTA TELL YOU A SECRET!
DON'T BOTHER ME NOW, YUSSIE
SLAM
HI, MOM,... POPPA...
SO, HOW'S UNCLE MAX... ??
SO, HOW SHOULD HE BE?? SINCE HE WAS BEATEN UP BY THEM UNION GOONS... HE JUST SITS THERE...A NOTHING!
LISTEN POPPA..I WANT TO GO UP TO A CAMP THIS SUMMER...IN THE CATSKILLS.
NOT ONE OF THOSE LIBERAL COMMUNIST CAMPS AGAIN, WILLIE?!
LISTEN... WITH MAX, HIS HEAD AIN'T RIGHT... SO, I'M STRUGGLING TO KEEP THE SHOP GOING!!
BUT, POPPA!

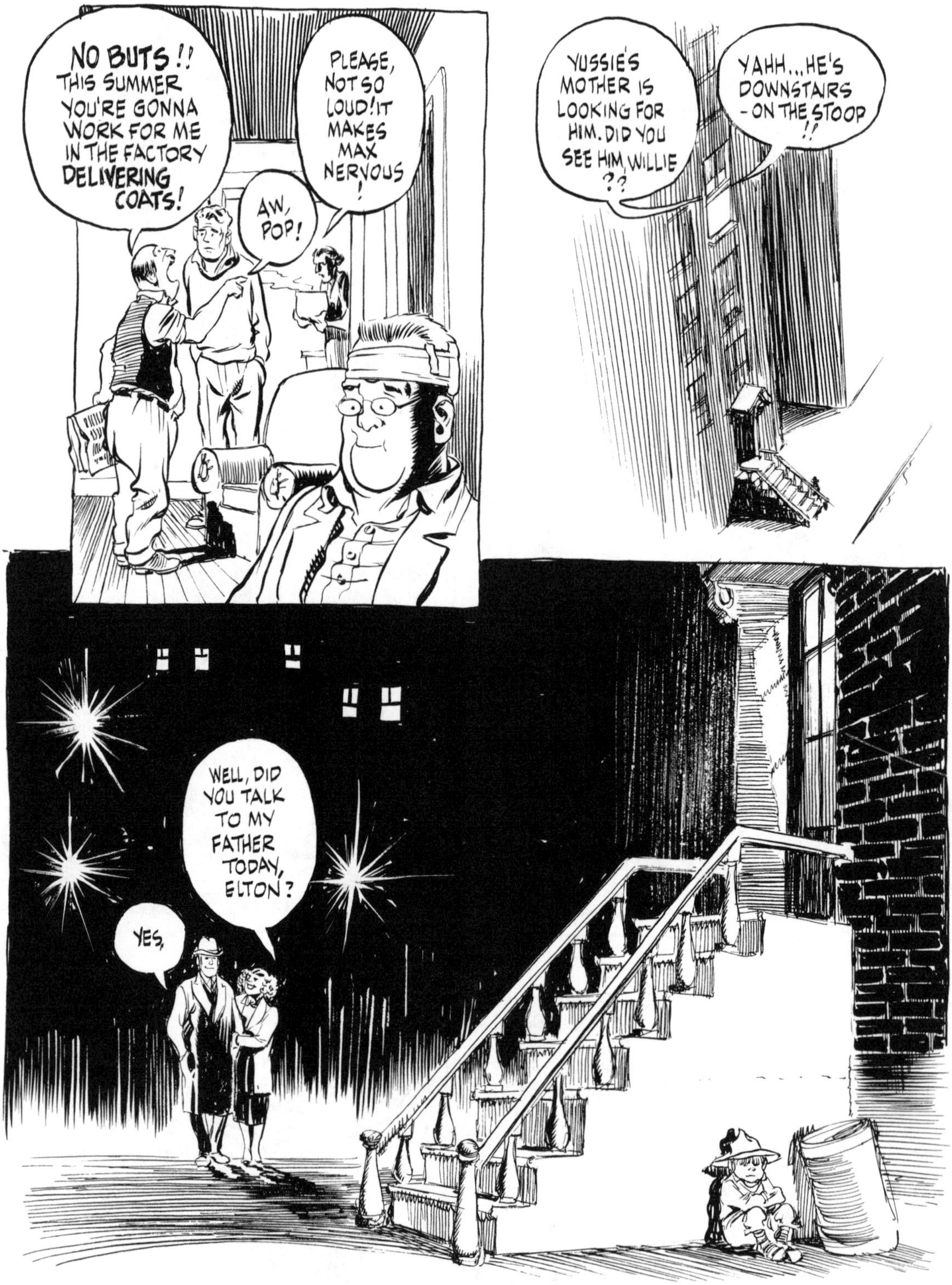
NO BUTS!! THIS SUMMER YOU'RE GONNA WORK FOR ME IN THE FACTORY DELIVERING COATS!
AW, POP!
PLEASE, NOT SO LOUD! IT MAKES MAX NERVOUS!
YUSSIE'S MOTHER IS LOOKING FOR HIM. DID YOU SEE HIM, WILLIE??
YAHH... HE'S DOWNSTAIRS - ON THE STOOP!!
WELL, DID YOU TALK TO MY FATHER TODAY, ELTON?
YES,

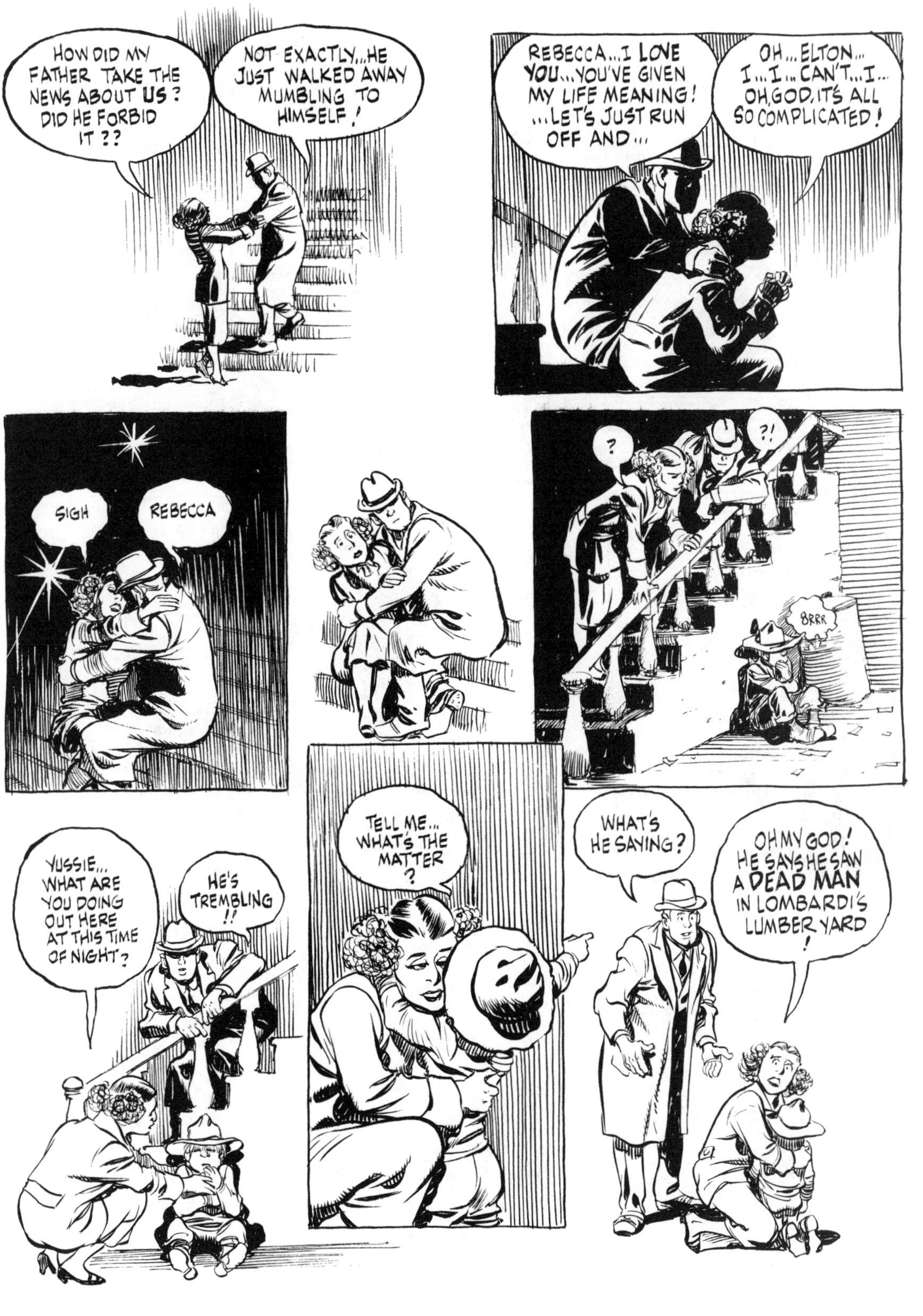
HOW DID MY FATHER TAKE THE NEWS ABOUT US? DID HE FORBID IT??
NOT EXACTLY...HE JUST WALKED AWAY MUMBLING TO HIMSELF!
REBECCA...I LOVE YOU...YOU'VE GIVEN MY LIFE MEANING! ...LET'S JUST RUN OFF AND...
OH...ELTON... I...I...CAN'T...I... OH, GOD, IT'S ALL SO COMPLICATED!
SIGH
REBECCA
?
?!
BRRR
YUSSIE... WHAT ARE YOU DOING OUT HERE AT THIS TIME OF NIGHT?
HE'S TREMBLING!!
TELL ME... WHAT'S THE MATTER?
WHAT'S HE SAYING?
OH MY GOD! HE SAYS HE SAW A DEAD MAN IN LOMBARDI'S LUMBER YARD!

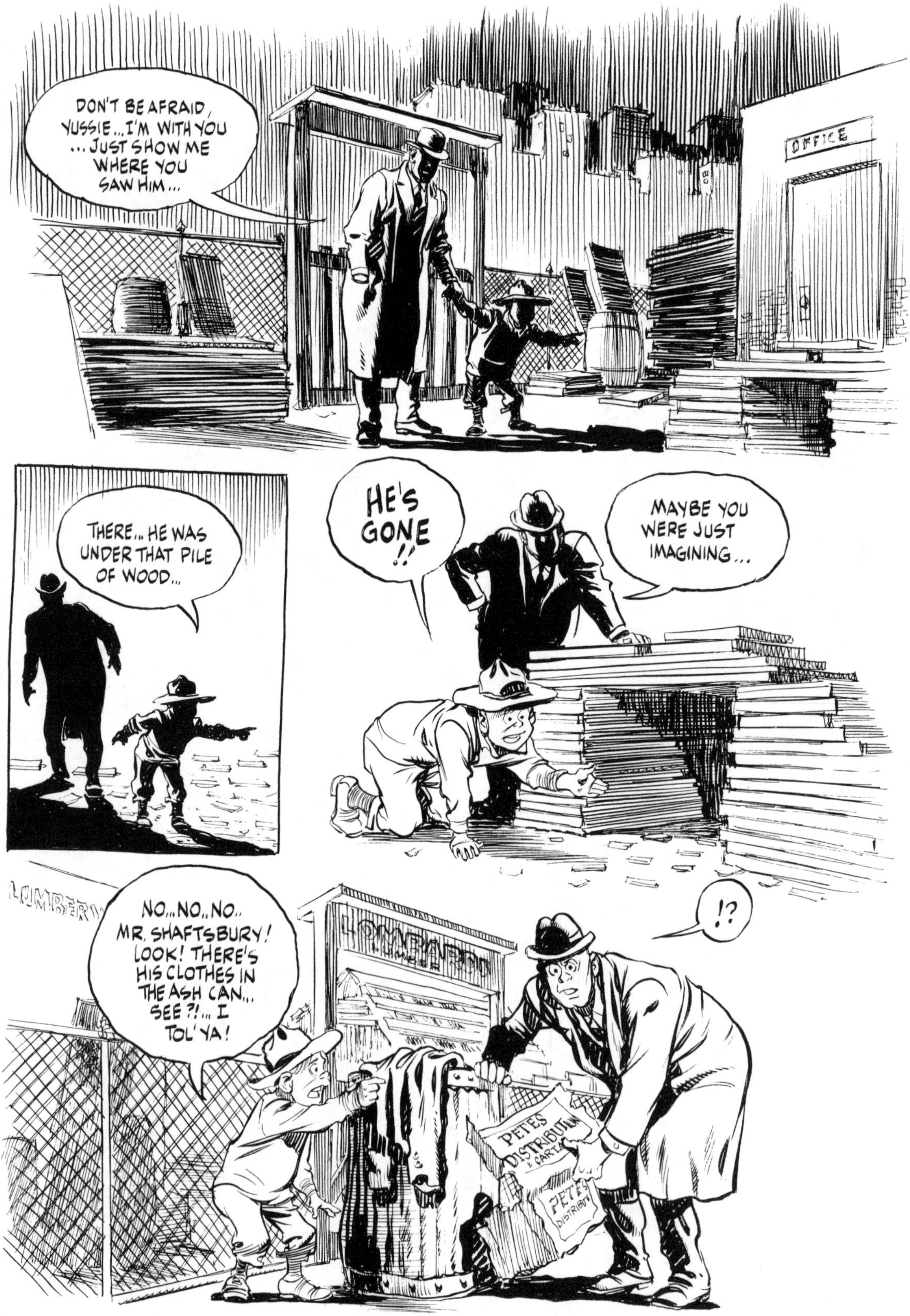
DON'T BE AFRAID, YUSSIE...I'M WITH YOU ...JUST SHOW ME WHERE YOU SAW HIM...
OFFICE
THERE... HE WAS UNDER THAT PILE OF WOOD...
HE'S GONE !!
MAYBE YOU WERE JUST IMAGINING...
NO...NO...NO... MR. SHAFTSBURY! LOOK! THERE'S HIS CLOTHES IN THE ASH CAN... SEE?!... I TOL' YA!
!?

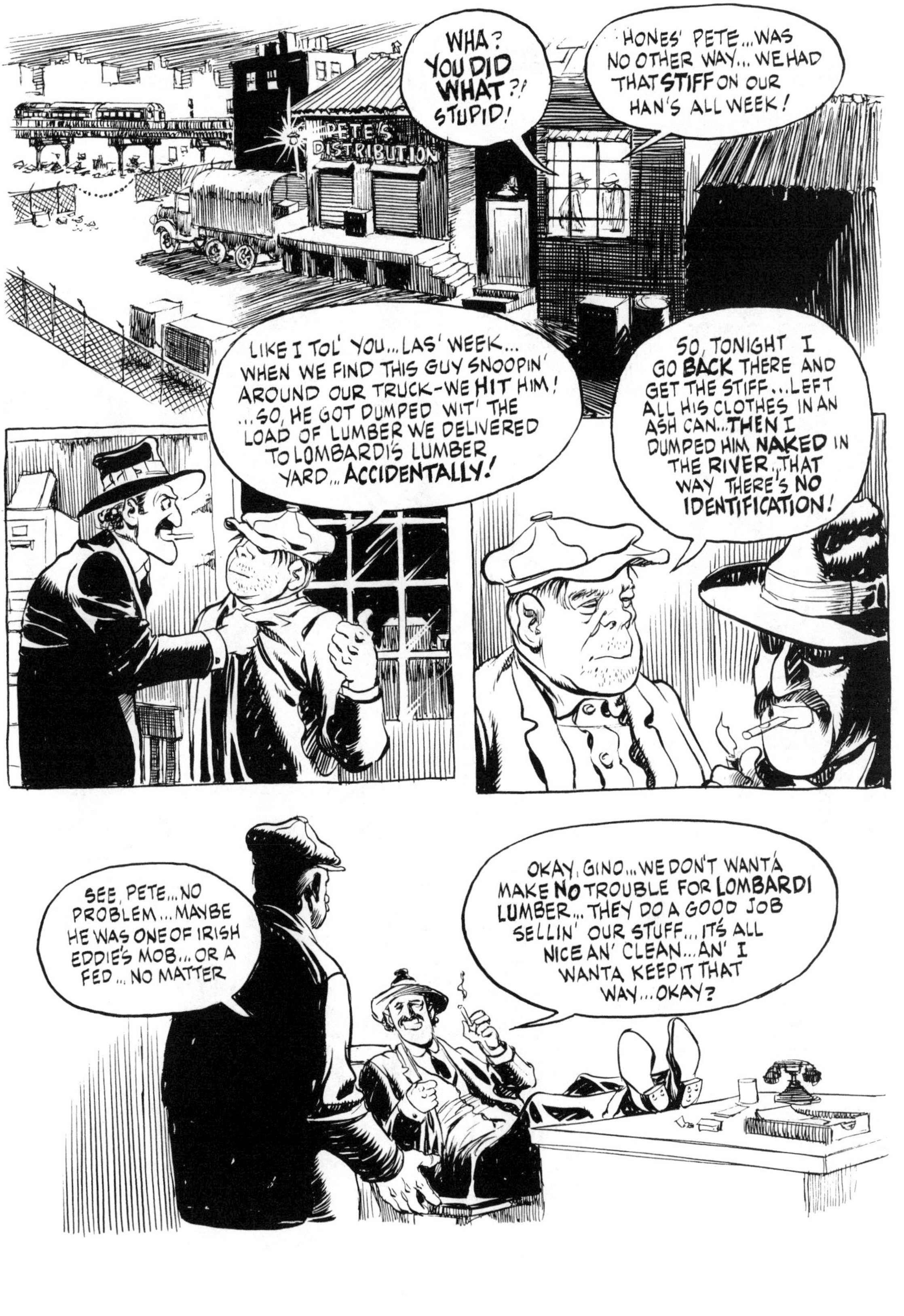
WHA? YOU DID WHAT?! STUPID!
HONES' PETE...WAS NO OTHER WAY...WE HAD THAT STIFF ON OUR HAN'S ALL WEEK!
PETE'S DISTRIBUTION
LIKE I TOL' YOU...LAS' WEEK...WHEN WE FIND THIS GUY SNOOPIN' AROUND OUR TRUCK-WE HIT HIM! ...SO, HE GOT DUMPED WIT' THE LOAD OF LUMBER WE DELIVERED TO LOMBARDI'S LUMBER YARD...ACCIDENTALLY!
SO, TONIGHT I GO BACK THERE AND GET THE STIFF...LEFT ALL HIS CLOTHES IN AN ASH CAN...THEN I DUMPED HIM NAKED IN THE RIVER, THAT WAY THERE'S NO IDENTIFICATION!
SEE, PETE...NO PROBLEM...MAYBE HE WAS ONE OF IRISH EDDIE'S MOB...OR A FED...NO MATTER
OKAY, GINO...WE DON'T WANTA MAKE NO TROUBLE FOR LOMBARDI LUMBER...THEY DO A GOOD JOB SELLIN' OUR STUFF...IT'S ALL NICE AN' CLEAN...AN' I WANTA KEEP IT THAT WAY...OKAY?

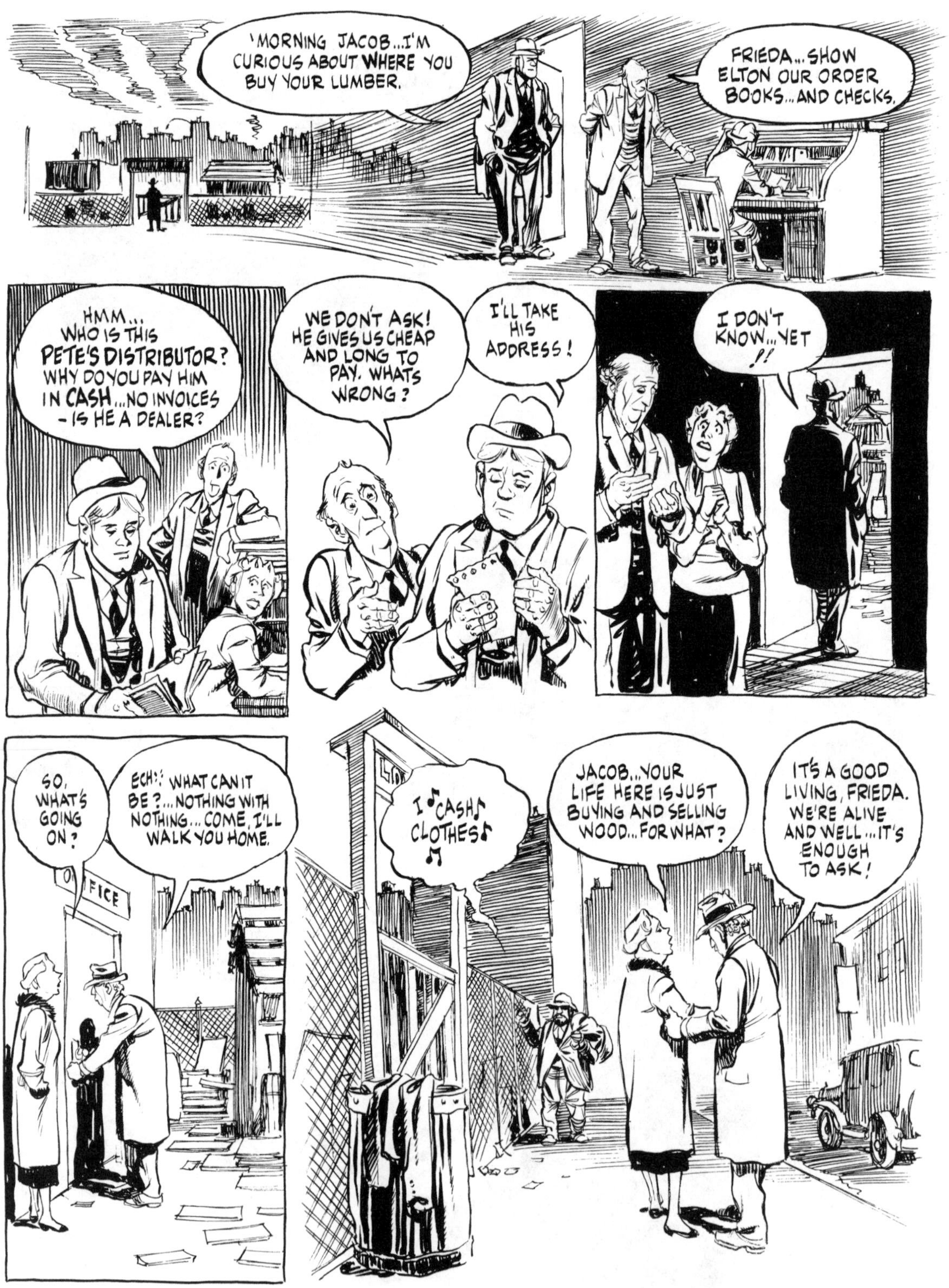

'MORNING JACOB...I'M CURIOUS ABOUT WHERE YOU BUY YOUR LUMBER.
FRIEDA...SHOW ELTON OUR ORDER BOOKS...AND CHECKS.
HMM... WHO IS THIS PETE'S DISTRIBUTOR? WHY DO YOU PAY HIM IN CASH...NO INVOICES - IS HE A DEALER?
WE DON'T ASK! HE GIVES US CHEAP AND LONG TO PAY. WHAT'S WRONG?
I'LL TAKE HIS ADDRESS!
I DON'T KNOW...YET !!
SO, WHAT'S GOING ON?
ECH! WHAT CAN IT BE?...NOTHING WITH NOTHING... COME, I'LL WALK YOU HOME.
OFFICE
I CASH CLOTHES
JACOB...YOUR LIFE HERE IS JUST BUYING AND SELLING WOOD...FOR WHAT?
IT'S A GOOD LIVING, FRIEDA. WE'RE ALIVE AND WELL...IT'S ENOUGH TO ASK!

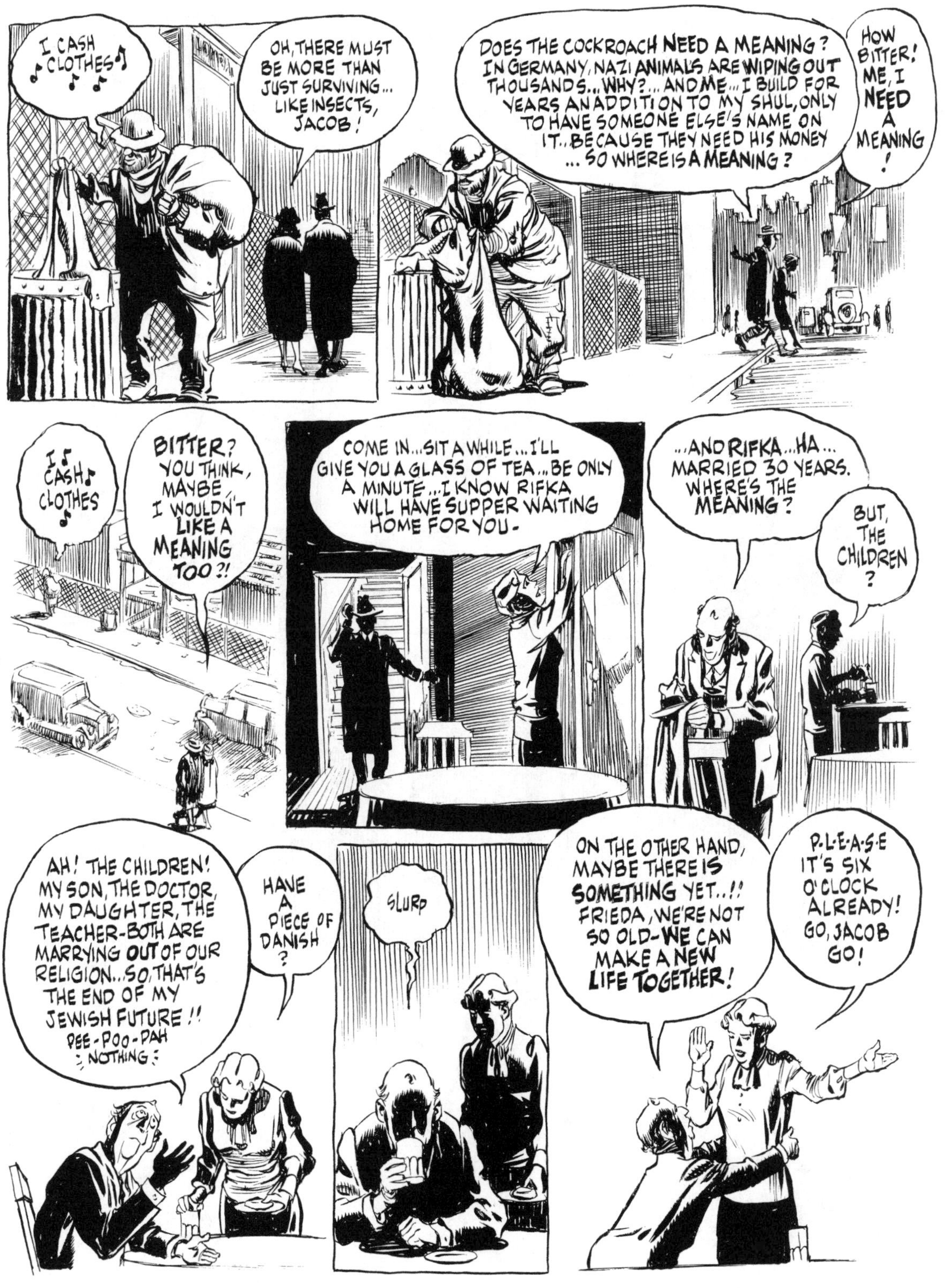

I CASH CLOTHES
OH, THERE MUST BE MORE THAN JUST SURVIVING... LIKE INSECTS, JACOB!
DOES THE COCKROACH NEED A MEANING? IN GERMANY, NAZI ANIMALS ARE WIPING OUT THOUSANDS... WHY?... AND ME... I BUILD FOR YEARS AN ADDITION TO MY SHUL, ONLY TO HAVE SOMEONE ELSE'S NAME ON IT.. BECAUSE THEY NEED HIS MONEY ... SO WHERE IS A MEANING?
HOW BITTER! ME, I NEED A MEANING!
I CASH CLOTHES
BITTER? YOU THINK, MAYBE I WOULDN'T LIKE A MEANING TOO?!
COME IN...SIT A WHILE...I'LL GIVE YOU A GLASS OF TEA...BE ONLY A MINUTE...I KNOW RIFKA WILL HAVE SUPPER WAITING HOME FOR YOU-
...AND RIFKA...HA... MARRIED 30 YEARS. WHERE'S THE MEANING?
BUT, THE CHILDREN?
AH! THE CHILDREN! MY SON, THE DOCTOR, MY DAUGHTER, THE TEACHER-BOTH ARE MARRYING OUT OF OUR RELIGION...SO, THAT'S THE END OF MY JEWISH FUTURE!! PEE-POO-PAH NOTHING
HAVE A PIECE OF DANISH?
SLURP
ON THE OTHER HAND, MAYBE THERE IS SOMETHING YET...!! FRIEDA, WE'RE NOT SO OLD-WE CAN MAKE A NEW LIFE TOGETHER!
P-L-E-A-S-E IT'S SIX O'CLOCK ALREADY! GO, JACOB GO!

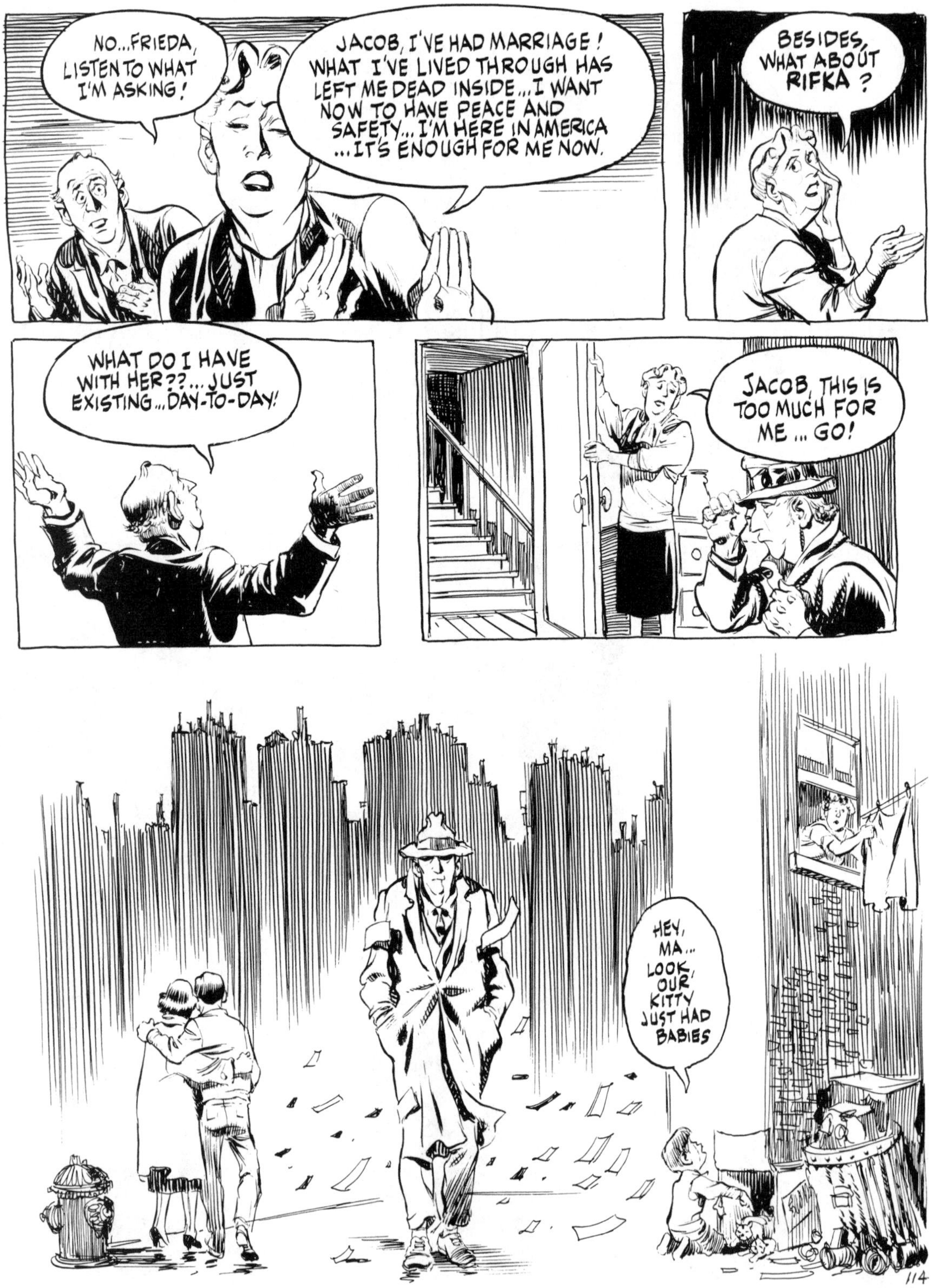
NO...FRIEDA, LISTEN TO WHAT I'M ASKING!
JACOB, I'VE HAD MARRIAGE! WHAT I'VE LIVED THROUGH HAS LEFT ME DEAD INSIDE...I WANT NOW TO HAVE PEACE AND SAFETY... I'M HERE IN AMERICA ...IT'S ENOUGH FOR ME NOW.
BESIDES, WHAT ABOUT RIFKA?
WHAT DO I HAVE WITH HER??... JUST EXISTING...DAY-TO-DAY!
JACOB, THIS IS TOO MUCH FOR ME ... GO!
HEY, MA... LOOK, OUR KITTY JUST HAD BABIES
114

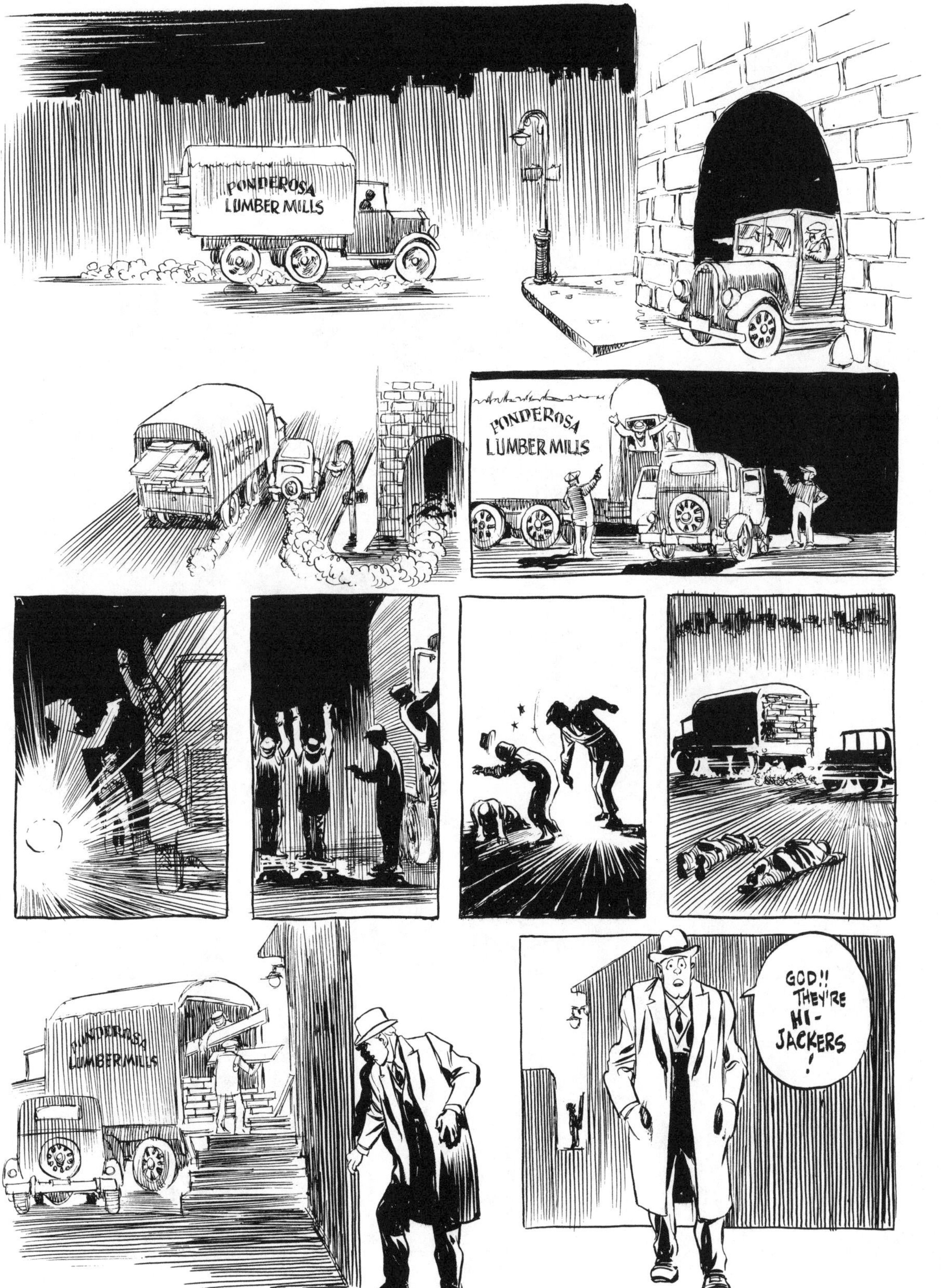
PONDEROSA
LUMBER MILLS
PONDEROSA
LUMBER MILLS
PONDEROSA
LUMBERMILLS
GOD!! THEY'RE HI-JACKERS!

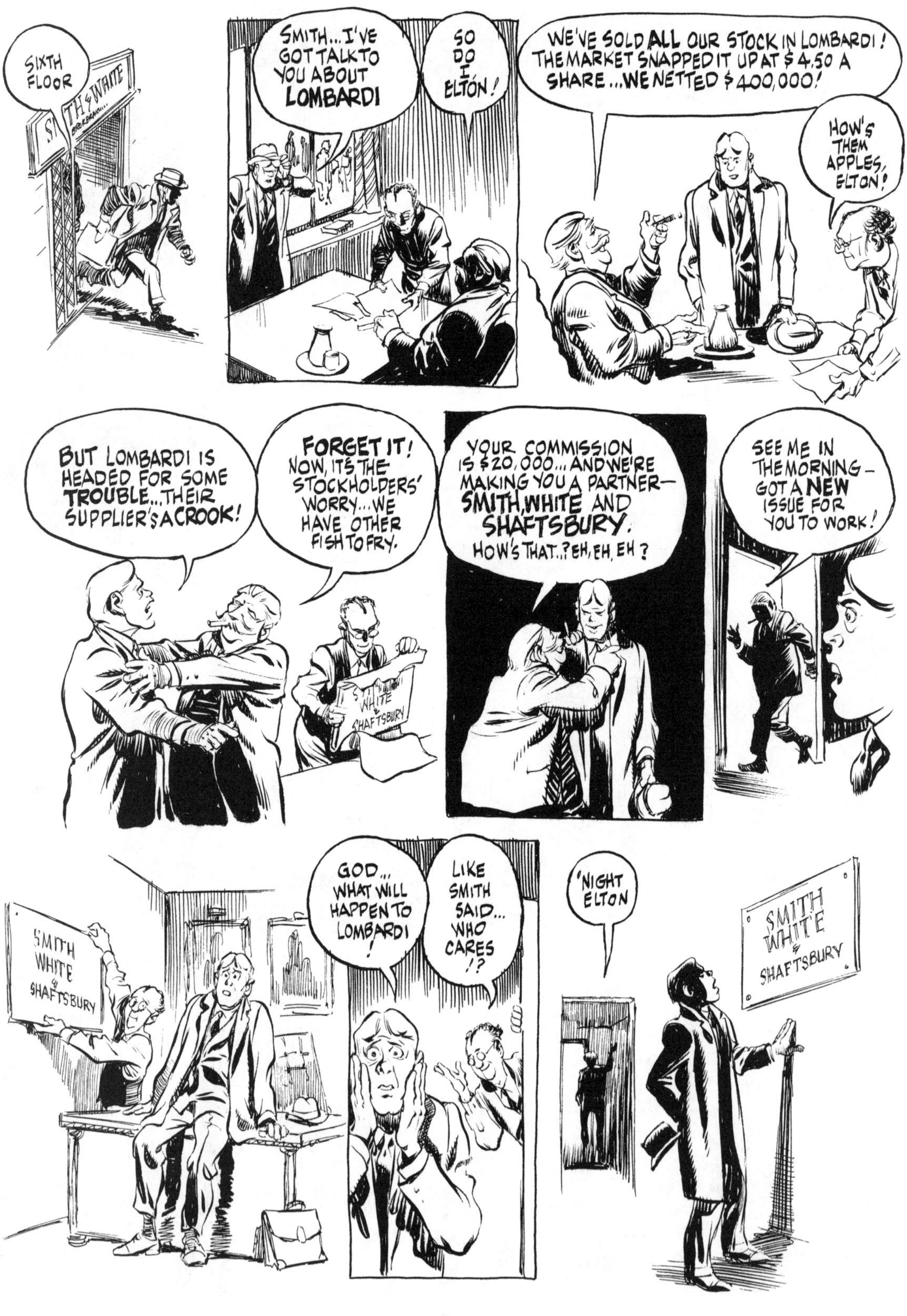
SIXTH FLOOR
SMITH & WHITE
SMITH... I'VE GOT TALK TO YOU ABOUT LOMBARDI
SO DO I ELTON!
WE'VE SOLD ALL OUR STOCK IN LOMBARDI! THE MARKET SNAPPED IT UP AT $4.50 A SHARE... WE NETTED $400,000!
HOW'S THEM APPLES, ELTON!
BUT LOMBARDI IS HEADED FOR SOME TROUBLE... THEIR SUPPLIER'S A CROOK!
FORGET IT! NOW, IT'S THE STOCKHOLDERS' WORRY... WE HAVE OTHER FISH TO FRY.
SMITH WHITE & SHAFTSBURY
YOUR COMMISSION IS $20,000... AND WE'RE MAKING YOU A PARTNER— SMITH, WHITE AND SHAFTSBURY. HOW'S THAT..? EH, EH, EH?
SEE ME IN THE MORNING— GOT A NEW ISSUE FOR YOU TO WORK!
SMITH WHITE & SHAFTSBURY
GOD... WHAT WILL HAPPEN TO LOMBARDI!
LIKE SMITH SAID... WHO CARES!?
'NIGHT ELTON
SMITH WHITE & SHAFTSBURY

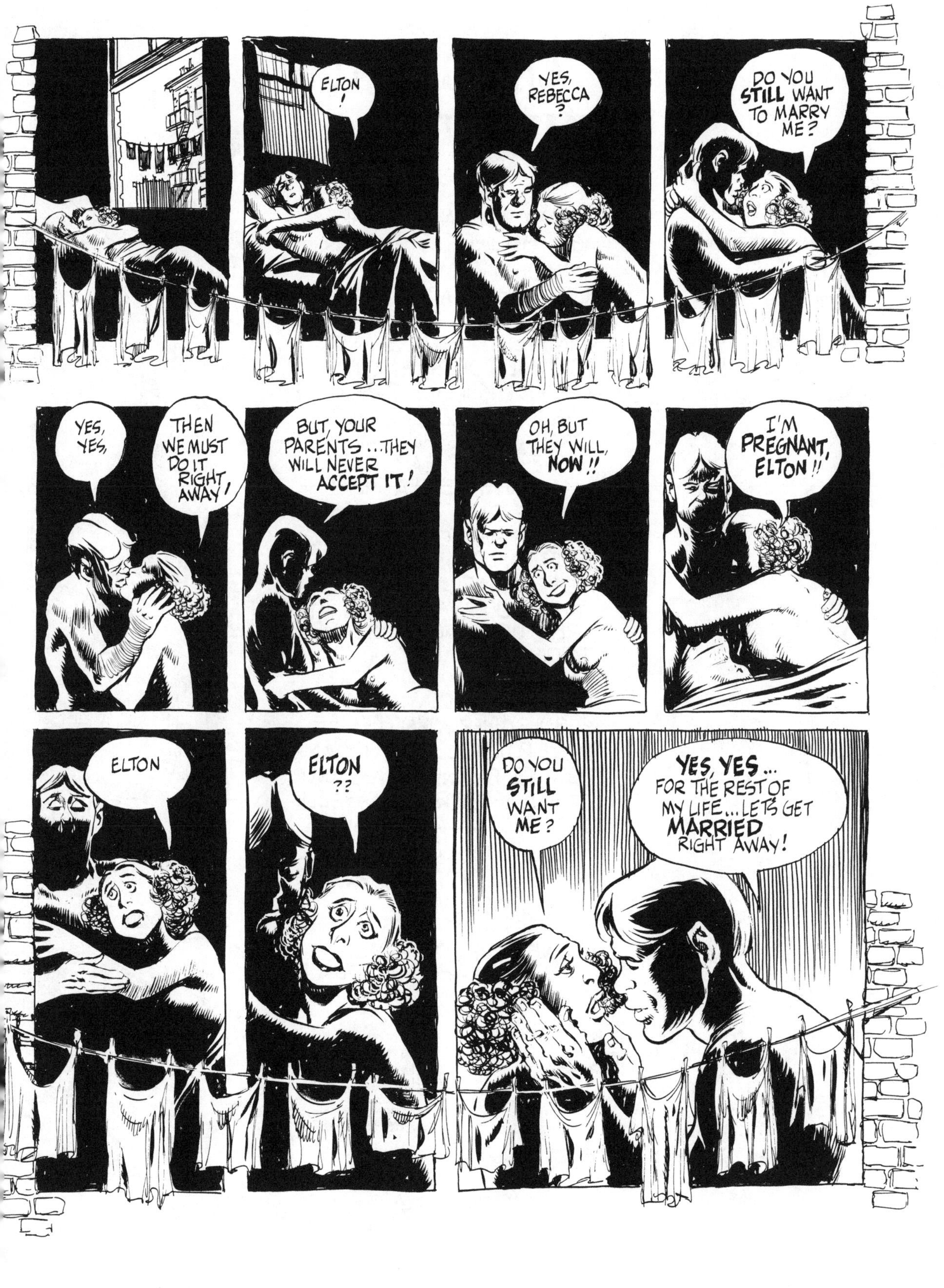
ELTON !
YES, REBECCA ?
DO YOU STILL WANT TO MARRY ME ?
YES, YES,
THEN WE MUST DO IT RIGHT AWAY !
BUT, YOUR PARENTS ...THEY WILL NEVER ACCEPT IT !
OH, BUT THEY WILL, NOW !!
I'M PREGNANT, ELTON !!
ELTON
ELTON ??
DO YOU STILL WANT ME ?
YES, YES ... FOR THE REST OF MY LIFE ... LET'S GET MARRIED RIGHT AWAY !

CHAPTER 11
SURVIVAL

MANY MILLIONS OF YEARS AGO... BEFORE THE FAMILIAR FORM OF WHAT WE KNOW AS HUMAN BEINGS APPEARED... THE **COCKROACH**, IN GREAT NUMBERS, INHABITED THE NOOKS AND CRANNIES OF THE EARTH...

IN THE ENSUING CENTURIES THESE INSECTS MANAGED TO SURVIVE LONG AFTER OTHER SIMILAR SPECIES DISAPPEARED!

MEANWHILE, IN A SHORT SPAN OF TIME... THE **HUMAN** SPECIES EVOLVED, AFFECTING THEIR ENVIRONMENT IN A MOST REMARKABLE WAY!!

WONDROUSLY, THESE UPRIGHT CREATURES ACTUALLY CAME TO DEAL WITH AND CONTROL NATURAL PHENOMENA ...THEY WERE ABLE TO DOMINATE OR SUBDUE OTHER FORMS OF LIFE MORE POWERFUL THAN THEY... AND DESPITE FAMINE, DISEASE AND OTHER DISASTERS SUCH AS SELF-DESTRUCTION... THEY HAVE MANAGED TO SURVIVE AND EVEN INCREASE THEIR NUMBERS MANY TIMES OVER!

THEY HAVE, IN COMMON WITH THE COCKROACH, A REMARKABLE LIFE FORCE!

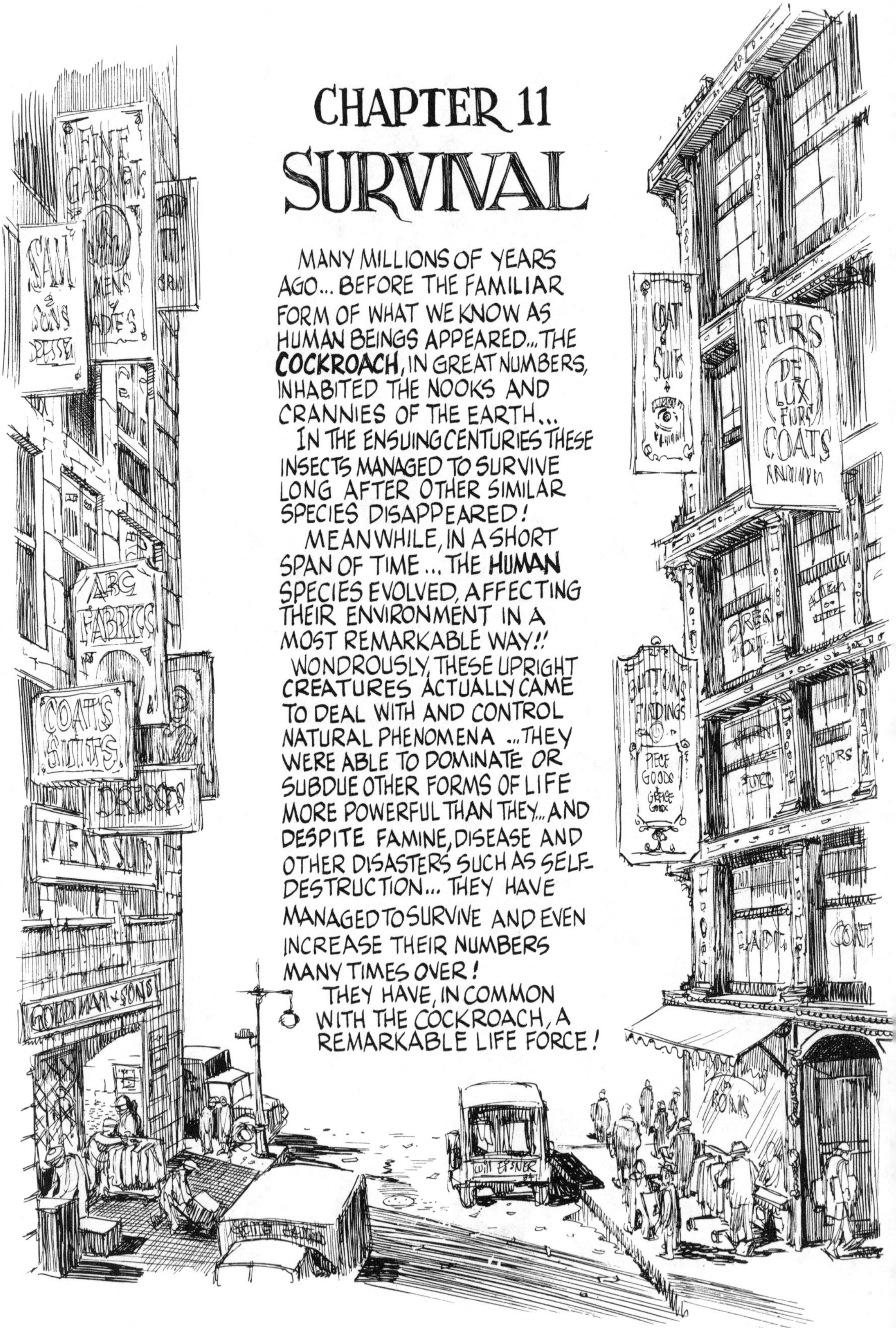

FINE GARMENTS
SAM & SONS
ABC FABRICS
COATS SUITS
MENS SUITS
GOLDMAN & SONS
COAT & SUITS
FURS DE LUX FURS COATS
BUTTONS & FINDINGS
PIECE GOODS
FURS

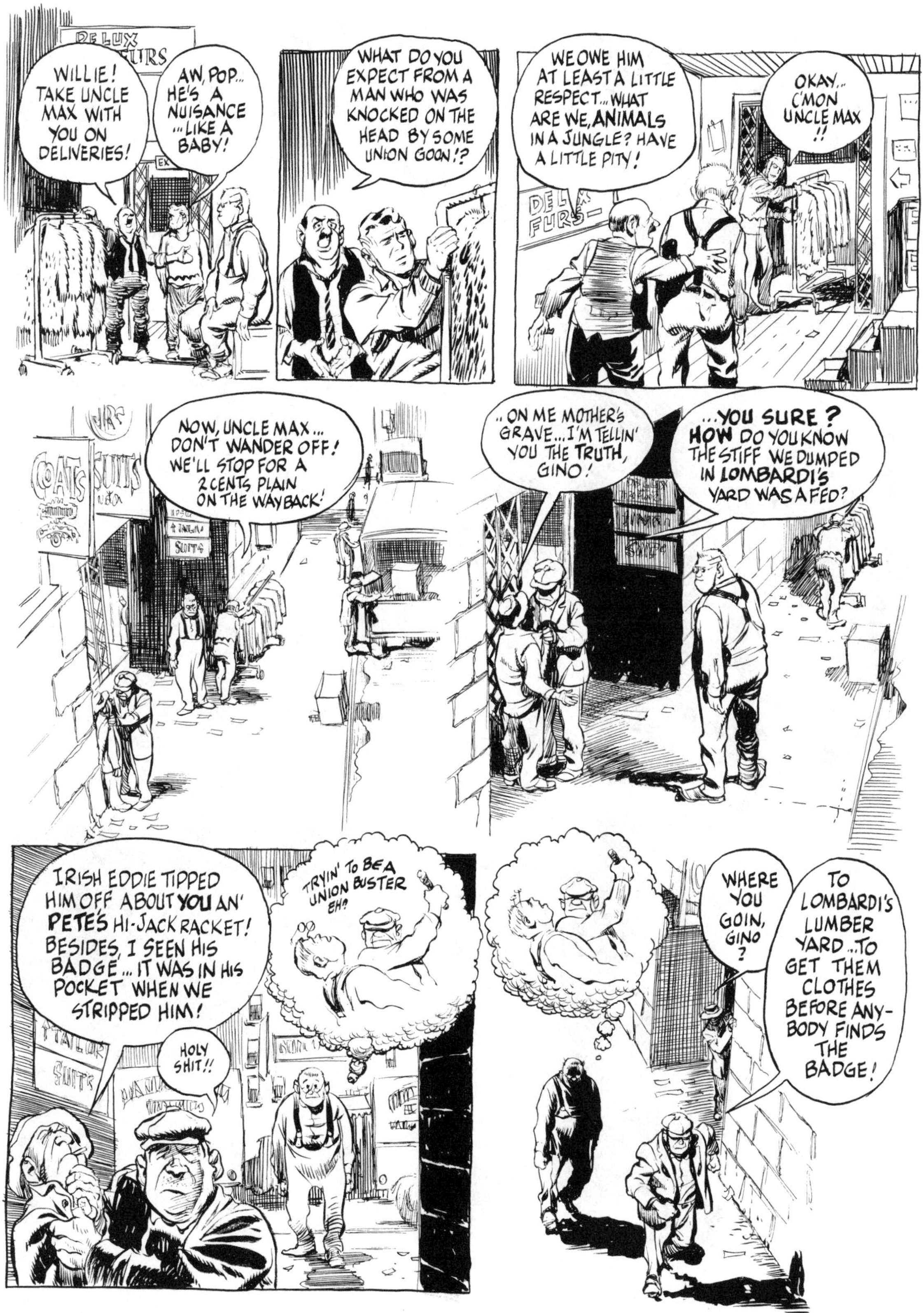
DE LUX FURS
WILLIE! TAKE UNCLE MAX WITH YOU ON DELIVERIES!
AW, POP... HE'S A NUISANCE ...LIKE A BABY!
WHAT DO YOU EXPECT FROM A MAN WHO WAS KNOCKED ON THE HEAD BY SOME UNION GOON!?
WE OWE HIM AT LEAST A LITTLE RESPECT... WHAT ARE WE, ANIMALS IN A JUNGLE? HAVE A LITTLE PITY!
DE LUX FURS
OKAY... C'MON UNCLE MAX!!
COATS
SUITS
NOW, UNCLE MAX... DON'T WANDER OFF! WE'LL STOP FOR A 2 CENTS PLAIN ON THE WAY BACK!
..ON ME MOTHER'S GRAVE... I'M TELLIN' YOU THE TRUTH, GINO!
...YOU SURE? HOW DO YOU KNOW THE STIFF WE DUMPED IN LOMBARDI'S YARD WAS A FED?
IRISH EDDIE TIPPED HIM OFF ABOUT YOU AN' PETE'S HI-JACK RACKET! BESIDES, I SEEN HIS BADGE... IT WAS IN HIS POCKET WHEN WE STRIPPED HIM!
TRYIN' TO BE A UNION BUSTER EH?
HOLY SHIT!!
WHERE YOU GOIN, GINO?
TO LOMBARDI'S LUMBER YARD... TO GET THEM CLOTHES BEFORE ANYBODY FINDS THE BADGE!

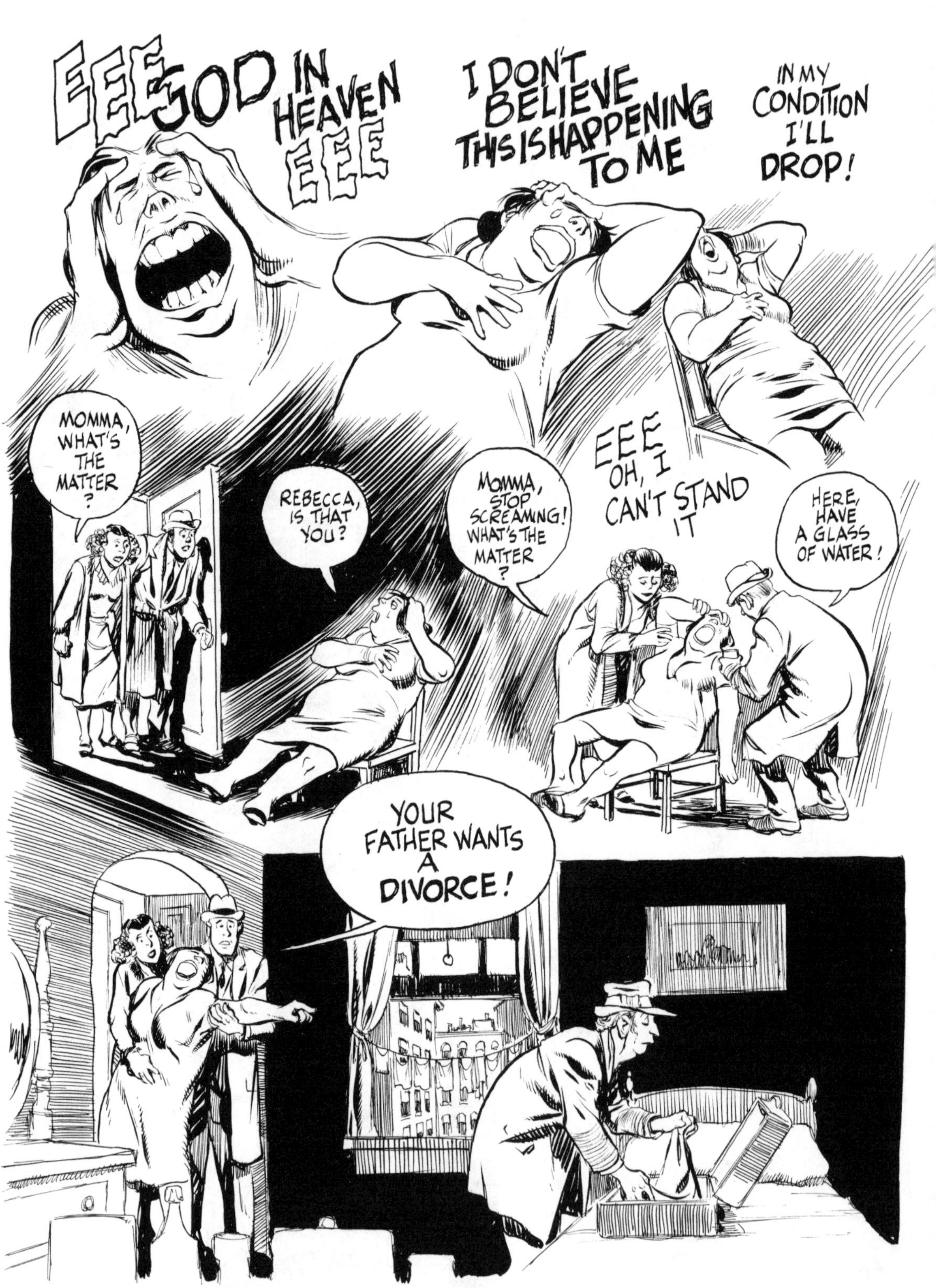
EEE GOD IN HEAVEN EEE
I DON'T BELIEVE THIS IS HAPPENING TO ME
IN MY CONDITION I'LL DROP!
MOMMA, WHAT'S THE MATTER?
REBECCA, IS THAT YOU?
MOMMA, STOP SCREAMING! WHAT'S THE MATTER?
EEE OH, I CAN'T STAND IT
HERE, HAVE A GLASS OF WATER!
YOUR FATHER WANTS A DIVORCE!

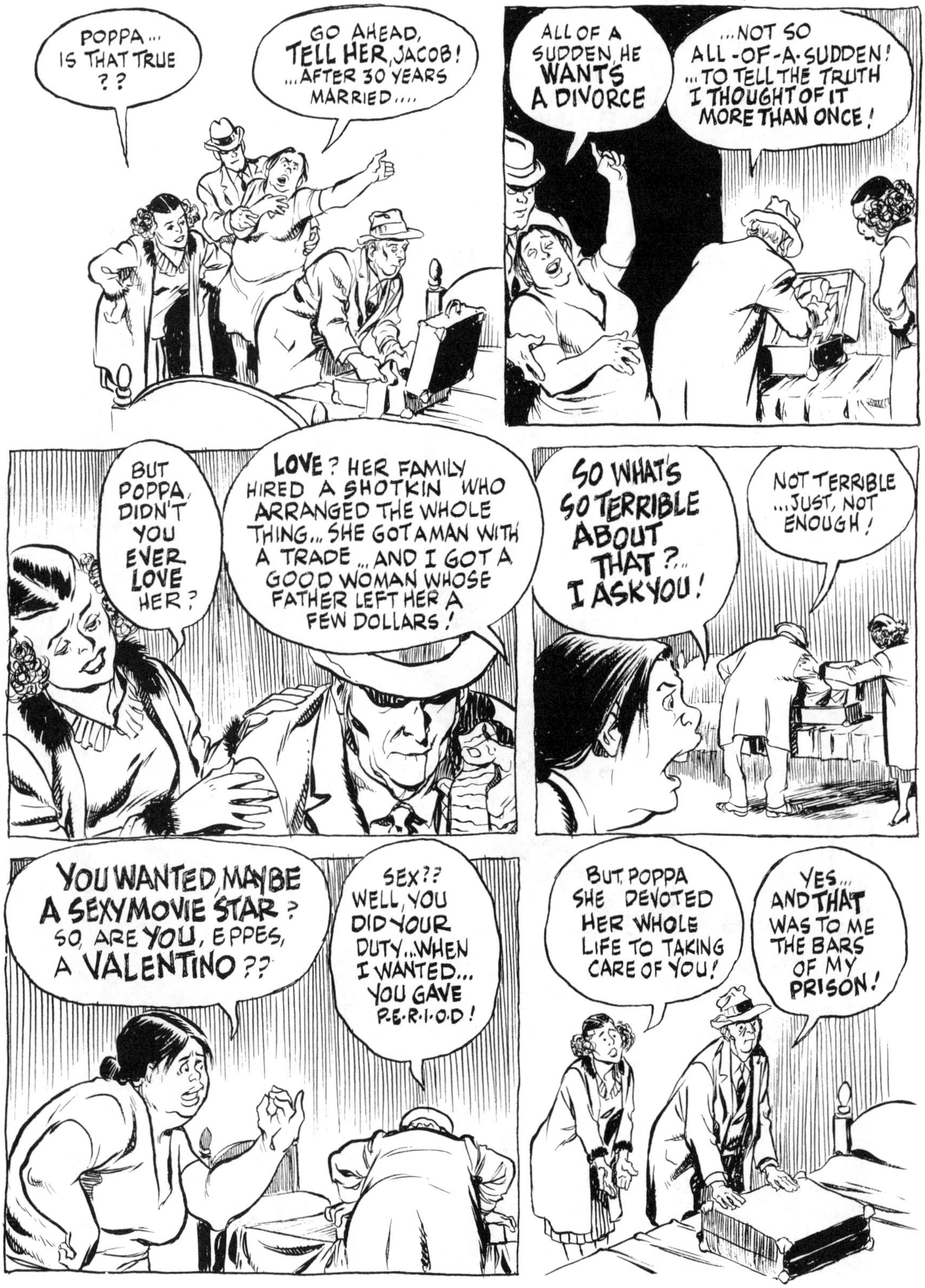
POPPA... IS THAT TRUE ??
GO AHEAD, TELL HER, JACOB! ...AFTER 30 YEARS MARRIED....
ALL OF A SUDDEN, HE WANTS A DIVORCE
...NOT SO ALL-OF-A-SUDDEN! ...TO TELL THE TRUTH I THOUGHT OF IT MORE THAN ONCE!
BUT POPPA, DIDN'T YOU EVER LOVE HER?
LOVE? HER FAMILY HIRED A SHOTKIN WHO ARRANGED THE WHOLE THING... SHE GOT A MAN WITH A TRADE ... AND I GOT A GOOD WOMAN WHOSE FATHER LEFT HER A FEW DOLLARS!
SO WHAT'S SO TERRIBLE ABOUT THAT?... I ASK YOU!
NOT TERRIBLE ...JUST, NOT ENOUGH!
YOU WANTED, MAYBE A SEXY MOVIE STAR? SO, ARE YOU, EPPES, A VALENTINO??
SEX?? WELL, YOU DID YOUR DUTY... WHEN I WANTED... YOU GAVE P.E.R.I.O.D!
BUT, POPPA SHE DEVOTED HER WHOLE LIFE TO TAKING CARE OF YOU!
YES... AND THAT WAS TO ME THE BARS OF MY PRISON!

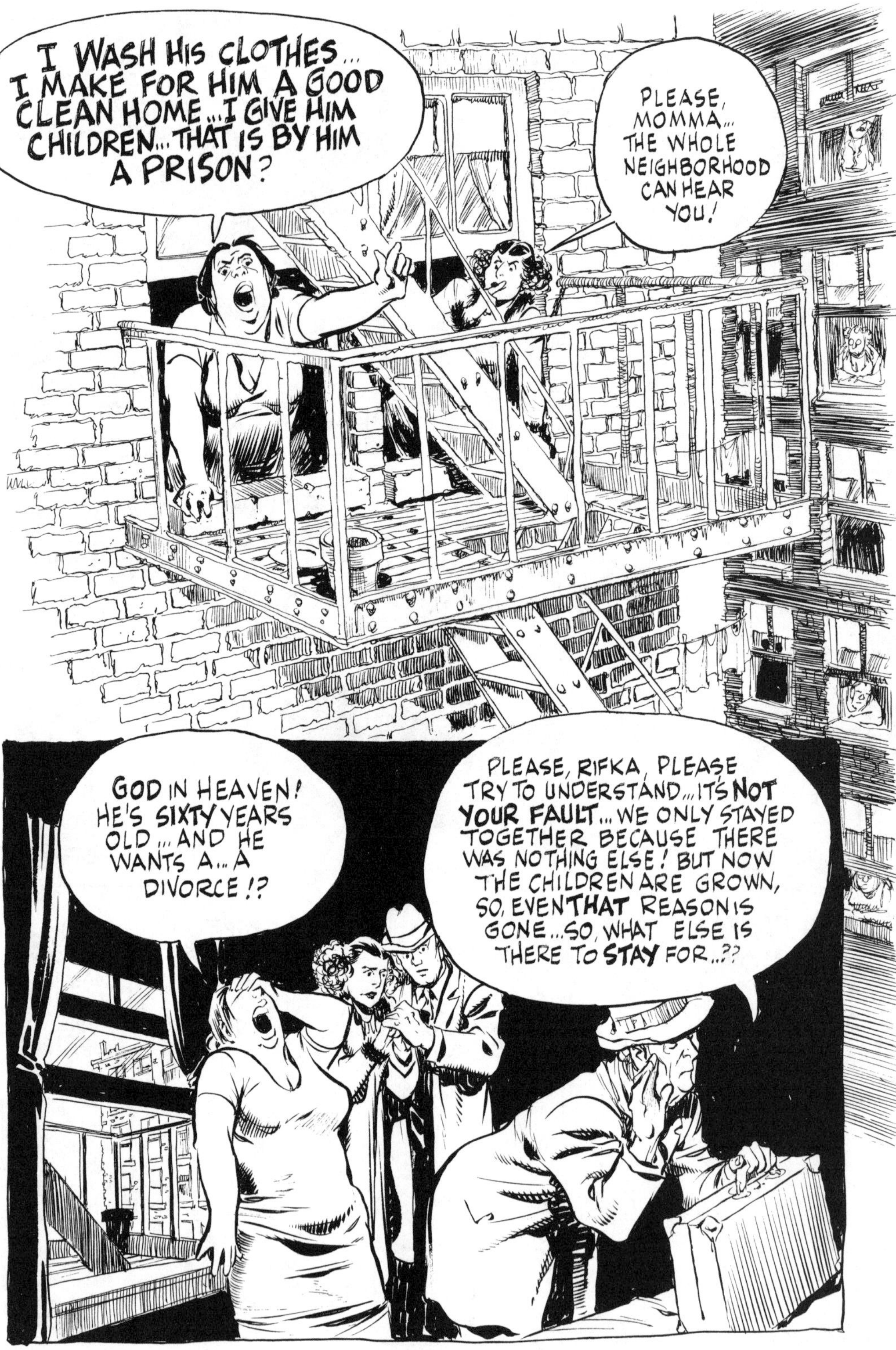
I WASH HIS CLOTHES... I MAKE FOR HIM A GOOD CLEAN HOME...I GIVE HIM CHILDREN... THAT IS BY HIM A PRISON?
PLEASE, MOMMA... THE WHOLE NEIGHBORHOOD CAN HEAR YOU!
GOD IN HEAVEN! HE'S SIXTY YEARS OLD... AND HE WANTS A... A DIVORCE!?
PLEASE, RIFKA, PLEASE TRY TO UNDERSTAND... IT'S NOT YOUR FAULT... WE ONLY STAYED TOGETHER BECAUSE THERE WAS NOTHING ELSE! BUT NOW THE CHILDREN ARE GROWN, SO, EVEN THAT REASON IS GONE... SO, WHAT ELSE IS THERE TO STAY FOR..??

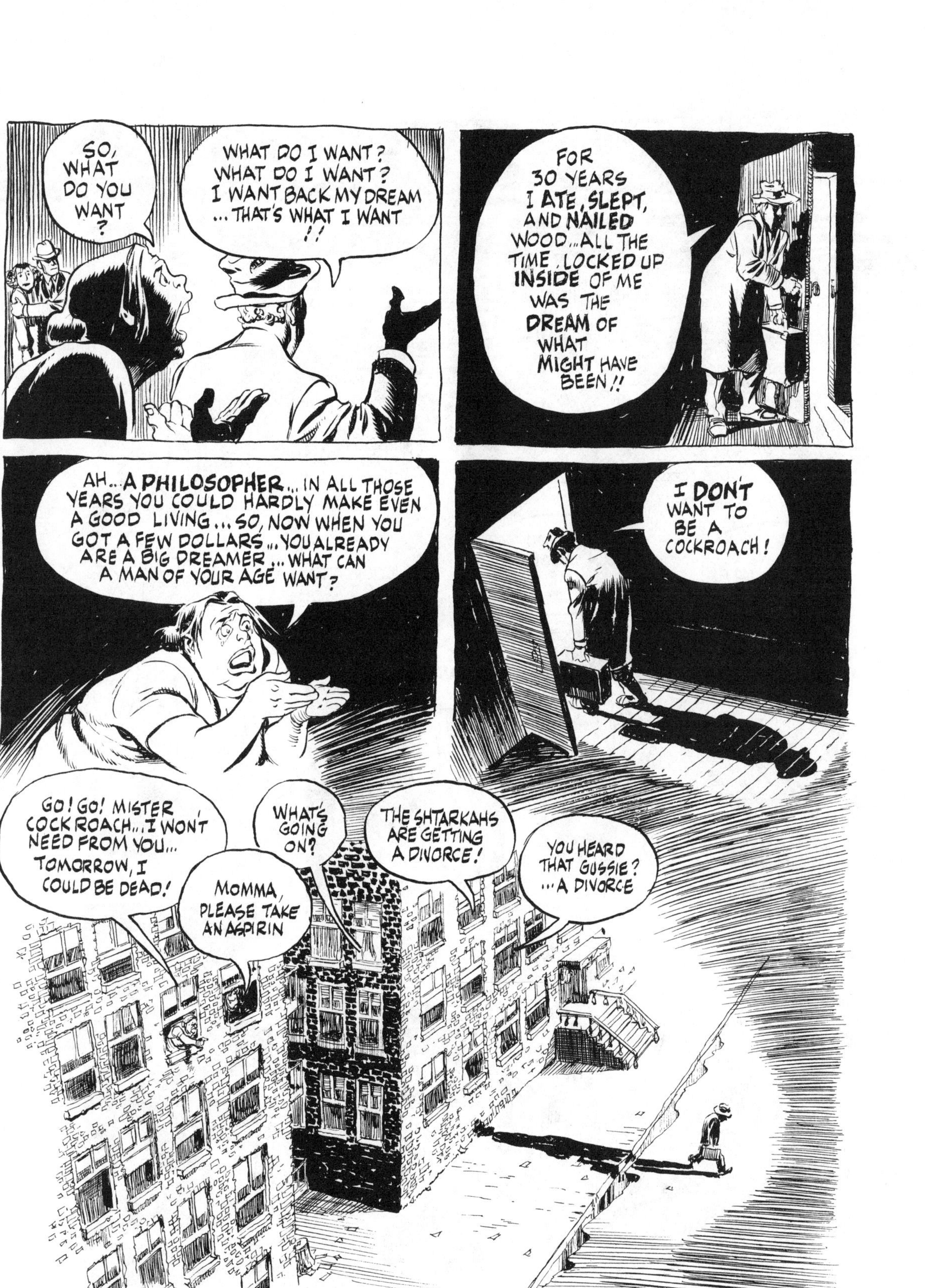
SO, WHAT DO YOU WANT ?
WHAT DO I WANT ? WHAT DO I WANT ? I WANT BACK MY DREAM ... THAT'S WHAT I WANT !!
FOR 30 YEARS I ATE, SLEPT, AND NAILED WOOD... ALL THE TIME, LOCKED UP INSIDE OF ME WAS THE DREAM OF WHAT MIGHT HAVE BEEN !!
AH... A PHILOSOPHER... IN ALL THOSE YEARS YOU COULD HARDLY MAKE EVEN A GOOD LIVING... SO, NOW WHEN YOU GOT A FEW DOLLARS... YOU ALREADY ARE A BIG DREAMER... WHAT CAN A MAN OF YOUR AGE WANT ?
I DON'T WANT TO BE A COCKROACH !
GO! GO! MISTER COCKROACH... I WON'T NEED FROM YOU... TOMORROW, I COULD BE DEAD!
MOMMA, PLEASE TAKE AN ASPIRIN
WHAT'S GOING ON?
THE SHTARKAHS ARE GETTING A DIVORCE !
YOU HEARD THAT GUSSIE ? ... A DIVORCE

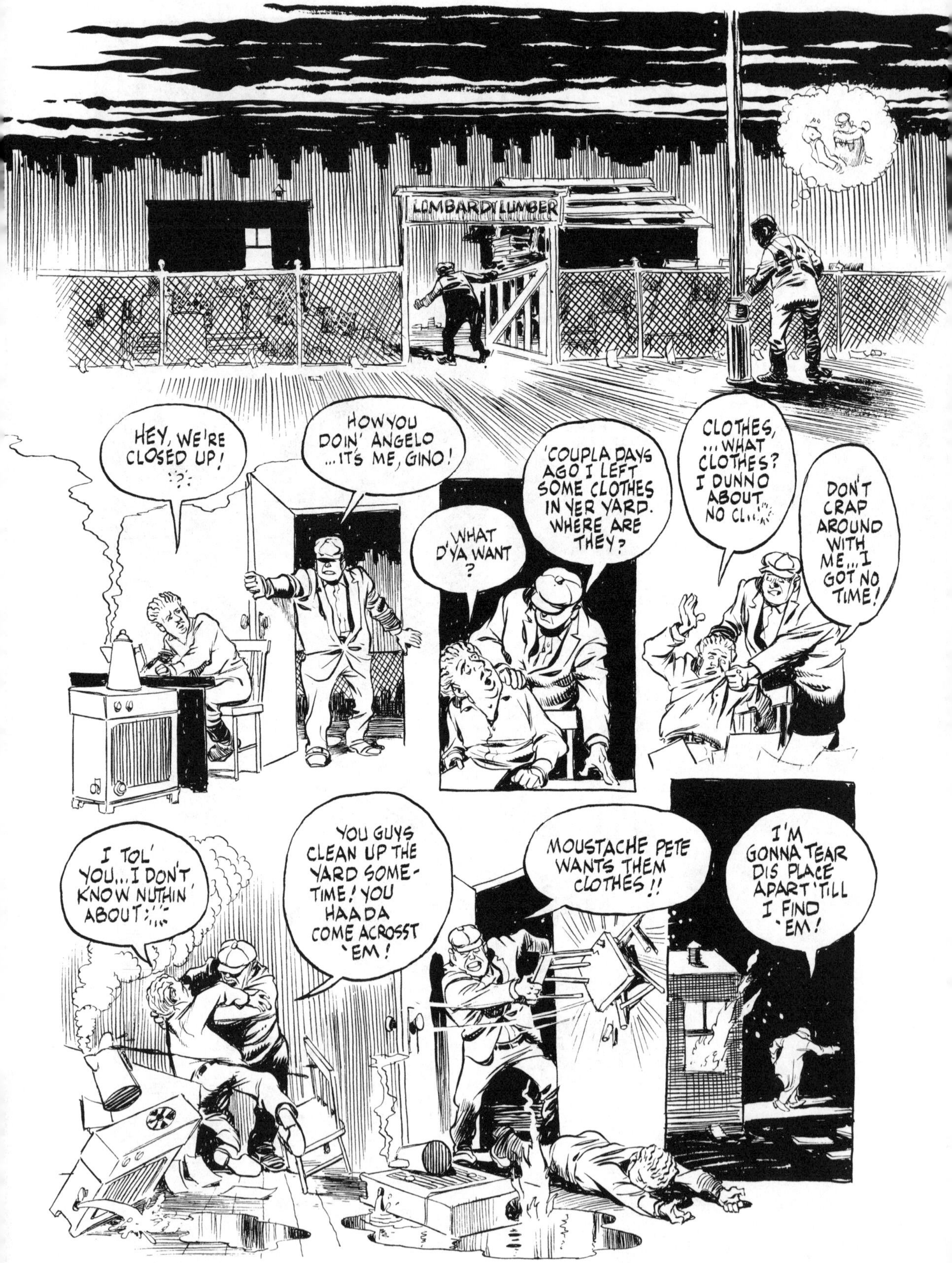
LOMBARDY LUMBER
HEY, WE'RE CLOSED UP!
HOW YOU DOIN' ANGELO ...IT'S ME, GINO!
WHAT D'YA WANT?
'COUPLA DAYS AGO I LEFT SOME CLOTHES IN YER YARD. WHERE ARE THEY?
CLOTHES, ...WHAT CLOTHES? I DUNNO ABOUT NO CL...
DON'T CRAP AROUND WITH ME...I GOT NO TIME!
I TOL' YOU...I DON'T KNOW NUTHIN' ABOUT
YOU GUYS CLEAN UP THE YARD SOME-TIME! YOU HAADA COME ACROSST 'EM!
MOUSTACHE PETE WANTS THEM CLOTHES!!
I'M GONNA TEAR DIS PLACE APART 'TILL I FIND 'EM!

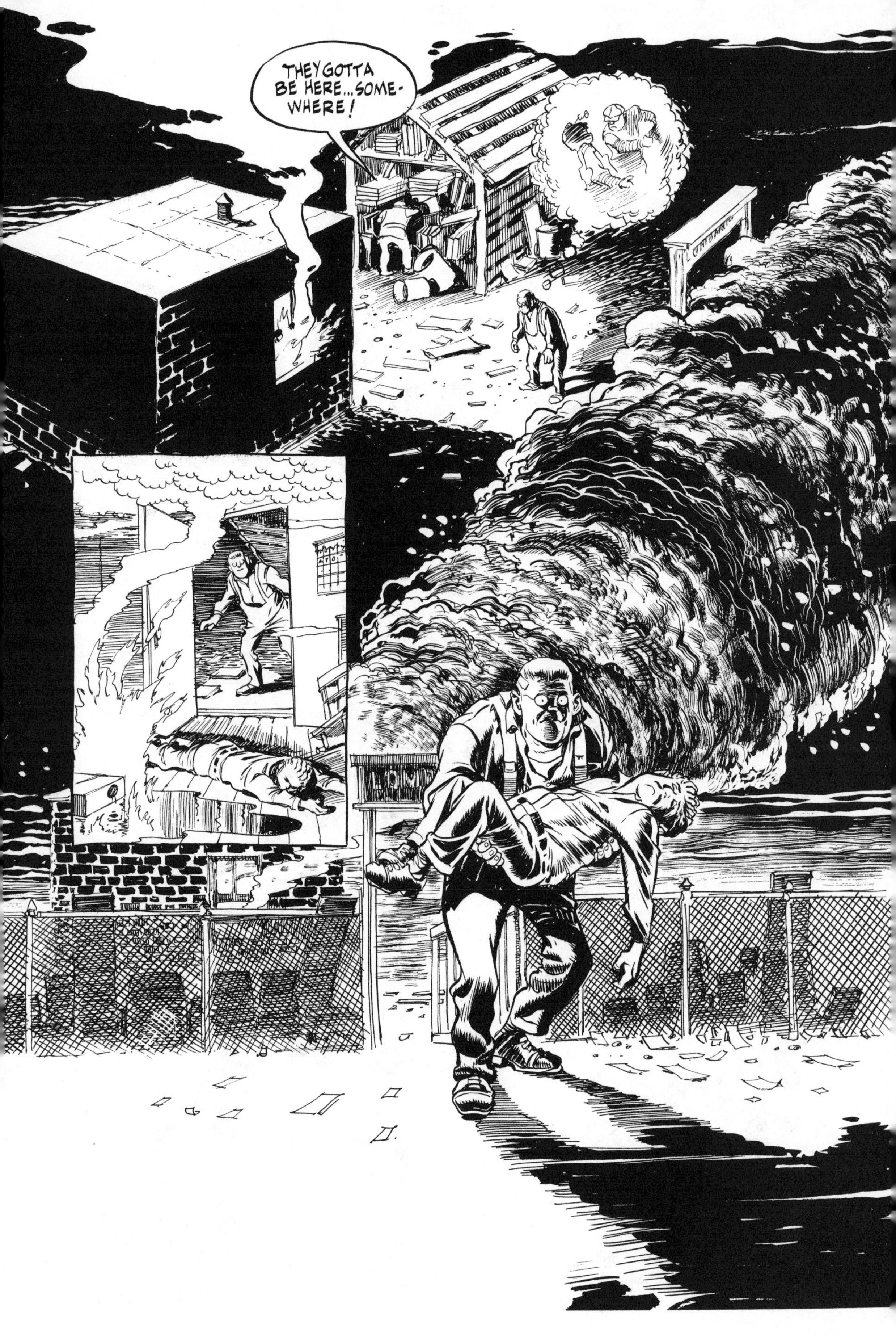
THEY GOTTA BE HERE... SOME-WHERE!

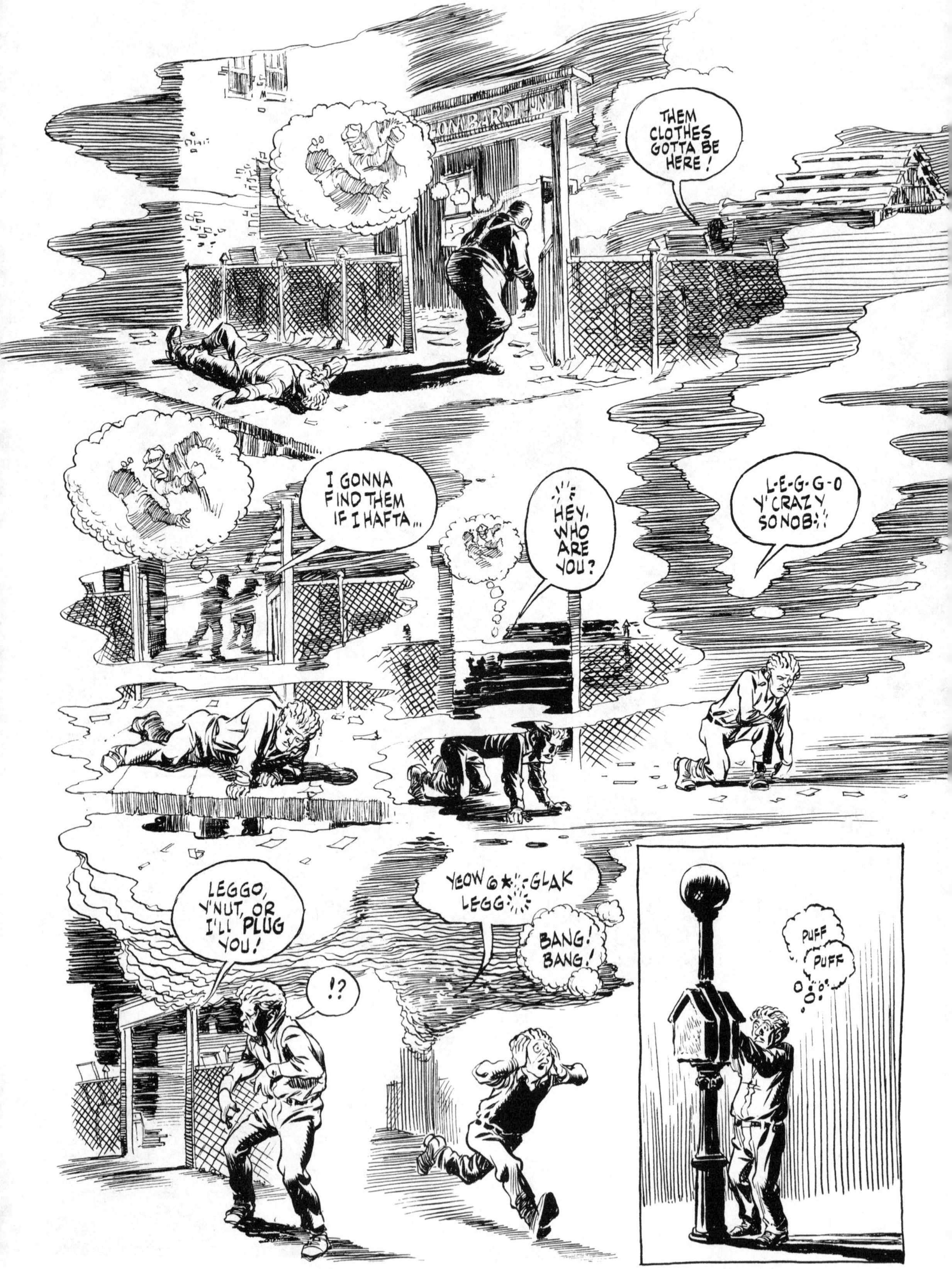
THEM CLOTHES GOTTA BE HERE!
I GONNA FIND THEM IF I HAFTA...
HEY, WHO ARE YOU?
L-E-G-G-O Y'CRAZY SONOB-
LEGGO, Y'NUT, OR I'LL PLUG YOU!
!?
YEOW -GLAK LEGG
BANG! BANG!
PUFF
PUFF

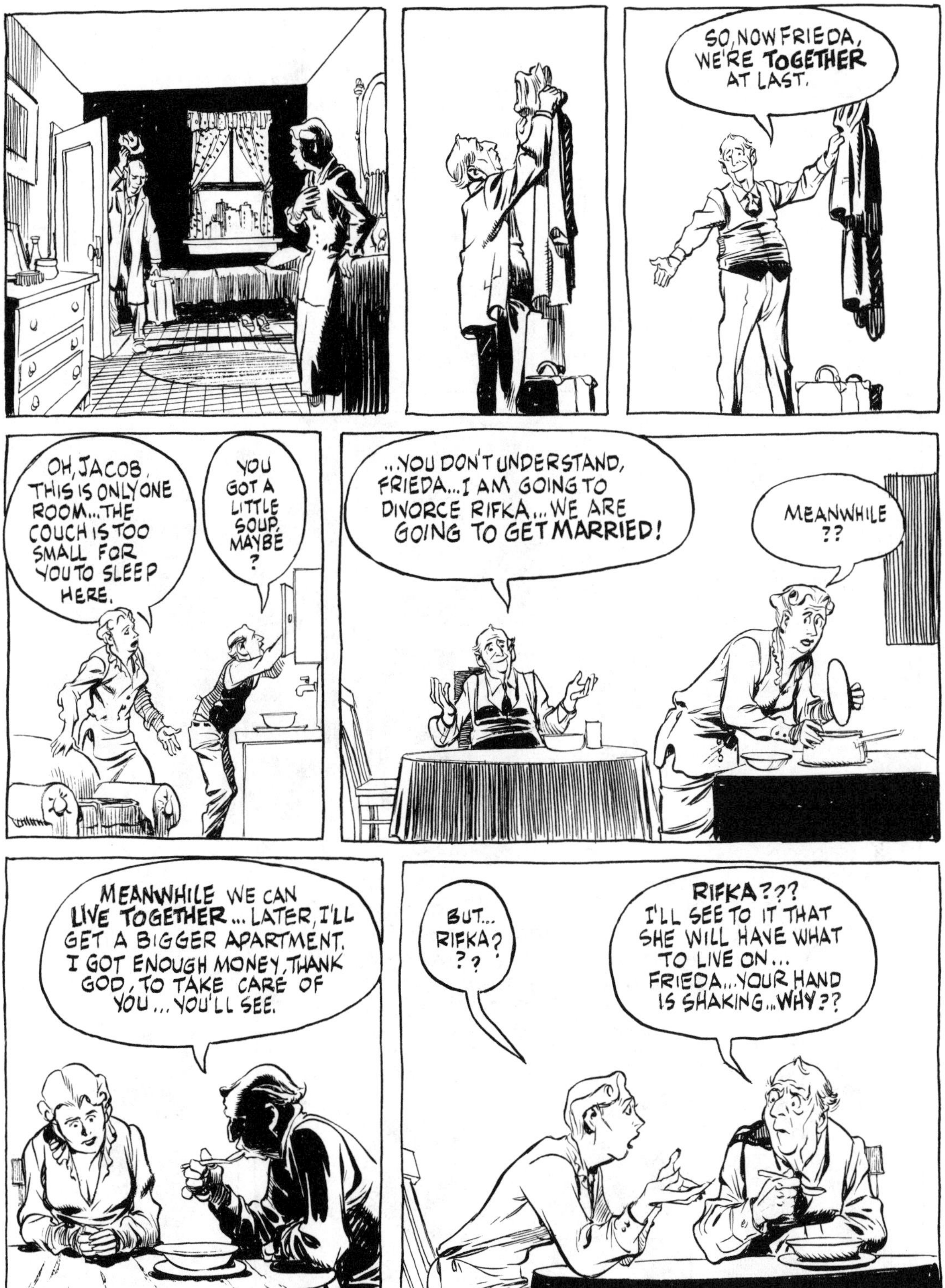
SO, NOW FRIEDA, WE'RE TOGETHER AT LAST.
OH, JACOB, THIS IS ONLY ONE ROOM... THE COUCH IS TOO SMALL FOR YOU TO SLEEP HERE.
YOU GOT A LITTLE SOUP, MAYBE ?
..YOU DON'T UNDERSTAND, FRIEDA...I AM GOING TO DIVORCE RIFKA... WE ARE GOING TO GET MARRIED!
MEANWHILE ??
MEANWHILE WE CAN LIVE TOGETHER... LATER, I'LL GET A BIGGER APARTMENT. I GOT ENOUGH MONEY, THANK GOD, TO TAKE CARE OF YOU... YOU'LL SEE.
BUT... RIFKA? ??
RIFKA??? I'LL SEE TO IT THAT SHE WILL HAVE WHAT TO LIVE ON... FRIEDA... YOUR HAND IS SHAKING... WHY??

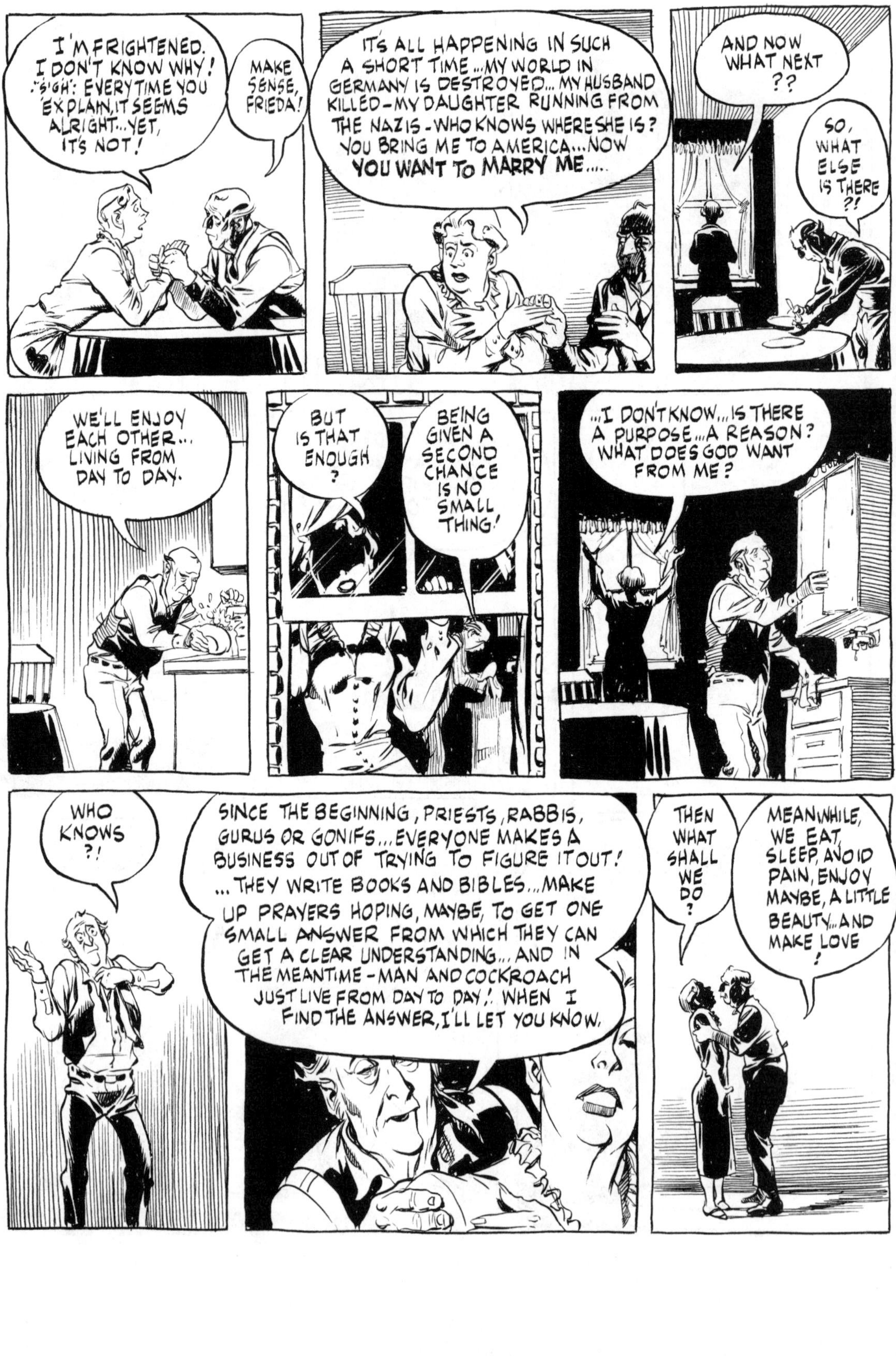
I'M FRIGHTENED. I DON'T KNOW WHY! :SIGH: EVERYTIME YOU EXPLAIN, IT SEEMS ALRIGHT...YET, IT'S NOT!
MAKE SENSE, FRIEDA!
IT'S ALL HAPPENING IN SUCH A SHORT TIME...MY WORLD IN GERMANY IS DESTROYED... MY HUSBAND KILLED-MY DAUGHTER RUNNING FROM THE NAZIS-WHO KNOWS WHERE SHE IS? YOU BRING ME TO AMERICA...NOW YOU WANT TO MARRY ME....
AND NOW WHAT NEXT ??
SO, WHAT ELSE IS THERE ?!
WE'LL ENJOY EACH OTHER... LIVING FROM DAY TO DAY.
BUT IS THAT ENOUGH ?
BEING GIVEN A SECOND CHANCE IS NO SMALL THING!
...I DON'T KNOW... IS THERE A PURPOSE...A REASON? WHAT DOES GOD WANT FROM ME?
WHO KNOWS ?!
SINCE THE BEGINNING, PRIESTS, RABBIS, GURUS OR GONIFS... EVERYONE MAKES A BUSINESS OUT OF TRYING TO FIGURE IT OUT! ... THEY WRITE BOOKS AND BIBLES...MAKE UP PRAYERS HOPING, MAYBE, TO GET ONE SMALL ANSWER FROM WHICH THEY CAN GET A CLEAR UNDERSTANDING... AND IN THE MEANTIME-MAN AND COCKROACH JUST LIVE FROM DAY TO DAY! WHEN I FIND THE ANSWER, I'LL LET YOU KNOW.
THEN WHAT SHALL WE DO ?
MEANWHILE, WE EAT, SLEEP, AVOID PAIN, ENJOY MAYBE, A LITTLE BEAUTY...AND MAKE LOVE !

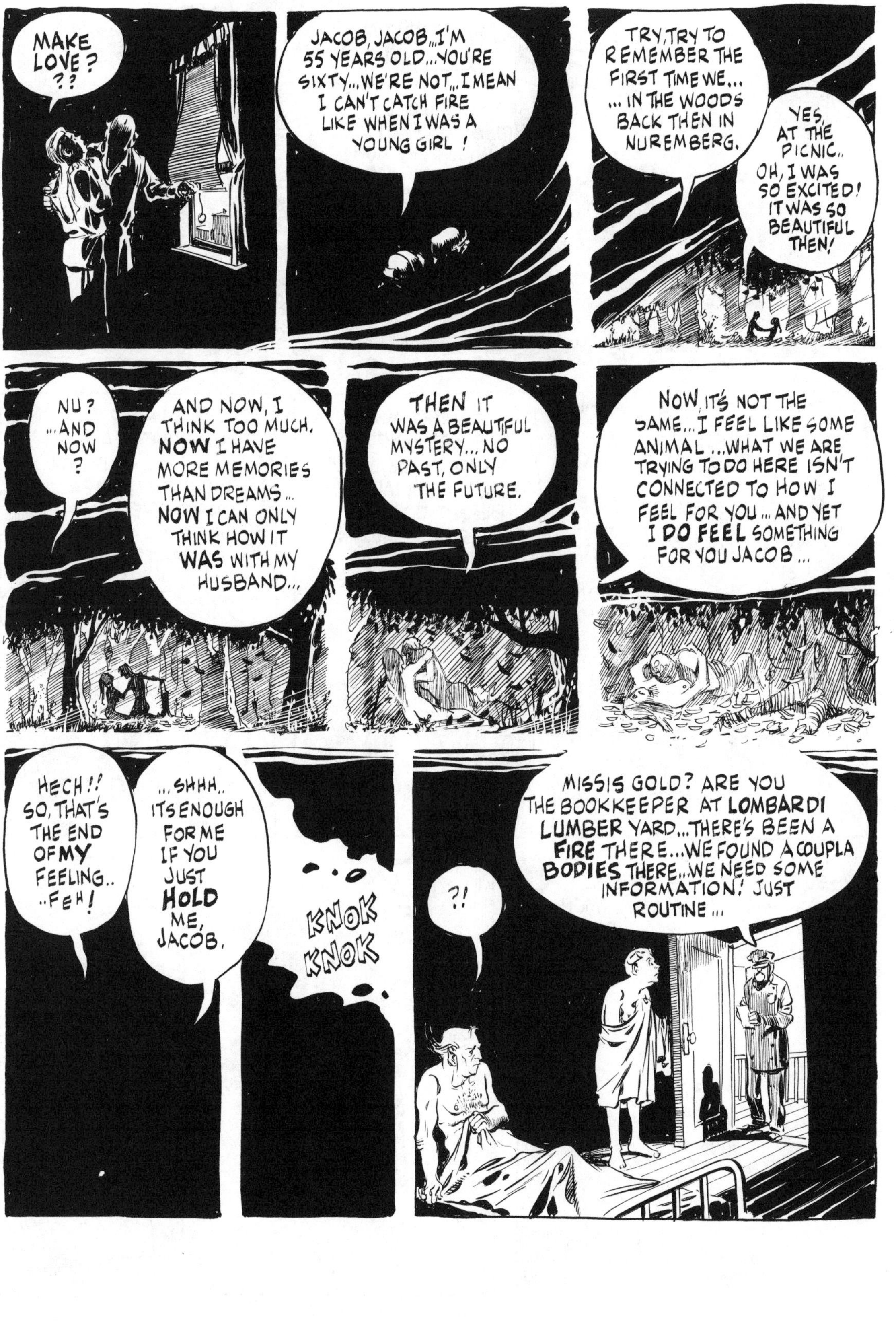
MAKE LOVE ? ??
JACOB, JACOB... I'M 55 YEARS OLD... YOU'RE SIXTY... WE'RE NOT... I MEAN I CAN'T CATCH FIRE LIKE WHEN I WAS A YOUNG GIRL !
TRY, TRY TO REMEMBER THE FIRST TIME WE... ... IN THE WOODS BACK THEN IN NUREMBERG.
YES, AT THE PICNIC.. OH, I WAS SO EXCITED! IT WAS SO BEAUTIFUL THEN!
NU ? ...AND NOW ?
AND NOW, I THINK TOO MUCH. **NOW** I HAVE MORE MEMORIES THAN DREAMS... **NOW** I CAN ONLY THINK HOW IT **WAS** WITH MY HUSBAND...
THEN IT WAS A BEAUTIFUL MYSTERY... NO PAST, ONLY THE FUTURE.
NOW, IT'S NOT THE SAME... I FEEL LIKE SOME ANIMAL ...WHAT WE ARE TRYING TO DO HERE ISN'T CONNECTED TO HOW I FEEL FOR YOU ... AND YET **I DO FEEL** SOMETHING FOR YOU JACOB ...
HECH !! SO, THAT'S THE END OF **MY** FEELING.. ..FEH !
...SHHH.. ITS ENOUGH FOR ME IF YOU JUST **HOLD** ME, JACOB.
KNOK KNOK
?!
MISSIS GOLD? ARE YOU THE BOOKKEEPER AT **LOMBARDI LUMBER** YARD... THERE'S BEEN A **FIRE** THERE... WE FOUND A COUPLA **BODIES** THERE... WE NEED SOME INFORMATION! JUST ROUTINE ...

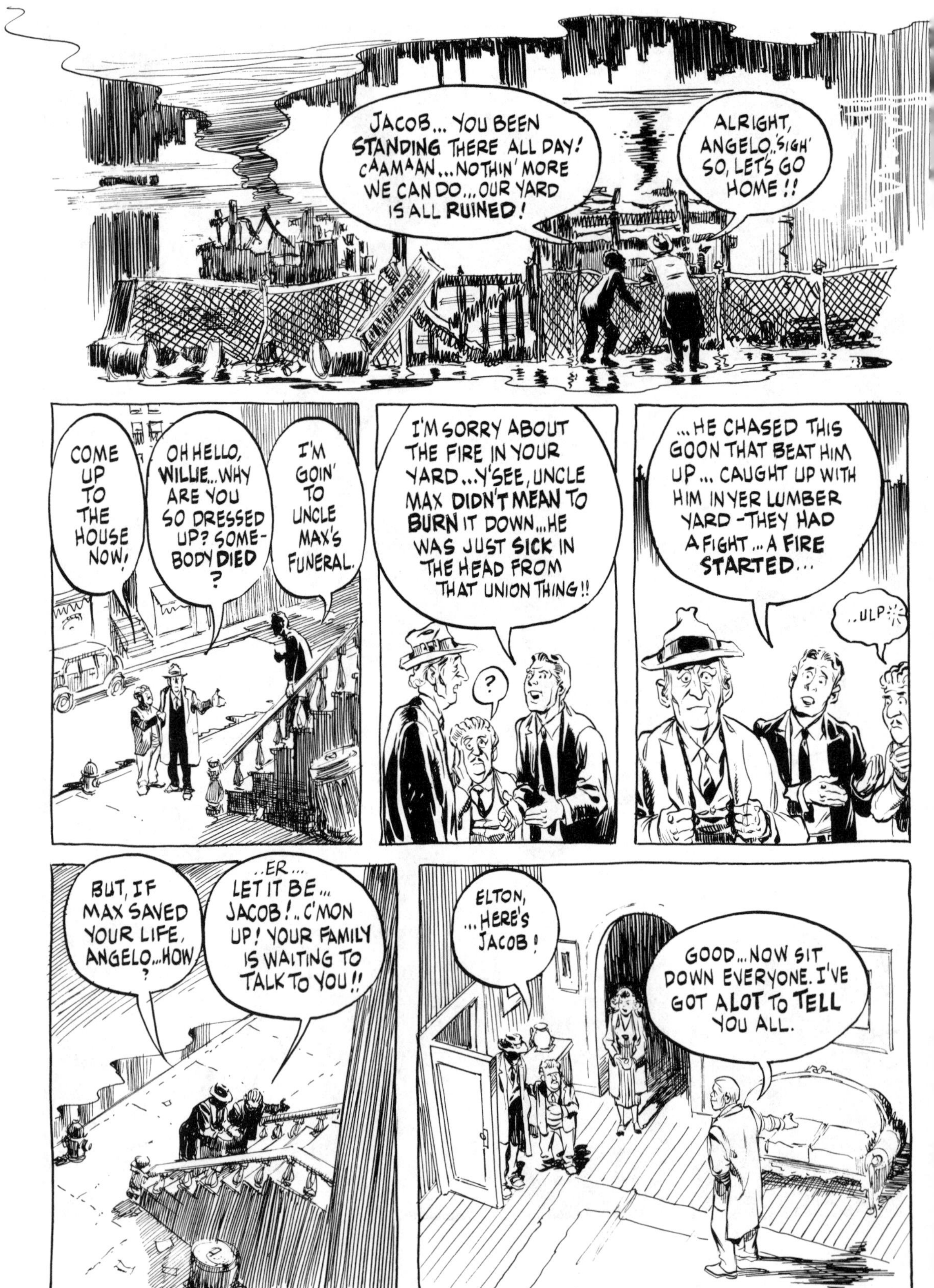

JACOB... YOU BEEN STANDING THERE ALL DAY! CAAMAAN... NOTHIN' MORE WE CAN DO... OUR YARD IS ALL RUINED!
ALRIGHT, ANGELO.. 'SIGH' SO, LET'S GO HOME!!
COME UP TO THE HOUSE NOW!
OH HELLO, WILLIE... WHY ARE YOU SO DRESSED UP? SOMEBODY DIED?
I'M GOIN' TO UNCLE MAX'S FUNERAL.
I'M SORRY ABOUT THE FIRE IN YOUR YARD... Y'SEE, UNCLE MAX DIDN'T MEAN TO BURN IT DOWN... HE WAS JUST SICK IN THE HEAD FROM THAT UNION THING!!
?
...HE CHASED THIS GOON THAT BEAT HIM UP... CAUGHT UP WITH HIM IN YER LUMBER YARD - THEY HAD A FIGHT... A FIRE STARTED...
..ULP
BUT, IF MAX SAVED YOUR LIFE, ANGELO... HOW?
..ER... LET IT BE... JACOB!.. C'MON UP! YOUR FAMILY IS WAITING TO TALK TO YOU!!
ELTON, ...HERE'S JACOB!
GOOD... NOW SIT DOWN EVERYONE. I'VE GOT ALOT TO TELL YOU ALL.

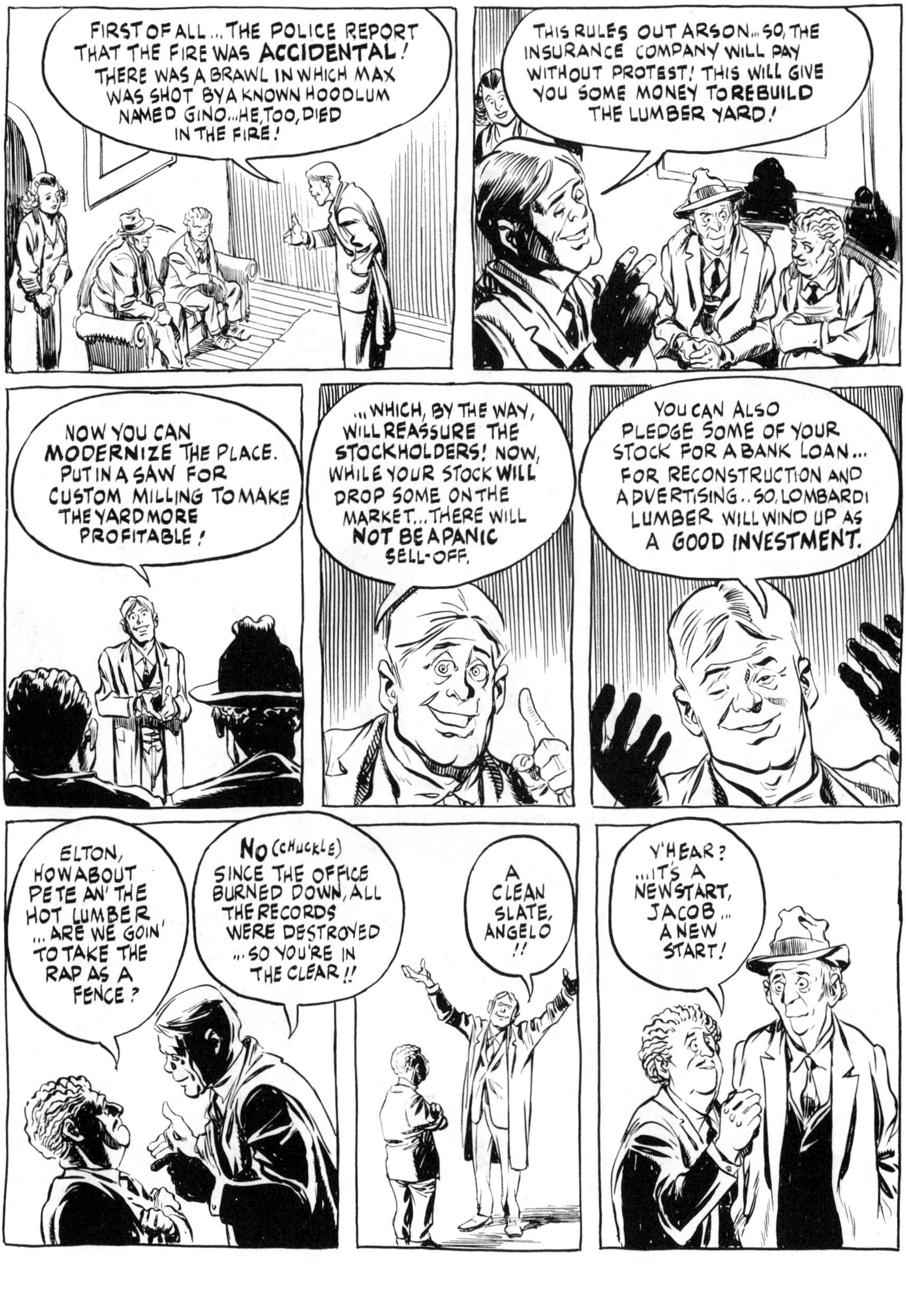
FIRST OF ALL... THE POLICE REPORT THAT THE FIRE WAS ACCIDENTAL! THERE WAS A BRAWL IN WHICH MAX WAS SHOT BY A KNOWN HOODLUM NAMED GINO...HE, TOO, DIED IN THE FIRE!
THIS RULES OUT ARSON... SO, THE INSURANCE COMPANY WILL PAY WITHOUT PROTEST! THIS WILL GIVE YOU SOME MONEY TO REBUILD THE LUMBER YARD!
NOW YOU CAN MODERNIZE THE PLACE. PUT IN A SAW FOR CUSTOM MILLING TO MAKE THE YARD MORE PROFITABLE!
...WHICH, BY THE WAY, WILL REASSURE THE STOCKHOLDERS! NOW, WHILE YOUR STOCK WILL DROP SOME ON THE MARKET... THERE WILL NOT BE A PANIC SELL-OFF.
YOU CAN ALSO PLEDGE SOME OF YOUR STOCK FOR A BANK LOAN... FOR RECONSTRUCTION AND ADVERTISING.. SO, LOMBARDI LUMBER WILL WIND UP AS A GOOD INVESTMENT.
ELTON, HOW ABOUT PETE AN' THE HOT LUMBER ...ARE WE GOIN' TO TAKE THE RAP AS A FENCE?
NO (CHUCKLE) SINCE THE OFFICE BURNED DOWN, ALL THE RECORDS WERE DESTROYED ...SO YOU'RE IN THE CLEAR!!
A CLEAN SLATE, ANGELO!!
Y'HEAR? ...IT'S A NEW START, JACOB... A NEW START!

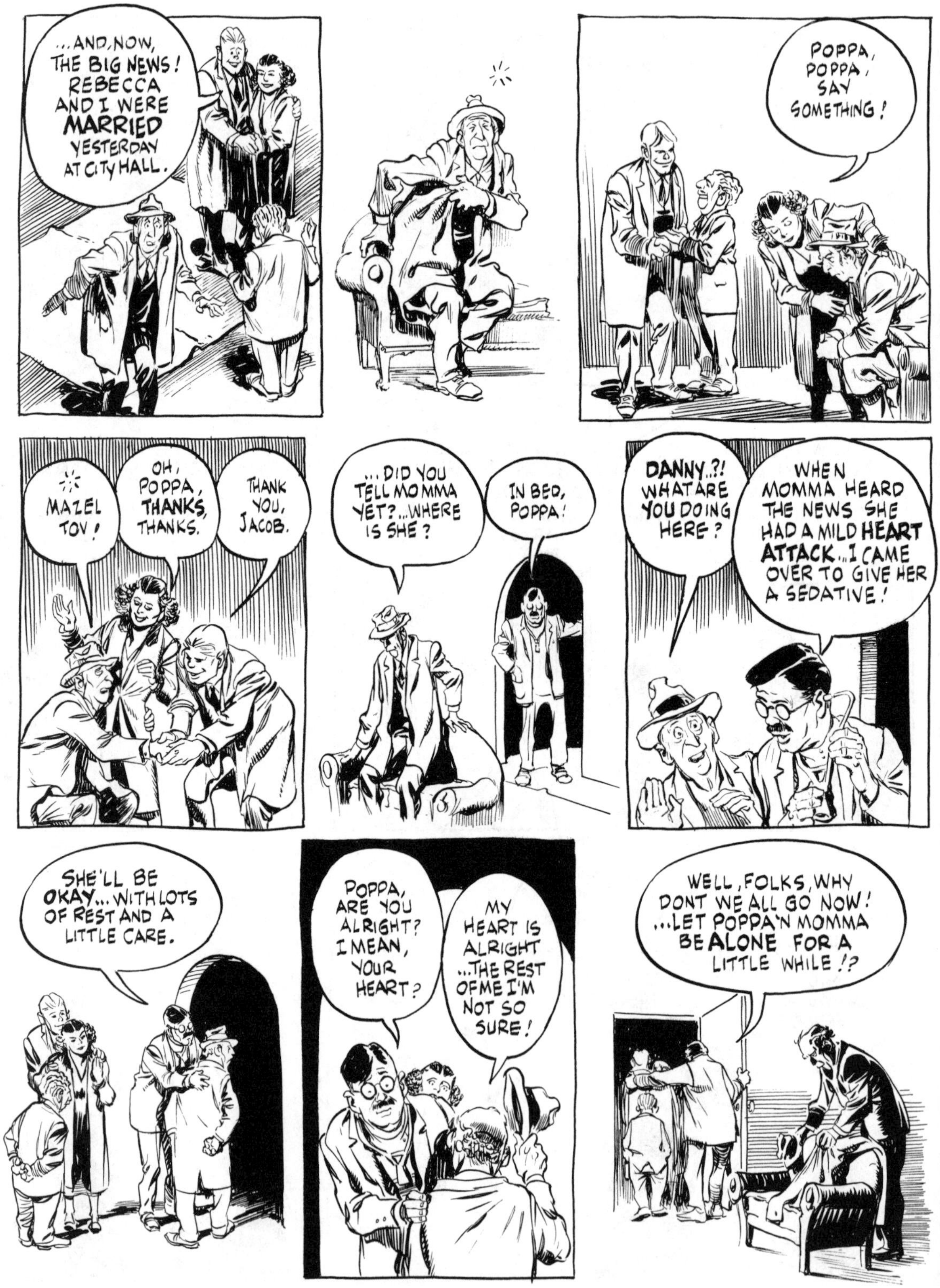
...AND, NOW, THE BIG NEWS! REBECCA AND I WERE MARRIED YESTERDAY AT CITY HALL.
POPPA, POPPA, SAY SOMETHING!
MAZEL TOV!
OH, POPPA, THANKS, THANKS.
THANK YOU, JACOB.
...DID YOU TELL MOMMA YET?...WHERE IS SHE?
IN BED, POPPA!
DANNY..?! WHAT ARE YOU DOING HERE?
WHEN MOMMA HEARD THE NEWS SHE HAD A MILD HEART ATTACK...I CAME OVER TO GIVE HER A SEDATIVE!
SHE'LL BE OKAY... WITH LOTS OF REST AND A LITTLE CARE.
POPPA, ARE YOU ALRIGHT? I MEAN, YOUR HEART?
MY HEART IS ALRIGHT ...THE REST OF ME I'M NOT SO SURE!
WELL, FOLKS, WHY DONT WE ALL GO NOW! ...LET POPPA 'N MOMMA BE ALONE FOR A LITTLE WHILE!?

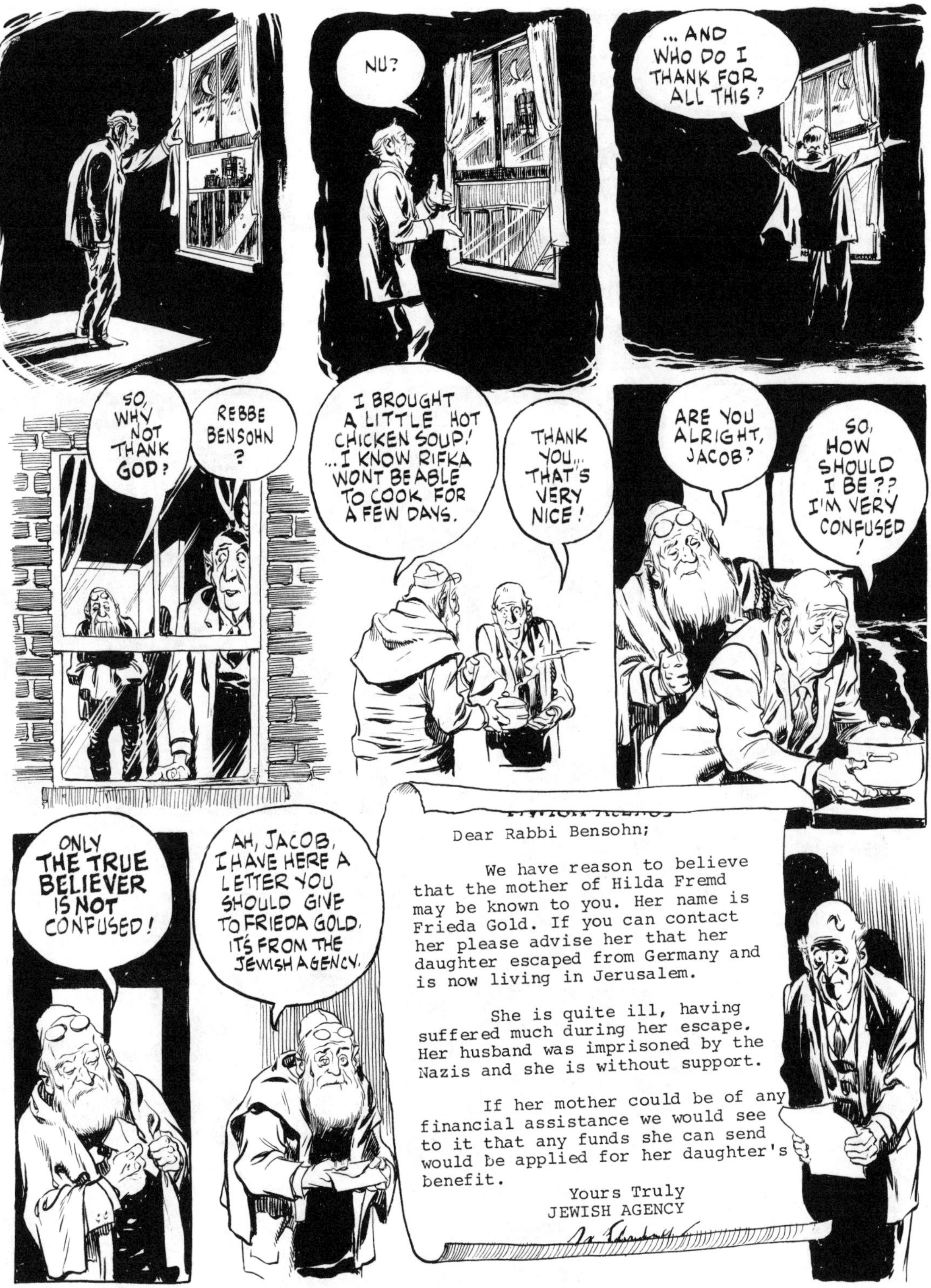
NU?
... AND WHO DO I THANK FOR ALL THIS?
SO, WHY NOT THANK GOD?
REBBE BENSOHN?
I BROUGHT A LITTLE HOT CHICKEN SOUP! ... I KNOW RIFKA WONT BE ABLE TO COOK FOR A FEW DAYS.
THANK YOU... THAT'S VERY NICE!
ARE YOU ALRIGHT, JACOB?
SO, HOW SHOULD I BE?? I'M VERY CONFUSED!
ONLY THE TRUE BELIEVER IS NOT CONFUSED!
AH, JACOB, I HAVE HERE A LETTER YOU SHOULD GIVE TO FRIEDA GOLD. IT'S FROM THE JEWISH AGENCY.
Dear Rabbi Bensohn;
We have reason to believe that the mother of Hilda Fremd may be known to you. Her name is Frieda Gold. If you can contact her please advise her that her daughter escaped from Germany and is now living in Jerusalem.
She is quite ill, having suffered much during her escape. Her husband was imprisoned by the Nazis and she is without support.
If her mother could be of any financial assistance we would see to it that any funds she can send would be applied for her daughter's benefit.
Yours Truly
JEWISH AGENCY

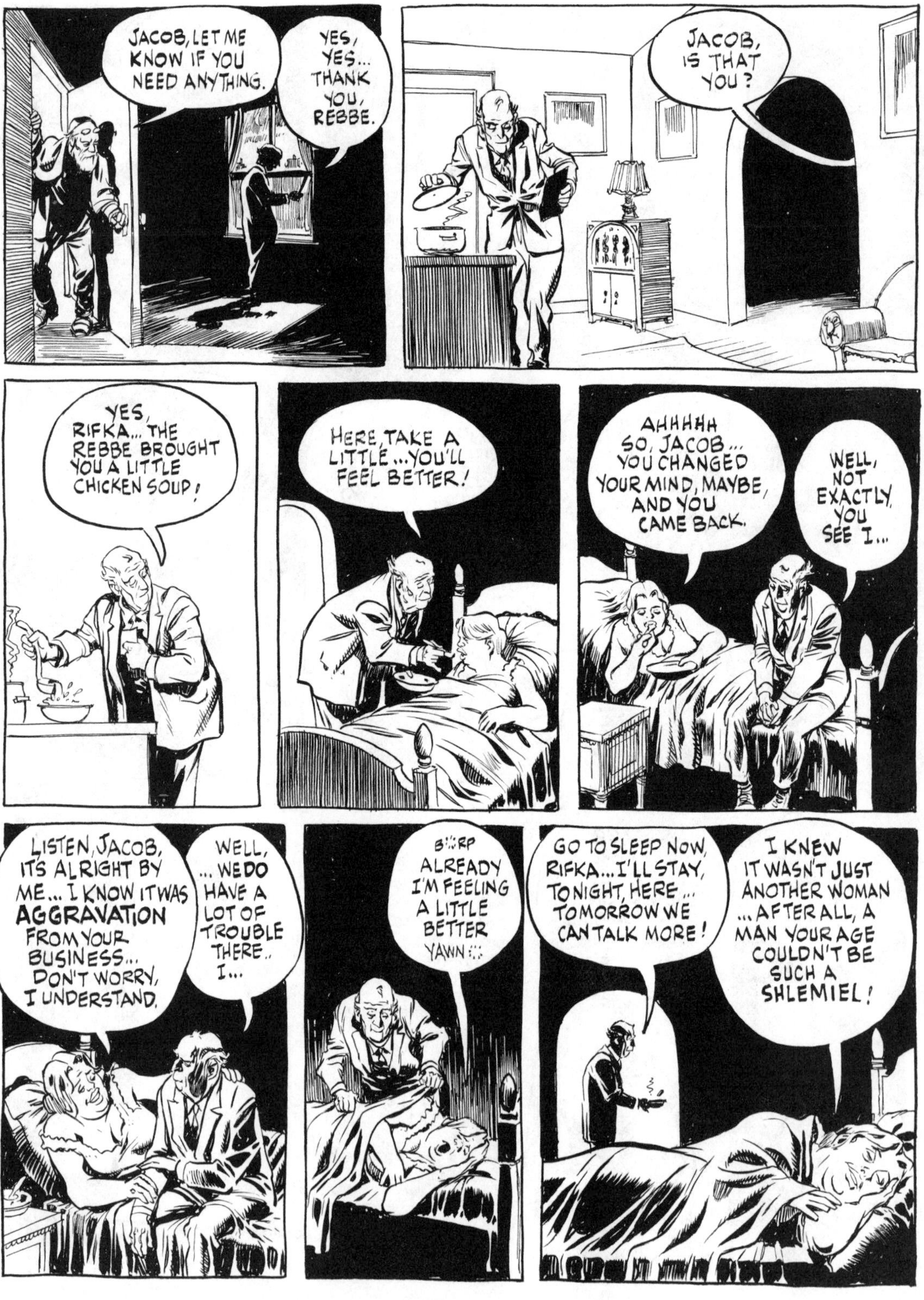
JACOB, LET ME KNOW IF YOU NEED ANYTHING.
YES, YES... THANK YOU, REBBE.
JACOB, IS THAT YOU?
YES, RIFKA... THE REBBE BROUGHT YOU A LITTLE CHICKEN SOUP!
HERE, TAKE A LITTLE... YOU'LL FEEL BETTER!
AHHHHH SO, JACOB... YOU CHANGED YOUR MIND, MAYBE, AND YOU CAME BACK.
WELL, NOT EXACTLY. YOU SEE I...
LISTEN, JACOB, IT'S ALRIGHT BY ME... I KNOW IT WAS AGGRAVATION FROM YOUR BUSINESS... DON'T WORRY, I UNDERSTAND.
WELL, ... WE DO HAVE A LOT OF TROUBLE THERE.. I...
ALREADY I'M FEELING A LITTLE BETTER
YAWN
GO TO SLEEP NOW, RIFKA... I'LL STAY, TONIGHT, HERE... TOMORROW WE CAN TALK MORE!
I KNEW IT WASN'T JUST ANOTHER WOMAN ...AFTER ALL, A MAN YOUR AGE COULDN'T BE SUCH A SHLEMIEL!

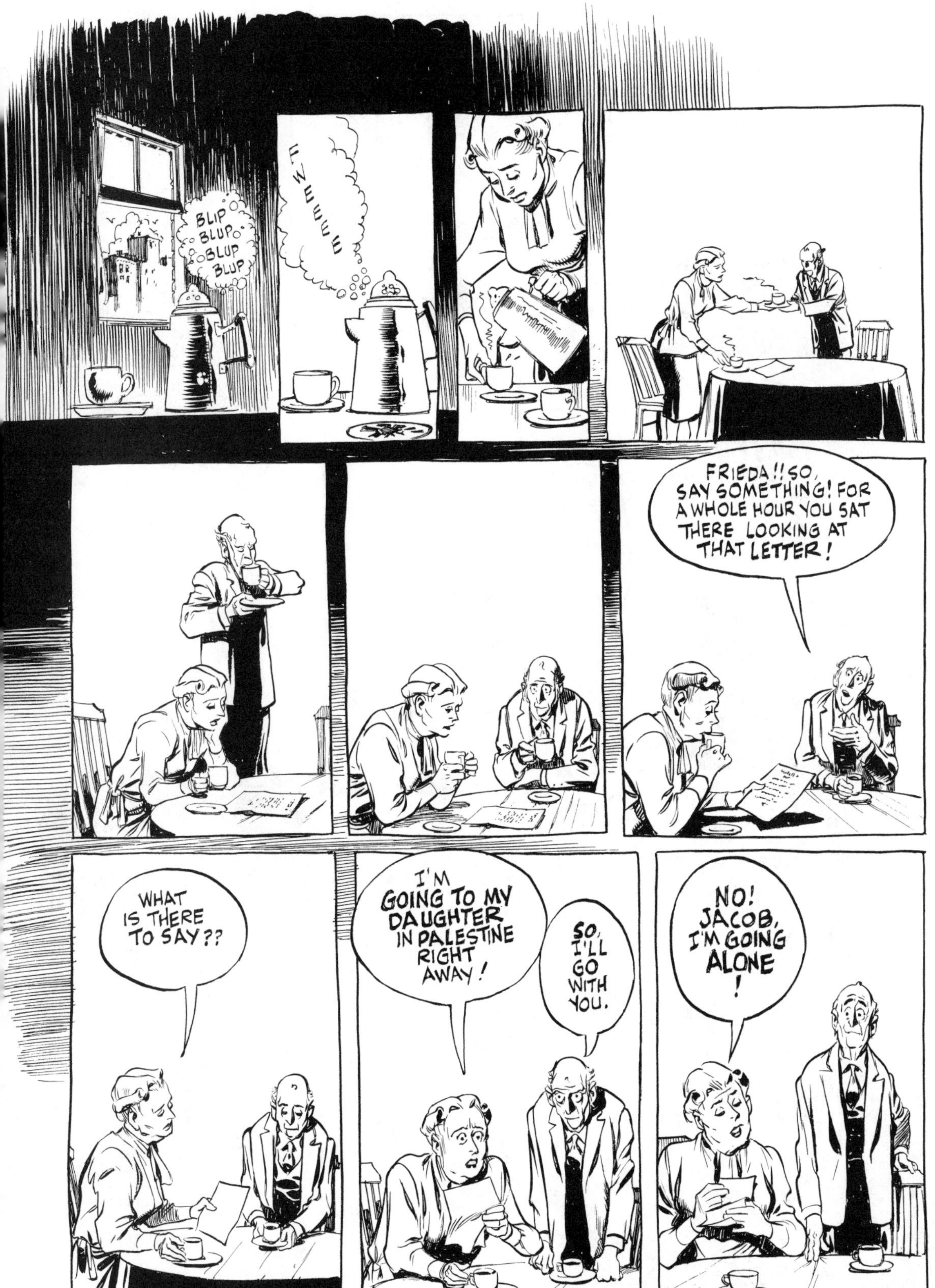
BLIP
BLUP
BLUP
BLUP
FWEEEE
FRIEDA!! SO, SAY SOMETHING! FOR A WHOLE HOUR YOU SAT THERE LOOKING AT THAT LETTER!
WHAT IS THERE TO SAY??
I'M GOING TO MY DAUGHTER IN PALESTINE RIGHT AWAY!
SO, I'LL GO WITH YOU.
NO! JACOB, I'M GOING ALONE!

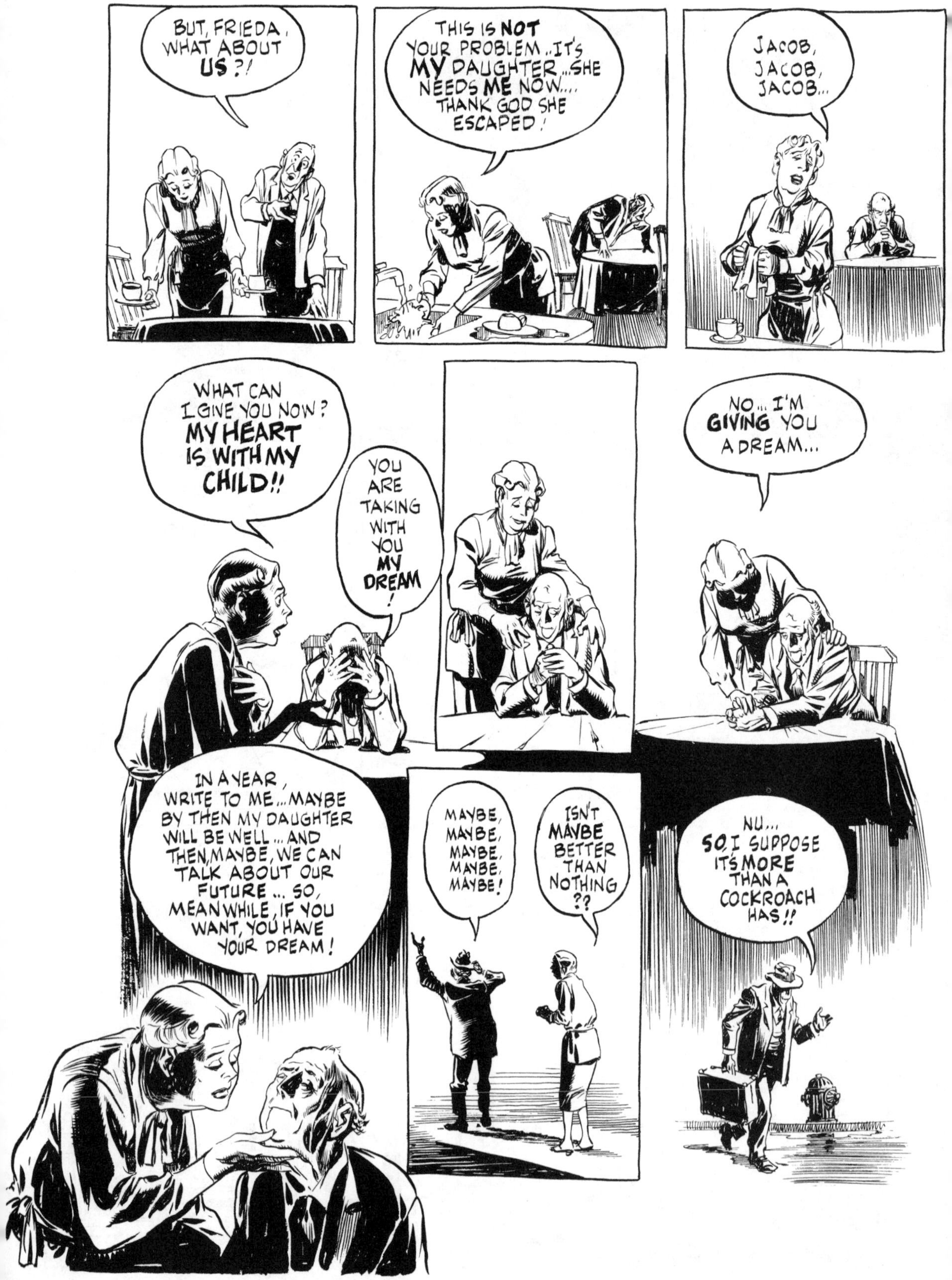

BUT, FRIEDA, WHAT ABOUT US ?!
THIS IS NOT YOUR PROBLEM ..IT'S MY DAUGHTER...SHE NEEDS ME NOW.... THANK GOD SHE ESCAPED !
JACOB, JACOB, JACOB...
WHAT CAN I GIVE YOU NOW ? MY HEART IS WITH MY CHILD!!
YOU ARE TAKING WITH YOU MY DREAM !
NO... I'M GIVING YOU A DREAM...
IN A YEAR, WRITE TO ME...MAYBE BY THEN MY DAUGHTER WILL BE WELL ... AND THEN, MAYBE, WE CAN TALK ABOUT OUR FUTURE ... SO, MEANWHILE, IF YOU WANT, YOU HAVE YOUR DREAM !
MAYBE, MAYBE, MAYBE, MAYBE, MAYBE!
ISN'T MAYBE BETTER THAN NOTHING ??
NU... SO, I SUPPOSE IT'S MORE THAN A COCKROACH HAS !!

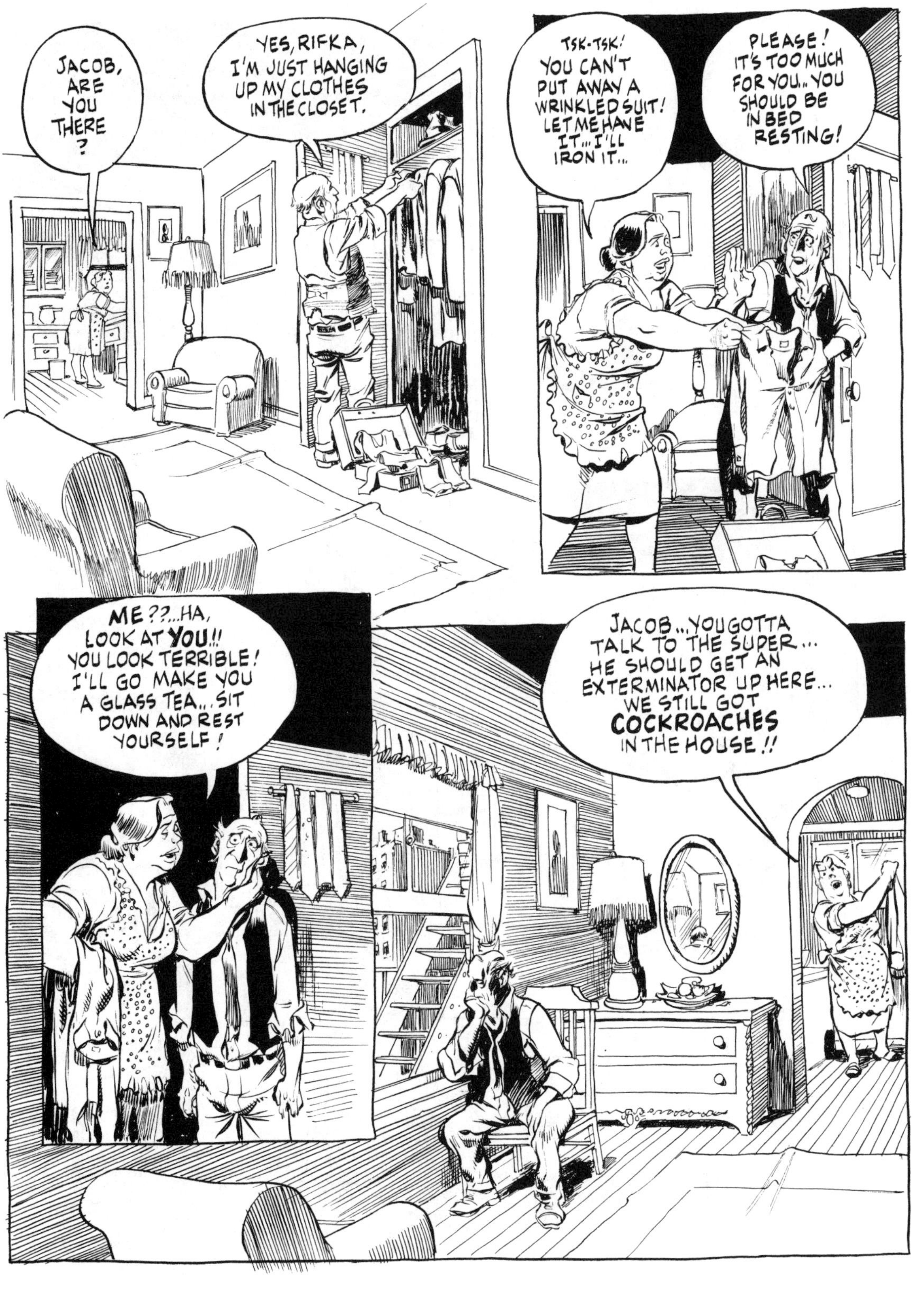
JACOB, ARE YOU THERE ?
YES, RIFKA, I'M JUST HANGING UP MY CLOTHES IN THE CLOSET.
TSK-TSK! YOU CAN'T PUT AWAY A WRINKLED SUIT! LET ME HAVE IT... I'LL IRON IT...
PLEASE! IT'S TOO MUCH FOR YOU.. YOU SHOULD BE IN BED RESTING!
ME??...HA, LOOK AT YOU!! YOU LOOK TERRIBLE! I'LL GO MAKE YOU A GLASS TEA... SIT DOWN AND REST YOURSELF!
JACOB...YOU GOTTA TALK TO THE SUPER... HE SHOULD GET AN EXTERMINATOR UP HERE... WE STILL GOT COCKROACHES IN THE HOUSE!!

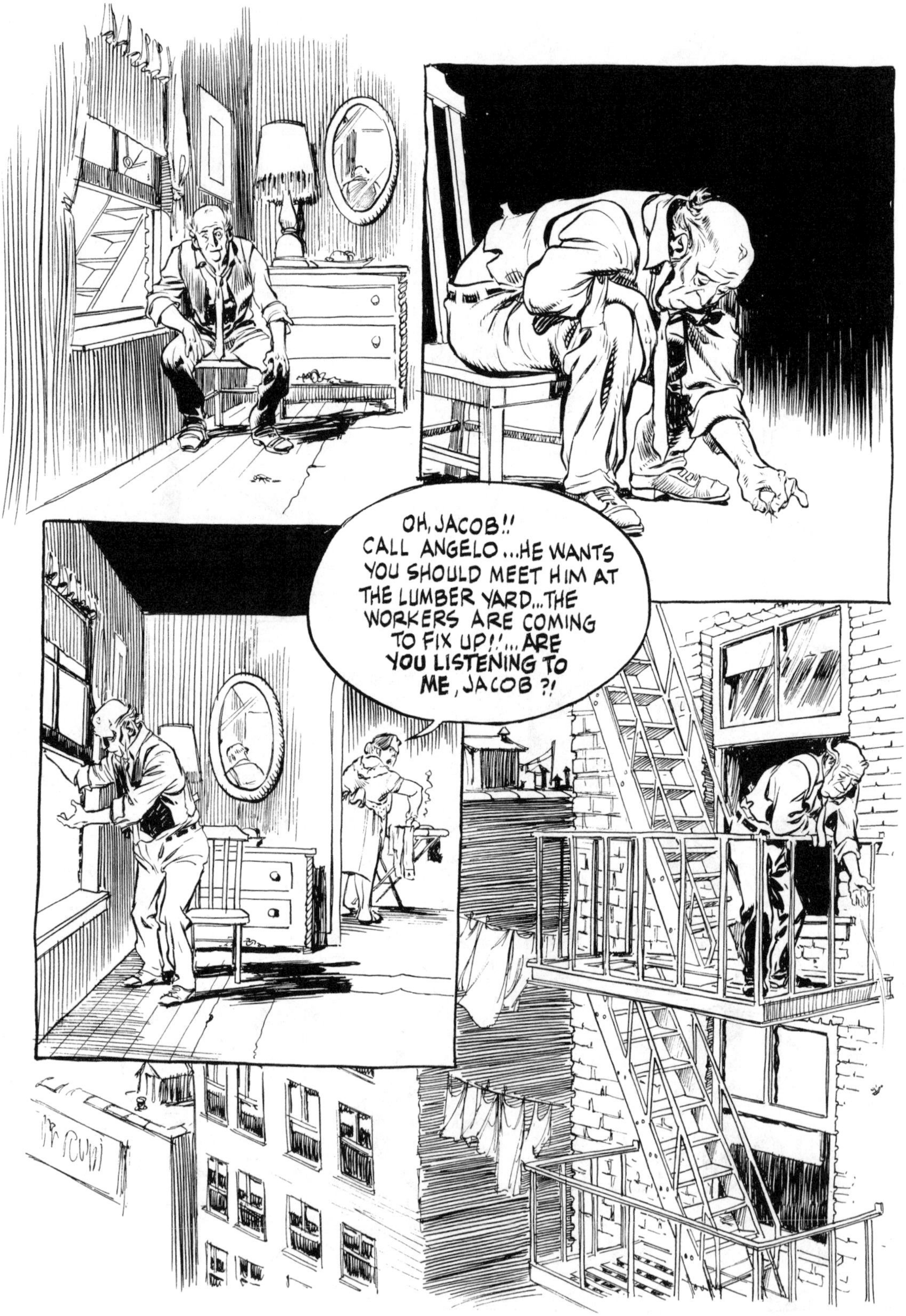
OH, JACOB!! CALL ANGELO...HE WANTS YOU SHOULD MEET HIM AT THE LUMBER YARD...THE WORKERS ARE COMING TO FIX UP!...ARE YOU LISTENING TO ME, JACOB ?!

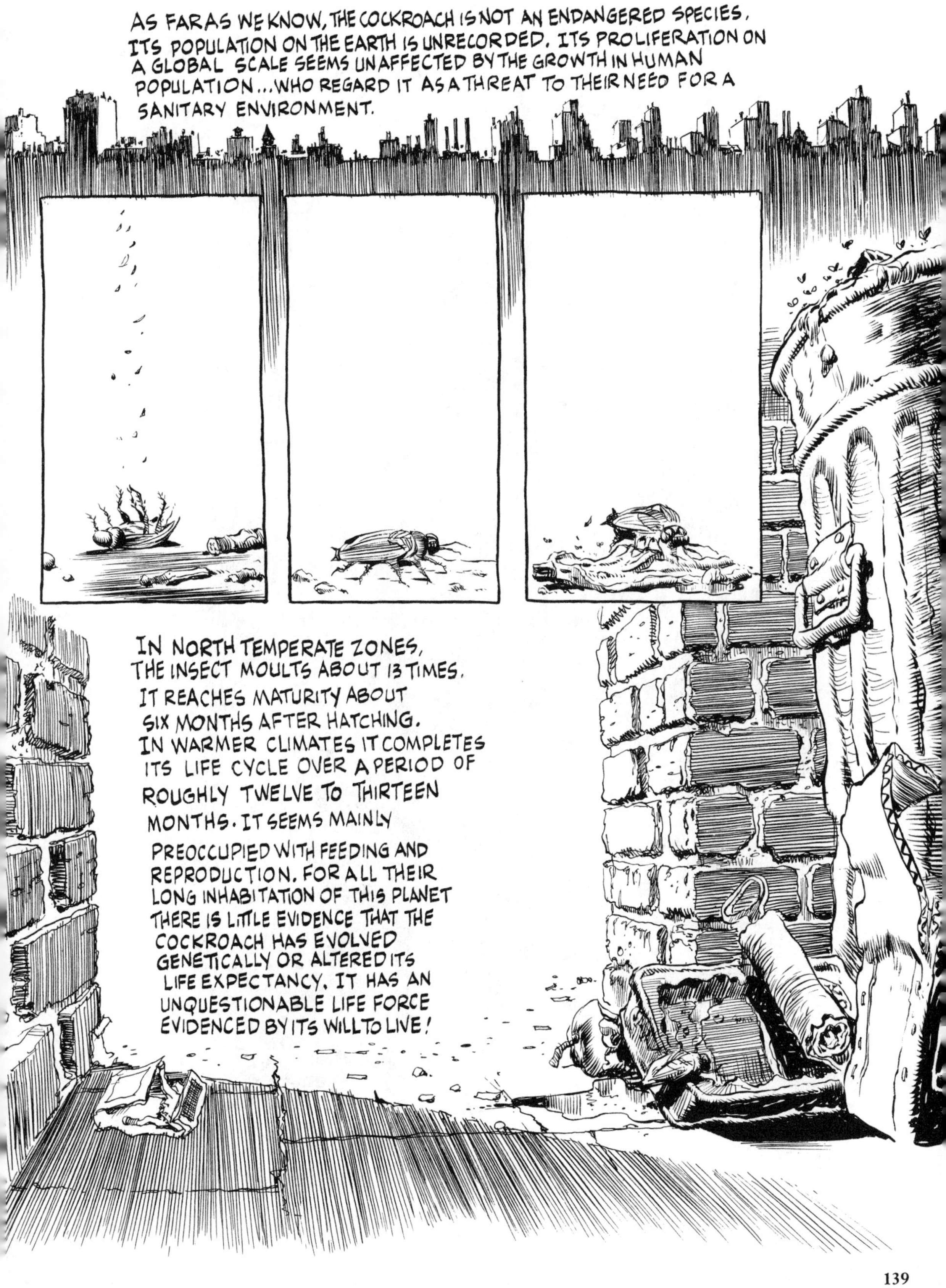
AS FARAS WE KNOW, THE COCKROACH IS NOT AN ENDANGERED SPECIES. ITS POPULATION ON THE EARTH IS UNRECORDED. ITS PROLIFERATION ON A GLOBAL SCALE SEEMS UNAFFECTED BY THE GROWTH IN HUMAN POPULATION...WHO REGARD IT AS A THREAT TO THEIR NEED FOR A SANITARY ENVIRONMENT.
IN NORTH TEMPERATE ZONES, THE INSECT MOULTS ABOUT 13 TIMES. IT REACHES MATURITY ABOUT SIX MONTHS AFTER HATCHING. IN WARMER CLIMATES IT COMPLETES ITS LIFE CYCLE OVER A PERIOD OF ROUGHLY TWELVE TO THIRTEEN MONTHS. IT SEEMS MAINLY PREOCCUPIED WITH FEEDING AND REPRODUCTION. FOR ALL THEIR LONG INHABITATION OF THIS PLANET THERE IS LITTLE EVIDENCE THAT THE COCKROACH HAS EVOLVED GENETICALLY OR ALTERED ITS LIFE EXPECTANCY. IT HAS AN UNQUESTIONABLE LIFE FORCE EVIDENCED BY ITS WILL TO LIVE!

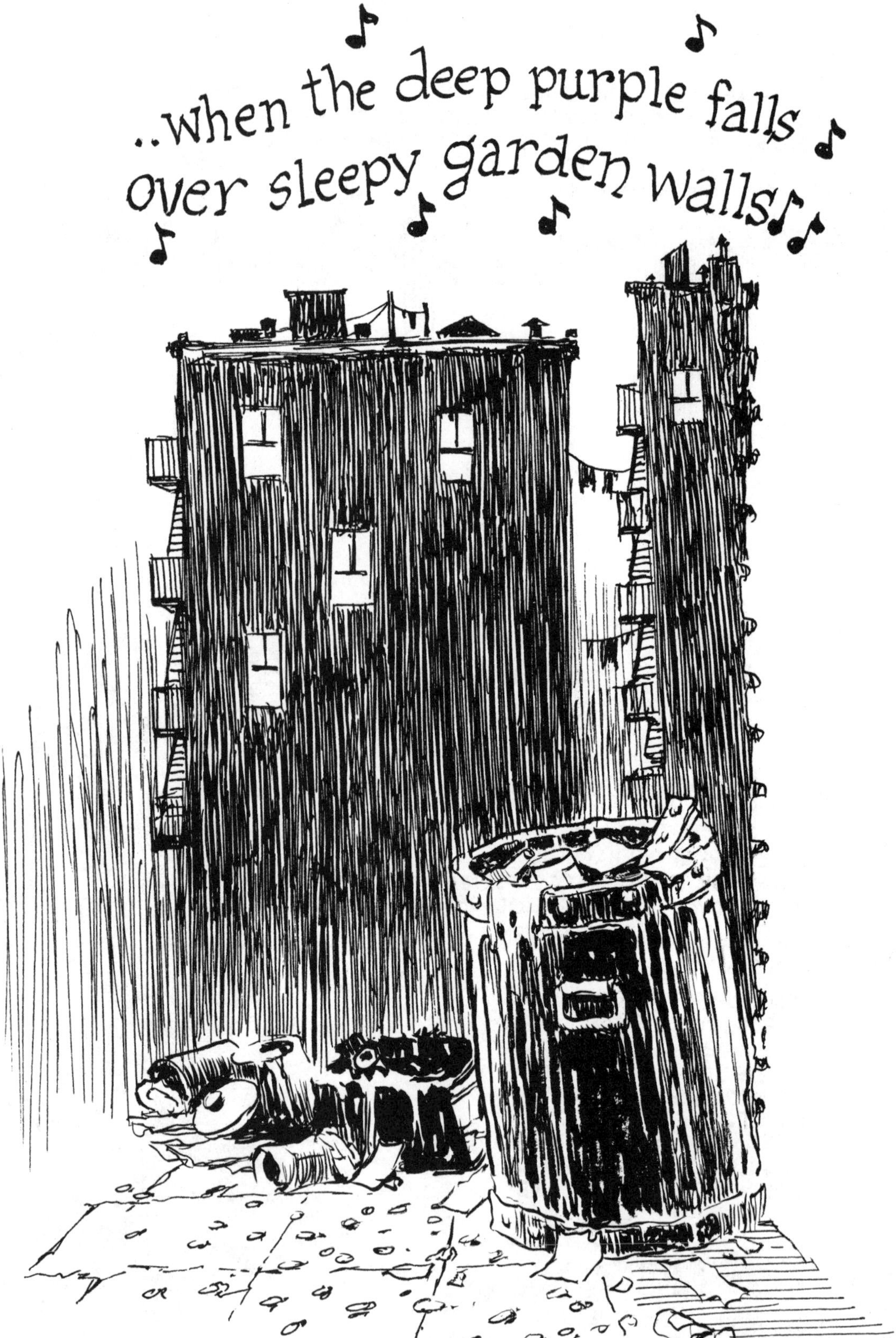
..when the deep purple falls
over sleepy garden walls

About the Author

Will Eisner (1917–2005) was present at the birth of the comic book industry in the 1930s, creating such titles as *Blackhawk* and *Sheena, Queen of the Jungle*. He created *The Spirit* in 1940, syndicating it for twelve years as a unique and innovative sixteen-page Sunday newspaper insert, with a weekly circulation of 5 million copies. As a Pentagon-based warrant officer during World War II, Eisner pioneered the instructional use of comics, continuing to produce them for the U.S. Army under civilian contract into the 1970s, along with educational comics for clients as diverse as General Motors and elementary school children.

In 1978 Eisner created *A Contract With God*, launching a bold new literary genre. Nearly twenty celebrated graphic novels followed, affirming his position as the grand old man of comics. Since 1988 the comic industry's top awards for excellence have been called "The Eisners." Throughout his career, Eisner received numerous honors and awards worldwide, including only the second Lifetime Achievement Award bestowed by the National Foundation for Jewish Culture (2002). In 2005, as one of his final projects, Eisner created *The Contract With God Trilogy*, which combined three of his great semiautobiographical novels all set on the mythical Dropsie Avenue in the Bronx— *A Contract With God*, *A Life Force*, and *Dropsie Avenue*. Michael Chabon's Pulitzer Prize–winning novel *The Amazing Adventures of Kavalier & Clay* is based in good part on Eisner.

Also available from the Will Eisner Library

A revolutionary novel, ***A Contract With God*** re-creates the neighborhood of Eisner's youth through a quartet of four interwoven stories. Expressing the joy, exuberance, tragedy and drama of life on the mythical Dropsie Avenue of the Bronx, *A Contract With God* belongs in the library of any graphic novel fan.

ISBN: 978-0-393-32804-2
Price: $16.95
204 pages

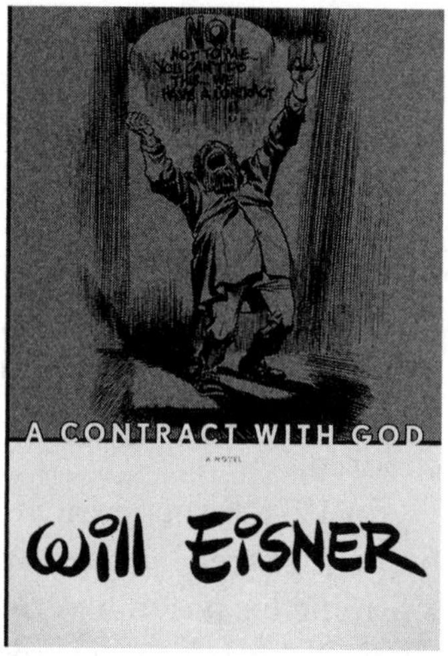
A CONTRACT WITH GOD
WILL EISNER

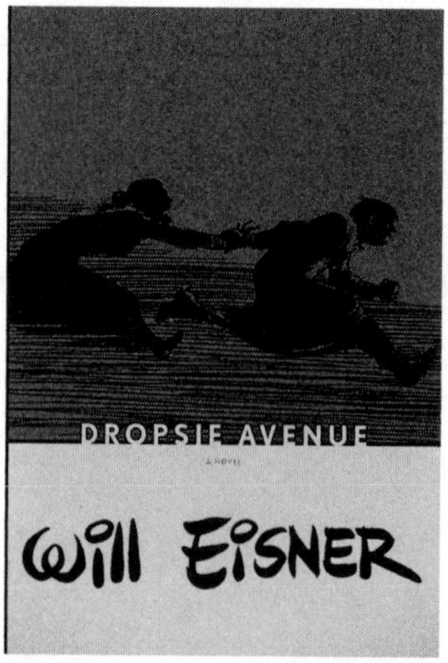
DROPSIE AVENUE
WILL EISNER

In ***Dropsie Avenue: The Neighborhood***, Eisner graphically traces the social trajectory of this mythic avenue over four centuries, creating a sweeping panorama of the city and its waves of new residents, whose stories present an unending "story of life, death, and resurrection."

ISBN: 978-0-393-32811-0
Price: $16.95
186 pages

DISCARDED